THE QUEEN'S PEACE

*The Origins and Development
of the Metropolitan Police
1829–1979*

DAVID ASCOLI

HAMISH HAMILTON

LONDON

First published in Great Britain 1979
by Hamish Hamilton Ltd
Garden House 57–59 Long Acre London WC2E 9JZ

Copyright © 1979 by David Ascoli

British Library Cataloguing in Publication Data

Ascoli, David
    The Queen's peace.
    1. Metropolitan Police – History
    I. Title
    363.2′09421   HV8196.L/
    ISBN 0–241–10296–0

Printed in Great Britain by
Western Printing Services Ltd, Bristol

'The safety of the people shall be the highest law.'

—Cicero: *De Legibus*

'The Police must always be suited to the Nature of the Government and Constitution of the Country where it is exercised. The Police of an arbitrary Government differs from that used in a Republic; and a Police proper for *England* must differ from them both; as it must always be agreeable to the just Notion of the Liberty of the Subject, as well as to the Laws and Constitution of this Country.'

—Sir John Fielding, 1768

'Law and arbitrary power are in eternal conflict.'

Edmund Burke: *Speech at the trial of Warren Hastings, 16 February 1788*

To the memory of
LT-COL SIR CHARLES ROWAN, KCB
and
SIR RICHARD MAYNE, KCB
without whom this would have been a very different book

CONTENTS

ILLUSTRATIONS

*All other photographs by courtesy of the Commissioner of the
Metropolitan Police*

FOREWORD

by

SIR DAVID MCNEE, QPM
Commissioner of Police of the Metropolis

WHEN on 29 September 1829 London's first police officers stepped on to the streets of the Metropolis it signalled the birth of modern policing as we know it. It is wholly appropriate therefore that David Ascoli's very readable history of the Metropolitan Police should be published this year to coincide with the 150th anniversary of the Force.

As the present Commissioner I was pleased to see that David Ascoli has paid proper tribute to Colonel Sir Charles Rowan and Sir Richard Mayne, the men to whom Sir Robert Peel gave the job of being the first joint Commissioners of the Metropolitan Police. A great debt is owed to these two men for the outstanding contribution they made not only to the survival and development of policing but to the consequent good order and stability of society as a whole. They laid the foundations of a policing tradition which depends upon public confidence and co-operation; from the outset they realised the need to make London's police (and consequently the British police) a part of the community they serve. That tradition, as David Ascoli rightly acknowledges, is as relevant today as it was 150 years ago.

Anyone who reads this history will soon realise what a colourful and varied existence the Metropolitan Police have led. Difficulties there have been, of that there can be no question. Some are of their own making but in the words of the author, 'The Metropolitan Police . . . is the most public institution in this country, its every action open to scrutiny, its every member personally accountable in law for the manner in which he executes his office' and he goes on to say, 'the politicians might care to reflect upon that'.

It is not true however, as David Ascoli suggests in his introduction, that I tried to make him put a *pibroch* into every page. My

idea was that he should write a concluding chapter about the
influence of Scotsmen in the Metropolitan Police. I can honestly
say that his failure to comply with my instruction has in no way
detracted from the admirable and informative history he has
written. There is a dearth of historical research about the British
Police service and David Ascoli has made a valuable contribution
to help remedy that. As Commissioner I read this book with great
interest coupled with a deep pride in the great Police Force about
which he has so ably written.

Introduction

IN HIS speech introducing the Metropolitan Police Bill to the House of Commons on 15 April 1829, Robert Peel had this to say: 'It is no longer possible to leave all the responsibility in connection with the detection of offenders, or the prevention of crimes, in the hands of the parochial authorities.'

Peel, a cautious man, chose his words carefully. The measure he was proposing was long overdue, but despite the accumulated evidence of generations of near-anarchy, the idea of a centralized civil institution for the maintenance of law and order had been bitterly resisted—for very different reasons—by Tories and Radicals alike. This antipathy—common to all classes—was in large measure a folk-reaction to Cromwell's ill-advised exercise in military dictatorship and to his suppression of traditional liberties. The English have long memories.

Peel's deliberately ambiguous words, 'all the responsibility', were intended to allay the worst suspicions of his friends, no less than his enemies; but his purpose from the outset was very precise, as anyone in his audience who had studied his Police Bill carefully would have realized. That intention, simply stated, was to divest parish vestries in the Metropolitan area of *all* responsibility for the prevention of crime and the preservation of law and order, and to concentrate those powers in a single Police Authority under the control of himself—and his successors—at the Home Office.

This, then, is the story of a unique exercise in social engineering. The Metropolitan Police is, above all, a very *English* institution, in the sense that Sir John Fielding intended in the passage quoted previously. It was brought into existence to give a fresh meaning to the old Anglo-Saxon concept of 'the King's Peace' and to protect the liberty of the subject against the licence of the ill-disposed. Its purpose was neither to make laws nor to sit in judgement on malefactors. It did not, as in Fouché's France, usurp the functions of the judiciary, nor was it, as in Tsarist and communist Russia, the servant of the executive. It survived—and will only survive—by public consent; by the temperate use of its considerable powers; and by its ability to walk the hazardous tightrope of public opinion. More than once it has come close to losing its balance.

The Metropolitan Police did not spring like some ready-armed Athena from the head of Zeus. On the contrary, during its early years it had to fight for its infant life, physically defenceless and politically traduced by its many opponents. That it succeeded against such formidable odds is a tribute to the two remarkable men who served as its first Joint Commissioners, and to the patience and courage of its founder members.

Historically, the creation of the Metropolitan Police has been attributed to Peel, although the principle that prevention is better than punishment had long been advocated by men like the Fieldings and later by Colquhoun and the Benthamites. It is certainly true that from the time he first entered the Home Office in 1822, Peel worked assiduously for reform of the criminal law and for a fundamental 'improvement' (another example of his careful use of words) of the police of the Metropolis; but his Police Act of 1829 was only an enabling instrument—admittedly of profound importance—setting up the legal and administrative framework of the proposed 'New Police'. The detailed organization, function, and training of the force he left to his Joint Commissioners[1] and thereafter—largely because of other preoccupations—he provided little more than paternal support, until his own departure from office in the following year.

The real architects of the Metropolitan Police were Charles Rowan and Richard Mayne, to whom history has been less than extravagant in its praise.

The two men had little in common beyond the fact that both were Irish, which was in itself a nice touch of native irony. Rowan, an Ulsterman, was a veteran of the Peninsular campaign and a convinced disciple of Sir John Moore whose prescription for good man management had been the simple, if then novel, military premise that humanity produces better soldiers than harshness. Mayne, fourteen years Rowan's junior, was a promising young Dublin

---

[1] On 20 July 1829 Peel wrote to the Commissioners setting out the approved pay and establishment. Apart from this directive, obligatory under the Act, Peel did not interfere in the planning process.

lawyer who had already established something of a reputation on the Northern circuit. They were not Peel's first choices, but whether by luck or good judgement,[1] he picked two men whose very different qualities perfectly complemented each other. And it is a measure of these two exceptional public servants, whose joint tenure of office lasted twenty-one years until Rowan's resignation for reasons of health in 1850, that their original concept of the organization and function of the Metropolitan Police—created without prior model or previous experience—has survived virtually unchanged to this day.

Plus ça change . . . In purely physical terms the Metropolis of Charles Rowan was very different from that of, say, David McNee; but, *mutatis mutandis*, the problems of policing it are basically the same. The anomaly of a separate and autonomous force for the City of London, devised by Peel as an emollient to soothe the conscience of his political opponents, has survived with no more justification now than then; Rowan and Mayne's original General Instruction Book of 1829 could, without the addition of a single paragraph still be issued to every newly-joined constable. The debate about freedom of speech and freedom of assembly is as old as Wilkes and as new as the National Front. The quality of villainy today has acquired a modern sophistication and sinister overtones; but on a comparative basis, the quantity of crime has probably not increased since the 'pre-statistical' violence of the eighteenth century. There have never been enough policemen adequately to enforce the law and there never will be. There have been black sheep in the flock and there always will be. But it is an indisputable fact that for 150 years the instrument which Rowan and Mayne forged with such patience and singleness of purpose has become the model for every other democratic society and the envy of less fortunate people. Therein lies the peculiar *Englishness* of this institution.

Throughout this book I have kept to my brief and, except where it is germane to the central theme, I have not widened the narrative to include the history of borough and county police forces which, within three decades of Peel's Act, were established on the pattern so successfully created in London; nor have I considered the different—sometimes very different—methods of law enforcement

---

[1] The appointments may have owed something to Peel's experience as Secretary for Ireland from 1812 to 1818. Equally, the choice of Rowan suggests the hand of the Prime Minister, Wellington.

practised in other countries. Law and its enforcement have exercised every community since the earliest times; I have therefore considered briefly how the Anglo-Saxon and Norman systems of public security in a rural English society developed and changed under the pressures of urban and then industrial constraints; in the words of Aristotle, 'law is a form of order; and good law must necessarily mean good order'. No less essential, he might have added, are the means by which good order can be preserved without loss of proper liberty; and liberty is a word capable of some very nicely balanced definitions. It is not possible to understand the eventual acceptance of Peel's 'New Police' without some knowledge of the legal jungle and climate of indiscipline which had for so long masqueraded as social democracy.

And the future? That is not strictly the province of this book; but since the public gets the police it deserves, it seems to me legitimate to speculate at the end about some of the fundamental problems which may face the Metropolitan Police in a society increasingly contemptuous of law and careless of order.

Acknowledging the help and cooperation I have had in writing this book is like Alice's 'caucus race', in which all should have prizes; but it would not be out of place to record my reply to a learned judge who asked me what my lasting impression was of the Metropolitan Police, as I laid down my pen. 'It was,' I told him, 'the pleasure of re-discovering the lost art of courtesy.' This is true— from the two Commissioners with whom I have been privileged to deal, down to the two traffic policemen, short in years but long in experience, who drove me round London for a day and in that time taught me more about the police function than anyone else. I should, however, like to emphasize that any political opinions are my own and not those of any Metropolitan Police officer.

If I name only a few names, it is for reasons of space, not ingratitude. First, Sir Robert Mark and his policy committee who fired the starting gun; and Bob Gregory and Mike Down of the former Public Relations Office, who launched me down the runway; Sir David McNee who, so to speak, inherited me and has tried, with persuasive charm but no success, to make me put a *pibroch* into every page; 'Jimmy' James, the Receiver, who has patiently fed me figures like a fruit-machine; Sir James Starritt, former Deputy Commissioner, wise policeman, and devastating raconteur; John Bliss, who lives too near to me for his comfort; and Bob Bryan, head of Special Branch and Roy Habershon, Commander of E District, who live too close to the job for theirs.

Throughout my journey I have been in the sure hands of John Maxfield and his colleagues in P.2; and of Patricia Plank and her cheerful team in the Commissioner's Reference Library. I have gone where I wished and spoken with police officers of every rank and shade of experience. From all of them I have had more help, patience, and consideration than any author is entitled to expect. And a lot of laughs. At Bramshill Police College the Librarian, Dennis Brett, has been especially kind and helpful. And I should record the most consoling remark of all, from Commander Gerry Lambourne—dean of dactyloscopy—who wished peace to my ulcers (not yet, I think, a conventional means of identification).

It has been a memorable experience. I suppose, like many outsiders, that I came half-expecting to bury Caesar. I have finished up by praising him almost unreservedly. Forget the long history of struggle for public acceptance. Forget the black sheep in the Old Bailey dock. Remember rather the young inspector at Albany Street who said to me: 'It's a wonderful and rewarding life. I wouldn't change it for all the money in the world.' The politicians might care to reflect upon that; so might my readers. Both have taken the Metropolitan Police for granted for far too long.

DAVID ASCOLI

Farriers
Shalford, Surrey
June 1979

Author's Note

THE WORD 'police' requires both explanation and definition. Despite its classical appearance, it was used neither by the Greeks nor the Romans; and Reith is right when he observes that 'modern historians now use it glibly, and sometimes very confusingly, in place of such names as "the young men", "the officers", "the officials", "the guards", and others, by which the existence of *policemen* has been obscured by earlier writers throughout the ages'.

Johnson in his *Dictionary* attributes its origin to mediaeval France and defines it in an abstract sense as meaning: 'The regulation and government of a city or country, so far as regards the inhabitants'. Yet the French word for the instrument of law enforcement was *gendarmerie* and it was the essentially military connotation of this name which aroused such universal antipathy in the francophobe England of the eighteenth century, and such suspicion of any movement towards a formalized 'police' institution, as witness the anonymous writer of a letter to the *Public Advertizer* in 1763:

> The Word *Police* has made many bold Attempts to get a Footing, but as neither the Word nor the Thing itself are much understood in London, I fancy it will require a considerable Time to bring it into Fashion; perhaps, from an Aversion to the French, from whom this Word is borrowed . . .

Towards the end of the eighteenth century, the word had certainly been brought into fashion, though almost always in the purely abstract sense of 'local government' or, even more loosely, of 'policy', in which context it was repeatedly used by Burke and Pitt. It was not until Patrick Colquhoun published his celebrated *Treatise* in 1796, that the word really acquired its modern usage of 'a civil force for maintaining public order, enforcing regulations for the prevention and punishment of breaches of the law, and detecting crime'. And in November 1829 Wellington could write thus to Peel: 'I congratulate you upon the entire success of the Police in

London. It is impossible to see anything more respectable than they [*sic*] are.'

Nevertheless, *pace* Reith and his glib historians, I have settled throughout for 'police', even where pedantry might suggest otherwise. They have been known by many names: affectionately as 'Peelers', 'Bobbies', or 'Coppers'; offensively as 'Peel's Bloody Gang', 'Pigs', or 'Fuzz'. At least the constable on the beat may have the satisfaction of knowing that *his* title has an old, distinguished and honourable pedigree.

A police constable has a unique legal status, tested in the celebrated case of *Fisher v Oldham Corporation* in 1930 and confirmed by the judgment of Mr Justice Macardie. This judgment was based on the declaration (as now worded under Schedule 2 of the 1964 Police Act) made by every constable on attestation: 'I do solemnly and sincerely declare and affirm that I will well and truly serve Our Sovereign Lady the Queen in the office of constable . . . and that while I continue to hold the said office I will to the best of my skill and knowledge discharge all the duties thereof faithfully according to the law.' In other words, the powers of a constable, whether confirmed by common law or statute law, are exercised by him by virtue of his office and cannot be exercised on the responsibility of any person but himself. The constable is nobody's servant except the Crown's. He executes a public office under the law; and it is the law which is his master.

Prologue

'THE PROBLEM of the human race,' observed Pascal, 'is that it consists of human beings.' The irony underlines a melancholy truth; for even as the sparks fly upwards, man was born to trouble. A strange creature, man: a rational animal, infinitely capable of irrational behaviour; instinct with a kind of divinity, yet ready to gamble it for the doubtful wages of sin; how like an angel—and how prone to fall. Small wonder that society, in its pursuit of civilized values, has long sought the means so to regulate human conduct that the dark side of human nature may be, if not exorcised, at least deterred from casting its disfiguring shadow across the face of innocence; for the makers of the law, the breakers of the law, and the keepers of the peace have one thing in common. They are all human beings. Pascal was right. Man's appetite for social indiscipline is not the least consequence of original sin.

The ascent of man from primitive hunter to peasant farmer was marked by the development of tribal communities. We have little certain knowledge of how these were organized, but the detritus of pre-literate society demonstrates that from the beginning a primitive system of government was evolved, a pecking-order of leaders and led, a social hierarchy charged with maintaining an orderly way of life; for Rousseau's noble savage was certainly more savage than noble. Rogue elephant and wolf-pack are not exclusive to the animal kingdom.

No community, however primitive, can long survive unless its members devise—*and enforce*—a code of conduct acceptable to the majority, a philosophy defined in the eighteenth century by the Italian Beccaria and the English Benthamites as 'the greatest happiness of the greatest number'. Indeed, the decline and fall of every great empire in history may arguably be said to have had its origin in the decay of public morality and the collapse of law and order. Absolute power breeds absolute tyranny. Absolute liberty invites reactionary licence; and it is the unique nature of civilized man that, while he will defy brutal repression, he will accept reasonable restraint. There could be no clearer illustration of this than the historic process by which the disorderly English arrived, by trial and error, at the first successful exercise in solving the equation which Samuel Johnson defined thus: 'The law is the last result of human wisdom acting upon human experience for the benefit of the public.'

In primitive societies the distinction between right and wrong grew infinitely slowly out of the interplay between tradition, custom and superstition. It varied, no doubt, between one community and another but the basic ingredients were then, as they are now, the common elements of human nature. If we take the book of Genesis as a universal allegory, then it is significant that the fall of man arose from an act of disobedience and that the first crime to be visited upon the seed of Adam was that of murder; and so it has remained. 'Thou shalt not kill' has become the prime commandment and the moral divide between rational man and the law of the jungle.

If communities were to exist—and co-exist—in peace, then there had to be acceptable rules for the maintenance of an ordered way of life; and penalties for those who broke the rules by individual crimes against persons or property or by disturbing the common peace. And from such primitive rules and customs emerged the concept of law and order. It was to take many centuries before society approached both the human wisdom and human experience of which Johnson wrote. It still has a long way to go.

'There are two, and only two, foundations of law—equity and utility.'[1] What Burke meant—and what he went on to say—was that law has no validity if it is not in accordance with natural justice, if it is not seen in the *public* regard to be fair and equitable; and all law is vanity if it cannot be enforced.

In the broadest sense, there are three means of law enforcement. The first is by authoritarian use of force, whether military or para-military. Its chief weapon is fear and its historic effect is demoralization, in every sense of that word. As a system it is self-defeating and counter-productive; and it is known as tyranny. The second is the delegation of responsibility for maintaining law and order to society itself, either within or outside a framework of judicial authority. Such a system bears the appearance of democracy. In

---

[1] Edmund Burke, *Tracts on the Popery Law.*

practice, it also bears the seeds of anarchy. The third means is the subject of this book: an impartial civil police institution, uninvolved in the processes of law-making and the administration of justice, but, to paraphrase Lincoln, charged solely with the regulation of public order of the people, by the people, and for the people. It is called democracy.

The English have inherited their system of government from the redoubtable Anglo-Saxon kings—from Alfred and Athelstan (*rex totius Britanniae*, so ran his proud title) and Edgar. This system was based on the idea of mutual pledging and collective security and it was to survive, through many changes (not always for the better), until its progressive collapse in the disorderly society of the eighteenth century.

In much the same way that the Roman Republic founded its legal authority on the Twelve Tables, so Anglo-Saxon England was given its basic, though much more flexible, guide-lines in Alfred's Book of Laws, which set out to blend the Mosaic code with Christian beliefs, ancient traditions, and old Germanic customs. Alfred set forth his principle thus: 'What ye will that other men should *not* do to you, that do ye not to other men', and he added: 'I have not dared to presume to set down in writing many laws of my own, for I cannot tell what will meet with the approval of our successors.' He cannot indeed have foreseen who his eventual successors would be, or how they would apply his simple principle. But Churchill had this to say: 'The Laws of Alfred, continually amplified by his successors, grew into that body of customary law which, under the name of the Laws of St Edward the Confessor, the Norman kings undertook to respect, and out of which the Common Law was founded.'

The 'social contract' which Alfred made with his people was called 'the King's Peace'. Like all good contracts it was short and unequivocal, understood by both parties and accepted by both parties. There was no small print.

In return for their unquestioned allegiance to his person and family and—by implication—his sovereign right to rule them, the king guaranteed the peace and security of his subjects. This uncomplicated formula for mutual assurance had two complementary elements. 'There was the public peace of the realm, common to all men; and there was the private peace proper to the king himself, designed to safeguard his person, to uphold his dignity and to secure his interests in every way.'[1] In an ideal society, such a contract would have been self-enforcing. But society has always had a fatal streak of indiscipline and thus, to honour his side of the contract, the king—in his capacity as chief magistrate—established a police system for the enforcement of the law and the maintenance of public order. This system, the basis of all subsequent police institutions in England, was perfected by Alfred's great-grandson Edgar (959–975 AD) after the unification of the country, and it enunciated the old Athenian principle of public security—namely, that 'the police are the people, and the people are the police'.[2] It is the first milestone in our story.

Under Edgar, the country was reorganized into shires, each under a king's representative, the shire reeve or sheriff.[3] The basic unit of the shire was the 'tything', a group of ten families, and these groups in turn were mustered in units of ten to form the 'hundred'.

The responsibility for local peace and security was thus firmly delegated by the king to the people themselves. Each tything,[4] under a 'tythingman' or 'headborough', was 'pledged'—that is to say, stood surety—for the good behaviour of its members, both jointly and severally. If any one person offended against another or against the community as a whole, it was the duty of the tything to inform the hundredmen and tythingmen of the district and pursue, arrest and bring the culprit to justice. The pursuit of a culprit—the 'hue and cry' of early Anglo-Saxon times—was obligatory on all members of a tything and failure to join the chase was itself a punishable offence.[5]

This effective system of maintaining the King's Peace was, by its

---

[1] W. Melville Lee, *A History of Police in England*.

[2] This principle was implicit in the General Instruction Book issued by Rowan and Mayne in 1829.

[3] The sheriff, as 'vice-regal' magistrate, had his own court of justice, while in his capacity as a police officer, he could, in the event of serious disorder, call out a primitive form of militia known as the *posse comitatus*.

[4] Every freeman of a community, other than the thanes, the clergy, the infirm, and widows, was obliged to be enrolled in a tything from the age of twelve. The remaining exception were the 'unfrith' or, literally, 'outlaws' whose criminal activities placed them outside the pale.

[5] In certain circumstances failure to assist a police constable in the execution of his duty is still an offence in law.

very nature, preventive rather than punitive since each member of a community had a vested interest in ensuring that the law—still in the process of evolving out of custom and tradition—was not broken. For the most part penalties consisted of collective and individual fines, levied in accordance with a neatly graduated scale in proportion to the gravity of the crime (a cut or wound caused by physical violence, for example, was assessed by the inch). There were only two capital offences: murder, the ultimate crime against the individual; and treason, the ultimate crime against the state. The fate of persistent law-breakers was outlawry, which—like the savage practice of transportation centuries later—was tantamount to a sentence of death.

Looking back across the years of social change and growing disorder, the Anglo-Saxon police institution, with its involvement of every citizen in ensuring the maintenance of law and order, seems to give the lie to Pascal's cynical aphorism, for it was based on trust rather than fear, on confidence rather than retribution, at once paternalistic and—as Christian influence spread—compassionate. But as a workable system, it was possible only in a predominantly static and rural society of communities with close ties of blood and kinship. Thus as early as the tenth century, the City of London, with its numerous and shifting population, and its growth as a centre of foreign trade, had become a special case, in which the tything system of village or parish was replaced by 'frith', or peace, gilds in which members of individual crafts or trades banded together not only to keep the peace, but to protect their traditional rights. The principle of mutual responsibility and mutal assurance differed little from that of provincial England, but once its special status had been established, the City, jealous of its privileged position, resisted—and has continued to resist—every attempt to diminish its authority or to absorb it into the growing Metropolitan area of which it is a geographical part but an administrative outsider.

*

The King's Peace of Anglo-Saxon England was soon to be rudely disturbed.

The Norman Conquest brought with it an alien culture, a foreign language, and a new concept of law and order derived from the continental feudal system. Much has been written about the destructive impact of the Norman occupation on the development of English institutions, but the practical result was quite otherwise, and the effect dynamic rather than stultifying.

As with every occupying power before or since, internal security and the maintenance of law and order were a paramount necessity; and William I had the wisdom and good sense not ruthlessly to dismantle a system which for so long had served the English character well.

The organization of tythings and hundreds remained the basic police institutions, the only superficial change being one of name whereby the tythingman or headborough was re-styled—in a Norman mis-translation—the 'chief frankpledge'. But there was one fundamental innovation.

The Anglo-Saxon shire-reeves had been invested with vice-regal powers within their own districts, and thus both judicial and police functions had been exercised at local level. This suited the temperament of rural English society well (and, for that matter, still does, for the English are jealous of their local institutions and hostile to the excessive concentration of power).

After the Conquest, this process gave way to a policy of centralization whereby the Norman sheriff, or 'vicecomes', became the agent rather than the local representative of the king, with the introduction of the circuit justice or 'Sheriff's Tourn', and the creation of counties. The Sheriff's Tourn travelled the country at Michaelmas primarily to administer justice in the hundreds, but in practice to levy substantial fines for the royal exchequer on a basis which had more to do with extortion than equity.

To the native English, this was anathema, and was met by widespread resistance which, as the *Anglo-Saxon Chronicle* sombrely records, was countered by savage reprisals. And within a hundred years of the Conquest, the decennary or tything system of local police administration had virtually ceased to exist.

But good institutions survive bad practices. The universal resistance to the oppressive conduct of the Sheriff's Tourn resulted in petitions to the king by some feudal magnates, or lords of the manor, for the re-establishment of local machinery for the exercise of justice; and thus there came into existence the Court Leet, whose very name proclaimed the revival of the old Anglo-Saxon concept of a localized judicial and police authority. It also marked the decline of the office of sheriff, for the members of a community were now answerable to their feudal overlord, as well as to each other. Indeed, it has been suggested that the whole history of English justice and police 'might be brought under the rubric, the decline and fall of the Sheriff'. It would be more accurate to say that English justice and police presently acquired a new sense of direction by a return to the old and tried Anglo-Saxon system and by the rise of the magistracy and the institution of parish vestries. This was to remain the working model for five centuries, until its progressive decay due to the corruption of the magistracy, the insularity of the vestries, and the growing lawlessness of the English people, most notably in the Metropolitan area.

The first two centuries of Plantagenet rule saw far-reaching developments. These changes dealt for the most part with constitutional issues and with the central judiciary, and do not concern us here; but they also rebuilt the foundations of our modern police system.

Henry II's Assize of Clarendon (1166) revived the obsolescent 'view of frankpledge' and the old institution of local responsibility for maintaining the King's Peace. Fifteen years later, the Assize of Arms reinforced the powers of local authorities by requiring all freemen over the age of fifteen to keep weapons in their homes, in accordance with their rank and status, for the purpose, when necessary, of preserving the peace and securing criminals. This measure was, at the same time, a remarkable act of faith on the king's part, for in a volatile social climate, it provided a ready means for armed rebellion. It also gave a new word to the English language.

The word 'constable' is of Roman-Frankish derivation, from *comes stabuli* or Master of the Horse. In origin, the holder of the title was a military officer of the highest rank and a figure of great power and authority. In twelfth-century England, however, the constable, while still of military rank, had—like many other Norman institutions—declined in authority and become little more than a royal staff officer; and it was in this capacity that the Assize of Arms appointed constables as inspectors of each household to ensure that the correct assortment of weaponry was being maintained. The title and its holder were soon to assume a new and significant function.

The next major change in police organization was the appointment by Richard I in 1195 of certain knights as 'Conservators of of the Peace'. Their duties were purely executive and their status superior to that of the local sheriffs. In the office of conservator we find the first instance of the peace officers who were within two centuries to assume judicial and police responsibilities throughout the whole country with the exception of the City; and in a writ of Henry III in 1251 there appears for the first time—the casual reference suggests familiarity—mention of 'high constables' and 'petty constables' as local officers under the direction of the conservators.

This random reference has been taken to imply that the two constabulary grades were a new or recent addition to the machinery for maintaining law and order, but it seems certain that they are only one further example of the prevalent use of French as the language of affairs of state. Time and custom had long since staled the high Norman office which had first carried this rank and style, but the word remained a useful symbol of authority, and thus the 'high constable' was synonymous with the hundredman, and the 'petty constable' with the tythingman or headborough. The English, not greatly concerned with a foreign vernacular, continued to use the native names and, indeed, the Parish Constables Act of 1872 indiscriminately uses the titles of tythingman, headborough, constable, parish constable, and police constable with a fine disregard for history and the statute book.

*

In 1285 the celebrated Statute of Winchester was passed under Edward I, of whom it has been said that 'he did more for the preservation of the peace in the first thirteen years of his reign than was accomplished by the thirteen monarchs next succeeding'.[1] It was to prove one of the most important, and certainly one of the most durable, of all constitutional measures. Indeed, five centuries later, a Commons committee set up in 1770 to inquire into the state of the nightly watch in Westminster querulously noted that 'the Statute of Winchester being very obsolete is a very improper regulation'. It still had more virtue than any comparable eighteenth-century legislation.

Edward I's measure was neither new nor radical. Its purpose, as the preamble runs, was 'to abate the power of felons' and what it achieved was to bring together, in a single statutory instrument, all the best and provenly effective elements of law enforcement from

[1] W. Melville Lee, *A History of Police in England.*

preceding centuries, while at the same time enlarging and strengthening the machinery of judicial and police administration.

First, it re-established the hundred as the local unit responsible for keeping the King's Peace, and also the system of frankpledge, thus once more delegating to the people the obligation of policing each other.[1] In so doing, it reverted to the old Anglo-Saxon axiom that prevention is better than cure, while ensuring proper retribution for law-breakers. To this end it revived the 'hue and cry' and the compulsory pursuit of criminals from hundred to hundred, on pain of prosecution for non-compliance.

From the Assize of Arms, the Statute borrowed the obligation of all freemen to carry arms for preserving peace and securing felons; and from a writ of 1233 came the practice of 'watch and ward'.

This was a reflection of the growth—still modest—of urban communities and the special police problems they created. Under the Statute, the gates of all walled towns were to be closed between the hours of sunset and sunrise, during which time strangers were permitted neither to enter nor to leave. In every city, a watch of six men was stationed at each gate (in boroughs the watch consisted of twelve men and in smaller towns, four to six) and suspected persons were to be brought before the peace officers for questioning. It was preventive policing with a vengeance.

The Statute of Winchester predictably did not apply to the City of London. Later in the same year, a separate measure[2] was introduced which divided the City into twenty-four wards with six watchmen, each under an alderman and answerable to the Lord Mayor. A novel feature was the addition of a 'marching watch' which moved from ward to ward and also exercised a police function during daylight hours.

By the date of Edward I's Statute, the office of constable had become firmly established. Its holders were appointed on an annual basis by the Courts Leet. Service was obligatory and, except for small fees and incidental expenses, unpaid. For at least two centuries, the constable was a figure of authority and dignity,

---

[1] The preamble—'cries shall be made in all counties, markets, hundreds . . . and all other places, where great resort of people is, so that none shall excuse himself by ignorance'—defined the long-surviving precept that ignorance of the law is no excuse. The wise and careful king could not have foreseen the ill-considered flood of modern legislation.

[2] *Statuta Civitatis London.*

respected as a local custodian of the law and an essential element of what had now become known as the 'parish'.

It is important, as our story develops, to understand the common law origin of the office of constable. It has never, either in theory or practice, been considered a privileged position or invested with powers greatly differing from those of other citizens. In the common law view, a constable 'is only a person who is paid to perform as a matter of duty acts which if he were so minded he might have done voluntarily'.[1] As we shall presently see, the decay of this most English of institutions led, under the Tudors and their successors, to a complete breakdown of the old order and a climate of indiscipline which threatened the very existence of democratic society. It was to arrest this formidable prospect that Peel addressed himself with such singular understanding when he entered the Home Office in 1822.

*

Until the middle of the fourteenth century the conservators were still only executive officers—'little more than constables on a large scale'[2]—and the Statute of Winchester had left the administration of local justice to sheriffs and the Courts Leet. But as the powers of the sheriff continued to decline, so those of the conservators were extended. By an Act of Edward III in 1344 they were given judicial functions, and a statute of 1361 decreed that 'in every county in England there shall be assigned for the keeping of the peace, one lord, and with him three or four of the most worthy men of the county . . . and they shall have power to restrain offenders, rioters and other barrators [trouble-makers], and to pursue, arrest, take, and chastise them, according to their trespass or offence; and to cause them to be arrested and duly punished according to the law and custom of the realm . . .' In these words was created the office of Justice of the Peace in which were combined both judicial and executive functions—those of magistrate and chief of police;[3] and in this statute was established a partnership of unique im-

---

[1] Stephen, *History of the Criminal Law.*   [2] *Ibid.*

[3] Under the Police Act of 1829, the Commissioners of the Metropolitan Police were appointed Justices of the Peace, though (as specifically defined) with no judicial powers. They remained so until the Administration of Justice Act 1973.

portance in the police history of England—that of justice and constable.[1]

Although appointed by the Courts Leet, constables—'the lowe and lay ministers of the peace'—were under the control of the new magistracy who swore them in and supervised their duties. From the outset, however, justices were nominated by the Crown, and since they were men of local standing and were duly required to have a property qualification (abolished in 1906), they were an effective link between king and people and therefore readily acceptable to a society which had so strongly resisted Norman attempts to centralize the powers of the judiciary.

With the establishment of Quarter Sessions two years after Edward III's statute became law, justices were paid four shillings a day for each day in sessions—a maximum of twelve days in the year.[2] Since they were then invariably men of substance, the sum was unimportant, but as we shall see, the decline in the quality of the magistracy, particularly in urban centres, and the derisory remuneration paid to justices led to increasing corruption, for which the office provided rich opportunities; and since imitation is the sincerest form of flattery, the contagion soon infected constables and their subordinates.

It is an axiom of the administrative process that the broader the back, the greater the load. It was not long, therefore, before the responsibilities and duties of justices began to assume formidable proportions, as functions which had nothing to do with their statutory role were delegated to them. In 1390 their numbers had been fixed at eight in each county and their staff, whether clerical or executive, was negligible. They were required, among a multitude of other things, to regulate wages, determine rates, administer the poor law, maintain roads and bridges, even supervise church attendance. In many respects they were in themselves *de facto* county councils—though these were not to be created until the Local Government Act of 1888. Not surprisingly, much of this excessive burden was offloaded onto their parish constables, still unpaid and still having to combine their parish duties with their normal occupations. The wonder is that the whole edifice did not

---

[1] In the City of London, the office of Justice of the Peace was—and still is—exercised by the Lord Mayor and aldermen.

[2] Payment of justices was abolished in 1854, except in the case of stipendiary magistrates.

collapse under its own weight. Yet, remarkably, the partnership of justice and parish constable survived two centuries of rebellion, pestilence and civil war; and it was not until the Tudor period that a social revolution began to reveal serious defects in the system.

*

With the disappearance of the feudal system the responsibilities of the magistracy—and the constabulary—grew still more onerous. The Tudors, mindful of the disarray into which the state had fallen during the civil wars, rode the country on a tight rein. 'The function of the Tudor Privy Council,' writes Trevelyan, 'was to teach not only Parliament to legislate but justices of the peace to govern.'[1] By these new standards, the magistracy seems to have been less than adequate, for one of the first acts of Henry VII was to issue a stern warning to the justices, while in 1539 Henry VIII addressed himself to them in these uncompromising terms: 'If you shall give such diligence as may satisfy your duty, leaving all disguised corruption, we shall be content the more easily to put in oblivion all your former remissness and negligences'—failing which, 'assure yourselves that the next advice shall be of so sharp a sort as shall bring with it a just punishment of those that have been found offenders.'

But other influences were at work. During the sixteenth century, England emerged as a significant commercial and colonial power and this in turn created a new middle class of merchants and artisans for whom the prospect of acquiring wealth had its natural attraction. At the other end of the scale, the dissolution of the monasteries and the physical symbols of prosperity created a very different class of vagrant criminals, with no means of subsistence other than what they could achieve by resort to robbery and violence. The result was a growing lawlessness and indiscipline which was to become a permanent feature of English life. The Tudor statute book is peppered with measures designed to deal with 'rogues, vagabonds, and sturdy beggars' and the law was administered with an increasing degree of savagery.[2] The busiest man in England was the public executioner.

Since time is money, and making money had now become a very

[1] G. M. Trevelyan, *History of England*.
[2] The Poor Law of 1601, the first true measure of social welfare, was an attempt to separate the genuinely deserving from the purely troublesome and work-shy.

desirable occupation, it was not long before the system of virtually unpaid public service which had worked so well and for so long began to break down. Members of the new class, particularly in urban areas, were not slow to see in the office of justice a useful status symbol and even if the pay for attendance at sessions was puny, there were obvious opportunities for self-enrichment on a grand scale. In rural England the justices were still, for the most part, drawn from the already wealthy class of landed gentry, but in London, especially, there grew up a new breed described with distaste by Lambard as 'men of small substance whose povertie made them both covetous and contemptible'. He did not add, as well he might have done, the word 'corrupt'.

Further down the scale the same disease infected the office of constable whose duties were now so time-consuming that he was virtually unable to carry on his normal trade or occupation. It therefore became the practice of many citizens elected to serve as constable to appoint deputies to carry out their duties in return for some modest payment. And since the prospect of public service no longer appealed to men of character or commercial acumen, the ranks were soon filled with the weak, the ignorant, the infirm and the senile.

The decline of the constable in Elizabethan times from a man of authority to a figure of fun is perfectly illustrated by Shakespeare. Elbow, the 'simple' Constable of *Measure for Measure* has no illusions after seven and a half years as a paid deputy: 'As they are chosen, they are glad to choose me for them; I do it for some piece of money and go through with all.' As for the garrulous and illiterate Dogberry in *Much Ado*, he is bumbledom personified, whether he be inspecting his motley crew of watchmen ('We will sleep rather than talk; we know what belongs to a watch', observes one of them), or reporting preposterously to his Justice: 'our watch, sir, have indeed comprehended two aspicious persons.' There speaks one authentic constabulary voice.

*

By the seventeenth century, Elbow and Dogberry had become symptoms of a universal disease, and corruption a way of life. A feature of the reign of James I was the appearance of the 'basket justice', so called after the basket prominently displayed on the bench for the 'voluntary' contributions of plaintiff and defendant alike. 'Justice,' wrote a contemporary, 'may be bought and sold as in the market-place. The law, which should be priceless, now has its price.' The system flourished until, 150 years later, Henry Fielding launched his campaign against 'the dirtiest money upon earth'.

London was then a squalid place, its unsanitary streets unpaved and unlit, policed—when parish vestries felt so inclined—by the occasional deputy constable and dozing watchman. It was a thieves' paradise, and there was no shortage of villainy. The City, with its older traditions and better administration, was by comparison an oasis of order in a sea of lawlessness, but it was still an odious comparison; and whatever vestige of social discipline remained was presently swept away by the tidal wave of the Civil War.

*

The end of Royalist resistance in 1651 left Cromwell with a divided and bitter country. War leaves its scars; civil war leaves wounds unhealed. And though Cromwell may have wished it otherwise, his supporters were resolved to pursue old vendettas.

The re-establishment of law and order was a task as urgent for the Lord Protector as it had been for William of Normandy. In general, justices and grand jurymen had supported the Royalist cause, constables and petty jurymen the Parliamentary.[1] Thus the old mediaeval partnership, already strained, was irrevocably debased. It is at least arguable that the roots of police reform in 1829 go back to the years when, without a king, the King's Peace became meaningless.

When Cromwell's attempt to revive the magistracy by creating a new commission of the peace failed, he turned to his only alternative weapon—the army. In 1655, the country was divided into twelve military districts under self-styled 'major-generals' and buttressed by a law-enforcement body of some 6,400 mounted troops. For the first time, England was under a military dictatorship.

Cromwell, the most English of men, understood the temper of the times, and had few illusions. His 'little poor invention', as he called it, was designed 'for the security of the peace of the nation, the suppressing of vice, and the encouragement of virtue', and his

---

[1] The curious exception was the City of London, which was a Parliamentary stronghold, partly from distaste for the fiscal policy of Charles I, but also for reasons of self-interest.

major-generals were enjoined to cooperate with 'the other [*sic*] Justices of the Peace'.

But Englishmen do not take kindly to puritan zeal. In their pursuit of virtue, Cromwell's men ignored the first principle of a successful police institution: public consent. The catalogue of repressive measures is too long to concern us here, but it ranged from the suppression of all traditional forms of sport, through fines for swearing and blasphemy, to the capital crime of adultery. Stage performances were forbidden, alehouses proscribed, and the celebration of Christmas frowned upon. 'Never,' wrote the French Ambassador, 'did I think so lively a people could be so shortly sunk in apathy.'

All this invasion of personal freedom might have been tolerated, except for one cardinal error of judgement which was to have a lasting effect on our social history and on the future of our police system. This was the introduction of political espionage. Years later Peel was to be reminded more than once of the universal hatred of such practices; and even today there remains a profound and proper public suspicion of anything savouring of a secret police.

*

With the Restoration, the problem of law and order assumed new and different proportions. In rural areas there was a general return to the old partnership of justice and constable, even if the impoverishment of the landed class meant a further decline in former standards. But in the growing Metropolis—to which all roads now led—the police system had virtually broken down. The reaction to puritan restraints and the king's riotous life-style combined to create a climate of public disorder and private degeneracy pursued against a background of municipal squalor. 'Thieves and robbers,' wrote a contemporary historian, 'are now become more desperate and savage than they have ever appeared since man was civilized.' In Westminster and its suburbs, the random proliferation of liberties, parishes and manors, all with their independent vestries, boards, trustees and commissioners, made a mockery of local government and of police administration. To escape the law, a thief had only to step from one parish into the next. One thing the Statute of Winchester had not reckoned with was the jealousy of petty authority.

The City, more compact and better administered, made a modest show of strength. In 1663, an Act of Common Council established a body of 1,000 paid 'bellmen' or, as they came to be affectionately —and derisively—known, 'Charlies'. Their pay was similarly derisory and their deterrent effect negligible as they dozed in their watch-boxes, emerging only to call the hour and the state of the weather. By the eighteenth century the 'nightly watch' had been extended to the whole Metropolis, and had become a public joke. Only two years before Peel's Police Act, the London 'Charlies' invited this description:

> Wanted, a hundred thousand men for London watchmen. None need apply for this lucrative situation without being the age of sixty, seventy, eighty, or ninety years; blind with one eye, and seeing very little with the other; crippled with one or both legs; deaf as a post; with an asthmatical cough, that tears them to pieces; whose speed will keep pace with a snail, and the strength of whose arm would not be able to arrest an old washerwoman of fourscore returned from a hard day's fag at the wash-tub; whose constitution is worn out in hard service, either in the army or navy, some unhealthy business, or from the effects of a gay and profligate life; and such that will neither hear nor see what belongs to their duty, or what does not, unless well palmed or garnished for the same.[1]

Small wonder that police reform had become a matter of profound urgency.

After the Great Fire, the sense of public shock resulted in many improvements in the condition of the Metropolis: street paving, a primitive form of street-lighting, better sanitation and—to cope with a new phenomenon—traffic regulation and the licensing of public vehicles (Christopher Wren's only memorial as a member of Parliament). By a curious coincidence the traffic office, under John Evelyn, was housed in Scotland Yard and its members were known as the Commissioners of Scotland Yard.

Yet the problem of London's police remained intractable. In 1673, an Act empowered justices to appoint constables, hitherto the prerogative of Courts Leet; and given the known reputation of most justices, it was not the wisest of measures. The same Act also gave justices the power to appoint special constables at times of emer-

[1] John Pearson, *The London Charleys of the Eighteenth Century, or half-past twelve o'clock and a very cloudy sort of morning.*

gency; and from this it has been adduced, with an English sense of the ridiculous, that the Special Constabulary pre-dates the Metropolitan Police by 150 years.

But there remained one other measure, as this turbulent century drew to its close, which was to have disastrous consequences. In 1692 a statute was passed—largely as a result of the growth of highway robbery—by which Parliament sanctioned the payment of rewards out of public funds for the arrest and conviction of felons. The practice has passed into the language as 'blood money', and instead of 'abating the power of felons' it was to create a new and sinister criminal class. And crime was now to become a social and political issue of formidable importance.

CHAPTER ONE

Liberty and Licence: the First Reformers

HISTORY IS full of paradoxes, and none more strange than that of London in the eighteenth century.

The conventional image is of an age of wit and elegance; of classical architecture and gracious living; of Handel at the Haymarket and the child Mozart in Ebury Street; of Swift and Sheridan, Burke and Samuel Johnson; an age of reason and of studied mannerism in literature and the arts, and a century of dazzling imperial achievement overseas.

But—and herein lies the paradox—this comfortable picture of a prosperous and civilized society concealed a deep-seated domestic sickness. At no time in its long history was London a more dissolute or disorderly place, ill-governed and at times virtually ungovernable, in which crime became the principal industry and corruption the accepted practice. The pursuit of money was an obsession common to every class, and it took every conventional form and many ingeniously novel ones.

In high society, the public purse, before the introduction of proper public accountability, was a happy hunting-ground. Walpole, when chief minister, built himself a handsome house at Chelsea out of funds assigned for the maintenance of the Royal Hospital, while Paymaster-General Henry Fox founded the fortunes of the house of Holland by appropriating the substantial exchequer fees charged to army estimates. 'Patronage' and 'place-men' were the contemporary symbols of the widely acceptable face of capitalism.

The middle class as typified by the magistracy, without access to the public purse, resorted to private corruption, for this was the age of the 'trading' justice who administered the law with complete impartiality, which only meant that all parties were treated alike as sources of personal profit. Blackmail, extortion, the sale of warrants and summonses, improper bailing, conspiracy—the catalogue of judicial crime was as varied as the nature of crime itself; and both constable and watchman were quick to imitate, however modestly, the example of their superiors. 'The greatest criminals in the town,' wrote Horace Walpole, 'are the officers of justice. There is no tyranny they do not exercise, no villainy in which they do not partake.'

The incentive for much of this malpractice was the recently devised system of blood money or parliamentary rewards for the apprehension and conviction of criminals, assessed on a graduated scale (for example a highwayman was valued at £50, an army deserter at £1). An ingenious refinement was the 'Tyburn ticket' which was sometimes the whole reward or, as in the case of a conviction for housebreaking, a 'ticket' and a £10 sweetener. The Tyburn ticket exempted the holder for life from all parochial duties such as constable, beadle or watchman, and since it was transferable it soon acquired a substantial market value. Thus, at least during the first half of the eighteenth century, both the officers of the law and the breakers of the law were in effect officially paid to pursue their nefarious activities. The system threw up one paragon of vice in Jonathan Wild, first of the so-called 'thief-takers', who, in his capacity as a self-appointed officer of the law, planned the crimes he claimed to solve, organized the first protection racket (and also the entire London underworld) and prospered so greatly that he acquired not only a warehouse for the storage of stolen goods, but even a ship with which to pursue a successful export trade. Eventually, in 1724, a combination of arrogance and excessive greed brought him to the gallows at Tyburn.

*

While the upper and middle classes exploited the financial possibilities of privilege and position, the lower orders—with no such advantages—resorted to crime on an unparalleled scale. Not only was there no longer any semblance of a preventive police system, but the rewards of blood money and the rich dividends of corruption actually encouraged criminal practices. Indeed, it was often more profitable to overlook minor misdemeanours in the hope that this would invite bigger and better felonies which carried a more lucrative price tag. In the jargon of the day, a criminal was scarcely worth apprehending until he 'weighed forty pounds'.

During the eighteenth century the population of the Metropolis doubled from 500,000 to 1,000,000, but the working class remained for the most part crowded into a vast warren of slums in the area around the Strand and Fleet Street. The suburbs were the highwayman's province; central London and the City the haunt of less glamorous but equally unprincipled criminals. To walk abroad by night in these narrow, ill-lit streets was to invite retribution, while daylight robbery was scarcely less commonplace. The houses of the wealthy became embattled fortresses, guarded by retinues of armed servants. In a very real sense the Metropolis was in a state of civil siege.

The causes of this collapse of law and order are many: the breakdown of the old preventive partnership of justice and constable; a squalid environment which aggravated the instinct for self-preservation; over-crowding, unemployment, hunger and destitution; the first real expression of revolt against social injustice; even that deep streak of social indiscipline which is endemic in the English character. But there were two other factors, both—in their extravagance—peculiarly English.

The first was gambling to which the English have immemorially been addicted as has no other nation (if the cynic suggests Australia as a close second, it can well be argued that the disease there was an English export); and gambling needs money. The second special factor was one of such profound social significance that it is necessary to consider it more closely. This factor was drink.

Until the eighteenth century, England had been largely a nation of beerdrinkers (wine and the more exotic forms of continental liquor had, for reasons of money as much as taste, been the prerogative of the upper classes). The licensing of alehouses dates from an Act of 1552 'to remedy the intolerable hurt and trouble to the Commonwealth of the Realm of common alehouses and other houses called Tipling-houses'. There was no excise duty on alcohol until 1643 when, with characteristic lack of judgment, it was levied by Charles I to help finance the Royalist cause.

With the outbreak of war with France at the end of the seventeenth century, a heavy duty was imposed on imported brandy. But the English are not so easily defeated and duly invented a substitute called 'English brandy', distilled under royal licence and compounded of a blend of materials so noxious as to defy analysis. It was cheap, it was lethal, and its sale was unrestricted. It was also

very largely a London phenomenon and it was estimated that, by
1698, every fifth house in the Metropolis was purveying English
brandy at 1d a quartern and even, in some shops, free of charge like
a primitive kind of trading-stamp.

It was soon replaced by a new and equally potent competitor, a
distillation of grain and juniper berries which the Dutch called
'geneva' and the English called 'gin'; and within ten years a beer-
drinking London had become a gin-swilling city.

The scale of this alcoholic explosion may be judged by two
statistics. In 1730, there were 16,486 licensed alehouses and 171
breweries in the Cities of London and Westminster alone (the
number of unlicensed 'dram shops' is not recorded, but must have
been at least as great). In the year 1735, when the population of
the Metropolis was about 650,000, the consumption of gin was
5,500,000 gallons. People were drinking themselves to death on a
grand scale.[1]

The Government made several ineffective efforts to legislate
against this social evil, but since the basis of gin was home-grown
grain, the strong agricultural lobby in Parliament successfully
opposed every measure; indeed, the Gin Act of 1736 resulted in
widespread riots under the slogan: 'No Gin, no King!' Excessive
drinking was common to all classes, but it was at the lower end of
the scale that the practice became—in the most literal sense—a
vicious circle. Men, women and (by no means least) children
resorted to crime as a passport to gin shops, and, when suitably
stimulated, resorted to more crime as a further passport to further
gin shops. Food seems to have been a secondary consideration and
in 1730 it was estimated that twenty people were dying nightly of
starvation in the Metropolis alone.[2] How many died of acute
alcoholism is not recorded.

But public drunkenness produced another Metropolitan phenomenon which was to have perhaps the most significant of all
influences on the gradual movement towards a reformed and re-

[1] At the end of the century, even after the control of distilleries,
Colquhoun notes with astonishment that the expenditure on Ale, Porter,
Gin and 'Compounds' in the Metropolis (1794) amounted to £3,286,466
15s 10d. This is probably an underestimate by 50 per cent.

[2] Here is another strange paradox. On p. 34 of his *Treatise*, Colquhoun
has this odd footnote: 'The chief consumption of oysters, crabs, lobsters,
pickled salmon, etc, when first in season, and when prices are high, is by
the *lowest* classes of the people.'

vitalized police institution. This was the emergence of the notorious 'London mob', easily assembled—on any or no pretext—to achieve by intimidation what could not be resolved by reason or the law. Parish constables and their decrepit 'Charlies', incompetent to deal even with elementary crime, were no match for a drunken and disorderly mob. In such situations (and they were to become a regular feature of the London scene) the one defence against anarchy was to meet violence with superior violence; and that meant the use of military force. It was a confrontation which was to bedevil every rational attempt to convert public and parliamentary opinion to an acceptable means of preventing crime and preserving law and order.

Typical of the spirit of the times was the introduction of the Riot Act in 1715,[1] a classic example of misconceived, and virtually unenforceable, legislation. The Act conferred special powers on justices to require 'in the King's name' that riotous assemblies of twelve or more persons disperse within one hour of being so ordered. Failure to comply was visited with a brutally simple remedy: 'The offenders therein shall suffer death as in the case of felony without benefit of clergy.' It is impossible not to feel some sympathy for the unfortunate George I. The Riot Act was the first statute of his reign and the King, lately arrived from the peaceful and law-abiding Electorate of Hanover and speaking little English, might be forgiven for wondering what manner of people he had been summoned to rule. He could not have been left long in doubt that the King's Peace was in urgent need of repair.

*

What manner of people, indeed? It is a question which must have exercised not only Hanoverian George. The answer provides yet one more historical paradox and goes some way towards explaining the eventual nature of the police institution for the Metropolis. The English—and in particular, Londoners—have long cherished a romantic notion that they are a breed apart, and that democracy was a private invention of the island race. Not for them the restraints of absolute rule or state authority, but rather the splendid vision of Shakespeare's John of Gaunt.

The truth is otherwise. The English have long confused liberty

---

[1] It has since been repealed by the Criminal Law Act 1967. The last time the Riot Act was read by a magistrate seems to have been on the occasion of the disorders following the police strike in Liverpool in 1919.

with licence. Peel summed it up exactly when he wrote to Wellington on 5 November 1829 about his 'New Police': 'I want to teach people that liberty does not consist in having your house robbed by organized gangs of thieves, and in leaving the principal streets of London in the nightly possession of drunken women and vagabonds.' It is a sentiment which, with different political and social overtones, is no less valid 150 years later.

By the eighteenth century there was no city in Europe more urgently in need of a preventive police force than dissolute, disorderly London. Instead—for such is the dangerous illusion of assumed freedom—government and the judiciary resorted to repression in its most savage form. 'The price of liberty,' wrote Smollett, 'is public degradation.' The price of licence became public entertainment; the gallows (a major attraction for young and old alike), the pillory, the stocks, public whipping, transportation— the calendar of retribution reflects with uncomfortable accuracy the dark side of the English character. It also reflected once again the truth of Pascal's aphorism. Desperate human beings are not deterred by desperate remedies. If stealing from a dwelling-house to the value of 40s was accounted a capital crime, the thief had nothing to lose if, to avoid detection, he committed murder in the course of theft. It is an equation to which intelligent men presently began to address themselves, and one which we shall have cause to examine in due course. Meanwhile, London and its riotous citizens continued on their lawless way and the Tyburn gallows enjoyed an ever brisker trade.

In this critical situation, there appeared upon the battlefield (the word fairly describes the London scene) the first of a small task-force of dedicated men who, during the next hundred years, were to devote themselves to arresting the decline into anarchy and to re-establishing the rule of law.

Thomas de Veil was appointed a justice for Middlesex and Westminster[1] in 1729—by coincidence, exactly 100 years before Peel's Act. He was then forty-five and an officer on half-pay, whose military career had been undistinguished (he was later given the nominal rank of Colonel in the Westminster Militia). By the time of

---

[1] He was the last magistrate to hold the title of 'Court Justice', an appointment dating back to Elizabethan times and signifying a special relationship to the Court and the Ministry. It carried a stipend paid out of secret service funds.

his death in 1746, he had established a reputation, unique in his day, as a fearless dispenser of justice and, by contemporary standards, an honest broker in a profession notorious for its gross dishonesty. When, in 1739, he moved from his house in Frith Street to No. 4 Bow Street and there established his 'public office', he set in train a course of events which was to have a far-reaching influence on the slow but certain establishment of a proper and effective police institution for the Metropolis.

De Veil was an authentic eighteenth-century character and an ambitious one. His first step towards the corridors of power had been to open an office—by yet another coincidence, in Scotland Yard—where he acted as a commission agent for officers and others who were seeking, with or without justification, grants, privileges and favours from the War Office and the Treasury. In financial terms, he prospered greatly. He needed to, for in his time he had four wives and fathered twenty-five legitimate children, and—in the words of his anonymous biographer—'he loved money and affected magnificence; he was a man of pleasure and never wanted resources, for what it constantly requires unbounded expense'.

But his sights were set on higher things; and he was as thorough as he was ambitious. So, before accepting the offer of a seat on the Bench, he made a careful study of the nature and powers of the office of justice of the peace, so that when he felt ready to take up his new duties, he was certainly better equipped for the task than any other member of the Metropolitan magistracy. He also took the wise precaution of making friends at court. While he was never chairman of the Westminster Bench, he came to be regarded as the chief magistrate in the Metropolis and the principal scourge of the criminal class. 'Indeed,' writes his biographer, 'there was hardly ever a magistrate so dreadful in this respect to these sort of people, for the very name of him was sufficient to frighten them, and they fancied his intelligence to be so good, that they were never safe from him.'

De Veil was, like all his contemporaries, a trading justice, but 'he possessed his own kind of integrity and took only what he held to be fair profit, and he kept the most scrupulous accounts. He knew his law and endeavoured to administer it with fairness.'[1] He found other ways of supplementing his income; for example, his appointment

---

[1] Browne, *The Rise of Scotland Yard*.

in 1738 to the sinecure office of Inspector-General of Exports and Imports at a salary of £500 a year with a supplement of £280 for his clerk; and the records show that his diligence as a justice was rewarded with various grants from government sources, including, in 1744, a knighthood. Such monies as he received were confidential, since, before the appointment of stipendiary magistrates in 1792, the payment of justices out of public funds would have been a breach of the constitution. It does not seem to have occurred to the legislators of the time that a paid magistracy would have effectively scotched one of the principal scandals of the day.

De Veil's seventeen years as a magistrate coincided with an un-precedented growth in the rate of crime and an explosion of mob rule in London; indeed, he is said never to have been without a copy of the Riot Act in his pocket. During this time he became, in effect, the first Commissioner of Police of the Metropolis despite the non-cooperation of the parish vestries with their jealously guarded rights and their ineffective constabulary. He was thus obliged to rely on his personal courage, his knowledge of the law, his exceptional detective abilities and, in extreme cases, the inter-vention of the military. He could not prevent crime; but he could, by his example, show that crime did not pay, a fact which he was not slow to impress upon criminals and upon unscrupulous lawyers. In a memorial, he claimed that in fifteen years he had been respons-ible for the execution or transportation of 'above nineteen hundred of the greatest malefactors that ever appeared in England'. Given the temper of the times, it was a remarkable single-handed achievement.

We need not here concern ourselves with De Veil's case-book, except to record an event in 1737 which was to provide one more link in the curious chain of coincidence which marks the police history of the Metropolis.

In that year, the Government turned aside briefly from its pre-occupation with public drunkenness to pass an Act licensing all theatres other than Covent Garden and Drury Lane, which enjoyed a royal patent (it was a measure which was not to be repealed for over 200 years). In 1736 Henry Fielding had formed a 'company of comedians' and had leased the Little Theatre in Haymarket. He was then thirty. During the previous seven years he had written and staged some twenty comedies which in their savage and satirical wit were the dramatic counterpart to Hogarth's visual commentaries on the immorality and degradation of the day. Nothing escaped his caustic pen: the prevalent vices of drink and gambling; sexual permissiveness; idleness and opulence. But above all his target was the judiciary and, in particular, the ignorance, dishonesty and corruption of trading justices. 'Sir,' says a character in *Tumble Down Dick*, 'that's a Justice of the Peace . . . a very ingenious man and a very great scholar, but happen'd to have the misfortune in his youth never to learn to read'; and again in *Don Quixote*: 'Twelve lawyers make not one honest man.' Thus, by the time he came to lease the Little Theatre, Fielding was the toast of the town. He had also made some formidable enemies.

With his new company of comedians, Fielding now trod more dangerous ground. This time his target was Robert Walpole. The first such play was *Pasquin* which attacked election bribery and ministerial corruption and achieved a success rivalling that of the earlier *Beggar's Opera*. Despite some warning shots across his bows, he followed this first sally with an even more savage essay in satire, *The Historical Register*, in which he introduced Walpole himself as the incompetent Quidam, 'a poor, impudent fellow', engaged in bribery and corruption on a grand and criminal scale.

Walpole had had enough. On 20 May 1737 he himself introduced a Bill, innocent enough in its title, but containing a clause empowering the Lord Chamberlain to prohibit the production of any plays 'for hire, gain or reward' without prior submission and licence. It was the end of Henry Fielding as a dramatist.[1] The Little Theatre was closed and he turned instead to the study of the law. He was now embarked upon a road which was presently to lead him to the public office in Bow Street where, in his capacity as Chief Magistrate, he became in the six short years during which he held that office, the most celebrated pioneer of police reform.

There remains one footnote which, as an example of high comedy, is worthy of Fielding himself. The following year (1738), the Government, gratified by its success at censorship, re-opened the Little Theatre for a performance by a company of French players. But it had reckoned without the force of public opinion and the versatility of the London mob. The audience turned up armed with an arsenal of vegetable missiles. So did Colonel de Veil,

---

[1] It was also to prove the birth of Henry Fielding as a novelist, perhaps the greatest of the eighteenth century.

armed with the Riot Act, which, amid scenes of uproar, he attempted to read from the stage. Baffled by a brilliant verbal counter-attack from an audience wag, De Veil withdrew, the performers fled, and the curtain came down. Henry Fielding might have been excused a small, wry smile of satisfaction. Governments which champion the cause of liberty should be careful of inviting licence.

*

Henry Fielding took the oath as a justice for the City and Liberty of Westminster in the autumn of 1748 and moved into No. 4 Bow Street early in December. Increasing ill-health had forced him to abandon his legal practice, and it is probable that his appointment as a magistrate[1] was in some measure a reward from his Tory friends, George Lyttelton and the Duke of Bedford, for his campaign against Walpole and his subsequent literary efforts in support of the Government.

There is a certain irony in the fact that Fielding, the man who had pilloried the trading justices of his day and had created the character of Justice Squeezum, should now find himself the magistrate at Bow Street. There was no shortage of enemies lying in wait for him, convinced that here was a classic case of gamekeeper turned poacher and that his appointment to Bow Street was a piece of political patronage to enable him to enrich himself on the same scale as the other trading justices of the Metropolis. He himself commented that 'a heavier load of scandal hath been cast upon me, than I believe ever fell to the share of any single man'.

But Fielding was made of sterner stuff. He was that rare eighteenth-century figure, a man of high principles and social vision. Not only did he set his face against all forms of corruption ('I reduced an income of about five hundred pounds a year of the dirtiest money upon earth to little more than three hundred pounds; a considerable portion of which remained with my clerk'[2]), but he brought to his task a unique compassion and understanding. He was also probably the first Englishman to make a serious study of the *causes* of crime. To men of violence and to the destroyers of life and property he administered justice with the utmost severity, but

[1] He had earlier been nominated as a Middlesex justice in 1747; but lacking at that time a property qualification, did not take up his duties there until 1749.

[2] Henry Fielding, *Journal of a Voyage to Lisbon.*

for those whom he felt to be themselves the victims of social degradation he had an instinctive sense of pity and to them he showed a special leniency. For this alone, he deserves to be remembered. How many readers of *Tom Jones* today even know this other and greater claim to fame of its author? For without his pioneering zeal and dedication and, after his death, the continuing work of his blind half-brother, John, it is arguably certain that uninformed public opinion would have made Peel's Metropolitan Police Act impossible.

In some ways, Henry Fielding was fortunate. He came to Bow Street at a time when crime in the Metropolis had reached a formidable level and an impotent and frightened government was ready to clutch at any straw, short of recourse to the public purse. It is true that Fielding, with no private financial resources, managed to obtain a small pension out of secret service funds. But when it is remembered that in the year 1752 alone, crime was 'subsidized' by the payment of over £40,000 in blood money, what might the Fieldings have achieved if such a sum had instead been applied to the *prevention* of crime?

He was also fortunate that he had had a legal training and that he had a brilliant literary talent. In 1751 he published *An Enquiry into the Causes of the late Increase of Robbers*, 'to rouse', as he said, 'the civil power from its present lethargic state'. This document, long since forgotten, is a historic statement not only of the causes of crime, but of the imperfections of legal procedure and the equally serious imperfections of the legal profession. Not surprisingly, it referred to drunkenness as 'this odious vice, indeed the parent of all others', and dealt in similar terms with gaming, prostitution and 'idleness, the first cause of crime'. The *Enquiry* had a profound effect which was presently to be reflected in the statute book. But its true measure may be judged by its extraordinary relevance to the social climate of our own day. To it we owe the concept of a Public Prosecutor, the theory of legal aid, the proposition that law and order is as much the province of the public as of the police, and—of particular contemporary significance—the belief that the law is too heavily weighted in favour of the defence and of the unscrupulous lawyer. To Henry Fielding, liberty and permissiveness were clean different things.

The *Enquiry* was not Fielding's last word on the subject. In 1753, by then a dying man, he was invited by the Duke of Newcastle to prepare 'the best plan which could be invented for putting an immediate end to those murders and robberies which were every day committed in the streets'. Within four days his plan was ready. 'The principal and most material proposal was the immediately depositing of six hundred pounds in my hands: at which small charge I undertook to demolish the then reigning gangs and to put the civil policy in such order that no such gangs should ever be able . . . at least to remain any time formidable to the public.'

This money he required not for himself or for his already established handful of detectives, but for the encouragement of public cooperation and for bribing informers. In October he received a first instalment of £200 and at the year's end could astonishingly report that 'in the remaining part of the month of November, and in all December, not only no such thing as a murder, but not even a street-robbery was committed'. Fielding at no time considered the formation of a *preventive* police force; but he had conclusively proved that certainty of detection was a powerful deterrent and thus, by implication, an essential weapon in the prevention of crime. His brother, John, was soon to find that government words, however flattering, are not always matched by government deeds.

*

'Mr Fielding's People' or, as they came to be known towards the end of the century, the Bow Street Runners, were the tiny seed out of which the Metropolitan Police was to grow.

Shortly after taking office at Bow Street, Fielding enlisted as assistants his brother John, and Saunders Welch, the High Constable of Holborn and a man of exceptional character, cast very much in Fielding's own mould. All three men were aware of the collapse of the parish constabulary system and of the total lack of cooperation between parish vestries. They were equally aware that, to combat crime on the massive scale that was then prevalent, it was necessary to carry the war into the criminals' own camp.

Fielding accordingly recruited seven men, all (except one) ex-constables of Westminster and chosen because they were 'actuated by a truly public spirit against Thieves', to continue as volunteer thief-takers under the supervision of the Bow Street Office. There is some argument whether at the outset these men were salaried employees, but it seems more likely that they made their living out

of blood money for successful prosecutions and from rewards paid
by the gratified victims of convicted thieves and robbers.

The names of this intrepid band have not survived and indeed—
with good reason—their existence was not formally admitted for
several years. Not only was their occupation lonely and hazardous,
but the public, who were their sole beneficiaries, viewed them with
the same suspicion and hostility that they had shown towards the
unprincipled thief-takers of Jonathan Wild's day. Yet despite their
inadequate numbers, their diligence and efficiency resulted in a
remarkable success rate; and had the Government persisted with
Henry Fielding's 1753 plan, the pattern of organized crime might
have been very different by the end of the century.

Instead, by then the Bow Street Runners had degenerated into
something a good deal less romantic than the conventional image
which has survived them. 'It is certain that they were the source of
much evil. Actuated by the hope of gain rather than by any sense of
duty, their motives were as ignoble as their methods were shady.'[1]
Indeed, we even find their most celebrated member, James
Townsend, coolly describing to the Select Committee of 1816 the
system of improper bailing then current among justices, adding, for
good measure, some simple arithmetic—'a hundred girls at two
shillings and fourpence, that would make £11 13s 4d. They sent
none to gaol, for the bailing of them was so much better.' Townsend
should have known. At his death, he was credited with being worth
£20,000.

The Bow Street Runners survived the formation of the 'New
Police' and it was not until the 1839 Act that they were finally disbanded. For all their shortcomings, they had made a significant
contribution to the police idea.

*

It was a singular stroke of fortune that Henry Fielding was succeeded at the Bow Street Office by two such ardent, if different,
disciples as his brother and Saunders Welch.

Welch, with his intimate knowledge of the criminal classes, was
first and last a policeman rather than a judicial officer and his
primary concern was the supervision of the small force of thief-
takers. The year before becoming a magistrate, he published a

---

[1] W. Melville Lee, *A History of Police in England.*

pamphlet called *Observations on the Office of Constable* which was designed to provide a set of guide-lines for the conduct of petty constables in the many parishes of the Metropolis. 'Let the service of the public,' he wrote, 'be the great motive of all those actions which regard your office; this, properly attended to, will keep you from all officious, wanton acts of power.' He advised against provocation by ill-disposed members of the public and warned against 'passion and resentment' and the use of force except as a last resort in self-defence. This, written in 1754, was a revolutionary approach to the peace-keeping attitudes of the day and was firmly rooted in the ancient common law origins of the office of constable. If we compare his advice with the General Instruction Book issued to the first Metropolitan policemen in 1829, it is beyond argument that Welch's 'principles of police' provided an almost verbatim model for Rowan and Mayne.

Saunders Welch, whose natural charm and personal qualities attracted the respect and affection of men as different as Henry Fielding and Samuel Johnson, worked in harness with John Fielding for six years, until, following a clash of personalities, they parted company. Welch subsequently opened an office in Litchfield Street, where he continued to demonstrate his unique brand of expertise until his retirement in 1774.

John Fielding's long reign at Bow Street lasted twenty-five years and his contribution to police and penal reform is so great that it is not possible to do more than summarize it here. Despite his blindness, he was an indefatigable worker, although a good deal more pompous and egotistical than his half-brother; it was no bad fault, for it needed a man of formidable determination to penetrate the entrenched defence system of government in the latter half of the eighteenth century, and also a man of resolution to involve a hostile and demoralized public in the battle for social survival. This provides yet another paradox. Here was a great Metropolis, threatened by anarchy and by licentious mob rule, whose citizens preferred to believe that police protection of their just and lawful rights was an equal threat to liberty. The English scarcely deserved the Fieldings.

John Fielding's work at Bow Street was a logical extension of Henry's pioneering efforts. He shared his brother's views on the causes of crime, on the inadequacy of the parochial constabulary, and on the need for a salaried and professional magistracy and police. But in two significant ways he was an innovator in his own right: he was a convinced believer in the value of good public relations and, echoing the old Anglo-Saxon system, in involving the public themselves in the maintenance of law and order; and he was probably the first magistrate to advance the principle that prevention of crime was the surest way of keeping the King's Peace. Thus, in one of the many notices he inserted in the *Public Advertiser*, he expressed the novel view that 'preventing offences is not only a more agreeable office to the magistrates, but a more useful one to the public, than the punishing of offenders', while some years later he wrote: 'It is much better to prevent even one man from being a rogue than apprehending and bringing forty to justice.'

One of John Fielding's first actions was to persuade the Government to pay him and Welch an annual salary each of £200 (his own stipend was subsequently increased to £400). As in his brother's case, the money came from the secret service fund and illustrates again the almost pathological aversion of those in authority to any public acknowledgement of the advantages of a professional system for preventing crime and keeping the peace; and it is a singular and unexplained fact that despite the well-publicized operation of the Bow Street Office, no other Metropolitan magistrate saw fit to imitate the novel principles and methods which were being pursued there. 'Bow Street,' wrote Anthony Babington, 'reached its predominant position, not in competition but by default.'[1] The reason can only be that the great majority of the magistracy still consisted of inferior persons with no concern in 'abating the power of felons', but rather a vested interest in encouraging crime as a source of personal gain. To such men a stipend of £400 was a derisory reward. They were soon to be confronted in no uncertain way with the consequences of their apathy and corruption.

In 1755 John Fielding, realizing that crime was no longer a parochial matter, published a *Plan for Preventing Robberies within Twenty Miles of London*, which was another example of his belief in the value of public cooperation. This plan was based on the idea that residents living in outlying areas of the Metropolis should contribute two guineas each towards forming a protective group or club which would notify Bow Street of highway robberies in their district; upon receipt of which, the office would circulate full details

[1] Babington: *A House in Bow Street.*

and, where possible, dispatch peace officers to pursue and apprehend the criminal. It was a bold exercise in public involvement; and predictably it was still-born.

Instead, Fielding turned once more to the strengthening and improvement of his small team of detectives, and in 1757 he extracted from the Government an annual payment of £400 (invariably in arrears) for what would today be called 'support services' and the provision of two 'pursuit horses'; and the following year he instituted what was virtually a national register of known criminals, a revolutionary innovation which anticipated by over 100 years the establishment of the embryo Criminal Record Office in 1869. It is ironic that this register, together with most of his other papers and those of his brother, were destroyed when, during the Gordon Riots, the mob sacked the Bow Street office.

Fielding's restless mind was soon at work again. In 1761, the year in which he was knighted,[1] he presented Newcastle—as his brother had done—with a master-plan for the reduction of crime which he called significantly 'a plan of police'. It was nothing if not radical and many of its proposals were subsequently adopted almost in their original form, although not by Newcastle who combined the political art of the impossible with a formidable capacity for inaction.

The main features of this plan were as follows. There should be appointed five or six stipendiary magistrates for Westminster and adjacent counties, all with proper legal qualifications in order to equip them effectively to handle the notorious attorneys of the day. These justices would be in regular attendance at public offices (of which Bow Street would be the principal one) and the scheme would be self-financing out of lawfully established fees and expenses. Next, he advocated the formation of a *unified*, though not uniformed, paid constabulary for the inner Metropolitan area, and a proper system of pavement lighting. The rural outskirts would be covered by special foot patrols operating after dark during the autumn and winter months; and a regiment of cavalry would be stationed near London to police the main access roads. This latter suggestion was treading on very delicate ground and Fielding was quick to emphasize that this military force, in keeping with the

---

[1] John Fielding was not noted for undue modesty. Five years earlier he had proposed to Newcastle that he should be thus honoured, citing the example of Sir Thomas de Veil. Since then, all succeeding Chief Magistrates of Bow Street, except one, have received a knighthood.

common law rights and responsibilities of 'all persons whatever', would be 'intended to cooperate with, *and act under*, the civil power'. Finally he asked for the most careful and scrupulous licensing of public houses, since such places were usually thieves' kitchens and therefore the seat and origin of much criminality. One single thread runs through this plan: it is the principal purpose of a police system to *prevent* crime.

Undeterred by Newcastle's apathy, Fielding concentrated on one aspect of his plan which seemed to him unassailable. For years the increasing activities of highwaymen on the approach roads to London had made all forms of travel a formidable risk. In October 1763, Fielding—whose powers of persuasion were considerable—extracted from the Treasury a small grant for the establishment of a Horse Patrol to police the approaches to the Metropolis. This consisted of eight (later increased to ten) non-uniformed men who were paid 4s a night with expenses. The scheme was initially sanctioned on an experimental basis for six months and its success was so dramatic that by the spring of 1764 travellers could come and go in complete safety. The Horse Patrol was continued for a further six months when, for no apparent reason other than economy, the Treasury terminated the grant. The cost had been a little over £1,000. The contribution to public tranquillity had been priceless.

This decision drew from Fielding one of his rare expressions of exasperation: 'There is nothing I so sincerely lament as the want of an opportunity of convincing Mr Grenville [First Lord of the Treasury] of the amazing importance of the police to the Government.' Mr Grenville was now to discover the amazing importance of a lack of police in the matter of law and order.

*

The affair of John Wilkes lasted for seven years. It was to prove a classic example of government ineptitude, of the perilous state of London's civil defences, and of a new phenomenon—the appearance of political and industrial militancy; and, given the nature of Londoners in general and Wilkes in particular, it had its moments of pure farce.

Briefly, Wilkes, the MP for Aylesbury, was charged in 1763 with publishing a libel on the King in his journal, *The North Briton*. Expelled from the House of Commons, he demonstrated the illegality of all proceedings against him with a wit and humour which effectively humiliated both the Government and the Court faction. Above all he made powerful friends in the City. And later that year he removed himself to Paris, on which pretext he was—again illegally—declared an outlaw.

By now, under the slogan 'Wilkes and Liberty', he was a public hero *in absentia* and the symbol for every kind of political and industrial grievance, real and imagined. At one end the City merchants ranged themselves against the commercial policy of the Government; at the other the mob, volatile as ever, took to the streets. The catalogue of riots was unique even by London's standards. Throughout these stormy years the civil power virtually ceased to exist. The unfortunate John Fielding was made the scapegoat for the shortcomings of public authority, but he had only to remind his critics of their apathy to his many previous proposals to silence them. Instead, the Government resorted to military force, with entirely predictable results. It could fairly be said that London had become ungovernable.

Wilkes's decision to return to London in 1768 resulted in an interlude of comedy, with the public hero winning a carefully manipulated election victory at Brentford and forthwith committing himself to gaol to save the Chief Justice, Mansfield, the embarrassment of conveying him there. Even from his luxurious quarters in the King's Bench prison, he continued to harass the Government and orchestrate the activities of the mob. And it was not until his release in 1770 that sanity and comparative peace were restored.

The Wilkes affair was to have far-reaching effects on such matters as press freedom and Parliamentary reform.[1] But it also had a profound influence on police history; and by yet another paradox, when ten years later the moment of truth arrived, John Wilkes was to be found on the side of the angels.

*

The traumatic experiences of the 1760s prodded the Government into some sense of duty. In May 1770 a Select Committee was appointed to inquire, as well it might, into the state of the police in the Metropolis (the City quickly ensured that it was not included in the terms of reference).

This was the first of eleven such committees which were to be

[1] One specific result was the printing of Parliamentary debates by Luke Hansard and William Cobbett.

convened before the passing of the Metropolitan Police Act in 1829; and all, except that of 1828, were marked by one striking similarity: inertia. Over the years, evidence was given by many sincere and experienced men who had devoted their lives to a study of the problems of police reorganization, and its vital prerequisite— criminal reform; men like Bentham and Colquhoun, Mackintosh and Romilly. The printed volumes of these Committee Reports are mute testimony to the incomprehension and lack of interest of political hacks who needed only to venture onto the London streets to watch anarchy in action. Not many of them would have known or cared about the squalid circumstances of three-quarters of their fellow-citizens. And very few would have been moved by an entry in the Newgate Calendar recorded as late as 1832.

At the Middlesex Sessions on Thursday, 17 May of that year, James Connor was sentenced to 'transportation for seven years'. It was a not unusual sentence—except that James Connor was aged twelve, that he was described as 'a labourer', and that his crime was 'the theft of a handkerchief, value four shillings'. During the six days of those Sessions, 269 persons were committed for trial, of whom 33 were sentenced to death for such crimes as 'stealing a shawl', 'stealing 16 shillings' and 'uttering a forged order for the delivery of 898 coker nuts'. Not only was the law in disarray. So too was that 'human wisdom and human experience' of which Johnson spoke.

*

The 1770 Committee duly called John Fielding as a witness (they need scarcely have troubled to call anyone else, except Saunders Welch). With exemplary patience, he rehearsed all the old arguments and proposals he had for so long advanced. His evidence, with the important exception of the plan for stipendiary magistrates, was duly recorded in the Committee's report; and the report was shelved.

Fielding returned to Bow Street to occupy himself with what he called 'the favourite object of my ambition'. This was the compiling of a bulletin, to be issued free to magistrates throughout the country and containing lists of wanted criminals believed to have escaped from the Metropolitan area. In his usual persuasive way, Fielding obtained a government subsidy of £400 to finance the project; and in 1772 there appeared the first issue of the *Quarterly Pursuit*. So great was its success that the indefatigable Fielding, despite his heavy load of magisterial work, converted it into the *Weekly Pursuit*. Six years after his death, a more elaborate version was produced by Sampson Wright, his successor at Bow Street, with the title *Public Hue and Cry*, and this in turn, with the formation of Peel's 'New Police', was to become the *Police Gazette*. Thus, slowly but surely, was forged another link in the campaign against crime.

*

In all historical processes, it is possible to identify a single event which proved to be a watershed. In the case of the Metropolitan Police, such an event occurred during the first week of June 1780.

The Gordon Riots lasted for seven days. During that time the Cities of London and Westminster were delivered to an explosion of mob violence so savage that it left the heart of the capital a smoking ruin and the forces of law and order shattered and discredited. Out of the ashes grew, infinitely slowly, and despite every vested interest, the realization that a civilized society was only possible if it took steps to civilize itself. It was to take another forty-nine years for the phoenix to rise.

The riots of 1780 had their notional origin in a parliamentary Bill to remove certain Catholic disabilities.[1] So much for history. The truth, despite all historical argument, is more stark. The English, as we have already seen, need little incentive to indiscipline. In 1736 the cry was 'No Gin no King!' In 1763, it was 'Wilkes and Liberty!' Now it was 'No Popery!' Since William of Orange, the Catholic debate had been a dormant issue; but the London mob never cared much about principles. In the eighteenth century it was more concerned with gin, with destitution, and with social frustration. Bonfires of dissent are built to be lighted.

Lord George Gordon was an improbable lighter of bonfires. He was twenty-nine, he was rich, he was a wit, and he was not notably anti-Catholic. Historians have suggested that he was mad, but at his eventual trial for high treason, he objected to one juryman, who was a ropemaker, on the grounds that he might be professionally biased. That sounds less like a madman than an authentic wag.

Reith[2] has suggested more plausibly that he was the tool of City

---

[1] The classic account of the events of June 1780 is to be found in J. F. de Castro, *The Gordon Riots*. But see also Charles Reith, *The Police Idea*.
[2] Reith, *op. cit.*

merchants determined to bring down a government involved in a commercially disastrous war with America;[1] and certainly the activities of the mob were planned—at least for the first three days —with a tactical skill which could not have been the work of one man. Thereafter the mob took control.

The ineffectiveness of counter-measures was marked by an absurd legal dilemma. According to Stormont, the Home Secretary, military force could only be used at the request of a magistrate; and since virtually every Metropolitan magistrate had decided that discretion was the better part of valour and had discovered urgent business commitments outside London, there was no way of ensuring proper constitutional procedure.[2] The Riot Act was shown to be a very blunt instrument indeed. Eventually it fell to the King himself, through a neat piece of legal sophistry, to override the constitution by authorizing military commanders to use their own discretion and to open fire on the mob without waiting for magisterial authority, a decision which culminated in 'Bloody Wednesday' when troops used their weapons against an inebriated crowd attacking the Bank of England. At least 250 rioters were killed, but the effect was salutary and the disorders gradually ceased.With soldiers patrolling the streets, a great peace descended on London. Nevertheless the final confrontation left deep scars.

*

After the riots, the debate. No citizen of the Metropolis could any longer doubt that, with the present state of its civil defences, the capital was at the mercy of any mob which chose to take the law into its own hands. Words like 'liberty' and 'just rights and freedoms' were bandied about, but there was little mention of 'licence' or 'breaches of the peace'. Shelburne's daring suggestion that the hated French might, after all, have found the proper answer was greeted with disgust, while Sheridan's demand for a full inquiry into 'the defective state of the magistracy' was rejected by the Solicitor-General on the dangerously specious grounds that the

[1] The Lord Mayor of London at the time of the riots was Brackley Kennet, a brothel-keeper turned wine-merchant.

[2] Throughout the riots John Fielding was lying seriously ill at his house at Brompton. Saunders Welch was in retirement. Justice Hyde, the only Westminster magistrate to attempt to do his duty, had his house burned down for his pains.

riots had been 'a single instance of a defect in the civil power' which would probably not occur again,[1] an observation which must have caused some surprise to the now respectable City dignitary, John Wilkes. Underlying every argument was a backward glance at the shade of Cromwell and the obsessional fear of a military regime. There were sincere men like Vincent, Hanway and Sayer who advanced the proposal of an armed citizenry without realizing that this was merely a euphemism for a citizen army. Only a very few thinking men—notably, in due course, Jeremy Bentham—argued that the savagery of the criminal law·might be a major contribution to the savage lawlessness of the community. The debate continued.

*

Back at Bow Street, John Fielding's successor, Sampson Wright, now managed to translate words into action. He was one of the few men to believe—probably correctly—that the presence of even a small, well-trained force of preventive police would have been able to break up the demonstration during the first day, and before drink, professional agitation, and the intervention of troops had converted a dangerous situation into an uncontrollable riot.

In 1782 the Government sanctioned the formation of a Bow Street Foot Patrol, consisting of sixty-eight men divided into parties of four or five, each under a 'captain', and controlled by the Bow Street Office.[2] During the hours of darkness, eight parties of this small force patrolled the outskirts of the Metropolis to a distance of four miles from Charing Cross, while five more covered beats within the City of Westminster. Of their relationship—or lack of it—with the existing parish constabulary, nothing is known, but it is a fair assumption that the vestries, when not actually hostile to this invasion of their territory, provided no cooperation.

The Foot Patrol is of particular importance for a number of reasons. First, it was, together with John Fielding's short-lived Horse Patrol, the earliest example of a purely preventive police force and thus an active expression of the principle for which Fielding had fought so long. Secondly, the patrols were paid out of public instead of secret funds, the captains at a rate of 5s a night

---

[1] Between 1780 and 1829, there were another eighty-one more or less serious riots in the Metropolis alone (*Annual Register*).

[2] Pitt's 1798 Committee on Police Finance put the annual cost at a little under £4,000.

and the men 2s 6d each. Thirdly, they were armed, a fact which contradicted most of the pious arguments generated by the Gordon Riots.

They seem to have been an immediate success, for soon they were being used to supplement the handful of Bow Street Runners, and the 1798 Report observed that, among other duties, 'they are also employed to keep the peace upon all public occasions'. The strain upon their modest numerical resources presently encouraged the authorities to increase their establishment until, by the early years of the next century, it had risen to 100 men. The Foot Patrol continued under the direction of the Chief Magistrate at Bow Street until 1839 when, together with the Runners, it was absorbed into the Metropolitan Police.

Meanwhile, other minds were at work on the problems raised by the Gordon Riots; and in 1785, Sir Archibald Macdonald, the Solicitor-General in the younger Pitt's administration, introduced 'a Bill for the Further Prevention of Crime and for the more speedy Detection and Punishment of Offenders against the Peace in the Cities of London and Westminster, the Borough of Southwark and certain parts adjacent to them'.

This measure, which came to be known as 'Pitt's Bill', was, in the context of its time, a very remarkable document, for virtually every clause was to be embodied in substance in Peel's Act forty-four years later. Its main proposals were these: the area defined in its title was to be made into a single 'District of the Metropolis' divided into nine 'divisions'; three Commissioners were to be appointed to execute the laws for the prevention of offences, and while each Commissioner would have the powers of a justice of the peace, he would take all offenders before the existing justices;[1] the Commissioners would have powers over all parochial authorities and their peace officers and would be responsible for the establishment of public offices and the selection of qualified justices; the duties of the new police force would include patrolling; the system of blood money would cease forthwith, the whole establishment, including commissioners and justices, would be paid, and the entire exercise would be financed out of properly legalized fees.

But Pitt had reckoned without the City of London. Even while the Bill was still being debated, the Lord Mayor and Sheriffs arrived

---

[1] This is the first instance of a deliberate intention to separate the judicial and executive functions of the magistracy.

hot-foot at the Commons armed with a petition, couched in language so intemperate as to have justified a motion of breach of privilege. The petition bristled with phrases like these: 'mischievous and dangerous Effects of a Law which . . . goes to the entire Subversion of the Chartered Rights of the greatest City in the World'; 'the Destruction of the Constitutional Liberties of above a Million [*sic*] of his Majesty's subjects'; 'a System of Police altogether new and arbitrary in the Extreme'; 'an immediate Rejection of the Bill, to quiet the Minds of His Majesty's Subjects and relieve them from the Dread of being reduced under the Scourge of such a System'. Alderman Hammet went so far as to say that the Bill frightened the City so much that 'if a torch had been applied to the buildings there, it could not have created greater alarm'. As Reith points out,[1] it was an unfortunate metaphor, for only five years earlier the City had suffered precisely that experience, entirely as a result of the lack of an organized police force.

Pitt, much occupied with other pressing affairs of state and short in years and experience, beat a tactical retreat. He was dependent on City support—and the City knew it. Observing that he was not 'perfectly master of the subject', he withdrew the Bill, and a measure which would have ensured the peace and security of the most disorderly, as well as the 'greatest', city in the world died an unnatural death. The City Fathers have much to answer for.

*

Just as Sampson Wright had salvaged something from the wreckage of the Gordon Riots debate, so now one small element of Pitt's Bill survived the arrogant hostility of the City. The chosen area for reform was one with which few could argue, although Fox and Sheridan deployed their considerable skills to suggest that the Government was embarked on a shabby conspiracy against the defenceless poor of the Metropolis, a charge which had more to do with hypocrisy than rational argument.

The Middlesex Justices Act was introduced in March 1792 with the purpose of ending the age-old scandal of magisterial corruption in the Metropolis. The fact that its prime mover was William Mainwaring, chairman of the Middlesex Sessions and himself one of the most corrupt and distasteful characters to have disgraced the

[1] Reith, *op. cit.*

Bench, was a fair commentary on eighteenth-century morality. But remarkably—in view of past precedents—the measure became law, at first on a temporary basis, but finally made permanent in 1812.

The Act established seven 'police offices',[1] each with three stipendiary magistrates at £400 a year, and six police officers at 12s a week. Justices and constables were strictly forbidden, on pain of dismissal, to indulge in private peculation, and a Treasurer—the forerunner of the Receiver for the Metropolitan Police District—was appointed to handle authorized fees and disbursements. It had taken forty years for Henry Fielding's cardinal reform to reach the statute book, even in an experimental and imperfect form; and Pitt, mindful of his earlier humiliation, made certain—by the inclusion of a long and specific clause—that the measure would neither injure nor insult the sensitive dignity of the City.

The twenty-one new justices were selected by the Home Secretary, Dundas. They were an odd assortment, with few special qualifications, and included an ex-Lord Mayor, a starch-dealer, a clergyman, a Poet Laureate, and sundry lawyers. But one man among them was to leave an indelible mark on the history of the Metropolitan Police. In June 1792, Patrick Colquhoun was appointed a justice at the new Worship Street office. In his time, he was to create what he himself called 'the new science of police'. And in this sense, the turn of the century belongs to him.

[1] The seven new offices, additional to Bow Street, were located at Great Marlborough Street, Queen Square, Hatton Garden, Worship Street, Whitechapel, Shadwell and Southwark. The Marine Police office in Wapping was added in 1798.

CHAPTER TWO

'An Act for Improving the Police in and near the Metropolis'

PATRICK COLQUHOUN was a native of Dumbarton, near Glasgow, where, for three consecutive years, he was Lord Provost. He had made his name and fortune in the cloth trade and had acquired the formal title of 'Father of the City of Glasgow' when, in 1789, he moved to London to develop and advance the commercial interests of his native city. He was then forty-four.

As we have seen, with the passing of the Middlesex Justices Act, he was nominated as a stipendiary magistrate at the new police office at Worship Street. There is no obvious reason why Henry Dundas should have chosen him beyond the fact that he was a fellow Scot and, by reputation, a man of known integrity and public spirit; and that—in 1792—was a very singular recommendation indeed. During the next twenty-five years he was to devote his exceptional talents and his qualities of compassion and understanding to the problems of criminal law reform and to the pursuit of what he called 'the new science' of a preventive police. He was, beyond argument, the most influential advocate of this new philosophy, and the chief instrument through whom Henry Fielding's vision of an ordered society was translated into Peel's historic assertion of the primacy of law and order.

The Metropolis to which Colquhoun came was as lawless and disorderly as at any time during the century. It may be that the years spent in the comparative tranquillity of Glasgow allowed him to take a dispassionate view of his magisterial duties;[1] but as the daily spectacle of vicious and degraded humanity was paraded before him and as he handed down the punitive sentences which the law demanded, he began to ask himself the same questions which had exercised the Fieldings and which for so long had met with, at

[1] He was just in time; for, within a decade, the London disease had spread to every city in the kingdom, with Glasgow in the vanguard.

best, cosmetic answers. Why do men, women and—especially—children resort to crime? Might it be possible that the very savagery of the criminal code was itself, by a terrible paradox, one of the causes of crime? How best could this decline into anarchy be arrested? And what manner of defensive mechanism was best suited to prevent crime and protect society? It is not the least of the many ironies of police history that it was a Scotsman who mapped out for the English a road through this hitherto impenetrable jungle of prejudice and apathy.

In 1796, Colquhoun published his findings. The *Treatise on the Police of the Metropolis* ran through seven editions in ten years, which throws an interesting light on the true extent of public concern about the collapse of law and order, a concern dramatically underlined by the course of events on the other side of the Channel. If the French, despite the existence of a para-military police system, could overthrow the established regime, how much more vulnerable were the English, with no effective police force, to the threat of revolution?

In his Introduction, Colquhoun set out as his purpose 'to suggest means for the prevention of crimes, that punishment may very seldom be necessary', a brave sentiment which, given the nature of man, was unlikely to be achieved this side of paradise. But at least, he argued, life in the Metropolis need not—indeed must not—be unmitigated hell. He had studied the work of the Fieldings to whom he paid due tribute; and he took careful account not only of Pitt's abortive Bill, but of the part played by vested interests in the City in frustrating its passage. Thus when outlining his proposals for a unified police system, he deliberately underlined the words '*in every part of the Capital*'.

The *Treatise*, with exemplary logic, dealt with cause and effect; the causes of crime and the effects of criminality, which were to create public disorder on a scale which demanded a proper and effective police system. He supported his argument with a wealth of chilling statistics[1] and he advanced the novel theory that working-class extravagance was a greater source of evil than working-class poverty (see footnote on p. 30.) After parading in detail the different types of criminal organization and the elaborate network

---

[1] His figure of £2,000,000 as the annual 'turnover' of stolen property and forgery could only be an educated guess, since it did not include any allowance for unreported crime.

of receivers of stolen goods, he set out, on the other side of the ledger, a list of the existing forces of law and order in the Metropolitan area, including the City. These he observed, with tongue in cheek, amounted to 3,044 men, but by the time he had deducted the useless and often criminally-inclined parish constables and watchmen, he arrived at a total of 117 effectives or, in other words, the peace officers attached to Bow Street and the seven new police offices. In passing, he warned—with deadly accurate foresight—that the end of hostilities with France would result in the discharge of thousands of men from the army and navy, for many of whom a life of crime would be the inevitable consequence. Time was therefore of the essence.

Colquhoun's proposals were clear and concise:

1. An immediate mitigation in the severity of the criminal code.[1]

2. An enlarged system of stipendiary magistrates to cover the whole of the Metropolis, including the City.

3. A considerable increase in the number of constables attached to such public offices.

4. A fund for financing the new organization, created out of extensive licensing of dealers, traders and public houses.

5. The establishment of a central Board of Control to administer and direct all police activities.

It was a simple and workable plan and the arguments which Colquhoun advanced in its support were irrefutable. The Police Finance Committee of 1798 went so far as to adopt his recommendations; but no action was taken. The aldermen of the City soon saw to that.

＊

But in one particular area, Colquhoun now met with success. By the end of the eighteenth century, London had become the largest commercial port in the world with an annual traffic of over 13,000 vessels and, in 1798, an export and import trade valued at over £60,000,000. Predictably this rich harvest was subject 'to acts of

[1] Notwithstanding, at the date of Colquhoun's retirement in 1817 the number of crimes which carried the death penalty was 223, of which no fewer than *160* had been added to the penal code in the hundred years since the accession of George I. It is a fearful commentary on the English sense of human values.

peculation, fraud, embezzlement, pillage and depredation, through the medium of various and numerous classes of depraved characters who are employed on the River'.[1] In his earlier *Treatise*, Colquhoun had estimated the figure of thefts from ships in the tideway at £500,000 a year, and from dockyards on the river at £300,000. Here was a field ripe for action.

In 1797, Captain John Harriott, an adventurous, if unsuccessful, sailor of fortune, came upon the new edition of Colquhoun's *Treatise* with its embryo plan for a River Police, a project which had been enthusiastically received by the West India merchants who for long had been the chief victims of the river gangs. Harriott, whose experience of public affairs clearly did not include a knowledge of City bigotry, submitted a plan of his own for policing the Thames to the Lord Mayor, among whose nominal duties was that of Conservator of the river. The answer was a dusty one and Harriott's plan would have met an equally dusty death but for a stroke of luck. Through the medium of John Staples, a magistrate at the Shadwell police office, a copy of Harriott's plan was sent to Colquhoun, and in April 1798 the two men met. Colquhoun, in a letter dated 22 April, expressed his enthusiasm and engaged the support of his mentor, Dundas, in promoting government acceptance of his own proposals and those of Harriott.[2] The sequel was as rare as it was unexpected. A month later formal approval was given for the setting-up of a Marine Police Institution.[3] It was an historic moment.

The Marine Police Office was established on 26 June 1798 at 259 Wapping New Stairs, the site of the present Wapping Police Station and headquarters of the Thames Division of the Metropolitan Police. It can thus claim to be the first officially-sponsored police organization in the Metropolis exclusively devoted to the prevention of crime, and it was to continue its independent existence until 1839 when, together with the various Bow Street bodies, its executive functions were taken over by the 'New Police'.

Harriott was appointed Resident Magistrate, with Colquhoun—

[1] Colquhoun, *Treatise on the Commerce and Police of the River Thames.*
[2] Years later Colquhoun and Harriott fell out, both claiming credit for the formation of the River Police. The likely truth is that the details of the plan were Colquhoun's work, and the successful operation of it Harriott's.
[3] By Act of Parliament in 1800, the River Police was put on a statutory basis, and the full cost met out of public funds.

recently translated to the Queen Square police office—as 'Super-intendent Magistrate'. The establishment consisted of a permanent staff of 80 and a part-time paid force of 1,120 'lumpers', or men engaged in the physical handling of cargoes, an ingenious example of the old theory of setting thieves to catch thieves. The cost of the whole operation was split, with the Government contributing £1,000 to finance the judicial side of the office and the remaining cost of about £4,000 being met by the West India merchants. Two official ship's constables were assigned to each vessel in process of unloading, and the whole chain of cargo-handling and delivery was policed at each stage by Surveyors and River Guards. Two years later, when Colquhoun published his lapidary account of the operation of this scheme[1] he noted that during its first nine months it had reduced losses through pilferage and theft by over £100,000. The Lord Mayor, Brook-Watson, whose unprotected City wharves were still fair game for river gangs, might well have regretted his dusty answer to John Harriott.

*

For another twenty years, Patrick Colquhoun devoted himself to promoting his passionately held views on reform of the criminal code and the police. Surprisingly, in view of his established reputation, he was not appointed Chief Magistrate at Bow Street on the resignation of Sir William Addington in 1800.[2] The new occupant of Henry Fielding's house and office was Richard Ford who for some years had been Addington's assistant.

Since the turn of the century, highway robbery on the approach roads to the Metropolis had greatly increased, for with the end of John Fielding's short-lived experiment, travellers outside the inner perimeter of London were left without protection. In 1805, Ford persuaded the Government to revive the Bow Street Horse Patrol, but on a considerably larger scale. The new establishment consisted of 2 inspectors and 52 constables, all (for some unexplained reason) married men over thirty-five.[3] All were ex-cavalrymen. At the same

---

[1] Colquhoun, *Treatise on the Commerce and Police of the River Thames.*

[2] Even more surprisingly, he was never knighted despite the fact that the Government came to treat him as its principal adviser on matters of law and order.

[3] The men were paid 28s a week, with an allowance for fodder. They were provided with quarters in the area of their patrol beats.

time, a reserve force was formed with the quaint title of the Dismounted Horse Patrol. The two patrols worked in close association, the former operating on an outer perimeter up to twenty miles from the centre of the Metropolis and the latter on a five-mile perimeter; as a result, the old Bow Street Foot Patrol was withdrawn into the city centre. Within a year Ford could report that the approaches to London were free of highwaymen. The idea of a preventive police was beginning to take shape, and several sacred cows were being slaughtered in the process.

There are two particularly significant features of the Horse Patrol which were unusual: they were uniformed and they were armed. The uniform was a double-breasted blue coat with gilt buttons, leather stock, white gloves, black leather hat, top boots and a scarlet waistcoat, from which they acquired the nickname of 'Robin Redbreasts', a sure sign of public approval. The arms were pistol, sabre, and truncheon.[1]

No police historian has commented on this extraordinary departure from the tradition which time and public obduracy had hallowed; for the Horse Patrol was, by any definition, a French-style *gendarmerie*. There was no adverse press comment. No protesting voices were raised in Parliament. No one even complained that the cost to public funds was £8,000 a year. The only rational answer is that the Patrol was limited to a single and highly desirable function, that the cry of 'Bow Street Patrol!' was comforting to the class who travelled by coach, and that the men operated individually over an area removed from the normal centres of public lawlessness. None the less, the Bow Street Horse Patrol created a notable precedent; and precedents are the father of progress.

*

There was certainly precious little progress in Parliament during the next twelve years despite the appointment of a Select Committee on the Police in 1812 resulting from the general panic which followed the notorious Ratcliffe Highway murders; and of yet another Select Committee which met in 1816 and produced three long reports over a period of two years.

The endless debates which punctuated these years were marked

---

[1] The Dismounted Horse Patrol wore a similar uniform and carried pistols and truncheons. The two patrols were the first uniformed bodies in police history.

by the collision of two dogmas: the Tories bitterly resisting any attempt to mitigate the criminal code and the Whigs equally bitterly resisting any proposals for reforming the police. It was a classic impasse. But these debates were dominated by one man, the Whig Samuel Romilly, who almost alone—except for the support of Wilberforce—campaigned for the mitigation of the criminal law in the context of capital punishment. His suicide in 1818 was in great measure the result of years of fruitless endeavour.

Romilly launched his campaign in May 1808 with a Bill to abolish the death penalty for picking pockets to the value of 1s—a sentence rarely carried out since most of the offences were committed by children. Against all the odds—and Tory opposition of the most reactionary kind—the Bill was passed, with a maximum alternative sentence of transportation for life. This gleam of light on a sombre scene was a historic event for it was the very first measure which actually abolished, rather than created, a capital crime.

Romilly returned to the attack with five more Bills dealing with the mitigation of minor capital offences. His one success was a measure to abolish the death penalty for the curious crime of 'begging by soldiers and sailors without a permit from their commanding officers'. And the quality of opposition in these debates is well illustrated by the following intervention from a Tory MP, Frankland: 'I never look at the people without feelings of respect, affection and admiration; kind, generous, magnanimous, yet full of compassion; with a courage dauntless and inexhaustible; but with hearts tender as the bosom of a dove.' This catalogue of saintly virtues, concluded the Hon. Member, was entirely the product of the eighteenth-century criminal code. Hansard records neither gasps of astonishment nor even cries of dissent—and understandably so. There are degrees of fantasy best greeted by uncomprehending silence.

*

But there was another eighteenth-century phenomenon which could no longer be treated with either sentiment or silence, for it involved not only the state of the Metropolis but the entire structure of English society.

The Industrial Revolution marked the transition of Britain from a great granary into an even greater workshop, as the harnessing of steam power and native ingenuity transformed old industries and created new ones. The machine age had dawned. A country whose economy had for centuries been based on rural crafts now witnessed the phenomenon of rapid urban development, largely uncontrolled and entirely unplanned,[1] and traditional forms of domestic manufacture gave way to the factory system. For the new breed of industrial magnate, this revolution created opportunities for acquiring immense wealth; for the artisan and working classes it meant unprecedented squalor and misery, widespread unemployment, and ruthless exploitation.

The realities of the Industrial Revolution released a massive reaction which manifested itself in extreme forms of civil disorder and violence. More significantly, they created a climate of opinion in which a new social consciousness and political awareness began to assert itself. This was something novel in English life where the franchise had been traditionally limited to property-owners and the lower classes had neither the means nor the incentive to organize themselves in self-defence. Now, however, in the last decade of the old century, working men began to band together in an attempt to protect their living standards and improve their conditions of employment, and thus the first embryo trade unions were formed.

The authorities countered these demonstrations of social indiscipline by direct methods. To violence they replied with superior violence, and since no police organization existed, they resorted to the use of military force to deal with public disorder, a primitive and effective weapon which served only to breed a deeper sense of injustice. The growth of unionism had been answered in 1799 by the passing of the Combination Law[2] which declared all forms of workers' association to be 'in restraint of trade' and made illegal strikes and any other organized action designed to coerce employers into improving wages or working conditions. The penalty upon

[1] In fifty years, the population of London grew from 650,000 to 1,100,000. Manchester, Glasgow and Birmingham—little more than a straggle of villages in the mid-eighteenth century—had, by 1815, populations respectively of 140,000, 125,000 and 100,000. Bristol and Norwich, which a century before had been the second and third cities in England, were now by comparison no more than modest towns.

[2] In 1800 a second Combination Law was passed forbidding employers to join together in association. It was scarcely more effective than the earlier Act.

conviction was simple and draconian: transportation for life. But when men are driven to desperation by intolerable injustice and exploitation, the law is a blunt and ineffective weapon, and thus illegal combinations continued to flourish in the form of secret societies, while the law, largely denied its proven victims, transported a steady quota of presumed ringleaders on the principle of discouraging the others.

The explosive forces thus generated were held in check by the overriding necessities of the long war and by the demands which these made on the industrial capacity of the country, although the undercurrent of unrest continued to show itself in such public demonstrations as the Luddite riots of 1812. The government of the day, despite Colquhoun's prophetic warning, seems not to have considered the social and economic consequences of peace, whenever that might come; but this is not so remarkable, for the situation was historically unique and the ruling class had long been reared in a belief in its divine infallibility. On 18 June 1815, Europe's long, dark night ended.

*

The moment of victory had seen England at the summit of her power and prestige, the acknowledged leader of Europe and the acclaimed saviour of a subject continent. At home, despite her costly exertions, she seemed capable of riding out any imaginable domestic storm. Yet within a few months her economy was in ruins and her people reduced to unexampled depths of misery and distress. Marriott has described it thus:[1]

> The outstanding features of the situation by which the rulers of England were confronted after the conclusion of the great war were these: a labour market congested and dislocated; trade suddenly arrested after a period of abnormal inflation; a gigantic debt;[2] a falling revenue; a disordered currency; a peasantry demoralized by reckless administration of relief; a populace discontented and ripe for disturbance; all classes involved in a common ruin, landlord and tenant-farmer, capitalist and manufacturer, banker and merchant, skilled artisan and agricultural labourer.

[1] Marriott, *England since Waterloo*.
[2] Between 1793 and 1815 the value of the £ was halved and the national debt increased from £239,663,421 to the staggering figure of £831,171,132.

It was a situation which the rulers of England had not contemplated and which, by nature and background, they were slow to recognize and powerless to arrest. Since the Glorious Revolution of 1688 the country had been governed by a small elite of aristocrats or wealthy (not always the same thing) landowners, remote from the common people and wedded to traditions of privilege and patronage. It had worked tolerably well. The English had no great love for their aristocrats but at least, unlike the temperamental French, they had not felt it necessary to chop off their heads. The popular native sport was the sacking and burning of their elegant town houses. Now, however, the shift of population from land to city and the miseries to which the new industrial society was exposed had laid the foundations of a bitter class struggle; and the precipitate disbandment of the army after Waterloo threw upon an already unstable labour market thousands of men to whom violence and hardship had become second nature. It was a situation ripe for anarchy; and anarchy was the outcome.

The Government to which the responsibility for dealing with this explosive situation fell had taken office under Lord Liverpool in 1812, and for three years had presided over the final chapter in the decline and fall of Bonaparte. For its success it owed everything to the military genius of Wellington and the diplomatic brilliance of its Foreign Secretary, Castlereagh. Liverpool himself was a typical product of his time, an aristocratic Tory with little imagination and less vision, a kind of Georgian Baldwin for whom inaction was politically safer than reaction. His distaste for heroics is reflected in the fact that the composition of his original Cabinet remained virtually unchanged for ten years, even though it contained as Chancellor the disastrous Nicholas Vansittart whose fiscal blunders —among them the continuance of Pitt's controversial Sinking Fund, the abolition of the property tax, and the institution of the Corn Laws—contributed significantly to the great depression which marked the post-war years and to the collapse of law and order throughout the country.

Law and order was the province of Lord Sidmouth. As Henry Addington, he had been successively Speaker of the House of Commons for twelve years, Chancellor of the Exchequer, Prime Minister between Pitt's two administrations, Lord President of the Council, and Lord Privy Seal. Now this unremarkable but durable man was confronted by a challenge for which there was no

precedent. 'Reform or Revolution!' was the new popular cry. To
the first Sidmouth turned a deaf ear,[1] and in so doing came close
to inviting the second.

*

During the winter of 1815–16 London was in a state of virtual
siege, as rioting mobs and smaller gangs roamed the streets, burning
and looting property. The contagion quickly spread to field and
factory.

If employers had wealth, the men had numbers; and though the
penalties of the law, when it could be enforced, were savage, the
men had methods of their own—arson, machine-breaking, vitriol-
throwing, gunpowder, and assassination—even more ferocious.
Industrial disturbances tended, therefore, to be a compound of
private economic disputes, genuine distress, semi-illegal organ-
isations, potential disorder, and specific crime.[2]

In the face of this growing threat to life and property, Sidmouth
assumed a posture of masterly inactivity. Industrial disorder on this
scale was a novel social phenomenon; but it remained a matter for
local magistrates and not for government intervention. It was,
however, accompanied by something even more novel and potentially more dangerous—organized political disturbances. Feeding
on popular discontents, a new breed of mob orators and radical agitators stumped the country preaching the gospel of sedition to large
and highly inflammable audiences. Violent riots became commonplace—on Tyneside, in Glasgow, Manchester, Birmingham and
Swindon. These demonstrations were far beyond the control of
local constabularies and the authorities resorted to the traditional
method of restoring order by calling in the military, a prescription
which merely served to inflame existing passions.

To Sidmouth and his High Tory Cabinet colleagues, the agitation for social and political reform raised critical issues. To yield to
public pressure might well encourage the extremists, nor was it
clear whether political unrest was the cause or the effect of economic

---

[1] During his last two years of office, Sidmouth did at least do something
to strengthen the defences of the Metropolis by creating sixteen police
districts, and by almost doubling the total number of men attached to the
Bow Street office, concentrating them within the inner perimeter and
putting them under the overall control of the Home Office.

[2] Gash, *Mr Secretary Peel.*

distress. For years men like Bentham, Colquhoun and Romilly had argued radical solutions, but the oligarchy of ruling aristocrats resolved to maintain the *status quo* until the storm had blown itself out. And so the country continued on its turbulent way.

*

There was another manifestation of the distressful state of the nation which was presently to prick the conscience of the Government.

Poverty, hunger and unemployment had led to an ever-escalating increase in organized and casual crime, and in the years immediately following the end of the war the number of indictable offences more than doubled. For centuries the English had indulged in a native taste for indiscipline and now, under the pressures of the day, the taste became a national obsession.

The reformers had strenuously advanced the case for prevention rather than punishment, but this presupposed a police organization a great deal more effective and reliable than the corrupt and antiquated parochial system, and Parliament remained resolutely opposed to any such dangerous devolution of authority. Wise men continued to argue that certainty of detection was a more formidable deterrent than savage penalties; but there were not many wise men.

It is a measure of the insularity of the Government that, despite the growth of provincial anarchy, all the Select Committees concerned with law and order during Liverpool's administration were restricted by their terms of reference to the Metropolitan area alone, and while the new Luddites rampaged throughout the country, the Commons confined their debates to the problems of absent constables and sleepy watchmen, and to profound issues such as the death penalty for crimes as violent as the cutting down of trees, the writing of threatening letters, and the impersonation of Chelsea Pensioners. Sidmouth preferred to emulate Pilate. Even the Peterloo 'massacre' of 1819 elicited no response from him beyond a letter to the Manchester magistrates warmly commending them for their handling of the situation.

At last, in January 1822, Sidmouth resigned. In his place at the Home Office, Liverpool appointed Robert Peel. A second Daniel was come to judgement.

*

Robert Peel was a new kind of political animal. He was born in 1788 near Bury in Lancashire, the eldest son of a self-made cotton manufacturer who may be said to have created the modern textile industry, and—in the process—a vast personal fortune.[1] An ardent Tory and devoted disciple of Pitt the elder, Peel had entered Parliament in 1790 as member for the pocket borough of Tamworth. His political career, which overlapped that of his celebrated son, was undistinguished, although a measure which he carried through in 1802—the Health and Morals of Apprentices Act—can claim to have been the first of a long line of legislative reforms designed (however tentatively) to improve the status and conditions of factory workers. He died in 1830 shortly after his son's greatest political achievement, the passing—against all the odds and against every ingrained conviction of the Peel family—of the Catholic Emancipation Bill.

The younger Peel was trained and educated from boyhood for a career in politics.

He was brought up by his father in the traditions of the 'nineties to think that the French Revolution was the greatest disaster in history; to think that revolution and reform were indissolubly connected; that concession meant disaster; that to give the lower classes in the State a hand in the government was to court destruction; that to keep down the forces of anarchy with the strong hand was the first duty of government and the first condition of national prosperity. Nothing in his education had counteracted this teaching. He had never associated with members of the other political party. The Whigs were still so much discredited that he had but little opportunity of seeing their case fairly stated in the public press. The Radicals were as yet almost non-existent. 'Democracy' meant for him the mob that had sacked Birmingham; 'Reform' was the catch-word of the Jacobin clubs.[2]

In short, it was the classical education of a reactionary Tory of the late eighteenth century.

Yet this middle-class son of a self-made man, lacking the aristo-

---

[1] According to Greville, he left a fortune of £2,100,000; and at the time of his death, 15,000 men, women—and children—were employed in his factories.

[2] A. A. W. Ramsay, *Sir Robert Peel*.

cratic breeding and landed interests of the ruling Tory oligarchy, was to become Prime Minister and one of the greatest reforming statesmen of his time; and to destroy his party in the process. His relationship with colleagues and opponents was never easy, for he was intensely reserved and sensitive, easily moved to anger and to moods of black depression. He was also exceedingly ambitious. But, unlike many of his contemporaries, he was a brave and honest man who pursued what he believed to be the right course, even when this ran counter to his earlier convictions or to the political philosophy of his party; for, as he himself once recalled, Pitt had said that to maintain a consistent attitude amid changed circumstances was to be 'a slave to the most idle vanity'.

Disraeli said of him that he was 'a burglar of other men's ideas', and a more recent critic has claimed that 'most of the constructive plans and achievements for which he is deservedly famous originated almost wholly in the minds of others'.[1] And why not? All reform, every measure of social advance, has been a distillation of many minds, a process of selection and refinement, and ultimately of decision and action. Winston Churchill, in his greater wisdom, once said: 'There has never been an original idea except that of sin.' Nowhere is this more true than in Peel's chairmanship of the Bullion Committee of 1819, his reform of the criminal law, and his Metropolitan Police Act of 1829. These were all controversial issues, long argued and promoted by others, and all contrary to fundamental Tory principles and indeed to Peel's own training and political philosophy. Yet he had the intellectual ability—and honesty —to see that they were in the best interests of the country, and the administrative skill—and patience—to see them finally committed to the statute book; and that, so far as police reform is concerned, was a unique achievement. Guizot summed him up neatly when he described him as 'the most liberal of conservatives, the most conservative of liberals, and the most capable man of all in both parties'.

*

Peel's education—Harrow and Christ Church, Oxford—was that of any typical young man destined for a career in politics. And on his twenty-first birthday his father presented him with the

[1] Reith, *A New Study of Police History*.

pocket borough of Cashel in Tipperary, a constituency priding
itself on precisely twelve voters who, in the words of the elder Peel,
'should not be unamenable to a modest financial persuasion'. And
in April 1809, the son joined his father on the Government back
benches.

The following year he was invited to make his maiden speech in
seconding the Address to the Throne and so profound an impression
did he make that Perceval, the Prime Minister, offered him an
Under-Secretaryship at the Colonial Office. He had been a member
of Parliament exactly one year, and he was just twenty-two. At the
Colonial Office he served under Lord Liverpool and when, in 1812,
the latter succeeded to the premiership on the assassination of
Perceval, Peel was fortunately placed for preferment; and Liverpool, with more discernment than he was to show throughout most
of his period of office, at once offered him the Secretaryship of
Ireland.

It was a formidable challenge for a young man with no knowledge
of Irish affairs and little experience of the pitfalls of politics. Yet
his very inexperience was perhaps his greatest asset. In June the
Lord Lieutenant of Ireland, the Duke of Richmond, had written to
Bathurst in London: 'Pray don't let them send me a Catholic or a
timid Man.' Richmond's prayer was handsomely answered, for
they sent him not only a devout Protestant but a man who was to
demonstrate not only firmness but physical and political courage.

Peel took office twelve years after the Act of Union and at a time
when Canning and his friends had revived the burning issue of
Catholic emancipation. He therefore inherited a situation which
was explosive even by Irish standards—an administration riddled
with corruption and a country ripe for revolution.[1] This is not the
place to examine Peel's original and—in its own way—revolutionary approach to the Irish problem. But there is one aspect of
his conduct of affairs which was to foreshadow his later achievements at the Home Office.

Within months of his arrival in Dublin, Peel was left in no doubt
of the climate of violence and lawlessness which gripped the country.
By comparison, the industrial and political disorders which he had

---

[1] To preserve his credibility, Peel wisely relinquished his constituency
of Cashel (which he had never seen) and persuaded his father to purchase
for him the pocket borough of Chippenham (which likewise he never
visited).

left behind in England were merely ripples on the surface of a
peaceful pond.

> From magistrates, peers, landowners, clergy, police officers, and
> military commanders, came a steady stream of reports whose
> contents seemed endless and unvarying: attacks on revenue
> officers and tithe collectors, private vengeance, burning of houses
> and ricks, robbery of houses and mail-coaches, plundering of
> food, theft of arms, intimidation and assault, murder, rape,
> mutilation, abduction, maiming of cattle, riot, nocturnal assem-
> blies, firing on sentries, killing of stragglers on the line of march,
> rescue of prisoners, and assassination of hostile witnesses.[1]

The catalogue is not unfamiliar to modern ears; and to Peel the
reduction of anarchy on such a scale was an imperative prerequisite
to the establishment of orderly government.

Early in 1814, he introduced two measures in the House of Commons. The first was a revival of the Insurrection Act which had
lapsed in 1810 and which, in its amended form, gave the Lord
Lieutenant powers to proclaim a state of emergency. The second—
and more strongly contested—measure was the Peace Preservation
Act[2] which provided legislation for the establishment of an organized police force to replace the old baronial constables or 'Barneys',
a system as useless and ineffective as the parochial 'Charlies' in
England.

This second measure—innocently styled by Peel to allay popular
suspicion—met with considerable opposition on both sides of the
House. The very word 'police' was anathema to a society which
feared and resented invasion of privilege and the extension of
executive power, and which had before it the example of Fouché's
ruthless operation of the Napoleonic code in France. Against this
native antipathy the Fielding brothers and Patrick Colquhoun had
fought in vain.

Thus it is evidence of Peel's political skill and firmness of purpose

---

[1] Gash, *op. cit.*

[2] History here provides a curious footnote. In 1786, after the failure of
Pitt's Police Bill, the main features of that revolutionary but ill-fated
measure were adopted in Dublin, where a small force of salaried police
under three Commissioners was introduced. By the date of Peel's arrival
in Dublin, corruption and inefficiency had reduced this experiment to a
mockery of both peace-keeping and law enforcement.

that both these measures had become law by the end of July. The main provisions of the Peace Act were these: the appointment of stipendiary magistrates with authority to override local justices; the recruitment of a permanent force of special constables under magisterial control; and the provision that the cost of this establishment should be met out of a levy on each disaffected area where its services might be required. Magistrates received £700 a year and constables £50.

Peel, with his knowledge of the corruption and inefficiency which had long marked the Irish judicial system, reserved to himself the sole responsibility for appointing the new magistrates and for ensuring that neither patronage nor local influence had any part in such appointments. The new constabulary was recruited from former non-commissioned officers of the regular army of good character, and since his police force needed to be mobile, he gave preference to ex-cavalrymen.

The new organization—and this is sufficient answer to those critics of Peel's originality of mind—was entirely his own idea. That it should have taken root and grown in a soil so fertile to lawlessness and indiscipline is a remarkable testimony to his sureness of touch in handling delicate political issues. He had wanted, as he explained to Wellesley, to create from the outset a force capable of policing the whole country on a fully-manned basis, but his problem was to find sufficient magistrates and constables to match his imperative standards of conduct and reliability; and such men were not easily come by. Thus he proceeded on the basis of 'few but good'.

Despite inevitable teething troubles, the new police force was an immediate success (by a curious irony, one of its first interventions was in Cashel, Peel's old constituency); more importantly, it proved to be a popular innovation in a country which had grown weary of the sight of death and destruction.[1] Peel had laid a firm foundation. In 1822 (by which time he had become Home Secretary) the Irish Constabulary was established on a regular national basis by his successor, Goulburn; and in 1836 a consolidating Act was passed by Drummond giving statutory authority for the 'Royal Irish Constabulary'. By then Peel had written a more important page in the statute book.

*

[1] It was the Irish who first coined the affectionate nickname of 'Peelers'.

In 1818, after six difficult but rewarding years, Peel resigned the Irish Secretaryship. His uncompromising attitude to the Catholic church had earned him great unpopularity—Daniel O'Connell, his chief scourge, had rudely nicknamed him 'Orange Peel'—but his honesty and compassion had earned him the respect of his opponents, and he left behind him a country more tranquil and ordered than it had been for generations. For four years he now chose the comparative anonymity of the back benches; none the less during this period he made his most significant mark yet upon the political scene with his passing of the Bullion Act—'Peel's Act', as it came to be known—a measure which ended a decade of financial profligacy and ushered in a new era of national prosperity and industrial peace. Such a man could not long remain in the political wilderness and when, in January 1822, Sidmouth resigned in Liverpool's long-overdue Cabinet reshuffle, Peel accepted the post of Home Secretary. Except for a short period in 1827, he was to hold that office for eight years and to establish himself as one of the first and certainly one of the most courageous of political reformers.

His Irish experience had taught him all he needed to know about the benefits of a properly organized system of police. But he was wise enough, politically, to realize that Westminster was not Dublin; and so he turned first to the essential prerequisite—a revision of the criminal law.

By the early nineteenth century the legal system of England had become an impenetrable jungle, scarcely codified, and based—as earlier reformers had hammered home—on the doubtful premise that the more savage the penalties, the greater the deterrent effect on criminals. It was a typically reactionary philosophy which was summed up in the Tory cliché that the law existed to break those who broke the law. The Newgate Calendar provided a grim and contrary answer. And it was on the Opposition benches that Peel was to find a powerful advocate of his own compassionate philosophy.

In March 1819, James Mackintosh, a close friend and disciple of Romilly, had taken up the torch which his colleague's suicide had extinguished the previous year, and had proposed a motion 'for the appointment of a Select Committee to consider of so much of the Criminal Laws as relates to Capital Punishment in Felonies'. In his speech he rehearsed the lessons of history, quoting Henry Fielding and Colquhoun, and the irrefutable statistics of current crime in the Metropolis. Two contributions to the debate are sufficient to illustrate the nature of ministerial attitudes. Castlereagh, in an attempt to frustrate the motion, insisted on the death penalty in the absence of alternative punishment 'which should produce the same effect of impressing offenders with a salutary terror'; while Canning, in arguing that Romilly's success in abolishing the death penalty for picking pockets had resulted in an increase in the crime, neatly confused cause and effect. Not one voice was raised in support of the patent alternative: prevention of crime. No mention was made of the inadequacy of the police system.

Mackintosh persisted; but it was not until Peel's arrival at the Home Office that two apparently contradictory events combined to resolve, however tentatively, the political dissonance.

In March 1822 Peel set up a Select Committee—the fifth to report in ten years—to examine the police organization in the Metropolis. In introducing his proposal, Peel trod very carefully indeed. 'He hoped,' reported Hansard, 'that the inquiry would be prosecuted with but one view—the obtaining for the Metropolis as perfect a system of police as was consistent with the character of a free country.' He sat back and waited.

In June 1822, the Committee reported. And its final conclusion represents one of the classic examples of bigotry in the English language:

> It is difficult to reconcile an effective system of police with that perfect freedom of action and exemption from interference which are the great privileges and blessing of society in this country; and Your Committee think that the forfeiture or curtailment of such advantages would be too great a sacrifice for improvements in police, or facilities in detection of crime, however desirable in themselves if abstractedly considered.

'Abstractedly' considered, this quaint expression of democracy must have caused some tremors of dismay, even among the most obdurate City Fathers.

Whether James Mackintosh knew the substance of this Report or not, a fortnight before its publication he proposed a Resolution to the effect that the House should consider 'the means of increasing the efficiency of the criminal laws by abating their undue rigour; together with measures for strengthening the police, and for rendering the punishment of transportation and imprisonment more effective for the purposes of example and reformation'.

Peel, still unaware of the massive rebuff which his own committee was about to deliver, accepted Mackintosh's Resolution in principle, although the reference to police reform must have surprised him, coming as it did from a party which had long argued that any such strengthened institution would be a grave encroachment on the liberty of the subject and a dangerous extension of executive power. He could not have imagined that he would be caught in quite so unexpected a cross-fire.

Yet (such are the ironies of politics) Mackintosh's proposal provided Peel with a providential escape from his dilemma. He had always known that only when he had cleared up the tangled undergrowth of statute law and abated its severity could he return to the vital issue of a preventive police organization. If his Select Committee insisted on behaving like Whigs, then he would pursue the line of action proposed by Mackintosh, a Whig who insisted on behaving like Peel.

He moved with some circumspection, not least in the area of capital punishment, where radical reformers were most vociferous. To his cautious, Tory-trained mind an excess of leniency could easily be self-defeating. Nevertheless, by the end of 1823 he had succeeded in passing five Acts which reduced the number of capital offences by more than 100, and one of which wisely—and ingeniously —relieved judges of the obligation to pass the death sentence for capital convictions except in cases of murder.

In March 1826,[1] he turned to the general revision and consolidation of the statute law in its criminal context. We need not concern ourselves here with the complex details of Peel's legislation beyond summarizing his achievement.

He concentrated on three main areas: theft and offences against property (by far the largest field of criminal activity); offences against the person; and forgery. As an indication of the scope of these reforms, he reduced the 130 existing statutes relating to larceny to a single Act of thirteen pages, and the 214 statutes covering offences against the person to two short measures. At the same time he consolidated several branches of the civil law and

[1] In 1825, he had introduced the Juries Regulation Bill which consolidated into a single measure eighty-five existing Acts relating to the empanelling of juries.

introduced a complete overhaul of the complicated tangle of legal procedures.

It was an extraordinary undertaking, carried through with the minimum of opposition from those reactionary quarters where he might reasonably have expected it. Throughout he was guided by a desire to simplify and to mitigate on the principle that, if the law was intelligible and the penalties less severe, the level of criminal activity would be sensibly reduced. Yet by one of the great ironies of social history, the immediate result of Peel's reforming zeal was a startling increase in crime. Comparative statistics for the periods 1811–17 and 1821–7 showed an increase of 86 per cent in commitments and 105 per cent in convictions.[1] The lesson was inescapable. The sanction of punishment was not enough where social conditions and grinding poverty drove men to desperate remedies. The answer lay—as Peel had always believed—in an organized system of crime prevention.

*

While Peel was thus engaged on his formidable programme of legal reform, events elsewhere conspired to confound the opponents of his plan for reorganizing the existing police institution in the Metropolitan area.

In 1824, the Combination Laws, which Pitt had introduced in very different circumstances, were repealed. As amended the following year, the new Act held men and masters subject only to common as opposed to statute Law and effectively legalized strikes. The supporters of the Act had argued that, freed of legal sanctions, men would no longer seek to associate together in restraint of trade; but the reality was to prove quite otherwise. The passage of the Act was marked by widespread industrial action and in every part of the country the military were called in to deal with public disorders. It was a form of repression which, as we have seen, ran counter to all Peel's convictions about the preservation of law and order.

Yet before he could revive his campaign for a preventive civil organization, the country was struck by an economic depression even more violent than that which had followed the Napoleonic

---

[1] Capital sentences over these two periods rose from 4,126 to 7,770, although Peel's policy of mitigation was reflected in the figures for actual executions: 536 against 579.

wars. The cause of the depression of 1826 was, ironically, an excess of prosperity; and, in such circumstances, the question of strikes was purely academic. Instead, the country was thrown into a state of industrial turmoil as banks and businesses failed and unemployment soared. There were bloody riots in the large industrial centres and bloody intervention by the Yeomanry. In the Blackburn area more than 1,000 power-looms were smashed, while in Macclesfield the mob sacked the centre of the town with the thoroughness of an invading army.

Curiously, this explosion of anarchy was not accompanied by political agitation, a fact which Peel was quick to recognize. 'The great cause of apprehension,' he wrote, 'is not in the disaffection, but in the real distress of the manufacturing districts. There is as much forebearance as it is possible to expect from so much suffering.' There was nothing for it but to organize relief on a massive scale, and to ride out the storm until a revival of trade should bring the country into calmer waters.

*

The revival was two years coming, and by then Peel was out of office. With the resignation of Liverpool in 1827, the King had invited Canning to form a government. Peel felt unable to serve under a prime minister whose support for Catholic emancipation he so radically opposed, and also resigned. But within a few weeks Canning was dead, and his successor, Goderich, after four months of insecure government, made way for the Duke of Wellington. In January 1828, Peel was back at the Home Office, but with the added responsibility—and prestige—of Leader of the House.

He now had a platform of enlarged authority from which to complete his programme of legal reform; and both the public disorders and the growing statistics of crime during the two previous years provided him with the incentive and the justification for tackling the thorny question of police reorganization. He already had Wellington's full support, but since he had to carry with him the reactionary elements in both Houses, he proceeded with his usual caution. And in order to limit the scope of controversy, he chose to restrict his proposals to the Metropolitan area. 'I do not think,' he wrote to Goulburn, 'that I should offer an apple until they have digested the cherry. Success here will earn a much larger reward later.'

On 28 February 1828, only a month after his return to the Home Office, he took up once more in the Commons his old theme of an inquiry into the state of the police and the causes of the growth of crime in the Metropolis. It was a shrewd speech, deliberately pitched in a low key and devoid of heroics or of controversial arguments likely to alarm his audience. With the growth of population and of the Metropolitan area itself, he suggested, the old police institutions were now manifestly inadequate (he was careful also to invite country and provincial members to reflect upon the implications for their own areas) and the time was ripe to consider a new kind of establishment rather than adapt the old. Society was entitled to protection from law-breakers beyond reform of the law itself.[1] It was a masterly performance. And it achieved its purpose with the setting up of a Police Committee to conduct the limited inquiry which Peel had proposed.

Its report was duly presented to the House of Commons on 11 July, and although it dwelt at some length on the many difficulties, it recommended, in terms which must have surprised even Peel, the unanimous conviction of the committee that the House should approve the establishment of a new system of police 'in this great Metropolis, for the adequate protection of property, and for the prevention and detection of crime'. The committee recommended the setting-up of a general police office under the direct authority of the Home Secretary and that all existing police bodies, including the night watch, should be subordinated to this office. Such were the bare bones of the matter.

If the committee's conclusion came as a surprise to Peel, it did not take him unawares. Even though he had given priority to reform of the criminal law, there is evidence from his letters, particularly to his friend Hobhouse, the Under-Secretary for Ireland, that he had been considering carefully the shape an eventual police organization for the Metropolis should take. He did not underestimate the power of the City nor its part in destroying Pitt's Bill. 'I should be afraid to meddle with it', he wrote to Hobhouse in 1826, probably

---

[1] In a speech to the House at the time of his resignation the previous year, he had said: 'Tory as I am, I have the satisfaction of knowing that there is not a single law connected with my name which has not had for its object some mitigation of the severity of the criminal law; some prevention of abuse in the exercise of it; or some security for its impartial administration.'

against his better judgement; but the chaotic situation in the rest of the Metropolis was another matter and he spoke of his intention of 'annihilating' the old parochial system. Above all, he was determined to seize the opportunity of separating the judicial and executive functions of the magistracy. No man should be both judge and jury, and the prevention and detection of crime was not the province of justices.

The Bill which Peel drafted was subject to careful revision to ensure the minimum of controversy. Even its title, 'An Act for improving the Police', studiously avoided any suggestion of radical innovation or offence to tender consciences, and the deliberate omission of the City of London was a clear concession to his most vocal opponents. But Peel, having worked so long for this reform, was determined to have no half-measures.

Under the terms of the Bill, the Home Secretary became the Police Authority for the Metropolitan area. A new Police Office was to be created in Westminster under the control of two 'Justices' (later renamed Joint Commissioners) whose powers, however, would be strictly executive and not judicial. All existing police institutions[1] were to be phased out and replaced by a single, unified force of paid constables, supervised and administered by the Joint Commissioners. The 'Metropolitan Police District' was defined and the new organization was to be financed out of a police-rate which would replace the old watch-rate. A 'Receiver' would be appointed to administer 'all monies applicable to the purposes of this Act'. The Bill finally provided powers for the extension of the Metropolitan Police District to include such additional parishes as might be judged desirable or necessary. It is impossible, in the light of all the earlier years of public and private obstruction, to imagine a more comprehensive or radical measure.

Peel introduced his Bill on 15 April 1829.[2] His speech was a remarkable exercise in political diplomacy. He had been here before, as had the handful of dedicated reformers who for a hundred years had laboured to create wisdom out of apathy and action out of

---

[1] The Bow Street establishment had been directly controlled by the Home Office since Sidmouth's time. In the event, this establishment and the River Police were not absorbed into the Metropolitan Police until the 1830s.

[2] Two days after the equally controversial Catholic Emancipation Bill had received the Royal Assent.

inertia. Babington[1] quotes a visiting foreigner who perfectly described the situation which Peel was now determined to resolve: 'The strange medley of licentiousness and legal restraint, of freedom and confinement—of punishment for what is done and liberty to do the same thing again—is very curious.' No Englishman could have described more accurately the reason and justification for the Police Act of 1829.

Peel carefully underplayed his hand. His Bill, he said, was not an invasion of liberty but a restraint of licence. He concentrated on the principle of 'improvement' rather than radical change, on consent rather than confrontation. Gently he dismissed the 'Charlies' in these words: 'So long as the present night-watch system is persisted in, there will be no efficient prevention of crime nor any satisfactory protection for property or the person.' Kensington, wealthy and vulnerable, was protected by six parish constables, several of whom were 'not invariably sober'. Deptford, at the other end of the scale, where the inhabitants had been subjected to 'atrocious and sanguinary crimes', had no parish police of any kind. Quietly, he involved every member of the House in the logic—of which each was aware—that what they were debating was the survival of a civilized society; and he ended thus:

> It is the duty of Parliament to afford to the inhabitants of the Metropolis and its vicinity, the full and complete protection of the law and to take prompt and decisive measures to check the increase of crime which is now proceeding at a frightfully rapid pace.

It was the first time that any politician had spoken of the 'duty of Parliament' in such a context. And it is a phrase which might well be remembered in our own time.

*

Peel's Act, originally known as the 'Metropolitan Police Improvement Bill', passed its first reading with virtually no opposition. It became law on 19 June 1829. And here is the preamble to this historic measure:

---

[1] Babington, *A House in Bow Street*.

An Act for improving the Police in and near the Metropolis. 19th *June* 1829.

WHEREAS Offences against Property have of late increased in and near the Metropolis; and the local Establishments of Nightly Watch and Nightly Police have been found inadequate to the Prevention and Detection of Crime, by reason of the frequent Unfitness of the Individuals employed, the Insufficiency of their Number, the limited Sphere of their Authority, and their Want of Connection and Co-operation with each other: And Whereas it is expedient to substitute a new and more efficient System of Police in lieu of such Establishments of Nightly Watch and Nightly Police, within the Limits hereinafter mentioned, and to constitute an Office of Police, which, acting under the immediate Authority of One of His Majesty's Principal Secretaries of State, shall direct and controul the Whole of such new System of Police within those Limits: . . .

Peel's patience and parliamentary skill had been well rewarded. The Act by which he had laid so much store was now on the statute book and the foundations of a unique organization had been laid. He had won the first battle. It now fell to others to win the war.

CHAPTER THREE

Rowan and Mayne

PEEL'S STUDIED moderation and his determination to hasten slowly reflect an unconscious identification of his 'New Police' with its distant Anglo-Saxon origins. He had willed the end—but not the means.

The Police Act had created a new statutory authority for the Metropolis in the office and person of the Home Secretary. The proposal to appoint two non-judicial magistrates had ended a tradition which went back six centuries. The decision to 'annihilate' the old parochial system of corrupt, independent, and uncoordinated peace officers and to substitute a unified police force gave practical effect to the work of Henry Fielding and successive reformers. And the new office of Receiver ensured that the finances[1] of the new organization would be administered under proper and efficient supervision. Of the forty-four clauses of the Act, more than half are concerned with good husbandry. So far, so good.

There is no evidence that Peel, when he introduced his Bill in April, had given any detailed consideration to the size or structure of his 'New Police', or to the nature and qualifications of the two Commissioners whose task it would be to translate the Bill into a practical reality. The extraordinary lack of parliamentary opposition to so radical a measure may well have blinded him to the subsequent attitude of press and public and to the hostility of the magistracy and the parish vestries. It was not long before this unnatural calm was to be broken by the sound of thunder off-stage.

At the beginning of May, while the Bill was still being debated in the Lords, Peel addressed himself to the urgent matter of choosing his Commissioners. The very novelty of the problem was to be underlined a century later by a distinguished Receiver of the

[1] Under the 1829 Act, the old watch-rate was replaced by a police-rate not exceeding 8d in the £. The Receiver had constantly to deploy a formidable artillery of threats and legal action to obtain payment of the new rate, which was bitterly resented by parish authorities.

Metropolitan Police who wrote: 'The appointment of Commissioner of Police of the Metropolis is among the most difficult upon which Ministers have to advise the Crown, and the holder of it is perhaps more exposed to criticism and the vicissitudes of fortune than any other member of the public service.'[1] In the light of history, there can be few holders of the office who would have disagreed with that opinion.

Peel had decided that he would not accept applications for the two posts. He no doubt listened to the suggestions of others, but strangely there is no correspondence to indicate how his mind was working until, on 29 May, he wrote privately to his friend Gregory, the Under-Secretary for Ireland. After outlining the purpose of his Act, he went on: 'It has occurred to me that if there were a military man conversant in the details of the police system in Ireland [*a system, of course, for which Peel had been largely responsible*], he might possibly be usefully employed here. But then, he must be a very superior man to what I recollect of Police Magistrates in Ireland.' He explained the qualities he was seeking—'great energy, great activity both of body and mind, accustomed to strict discipline and the power of enforcing it', and 'he must be a gentleman and entirely trustworthy'. For so exceptional a person he suggested the unexceptional salary of £800 with, perhaps, a residence; and he ended: 'There will be a force of between two and three thousand men ultimately under his command. With the soldier I would unite a sensible lawyer as the other magistrate.'

This letter is important since it is the first clear statement of Peel's intentions as regards both the two Commissioners and the projected size of the new police force. Not surprisingly, Gregory was unable to recommend a suitable candidate from the Irish establishment, for even a man of limited imagination must have realized the formidable task involved, while the salary offered was £200 less than that fixed seven years earlier for the Irish magistracy. Nor, towards the end of June, was Peel any more successful when he offered the 'military' appointment to a Lt-Col. James Shaw in a letter calculated to fill that gentleman with considerable apprehension. Shaw duly declined the 'flattering' offer; so Peel, whose Act had become law on 19 June, consulted his short-list and made his firm and—as it was to prove—inspired choices.

*

[1] Moylan, *Scotland Yard*.

Charles Rowan and Richard Mayne first met in Peel's office on 6 July, there to be sworn in as justices and to receive their appointments as Joint Commissioners.[1] Rowan, aged forty-six, had spent his entire active life in military service until his retirement from the army as a colonel in 1822, while Mayne, fourteen years his junior, was making his way with some success in the legal profession. They took an instinctive liking to each other and the twenty-one years in which they worked together in double harness seem to have occasioned no single instance of serious disagreement; indeed the public abuse and political chicanery with which they had to contend during the early years of their partnership must have cemented their feelings of mutual respect and affection. How they came to be chosen by Peel as the instruments to put his Police Act into effect (and he could ill-afford to start on the wrong foot) is largely a matter for surmise, since neither Rowan nor Mayne left any record of the circumstances; but two surviving letters provide a clue.

The day after the meeting at the Home Office, Peel wrote thus to Lord Rosslyn, the Lord Privy Seal: 'I have on the Recommendation of the highest Military Authorities taken for the Military Magistrate Colonel Rowan of the 52nd Regt.' As we shall presently see, this must arguably have been a reference to the Duke of Wellington; and on 2 July, William Gregson, one of Peel's undersecretaries, wrote to Mayne at his chambers in the Temple indicating that his candidature had been warmly endorsed by leading members of the judiciary.

There is no record of the discussions at the Home Office on 6 July, but it is not difficult to reconstruct the course they took. Neither Rowan nor Mayne had any previous experience of police work, although they were probably both well aware of the public debate, of the disorderly state of the Metropolis, and even of the published report of the 1828 Committee. They must certainly have familiarized themselves with the new Police Act. Peel, on the other hand, was not by nature a man to hire two dogs and do the barking himself. What we do know is that Peel asked that the two men should let him have a detailed plan for organizing the 'New Police'. And

---

[1] John Wray, the first Receiver, was appointed later in July 1829. To Wyndham, Peel wrote, with uncharacteristic exaggeration: 'The success of the Bill mainly turns on the office of Receiver.'

there is a note in Mayne's hand in the Public Record Office which says simply: 'We commenced operations immediately.'

*

Before we look at the backgrounds of the two Commissioners and the details and execution of their original plan, it is worth digressing briefly to record, as no historian of the Metropolitan Police has done, the extraordinary timetable which the two men set themselves—and carried out.

They began on 7 July with a blank sheet of paper, in a bare room at the Home Office, and with such clerical assistance as they could beg or borrow. In exactly *twelve weeks to the day* they had:

1. produced, within a fortnight, an approved establishment for the first six police divisions[1] and the supervising HQ;
2. agreed the pay structure;
3. devised a detailed divisional organization, broken down into sections, and precise beats;
4. written a General Instruction Book which remains today a model of its kind;
5. established a central Police Office at 4 Whitehall Place;
6. acquired, through the Receiver, suitable station-houses from which each divisional 'company' would operate;
7. recruited upwards of 1,000 constables and superior grades;
8. designed, contracted and arranged the manufacture of uniforms and equipment for the new force;
9. provided basic drill and elementary instruction for the force.

It says much for Rowan and Mayne's remarkable application and their grasp of what was a unique assignment; and it also says much for Peel's wisdom, once he had approved their plan, in leaving them to carry it through without interference or obstruction. By 29 September 1829 he had willed not only the end, but now also the means.

*

Charles Rowan was one of ten sons[2] of an improvident Ulster landowner. In 1797 he was commissioned as an ensign in the 52nd

[1] The General Instruction Book refers to only five divisions, but Rowan added another 'Company', attached to the Commissioners' Office 'for duty in the immediate neighbourhood'.

[2] Two of his brothers also served in the 52nd, one of them, William, rising to the rank of field-marshal.

Regt of Foot, a choice which was to have far-reaching consequences; for in 1803 the 52nd (together with the 43rd and the newly-formed 95th) was selected by Sir John Moore for what became known as the 'Shorncliffe experiment'.

In purely military terms, the Shorncliffe experiment was designed as an answer to the French tactics of using a highly mobile force of skirmishers as advance or rear guard to main bodies of infantry. Out of this experiment grew the Light Division which was to play so decisive a part in the Peninsular campaign and at Waterloo. And twenty-six years later Charles Rowan was to apply the lessons of Shorncliffe to a very different set of tactical problems.

But from Sir John Moore, Rowan was to learn something of much greater significance. He was to have a lesson in human nature.

By the end of the eighteenth century, the British army had become thoroughly infected with the London disease—drunken, disorderly, and brutalized by a system which handed down a sentence of 500 lashes as a minimum penalty for a minor offence. The enforcement of discipline—like the enforcement of law—relied on a single, unreliable weapon: fear.

Moore, like his civilian contemporary, Colquhoun, had a clear and uncomplicated view of crime and punishment which amounted to the simple proposition that if men did not commit crimes, punishment would become unnecessary. In 1803 he had set down his thoughts in a two-part plan: *Military Training* and *Moral Training*. Both elements of this plan were revolutionary in the context of their time, but it is the second part which marked a total departure from the ossified army attitudes of the day and which was so profoundly to influence the young Charles Rowan.

The essence of 'moral training', as Moore demonstrated, was the art of man-management. Officers who were not masters of their profession were not fitted to command soldiers (an opinion then so novel as to have amounted to heresy). Discipline, imperative in any uniformed body of men, should proceed from a sense of duty, pride and mutual respect. And brutality served only further to brutalize. George Napier, a fellow officer of Rowan, was later to write: 'The great thing that Sir John Moore used to impress upon the minds of the officers was that our duty was to do everything in our power to *prevent* crime, as then there would be no occasion for punishment.' Colquhoun could not have put it better.

Charles Rowan could never have foreseen, throughout his distinguished military career,[1] the capacity in which his special training and talents would eventually be put to a test scarcely less
hazardous than the battlefield. Nothing is known of his life during
the seven years after his retirement in 1822. He was then only
thirty-nine and he was not by nature a man who could have spent
his days in idleness; nor could he have lived solely on the proceeds
of the sale of his commission. But something about Peel's concept
of the 'New Police' must have touched a chord in his memory and
suggested to him that Sir John Moore's proven theories of military
man-management would be equally applicable in this new and un-
proven civilian field; for early in May 1829, he was corresponding
about the post of Police Commissioner with Sir George Murray,
who had been Wellington's Quartermaster-General at Waterloo.
Murray, who was well aware of Rowan's outstanding ability, would
certainly have spoken not only with Peel (as he did), but also with
Wellington, and it is reasonable to believe that these were the
'highest Military Authorities' to whom Peel referred in his letter to
Rosslyn. It was indeed a fortunate conjunction.

*

Of Richard Mayne, much less is known. He was born in 1796,
the son of an Irish judge. He was educated at Trinity College,
Dublin and called to the English Bar in 1822. Thus at the date of
Peel's Act he was only thirty-three and had been in practice for less
than seven years. Peel, as we know, was looking for a 'sensible
lawyer' and not a legal luminary; and the salary of £800 which the
Police Act laid down for each of the Commissioners would not have
been much of a bait to lure any leading barrister from his lucrative
profession. The fact that Peel offered the post to one so young and
comparatively inexperienced can only reflect Mayne's growing
reputation and Peel's considerable judgement. Why Mayne threw
up a certain propitious future for a probable bed of nails is a matter
for conjecture. He had not even met Charles Rowan, nor were his
terms of reference clearly defined in the Act. But he had spent
enough time in the courts to know the size of the problem and Peel's
offer must have been an irresistible challenge.

[1] Brigade-major to Craufurd in the Peninsula; staff-officer to Wellington; second-in-command to Colborne at Waterloo; CO of the 52nd from
1815 to 1818 and again from 1819 to 1822; CB, 1815.

He was to occupy his office for thirty-nine years, the longest tenure of any Commissioner, the last thirteen of them in splendid and autocratic isolation. Chief Inspector Cavanagh recalls his interview with Mayne when he received his first promotion in 1857:

> He continued writing while I stood to attention for, I should say, ten minutes. At last he put his pen on one side . . . and looked me straight in the face—and he knew how to look. At length he said: 'Mr. Yardley has recommended you for promotion to the accountant's office. It is a very responsible position. I hope you will give him satisfaction'.

He must have done. Richard Mayne did not make chief inspectors out of unsatisfactory sergeants.

*

Within two weeks of their appointment, Rowan and Mayne had submitted to Peel their first plan for the establishment of six Metropolitan Police Divisions covering the City of Westminster and certain parishes to the west on the north side of the river. A schedule to the Police Act had defined the original Metropolitan Police District as an area covered by a radius of up to seven miles from Charing Cross and containing eighty-eight 'parishes, liberties and hamlets'.[1] Plainly any attempt to apply the new system to the entire district from the outset would have seriously delayed the implementation of the measure. The sooner the 'New Police' could make its appearance in the centre of London, the better; the outer areas could follow as experience was gained. Furthermore, Peel, who was no political innocent, was becoming aware that he had applied a small match to a very large powder barrel.

This was the establishment which the new Commissioners proposed, and which was authorised by Peel on 20 July:[2]

---

[1] This was approximately the area covered by the old Bow Street foot patrols.

[2] It is interesting to note that in his letter of 20 July to Rowan and Mayne, Peel already described them as 'Commissioners'. A virtually identical letter of the same date to John Wray is signed by Samuel March Phillipps, Peel's Under-Secretary, and illustrates the special status of the Receiver's office.

Office Establishment	*Police Force*
1 Chief Clerk	8 Superintendents
1 Second Clerk	20 Inspectors
1 Third Clerk	88 Sergeants
	895 Constables

Receiver's Office
1 Chief Clerk
1 Second Clerk

The plan which Rowan and Mayne submitted to Peel was duly incorporated in the General Instruction Book.[1] This was divided into two parts: Pt I, dealing with organization and duties and clearly written by Rowan; and Pt II, setting out the legal powers of a constable as defined by common law and Acts of Parliament, and equally obviously the work of Mayne.

Pt I is of particular interest since it illustrates on every page the way in which Rowan adapted the teaching of Sir John Moore—the only model of which he had any experience—to the requirements of an unarmed civilian force. Thus he approached the organization of the 'New Police' as if it were a regiment, with one 'company' allocated and corresponding to each 'division'. A division was divided into eight 'sections', and each section into eight 'beats' (or patrols). The idea of flexible and mutually-supporting beats (impossible under the old system of rigid parish boundaries) was borrowed directly from Light Infantry outpost training.

In defining the command structure, Rowan borrowed the senior ranks of Superintendent (wrongly corrected by Peel to Super-intend*a*nt in the surviving proof copy of the Instruction Book) and Inspector from the old parochial and public-office systems; the rank of Sergeant came straight from the army; while that of Constable was deliberately intended to revive and dignify the ancient and familiar office which had fallen into such disrepute.

The company (of which there were initially six) was divided into sixteen parties, each consisting of one sergeant and nine men, four

[1] Reith states that the General Instruction Book was printed and issued to all members of the force by 26 September. But on that date, Phillipps wrote to Peel regarding a serious legal error on pp. 50 and 51. The book was withdrawn; and inserted at the back of Rowan's copy at Scotland Yard is a note signed by Phillipps and dated *October 16th*, authorizing the issue of amended copies.

such parties forming an inspector's party. Sixteen men, one from each party, formed a company reserve at the station-house.

Some simple arithmetic will show that the establishment created under the above organization differs slightly in each rank from the numbers submitted for Peel's approval (for example, 2 fewer superintendents and 31 fewer constables). There is no obvious explanation for this discrepancy.

Rowan then went on to explain the duties of each rank and it is here that his own personal qualities and his understanding of the proper management of men are strikingly illustrated. Here, for example, is part of his instruction to the superintendent: 'He should make himself well-acquainted, by frequent personal intercourse, with the Inspectors and Serjeants, and through them with the character and conduct of every Man in the Company under his orders; he will be firm and just, at the same time kind and conciliating towards them, in his behaviour, on all occasions.'

'Firm and just'; 'kind and conciliating'. This was indeed a new language of leadership. Nor was it simply a form of words. During the early years of stress, when it seemed that every man's hand was turned against him and Mayne, Charles Rowan held steadfastly to this simple philosophy. He accepted a personal, almost paternalistic, responsibility for every man under his command, and had there not been so firm and just a hand on the helm, Peel's 'New Police' would assuredly have foundered within two years of its formation.

To his constables, Rowan addressed himself with equal care and understanding, for he appreciated, perhaps more clearly than the younger Mayne, that the man on the beat was in the firing-line; that the future of the 'New Police' depended entirely on public acceptance; and that the constable—and his conduct—were the yardsticks by which the whole police concept would be judged.

Thus in his Instructions to constables, Rowan enjoined them to be 'civil and attentive to all persons, of every rank and class' and to to be careful of idle and unnecessary interference; but that, when required to act, to 'do so with decision and boldness'. Finally: 'He must remember that there is no qualification more indispensable to a Police Officer than a perfect command of temper, never suffering himself to be moved in the slightest degree by any language or threats that may be used; if he do his duty in a quiet and determined manner, such conduct will probably induce well-disposed by-standers to assist him should he require it.' It is a classic statement of the art of public relations in its widest sense, and reiterates with curious exactness the precept laid down by Saunders Welch in his *Observations on the Office of Constable* eighty years earlier. It is evidence enough that great minds do think alike.

This bible of police organization and procedure must have occupied Rowan and Mayne for no more than a month, during which they were working on other equally novel problems; and their whole policy is summed up in the concise introduction which prefaces the Instruction Book. It is of such importance to a proper understanding of the revolution in social engineering which they had set in train that it should be recorded here:

> The following General[1] Instructions for the different ranks of the Police Force are not to be understood as containing rules of conduct applicable to every variety of circumstances that may occur in the performance of their duty; something must necessarily be left to the intelligence and discretion of individuals; and according to the degree in which they show themselves possessed to these qualities and to their zeal, activity, and judgement, on all occasions, will be their claims to future promotion and reward.
>
> It should be understood, at the outset, that the principal[2] object to be attained is the Prevention of Crime.
>
> To this great end every effort of the Police is to be directed. The security of person and property, the preservation of the public tranquillity, and all the other objects of a Police Establishment, will thus be better effected, than by the detection and punishment of the offender, after he has succeeded in committing the crime. This should constantly be kept in mind by every member of the Police Force, as the guide for his own conduct. Officers and Police Constables should endeavour to distinguish themselves by such vigilance and activity, as may render it extremely difficult for any one to commit a crime within that portion of the town under their charge.
>
> When in any Division offences are frequently committed there must be reason to suspect that the Police is not in that Division properly conducted. The absence of crime will be considered the

---

[1] In the proof copy, Peel altered the original word 'Provisional' to 'General'.

[2] The word 'principal' was inserted by Peel.

best proof of the complete efficiency of the Police. In Divisions, where this security and good order have been effected, the Officers and Men belonging to it may feel assured that such good conduct will be noticed by rewards and promotion.

*

Next, the Commissioners turned their attention to the pay structure of the force and to the vital matter of recruiting policy.

The salaries of the Commissioners (£800 each, paid out of the Consolidated Fund) and the Receiver (£700, paid out of the police-rate revenue) had been set out in the Act.[1] The pay of the four police grades was fixed as follows:

Superintendents	£200 p.a.
Inspectors	£100 p.a.
Sergeants	22s 6d p.w.
Constables	21s p.w. (less 2s towards the cost of uniforms)

The clerical scale was thus:

Chief Clerk	£200 p.a.
Second Clerk	£150 p.a.
Third Clerk	£90 p.a.

The police rates of pay were decided by Peel, as his letter of 20 July shows, and those for sergeants and constables could not have been agreed to with much enthusiasm by Rowan or Mayne. If they were to recruit men of the calibre the job required, then these rates—well below those of a skilled artisan—were a positive disincentive, a point made with irrefutable logic by Peel's High Tory and very articulate friend Croker in a letter to him at the end of September.

Peel, however, was adamant. He was determined, as he wrote to Croker, to refuse employment to 'gentlemen—commissioned officers, for instance—as superintendents and inspectors, because I am certain they would be above their work . . . A Sergeant of the Guards at £200 a year is a better man for my purpose than a captain of high military reputation, if he would serve for nothing, or if I could give him a thousand a year. For somewhat similar reasons, a

---

[1] The salary of the Chief Magistrate at Bow Street was £1,200, an anomaly to which neither Rowan nor Mayne seems to have drawn attention.

three shillings a day man is better than a five shilling a day man.'

Apart from the curious logic of the last sentence, Peel was stubborn to the point of obsession that his 'New Police' should be seen to be free of all taint of militarism and indeed he made it a cardinal principle that, as the force grew, it should be 'filled up from below'. His thinking is understandable, but in deciding on a 'deterrent' pay structure he was sowing the seed of much future discontent, even to the point of mutiny.

Peel's decision greatly circumscribed the Commissioners in their recruiting policy, for only the highest standards could be considered if the new force were to operate with proper efficiency. These standards included: a signed recommendation as to character; physical fitness; a maximum age limit of thirty-five; a minimum height of 5 ft 7 in; and an ability to read and write (the last, in the context of 1829, a major limiting factor). Every applicant was personally interviewed by the Commissioners and the rejection rate, particularly among the old parochial officers who applied, was high. Even then, the turnover of men was startling. Within two years of the formation of the New Police, when the total strength was just over 4,000, 1,250 had resigned voluntarily and 1,989 had been dismissed, 80 per cent of them for drunkenness; and by 1838, over 6,000 constables had resigned and 5,200 had been dismissed. Of the original 3,000, only 850 still remained in the service. The problems of replacement and training must have been formidable and there is no doubt that Peel's refusal to reconsider the pay structure contributed significantly to the Commissioners' difficulties.

There is a general but erroneous idea that the greater proportion of recruits was drawn, *faute de mieux*, from the army and navy, but by 1 June 1830, when all the seventeen divisions envisaged in the Act had been formed and the total strength had risen to 3,314, the constabulary grade[1] was made up as follows: 135 butchers, 109 bakers, 198 shoemakers, 51 tailors, 402 soldiers, 1,154 labourers, 205 servants, 141 carpenters, 75 bricklayers, 55 blacksmiths, 20 turners, 152 clerks, 141 shopmen, 141 superior mechanics, 46 plumbers and painters, 101 sailors, 51 weavers, and 8 stonemasons.

---

[1] The ranks of superintendent and inspector were almost exclusively filled from former warrant-officers and NCOs of the Guards and the Cavalry, although Supt Thomas of F Division was a former parish constable from Covent Garden.

It is interesting to speculate as to why so many skilled and semi-skilled artisans should have joined a service which was ill-paid and the object of almost universal public hostility.

*

The question whether or not the New Police should wear uniform led to considerable discussion, as Rowan was later to explain to the Select Committee set up after the Popay affair (see p. 105). Peel, in a moment of extravagance, proposed a confection of scarlet and gold, which would have ill-accorded with his conception of a civilian institution. Eventually, as Rowan explained, the decision was taken to put the men into 'a quiet uniform' not greatly distinguishable from an ordinary civilian livery. The designer of this uniform is not known, for no drawings have survived; but it is reasonable to suppose that it was largely the work of the indefatigable Rowan.[1]

It consisted of a blue swallow-tail coat with white buttons; a collar worn over a stiff leather stock and fastened by a brass buckle; a broad leather belt; blue peg-top trousers (white for optional wear in summer); heavy half-wellington boots which were to be the subject of considerable Victorian mirth; a tall chimney-pot hat with a specially strengthened top so that it might serve as a platform on which the constable could, if necessary, stand; a rattle and a truncheon. Each man's divisional letter and number was sewn onto the collar as a mark of public identification. The whole outfit was 'quiet' and smart, but exceedingly uncomfortable, and it was to remain virtually unchanged for over thirty years. The contract for uniforms and equipment was awarded to Charles Hebbert of Pall Mall.

Constables and sergeants were provided with this uniform at a biennial cost of £11 6s 4d. Superintendents and inspectors were required to purchase their own. All ranks were obliged by Police Regulations to wear uniform at all times (a blue and white armlet denoting when they were on duty) and it was not until the arrival of Colonel Sir Edmund Henderson in 1869 that these regulations were relaxed.

*

[1] Despite repeated representations to the Home Office, Rowan and Mayne were not permitted to wear uniform until 1839.

Finally, the Commissioners went in search of an operational base.

On the east side of Whitehall stood an area known as 'Scotland', where—so the story went—Scottish dignitaries had been lodged when they came to pay their respects to the kings of England. With the destruction of the old Palace of Whitehall, the area had been developed as a residential close around a narrow court known as Great Scotland Yard. Inigo Jones and Wren lived here, and here also, as we have seen, Evelyn (as Commissioner of Traffic) and Thomas de Veil had set up their offices.

By the early nineteenth century, the developers had gone to work again and had built at the far end a row of houses called Whitehall Place, which backed onto Great Scotland Yard.[1] When, in July, the lease of No. 4 became vacant, Peel instructed the Receiver to acquire the premises for the new Metropolitan Police Office (Rowan, a bachelor, was provided with a set of furnished quarters on the top floor). At the same time, the back of No. 4 Whitehall Place was extensively altered to accommodate a station-house for the small additional division (A) which Rowan had formed 'for duty in the immediate neighbourhood'.

The men of this division were soon speaking of their station by the name of the little street on which it faced. It was not much longer before even those who had business with the Commissioners or the Receiver at No. 4 Whitehall Place ceased to refer to it as 'the Metropolitan Police Office'; and, Middle and Little Scotland Yard [the old adjacent courts] having vanished, the epithet 'Great' became redundant, and the whole headquarters was known, *tout court*, as Scotland Yard.[2]

Old habits die hard. Despite two moves—the size of the present monolith would have seemed inconceivable to Rowan and Mayne—the original name has persisted, to the point where it has become, in the public regard, synonymous with the Metropolitan Police rather than the Office of the Commissioner of Police of the Metropolis.

*

[1] The two remaining police connections with Great Scotland Yard today are the offices of A.5 (Mounted Branch) housed there in Lord Lonsdale's old livery stables, and those of the Diplomatic Protection Group.

[2] Browne, *The Rise of Scotland Yard.*

By early September, the all-important ranks of superintendent and inspector had been filled and the Chief Clerk, Charles Yardley —a Waterloo veteran—appointed. Most of the sergeants and constables had been selected, and in Pall Mall Charles Hebbert was working round the clock. Rowan, with a soldier's conviction of the relationship between drill and discipline, held a series of parades in Old Palace Yard. It was a brave but hazardous decision, for the sight of men drilling in public, albeit still in plain clothes, did not go unnoticed and was presently to become an important, if ridiculous, element in a carefully orchestrated assault upon the true motives of the Commissioners. Rowan, with his innate modesty and integrity, could hardly be blamed for offering so improbable a hostage to fortune. When the English are determined to be provoked, the nature of that provocation has never mattered much.

On 26 September, the six companies assembled in the grounds of the Foundling Hospital. Their terms of service were read out to them and they were duly sworn in as constables by Rowan and Mayne in their capacity as justices. Each company was then formed into its sixteen parties. The following day they were paraded again at their station-houses, issued with their uniforms and details of accommodation and messing, and acquainted with their individual beats;[1] and at six o'clock on the evening of Tuesday, 29 September, the first parties of the Metropolitan Police marched out of their station-houses to commence their duties.

For Peel it was the reward for years of patience and persistence. For Rowan and Mayne it was the visible result of twelve weeks of brilliant and meticulous planning. All three men had reason to be satisfied with their achievement. But they had made one dangerous error; they had reckoned without English bloody-mindedness.

---

[1] Rowan later described the definition of a 'beat' as a stretch or area which could be covered in fifteen or twenty minutes at a steady pace of $2\frac{1}{2}$ miles per hour.

CHAPTER FOUR

A Thin Blue Line

HOSTILITY TO the New Police was immediate and universal. The Whigs had consistently opposed the idea of police reform, to the accompaniment of much windy rhetoric about the invasion of civil liberties and dire warnings of a French-style *gendarmerie*, while conveniently forgetting that they had raised no protest to the passage of Peel's Bill. Their militant left wing, the Ultra-Radicals, hotfoot in pursuit of political reform, saw in an organized police force a serious obstacle to their chief weapon, intimidation by mob rule. Even the Tories were at best lukewarm, disenchanted with Peel and his about-turn on the Catholic issue.

Justices and parish vestries were similarly hostile, although for different reasons. Magistrates strongly resented the special status of the Joint Commissioners and the invasion of their own executive powers, and one justice, as we shall see, carried his personal animosity to the point of putting the entire future of the police in serious jeopardy. Parochial authorities, ignoring the fact that Peel's Bill was largely the result of their own arrogance and inefficiency, objected vociferously to the removal of their parish constables and 'Charlies', and to the imposition of the new and 'onerous' police-rate.[1]

Public opinion, volatile as ever, was swept along by a press campaign as malicious as it was hysterical. As early as April, when Peel introduced his Bill, *The Times* had advanced the curious objection to a centralized police force that it would 'provide increasing opportunities for political patronage'; and by September virtually the entire press, including those organs which had warmly supported the findings of the 1828 Committee, was embarked on a mindless witch-hunt, culminating in the novel assertion that Peel's true

---

[1] During the last year, under the old watch-rate, constables and watchmen cost the ratepayers of the parish of Hackney £3,380. The cost for the first year under the new police-rate fell to £3,164. (*1834 Select Committee Report*)

object was to marry the Duke of Wellington to the ten-year-old Princess Victoria and instal him on the throne. Throughout the Metropolis the storm-signals had been hoisted.

*

Rowan and Mayne were probably too preoccupied with their brief to notice the sound of the rising wind. Neither of them had any practical experience of the hazards of public office and it is reasonable to suppose that they were innocent enough to feel themselves entitled to the protection of the Government in general and their Minister in particular. In this they were sadly wrong. Politics are about power, and the pursuit of power is an occupation with little room for sentiment and less for paternalism.

Thus it is ironical that Peel, the father of the New Police, showed little understanding of the growing pains of his child. By November he was assuring Wellington, with a complacency that the facts did not yet warrant, of his faith in the future of the police, and of the labour pains he had so readily, if vicariously, suffered. Of the two midwives who had brought the infant into the world, he made no mention whatever.

Rowan and Mayne soon found that the Act which had created their joint office was a very imperfect instrument. In the first place, they had been given statutory responsibilities without any precise definition of their status and authority, particularly in relation to the magistrates and parochial authorities. The Act referred to 'such [other] duties as shall be herein-after specified'—and omitted to specify them. The Commissioners were made responsible for preserving law and order and controlling crime and riots throughout the entire Metropolitan Police District; but this had been the traditional province of magistrates and no attempt had been made to clarify the new relationship, nor formally to transfer to the New Police the peace officers attached to Bow Street and the other public offices. It is not surprising that the justices were incensed by the invasion of their prerogative. Despite repeated requests from Rowan and Mayne, Peel declined to arbitrate in this increasingly delicate situation. 'He gave them [the Commissioners] duties which usurped the powers of the Chief Magistrate and others and was adamant in refusing to give a ruling that on occasions of riots the magistrates were to take orders from the Commissioners or that these were to take orders from the magistrates.'[1] It was to take several years—and much bad blood—before the separate functions of the judicial and executive branches of the law were finally established.

*

Two men of lesser calibre than Rowan and Mayne would probably have fallen at this first hurdle; but relying on the policy of civility and moderation which informs each page of their Instruction Book, they refused to be distracted by overt acts of hostility and worked patiently towards their goal of building a police force which, by its conduct, would eventually achieve the ultimate accolade of public regard and acceptance.

For the men themselves, it was a baptism of fire. They had of necessity to learn their trade by trial and error, for there had been little time for anything more than elementary training and it is in the nature of a constable's duties that people have a perverse habit of behaving in accordance with no known text-book.

Physical assault[2] and every form of obstruction were commonplace, and the Commissioners were bombarded with complaints, both real and frivolous, against individual policemen.

In the matter of assault, Peel's refusal adequately to define the legal powers of constables led to an impossible situation. Since public prosecutors did not yet exist, a policeman was obliged to bring his own case and conduct it in the face of open hostility (and improper conduct) from the judiciary and the legal profession, to say nothing of the press and public. If the constable won—which was exceptional—the defendant could expect to escape with a derisory sentence. If he lost, then he risked a counter-action for wrongful arrest and an indefinite prison sentence since he was unable to pay the costs. Legal aid for prosecuting constables was only sparingly made available by the Home Office, and after Peel's departure from office at the end of 1830, seems to have been entirely withheld by his Whig successors. In such circumstances, it is remarkable that constables were prepared to bring a court action at all or that they resisted the temptation to resort to the corrupt

[1] Reith, *A New Study of Police History*.
[2] The first policeman to lose his life on duty was PC Long of G Division who was stabbed to death while questioning three suspicious characters on 18 August 1830. Public revulsion at this murder created a marked improvement in attitudes towards the police. It did not last long.

practices of their predecessors. We can only assume that Rowan and Mayne, by their example and their encouragement, succeeded in creating a completely novel sense of public duty among their men.

In the matter of complaints against the police, the Commissioners went to extraordinary lengths to ensure that justice was seen to be done. Every complaint—and they were many—was personally investigated without regard to time and trouble, and each complainant was invited either to bring an action in the courts, or to attend at 4 Whitehall Place for an impartial inquiry into the charges made. In most instances, the aggrieved party chose the latter course, and if the case was proved, the constable in question was fined or dismissed. If the charge could not be sustained, the complainant was at least left with the feeling that he had been treated with courtesy and impartiality.[1] It was a procedure which aroused the wrath of magistrates and press alike, but it met with general public approval and further served to strengthen the relationship between the Commissioners and their sorely-tried men.

In the light of early experiences, it is surprising that the New Police managed to survive as a coherent force. As we have seen, the wastage from resignations and dismissals during the first year was considerable, the former through disenchantment with public attitudes, poor pay and conditions, and physical hazards, the latter through Rowan's determination to maintain those impeccable standards of conduct which alone could disarm the criticisms of his enemies. Pensions were still in the future and payment to seriously disabled men was only occasionally and then grudgingly conceded, despite Rowan's constant pressure and despite Clause XII of the 1829 Act which directed that the Home Secretary could authorize the Receiver to pay sums out of the Police precept 'as a Compensation for Wounds or severe Injuries received in the Performance of their Duty', a vague act of piety which was eventually translated into a formal entitlement of £40 by Lord John Russell six years later. Yet despite obvious disincentives, a steady stream of acceptable recruits continued to come forward at a rate not only to replace

---

[1] In apparent contradiction of Peel's determination not to admit ex-officers to the New Police, Rowan had appointed a Captain Carden as Superintendent of S Division. His reason, which Peel seems to have accepted, was to have available the services of such a man to help the Commissioners in investigating the growing flood of complaints by the public.

wastage but to man the newly-formed divisional companies.[1] Only the most bigotted or politically-motivated could persist in the fiction of a ruthless *gendarmerie*. Even *The Times*, one of the first and fiercest critics of Peel's Act, could write thus on the anniversary of the first appearance of the New Police: 'We ourselves have seen nothing of the police but exemplary courtesy, forbearance and proprietary, great willingness to act and, when occasion calls for it, to refrain from acting. Overpaid, at a guinea a week each, no rational person can consider them.'

There is more joy in Heaven . . .; unfortunately there remained other, dangerously unrepentent sinners.

*

Statistics towards the end of 1830 proved beyond argument that in pursuance of their 'principal object'—the prevention of crime— the police had achieved remarkable success.[2] Indeed, there were growing complaints from provincial authorities that Peel's 'raw lobsters' had effectively driven the criminal population out of London and into the towns of the Midlands and the North, and the exodus of villains from Westminster across the City boundary evoked indignant protests from the Court of Common Council. Temple Bar had become Tom Tiddler's ground.

But if one epidemic had been checked, the old disease remained; and it now took on a new and critical form.

The burning issue which succeeded Catholic Emancipation was Parliamentary Reform, a subject tailor-made (literally, in the case of Francis Place, the moderate and influential Radical) for political extremists and militant agitators. On this issue the divide between Tories and Whigs was clear and unequivocal. If the forum of Parliament was the proper battleground, the streets of London provided a more fertile field for public demonstration; and this ground, for so long open territory, was now under the protection of the New Police.

Or was it? The strategy of the Ultra-Radicals, supported by rebellious parish vestries, was to confront the police with mob violence in the streets, and by defeating them in public, compel the

---

[1] Seven divisions were added in February 1830 and four more in May.

[2] The 1834 Committee noted that within five years an estimated annual figure of £900,000 lost through theft and robbery with violence in the Metropolis had been reduced to £20,000 a year.

Tories to fall back on the last resort of military intervention. That
way lay anarchy—and anarchy was the purpose of the Ultras.

For a year, the militants bided their time, relying meanwhile on a
campaign of slanderous abuse and vilification against the police in
the press and on public platforms. It was a deliberate softening-up
process designed to sap police morale and to prepare public
opinion for a final physical confrontation. With hindsight, it was a
tactical error of the first magnitude, for it provided Rowan and
Mayne with a breathing-space to establish a unified and disciplined
defensive system and to gain experience of the proper deployment
of their resources. To Rowan it must have brought back memories
of his Peninsula days, even if the enemy was now more elusive and
less easily identifiable. But there can be little doubt that if the militants had struck in the autumn of 1829, when the police was at its
most vulnerable, they would have carried the day. In the event, it
was not until October 1830 that the simmering cauldron boiled over.

The Moderate Radicals pursued their campaign for reform
through the legitimate channels of public and parliamentary debate,
but the Ultras—determined not on reform but on the complete
overthrow of constitutional government—embarked on a head-on
collision with the symbols of public authority; and the first demonstrations in Covent Garden and Piccadilly on 26 October were
accompanied by the slogan: 'No New Police!' When Parliament
reassembled the following day and it became known that the
Speech from the Throne had omitted any reference to Parliamentary
reform, there was violent rioting throughout Westminster and, on
28 October, a pitched battle with the police at Hyde Park Corner.

This was the first real test for Rowan and Mayne. For a year they
had contended with verbal attacks, with non-cooperation and active
opposition from justices and parochial authorities, and with assaults
on individual police officers. Now they were confronted with organized violence and they seem at first to have had no real plan for
dealing with such a contingency. Rowan's dilemma was clear. The
Commissioners were responsible for riot-control, but the police—
unarmed except for their truncheons—could not afford to over-
react in the face of provocation from whatever quarter, however
extreme. Thus during the October disturbances Rowan adopted a
defensive technique and the mob was met by only passive police
resistance, a tactic which seems to have bewildered the rioters who,
bent on violence, were hoping for violence in return.

Such tactics, however, could not be effective in the event of public disorder on a massive scale; and it was from a curious quarter that an alternative suggestion came. Alone among Radicals and Whigs, Francis Place, the tailor of Charing Cross and one of the most bizarre figures in the history of political reform, understood the essential role of the New Police in that maintenance of law and order to which the Ultras were implacably opposed; and to the admirable Superintendent Thomas, Place advanced the idea of organized counter-attack. Thomas did not have to wait long to try out this new technique.

9 November was Lord Mayor's Day and the militants chose this occasion, when the King would be attending the Guildhall banquet, to organize a giant demonstration. Their target was the police, as the following poster—one of many such—proclaimed:

LIBERTY OR DEATH! BRITONS!! AND HONEST MEN!!!
The time has at last arrived. All London meets on Tuesday. We assure you from ocular demonstration that 6,000 cutlasses have been removed from the Tower for the use of Peel's Bloody Gang. Remember the cursed speech from the Throne!! These damned Police are now to be armed.
Englishmen, will you put up with this?

Confronted by such incitement to riot and disorder, the Government advised the King not to attend the banquet, and the mob, denied the royal presence, marched upon the West End in search of trouble. Instead, they found themselves faced in the Strand by Superintendent Thomas and his men of F Division who, without waiting to be provoked, drew their truncheons and descended upon the rioters in a compact body. The startled mob broke and fled for safety beyond the City boundary. The first baton-charge had proved an unqualified success, without bloodshed or injury on either side.

During the next few days, there was continuing confrontation between police and militants and the new tactics proved so effective that even the hostile *Courier* felt disposed to congratulate the police on having so efficiently restored order without the usual intervention of the military. Peel had little difficulty in justifying this action to the House; and Rowan and Mayne must have been congratulating themselves on the growing success of their police organization, when suddenly, on 15 November, the Government resigned. It was succeeded by a Whig administration under Earl Grey, and Peel's place at the Home Office was taken by a very different kind of man.

*

Lord Melbourne was in his early fifties and without experience of office. Witty and somewhat affected, he combined a reputation for laziness with a formidable capacity for indecision, as the Commissioners were very shortly to discover, as also his dislike of committing himself in writing.

The Metropolitan Police provided Melbourne with something of a problem. He had inherited from Peel an organization the creation of which the Whigs had bitterly opposed for a century or more; indeed, they had been widely credited with an election pledge to disband the force. But even their moderate Radical wing could see daily evidence of the success of the New Police in combating crime and maintaining public order. To abolish them would leave the Government with no choice but to rely on the even more hated alternative of military intervention. It was a dilemma which must have given Peel a good deal of satisfaction.

Melbourne's course—and that of his successor at the Home Office, Duncannon—was to play politics with the police, and politics of a particularly distasteful kind at that. He needed the police—and the growing agitation for Parliamentary reform reinforced that need; but he could visit upon the Commissioners and their men every sin of omission and commission, real or imagined, by giving tacit support to dissident parishes and hostile magistrates, and by encouraging, not always with much subtlety, public complaints and press antipathy. Thus Rowan and Mayne were left to fight a lonely battle for survival. That they succeeded against such odds is tribute enough to their firmness of purpose and their refusal to be deflected from their statutory duty. At least Melbourne had the political sense not to dismiss them and thereby provide the Tories with a powerful electoral weapon, although his successor, Duncannon, came very close to forcing Rowan's resignation on an issue which would certainly have brought down the Government.

The year 1831 opened with further outbreaks of public disorder, and with the formation of the National Political Union of the Working Classes, a Radical body with branches or 'classes' throughout the Metropolis and which, though started by the Moderates, soon became the tool of the Ultras. Of all the revolutionary forces

generated by agitation for reform, the NPU was to provide Rowan
and Mayne with their most difficult and dangerous challenge.

Melbourne was well aware of this; and he was cynically prepared
to damage the Commissioners' credibility by every devious means
and by treating the police, not least in public, as a distasteful but
necessary evil. Wild allegations of brutality and corruption from
parish vestries were passed to the Commissioners without comment.
Each was carefully investigated and almost invariably refuted. To
their temperate and meticulous reports they received no replies. It
was a form of death by a hundred humiliations.

The Ultras made full use of the 'democratic' aspirations of the
NPU to foment disorder on an ever-increasing scale, and from
April onwards the police were extended far beyond their numerical
resources; for the militants now realized that while they could not
defeat police tactics on equal terms, they could overwhelm them by
sheer force of numbers.

Melbourne and his colleagues, despite their publicly professed
hostility to the Commissioners, could read the storm signals; and it
is typical of their equivocation that on 15 October they introduced
the Special Constables Act (applicable to the whole country) by
which magistrates were empowered to nominate citizens to be
enrolled for police duties in the event of a serious emergency. As
we have seen, special constables had been legalized—though never
embodied—in 1673, and the 1831 Act (which is still the basis of the
Special Constabulary[1]) was in fact a statutory re-statement of the
old mediaeval concept of the *posse comitatus*. So far as the Metropolis was concerned, Melbourne predictably gave no direction
regarding the operational responsibility for these stand-by policemen, although the wording of the Act makes it clear that they would
have come under the direction of the Police Magistrates. Fortunately
—for the confusion would have been devastating—the Act was not
invoked in London until 1848, by which time the purely executive
function of the Commissioners had at last been clearly defined and
the operational control of the Special Constabulary firmly vested in
them.

Less than a month after the passage of this Act, Rowan was provided with an opportunity to put Melbourne's true motives to the

---

[1] The legal obligation to serve as a special constable was not replaced by
the present voluntary system until after the First World War (Special
Constables Act 1923.)

test. The Ultra-Radicals advertised a mass meeting to take place on
7 November at White Conduit House, a large public hall in Penton-
ville. Rowan, surely with tongue in cheek, circularized all Police
Magistrates and suggested[1] that they swear in 'adequate' numbers
of special constables to assist in maintaining order (he had, of
course, made his own efficient dispositions and ensured that the
militants were kept well aware of police preparations). The bluff
worked; and the organizers hastily abandoned the meeting. Charles
Rowan was beginning to learn that politics was a game at which
two could play.

But Melbourne had kept one trick up his sleeve. Without reference to the Commissioners, he had instructed two Marlborough
Street magistrates, Frederick Roe and Allen Laing, to attend the
meeting in their official capacity. Roe demanded to be given full
details of police dispositions, which the superintendent in charge
readily provided, pointing out that they had effectively frustrated
the militants' plans. But Roe, a man who would have taken offence
at the word 'Welcome!' on the mat, decided to pick the quarrel he
had long been seeking and wrote to the Home Secretary complaining
of the superintendent's attitude, and the fact that the Commissioners had neither consulted him nor been present to receive him,
an impertinent observation which drew a sharp reply from Mayne.
It was to be the beginning of a long and unattractive vendetta.

*

In April 1832, Sir Richard Birnie, Chief Magistrate at Bow
Street, died and was replaced by Roe, a deliberately provocative
appointment on Melbourne's part. The personal campaign against
the Commissioners on which the new Chief Magistrate now embarked need not concern us in detail here. His meanest hour, and
final discomfiture, were to come two years later; but for the present
he made it his business to frustrate Rowan and Mayne by every
means at his command—and these included the continuing employment of the Bow Street Runners and Bow Street Officers whose
activities (now technically illegal under the terms of the 1829 Act)
were designed to embarrass the Metropolitan Police in the exercise
of their statutory duty. It did not matter to Roe—or Melbourne—
that his small private army at Bow Street were *agents provocateurs*,

---

[1] The suggestion was ignored, as Rowan knew it would be.

if not actually themselves involved in crime, so long as they successfully obstructed the regular police; and Melbourne made full use
of Roe's capacity for trouble-making.

Repeatedly Mayne sought a final and definitive clarification of
the respective judicial and executive functions of the magistrates
and the Commissioners. Between April and November he wrote
eleven letters to the Home Office on this subject. Only to the last
did he receive a reply—from Phillipps and not from Melbourne—
which, while giving the appearance of a formal recognition of the
Commissioners' status, was couched in language at once Delphic
and disconcerting. The letter ended: 'Lord Melbourne is fully
sensible . . . that all regulations for the general government as well
as for the particular services of the Officers of the Police are to be
made by the Commissioners subject to the approbation of the
Secretary of State.' Given Melbourne's ill-concealed support for
Roe, the sting was in the tail.

*

While this ritual dance dragged on, the political ferment continued to grow, with the defeat of the second Reform Bill in the
Lords. One small but significant event at this time served to illustrate the success of Rowan's 'firm and just' conduct of his office.
While the New Police continued to contain public disorders in the
Metropolitan District, the City of London, still dependent on the
old, discredited system of peace officers, had become a focal point
for militant activity. The City Fathers, well aware of the new
climate outside their boundaries, reluctantly decided to create a
force of 100 Day Police, organized on the Metropolitan pattern. It
was a tiny triumph for common sense over bigotry, for it was to
provide the nucleus of the City of London Police, the formation of
which was to be imposed on the City authorities by the 1839 Police
Act, under the threat of a compulsory take-over by the Metropolitan Commissioners in the event of non-compliance. Patience
has its just, if often unexpected, rewards.

*

On 7 June 1832, the Third Reform Bill became law; but the
militants were not to be deflected from their real objective by the
passage of a measure which they dismissed as little more than a

cosmetic palliative. And the following year a curious conjunction of events conspired to bring matters to a head.

In April 1833 a Select Committee was appointed 'to inquire into the State of the Police of the Metropolis within the Metropolitan District, and the State of Crime therein'. Whether the Government had an ulterior motive behind this decision—and Melbourne's attitude to the police suggests that this may have been so—the membership of the Committee was widely based and Rowan and Mayne must have welcomed the opportunity to present their own, unassailable case in open court. But hardly had the Committee started to take evidence than there occurred two *causes célèbres*.

Towards the end of February, a Sergeant Popay of P Division was instructed by his superintendent to be present in plain clothes at meetings of the extreme-militant Camberwell 'class' of the NPU in order to monitor the activities of the speakers. Popay, in an excess of constabulary zeal, so interpreted his instructions as to infiltrate the NPU class, posing as an impoverished painter with views so revolutionary and utterances so militant that he was soon accepted as one of the natural leaders of the movement. The deception might have passed unnoticed, had Popay not had the misfortune to be recognized at his desk in the station-house by one of his Union associates. The result was public uproar and all the old arguments about police espionage and invasion of privacy were taken down, dusted, and ventilated again in language hysterical even by the standards of the day; and while this battle of words raged, the Central Committee of the Union, now dominated by the Ultras, decided on a final resort to physical violence, as 'the only means of obtaining and securing the Rights of the People'.

A mass meeting was announced, to be held on 13 May at Coldbath Fields in Clerkenwell. The handbills accompanying this announcement were couched in language so inflammatory that the Home Secretary, frightened for once into decisive action, declared the meeting illegal. Melbourne summoned Rowan and Mayne and gave them the following *verbal* instructions (the word is important in a later context): an adequate force of police was to be assembled in the area but was, in the first instance, to remain concealed. No action was to be taken unless an attempt was made to address the meeting, in which event the crowd was to be dispersed and the leaders arrested.

Rowan made his usual careful dispositions. He assembled some

600 men in nearby stables and, probably mindful of the earlier behaviour of Frederick Roe, decided to take personal command of police operations.

In defiance of the ban, a small crowd gathered but the numbers were soon swelled by armed processions of NPU members shouting revolutionary slogans. The eventual size of the mob was disputed at the subsequent Inquiry, but seems to have been not less than 6,000; and when, at about 3 p.m., an NPU leader began to address the meeting, Rowan acted.[1]

A confused running fight ensued in which the police, heavily outnumbered and confronted by armed thugs, behaved with astonishing propriety. They sustained many casualties, two of their number were seriously injured, and one, PC Culley, was stabbed to death. Eventually the mob was dispersed and the police, though they did not then know it, had won their final and conclusive success over the Ultras. More importantly, they had won an even greater victory in the long term—the seal of public approval.

Events now moved fast. The jury at the inquest on Robert Culley, held improbably in the nearby Calthorpe Arms public house, returned a verdict of 'justifiable homicide', a perversion of justice so manifest that it was subsequently set aside by a higher court. Public and private subscriptions were organized for the widow of the dead constable and the Government took the unprecedented step of awarding her the sum of £200 in compensation. Even Melbourne must have recognized the wind of change.

None the less, the Popay affair and the battle of Coldbath Fields raised important issues, and during the summer of 1833, the Government temporarily adjourned the Police Committee and set up two separate inquiries.

The Popay committee, appointed to inquire into the complaint of 'the Employment of Policemen as Spies', resolved that 'the Conduct of the Policeman Popay has been highly reprehensible', and ended by saying that the committee, while accepting the necessity for the occasional employment of police in plain clothes, 'solemnly deprecate any approach to the Employment of Spies . . . as a

---

[1] The Commissioners' report to the Inquiry included this sentence, very much in character: 'The last words spoken by Colonel Rowan to those who alone were expected to take an active part in the affair, were to be cool and temperate, to hurt or strike no one unnecessarily, or unless they were resisted.'

practice most abhorrent to the feelings of the People, and most Alien to the spirit of the Constitution'. Sergeant Popay, the victim of his own excessive enthusiasm, was dismissed.

The inquiry into the Coldbath Fields meeting was a very different affair, for it was conducted by a committee which included Robert Peel, and which was plainly determined from the outset to establish the true facts. On 8 August, Melbourne was summoned to give evidence. It is tempting to quote here the entire and uncompromising cross-examination of his Lordship by Sir George Grey. Many of the exchanges were rightly concerned with the Home Secretary's refusal to give written, as opposed to verbal, instructions to the Commissioners. And the concluding questions and answers tell us all we need to know of the man with whom Rowan and Mayne had for so long contended:

> The police are entirely under the control of the Home Department, are they not?—Yes.
>
> Do you ever institute any inquiry into the conduct of the men, without communicating with the Commissioners?—Never, except through the Commissioners.
>
> Never on any occasion do you entertain any inquiry into their conduct, without the knowledge of the Commissioners?—No.
>
> Would your Lordship deem it proper to institute such an inquiry without communication with the Commissioners at the head of the Force?—I should deem it imprudent.

Unfortunately for Melbourne, he had omitted to acquaint himself with the rather different evidence given by his crony, Frederick Roe, on 10 May to the parent committee.

The original 1833 Select Committee was re-convened the following year and reported on 13 August. Since its membership was largely the same as that which had held the two special inquiries, it now approached its task in a very different climate of opinion and with the benefit of a wealth of new and recent evidence. The Report, among other recommendations, demonstrated beyond argument three essential areas for action:

1. The necessity of finally separating the judicial and executive functions of the Police Magistrates.
2. The desirability of implementing forthwith the requirement of the 1829 Act that *all* existing police organizations, including

the various Bow Street officers, should be incorporated in the Metropolitan Police and placed under the control of the Commissioners.

3. The City of London (and the responsibility for its policing) should be absorbed into the Metropolitan Police District.[1]

Between them, Frederick Roe and the City authorities contrived to frustrate these overdue reforms, and except for the incorporation of the Bow Street Horse Patrol into the outlying Metropolitan divisions two years later, no further action was taken until the passing of the 1839 Police Act. Ten years is a short time in politics.

But the real significance of the 1834 Committee Report lies in two unambiguous—and, in a sense, historic—statements of opinion. The first is a reference to 'Colonel Rowan and Mr Mayne ... who still continue to fill the arduous offices of Commissioners of Police'. The Report goes on:

On many critical occasions, and in very difficult circumstances, the sound discretion they have exercised, the straightforward, open and honourable course they have pursued whenever their conduct has been questioned by the Public [*and not only by the Public*], calls for the strongest expression of approbation on the part of your Committee.

The second and final observation is as follows:

Your Committee conclude with this expression of their Opinion; viz. that the Metropolitan Police Force, as respects its influence in repressing crime and the security it has given to persons and property, is one of the most valuable modern institutions.

It had taken five years of patient and courageous endeavour by the Commissioners and their men to win such singular approbation from such a quarter. Serious problems and one potentially fatal confrontation lay ahead, but the standing of the New Police was now assured beyond argument. No man could have signed the Report with greater satisfaction than Robert Peel.

*

[1] Quoted figures showed the annual cost of Day Police and Nightly Watch in the City of London to be £45,207 5s 1d. The cost of two extra divisions of the Metropolitan Police 'to perform the same duty' was estimated at £24,650—a saving of over £20,000.

In July 1834, while the Committee was still sitting, Grey resigned and was succeeded as Prime Minister by Melbourne. The new Home Secretary was his brother-in-law, Lord Duncannon, and if Rowan and Mayne thought they might now enjoy some respite from their years of harassment, they were soon to be rudely disillusioned.

Duncannon shared all of Melbourne's vices and none of his virtues. He was a bigoted Whig. He detested the Metropolitan Police and all it stood for. And he was on terms of closest intimacy with Frederick Roe. On the very day on which he assumed office, Duncannon—at Roe's instigation—showed his claws.

The circumstances were briefly thus. On 19 June a prostitute had been arrested in D Division for being drunk and disorderly. She was detained in a cell and the following morning, before Supt Lazenby, accused one of his inspectors named Wovenden of having raped her during the night. Her story was so patently untrue that Lazenby refused to accept it, but reported the matter to the Commissioners. Mayne, recognizing a potentially explosive situation, insisted that Wovenden should be formally charged before a magistrate to clear his name, but the prostitute refused to proceed against him.

On 30 July Duncannon—fully apprised of the course of events through a sergeant-clerk working undercover for Roe in Lazenby's office—demanded details of the case. Three days later the Commissioners learned that, without reference to them, Wovenden had been arrested on a warrant from Bow Street and that Roe had been instructed by Duncannon to conduct a private investigation. This inquiry, carried out with a contempt for truth and equity remarkable even by Roe's standards, resulted in Wovenden being prosecuted in a higher court. The grand jury took one look at the evidence and threw the case out. Wovenden was released.

Roe, however, was hell-bent on a final confrontation with the Commissioners. During September, they had presented Duncannon with the results of a detailed internal investigation into the case which proved beyond any argument that Lazenby and Wovenden were completely innocent of any impropriety or misconduct and that they had been the victims of Roe's bitter personal vendetta against the police. Whether Duncannon, left to his own devices, would have accepted this report is not known; but Roe intervened, and on 31 October the Commissioners were curtly instructed by the Home Secretary to dismiss the two officers.

It is clear from the correspondence that Roe's sole intention was to force the resignation of the Commissioners. For Rowan especially it was perhaps the most difficult decision of his life. Loyalty to Lazenby and Wovenden—both Peninsula veterans—argued that he and Mayne should resign; but there was another, wider loyalty to the whole police institution for which the Commissioners were responsible. Given two men of the character of Duncannon and Roe, their departure from office would have ensured the complete disintegration of the force which they had created and of which the recent Committee had so warmly approved. So on 6 November Rowan wrote to Phillipps at the Home Office. His letter was a dignified defence of Lazenby and Wovenden and a damning commentary on the conduct of Roe; and it ended with the words: 'The Commissioners beg . . . to acquaint you for his Lordship's information that [the two men] have been dismissed accordingly.' Despite many subsequent efforts from different quarters, they were never reinstated.

Roe had not finished yet. Baulked by Rowan's decision, he now chose a different tack and on 17 November Duncannon conveyed to the Commissioners a recommendation from Roe that in future the pay of superintendents should be reduced to £150. It was a mean and shabby suggestion, designed not only to cause trouble in the ranks, but to revive the question of resignation at the top. The threat, however, proved to be still-born for, providentially, the King dismissed Melbourne in December, and with him, into the obscurity from which he should never have emerged, went Duncannon.

For Rowan and Mayne, it had been their darkest hour; and despite occasional sniping from Bow Street, their authority was never again to be seriously challenged.

*

There followed a brief Tory interregnum until April 1835, when the Whigs returned to power. Melbourne was Prime Minister again and Duncannon's successor at the Home Office was Lord John Russell.

The new Home Secretary, although a convinced Whig, had much in common with Peel, not least in his passion for social reform and in his natural caution. The success of the Metropolitan Police had

resulted, as we have seen, in the exodus of many villains to provincial centres where responsibility for law and order and the prevention of crime still lay with the old and ineffective partnership of
justices and constables. Russell accordingly decided to apply the
successful London model to the provinces and on 9 September his
Municipal Corporations Act became law.[1] Under this far-reaching
measure, the 178 boroughs to which it applied were required to
appoint Watch Committees as local police authorities with the
responsibility for creating and supervising constabularies to maintain the King's Peace in their areas of jurisdiction. The cost was
initially to be borne on the rates and the Home Secretary had power
neither to inspect nor to interfere with their arrangements. The
Metropolitan Police were soon in great demand to provide professional assistance in setting up the new borough forces and their
proven system and methods were widely copied. Russell had acted
just in time, for within a year the country was faced by the growing
agitation of the Chartist movement.

Russell's attitude towards the Commissioners was a curious
mixture of grudging support and petty spite, as if he felt that no
true Whig should endorse a Tory-inspired institution, however
'liberal' (the new word by which his party now described itself).
This 'marvellous little man', as Greville described him, could be as
small in mind as he was in stature, but he was above all a political
realist and his six years at the Home Office left a mark upon the
police history of this country scarcely less enduring than that
imprinted by Peel.

With the Municipal Corporations Act on the statute book, he
turned his attention to the problem of the rural areas and early in
1837 a Royal Commission—no less—was set up to examine 'the
best Means of Establishing an Efficient Constabulary Force in the
Counties of England and Wales' (it should be remembered that the
formation of county councils was still fifty years in the future). For
the first time for many years, Rowan and Mayne were left in relative
peace to carry on with the task of consolidating their hard-won
victories. The demands upon their time and upon their experienced
men, as the new borough forces began to take shape, put a considerable strain on their limited resources, for the Metropolitan
Police establishment had not been increased since 1830, and to their

[1] For a detailed account of the development of borough and county
police forces, see T. A. Critchley, *A History of Police in England and Wales*.

repeated requests Russell turned a deaf ear. (In December 1837 he agreed, with ill grace, to the recruitment of an additional 100 men.)

The New Police was now universally accepted—by the public, by the press, and even by the parochial authorities. The prestige and authority of the Commissioners had never stood higher (even Frederick Roe had accepted defeat, a baronetcy, and the comfort of a well-pensioned retirement), but inevitably successful action breeds reaction. This was to take a form which, as we shall see, was to bedevil the Metropolitan Police to this day. And it raises issues of such importance that it is proper to consider it here.

The 1829 Act had named the Home Secretary as the Police Authority for the Metropolis 'to direct and controul such new System of Police within those limits'. Like most statutory instruments, it took no account of the vagaries of human nature or of the consequences of an imprecise use of language. We have seen how the failure to define the relationship between the Commissioners and the magistrates came close to destroying the New Police; indeed, it could be said that, between them, Melbourne, Duncannon and Roe effectively managed to defy the law. But as the prestige and popularity of the Commissioners grew, another—and more sensitive—area of controversy became apparent.

A literal interpretation of Peel's Act implied that the Home Secretary's authority over the Commissioners was complete and absolute, and Melbourne's evidence before the Coldbath Fields Committee showed that he, at least, believed this to be so (see p. 106). But such total authority presupposed the existence of a State Police, the very institution which both political parties had consistently rejected. Where, then, lay the line of demarcation?

The Commissioner of Police of the Metropolis is the servant of Crown and people, answerable to Parliament, in its capacity of *vox populi*, for the conduct of his office. He, and every member of his force, is subject to the same law of which they are the executive arm, even if that law is so altered as to subject him to political pressures. He is, by definition, as impartial in his field as the judiciary are in theirs; but it was not always thus, and the proper powers of a Commissioner were to prove a constant source of friction. More recently Sir Robert Mark has defined the position thus:

There is no question that, unlike other chief officers [*chief constables of borough and county forces*], the Commissioner is *administratively* under the control of the Home Secretary and, indeed, can be summarily removed from office, unlike a Chief Constable who, under the 1964 Act, enjoys the right to an enquiry. But no Commissioner worth his salt would tolerate interference in his *operational* role.[1]

During the formative years of the New Police, the status of the Commissioners was such that they were concerned only in a struggle for survival. From the outset, Richard Mayne and Samuel Phillipps, the indestructible Under-Secretary at the Home Office, had taken an instant dislike to each other. The letter-books in the Public Record Office tell us much about the character of the two men. Phillipps was afraid of Mayne, seeing in him a quality of intellect which he himself entirely lacked. Mayne despised Phillipps as the epitome of bureaucratic arrogance; and both men were right.

Phillipps may fairly be accused of having instigated the atmosphere of discord between the Home Office and the Commissioners which became more marked as the power and influence of the latter increased. Not once did Rowan or Mayne seek to abuse their power nor did they consider themselves anything other than servants of the public, with a statutory duty to preserve the King's Peace. That their repeated requests for a clear definition of their office and for increased resources with which to carry out their duties went largely unanswered is due to Phillipps's jealousy of their achievement and to his blatant manipulation of successive Home Secretaries. He was neither foolish nor naive, and recognized more clearly than his masters that the use—and abuse—of administrative control could circumscribe the operational freedom of the Commissioners. The undercurrent of antipathy persisted until fifty years later it was brought to a head by the resignation of Sir Charles Warren.

*

Fortunately, however, Russell had no taste for private intrigue and with his Royal Commission at work on the problem of policing rural areas,[2] he returned to the cultivation of his Metropolitan garden.

In March 1837 he set up another Select Committee to consider

---

[1] Letter to the author, 21 November 1977.

[2] The outcome was the County Police Act 1839, known as the 'Permissive Act'.

the state of the police in the Metropolis 'including the City of London'. This Committee, which again included Peel among its members, took as its starting-point the 1834 Report, the recommendations of which had been virtually ignored or frustrated by Roe's collusion with the Home Office; but there was now a new determination to translate pious intentions into decisive action. The Committee had before it the example of all that Rowan and Mayne had achieved despite official obstruction and provocation, and so thorough was its examination that it felt obliged to publish its preliminary findings at the end of the year and to re-convene to complete its task the following March. The final Report contained thirteen recommendations of which the following are the most important:[1]

1. The stipendiary magistrates should be required 'to execute such duties only as are of a judicial character'.

2. The public offices should become police courts of summary jurisdiction and police constables should attend upon magistrates for the serving of warrants and summonses.

3. The Marine Police should be incorporated as a new division of the Metropolitan Police.

4. The Bow Street Runners, the Bow Street Officers and the peace officers attached to the other public offices should be disbanded or, where suitable, absorbed into the Metropolitan Police.

5. The City of London should be incorporated into the Metropolitan Police District and operational control of its policing should be vested in the Metropolitan Commissioners.

All these recommendations were included in the draft of the new Metropolitan Police Bill when it was introduced early in 1839; and at once the City was up in arms. On 12 March 'the Lord Mayor, Aldermen and Commons of the City of London in Common Council assembled' decided to present a petition to the Queen which claimed that there already existed in the City 'a Police fully adequate to its wants and equal, if not superior, to the Metropolitan

---

[1] The XIIIth Recommendation contains one odd item where, in regard to various public nuisances, it refers to 'the cruel and disgraceful treatment of dogs employed in drawing carts or trucks in the street'. In a society which tolerated the scandal of child labour without many twinges of conscience, this seems a curious sense of priorities.

Police'. This manifest absurdity deceived no one, and Russell replied to it with an ultimatum: either the City Corporation would take immediate steps to introduce a police institution on the exact lines of the Metropolitan Police, or the City, notwithstanding its 'immemorial rights and privileges', would be incorporated into the Metropolitan Police District. The Corporation bowed to the inevitable and hurriedly introduced a Private Bill for the regulation of their own police—and the preservation of their rights and privileges. It became law on 17 August.[1]

On the same day the Second Metropolitan Police Bill, 'an Act for further improving the Police in and near the Metropolis', with the ten clauses dealing with the City of London duly deleted, was passed. It incorporated all the recommendations made by the 1837–8 Committee and included a number of additional 'improvements'. For example: the area of the Metropolitan Police District was enlarged to a radius of approximately fifteen miles from Charing Cross, and the establishment was increased to 4,328; the salary of each of the Joint Commissioners was raised to £1,200; and a Superannuation Fund was set up. This was funded out of contributions of not more than $2\frac{1}{2}$ per cent from pay, together with certain 'fines, fees and legacies'. The pension rate was initially fixed at a figure of not more than two-thirds of pay for twenty or more years of service, with a graduated scale for service above fifteen years.[2]

*

It had taken ten years for all the measures envisaged in Peel's pioneering Act to be incorporated in a single, comprehensive Bill. Except for the survival of an independent City Police, all the old anomalies had been swept away and Rowan and Mayne could at last turn to consolidating their hard-won gains; and the Metropolitan Police, which they had created and then defended against all comers, seemed now, in its solid respectability, to be a natural symbol of the new Victorian Age.

[1] The City of London Police Act 1839 created a force of 543 all ranks, divided into six (later four) divisions, with Headquarters at Old Jewry. The first Commissioner was Daniel Harvey.

[2] By 1849 the Fund was insolvent and another forty years were to pass before police pensions were established on a proper footing.

CHAPTER FIVE

'One of the most valuable modern institutions'

THE OPINION of the 1834 Committee was by no means universally shared, despite the obvious success of the New Police in maintaining the King's Peace in a Metropolis which had long since forgotten the meaning of the words and despite Rowan's determination to set a standard of conduct which would be beyond public criticism. His chief problem was the quality of the available human material and this was to remain so for many years; for the demon alcohol, among other frailties, was not to be exorcised simply by the assumption of a uniform or by the issue of strongly-worded police orders; but the true value of the London institution was reflected in the slow extension of the Metropolitan model to the rest of the country. It is yet another example of the many paradoxes of police history.

The Chartist agitation is a case in point. It was purely working-class in origin and, until the final confrontation in 1848, to which we will return, virtually confined to the provinces. There were many reasons for this, but not the least important was the existence of an organized police force in the Metropolis. Thus the provincial cities, still in the process of creating their own police institutions under the Municipal Corporations Act, were vulnerable to mob violence and fertile ground for political agitators; and this, by an odd chance, was to involve the Metropolitan Police in one of its few public defeats.

In the summer of 1839, the Chartists summoned a National Convention in Birmingham. Faced by the likelihood of public disorder and with no local police force yet organized, the city magistrates requested assistance from London, and Supt May of A Division was dispatched with ninety men to deal with any emergency. Predictably this precautionary measure was treated as an act of provocation by the Chartist leaders (the provision of so inadequate a force was in any event a debatable decision) and a confrontation duly took place in the aptly-named Bull Ring. May ordered the crowd to disperse, and when they refused to do so (no magistrate was present to read the Riot Act) the police made a baton-charge. Melville Lee takes up the story:[1]

> In the mêlée which followed, the police were worsted, and the situation was barely saved by the opportune appearance of the military. On the ensuing Monday evening, a second conflict took place, in which the policemen were victorious, though at the expense of an increase of bitterness on both sides. A spurious semblance of peace having been thus restored, fifty constables returned to London, and only forty were left to deal with any recrudescence of disorder.

> Trouble started again three days later and May's remaining handful of men were driven to take shelter, while the mob ransacked the centre of the city. Once more the military intervened, but it was not until a large body of special constables was hastily organized that the situation was brought under control. May and his men returned to London with little to show for their efforts except a bruised reputation. The lessons were obvious. The Metropolitan Police still had much to learn in the matter of handling unruly crowds. For Supt May, it had been shown that discretion is more often than not the better part of valour. And the Commissioners discovered that they would be well-advised in future not to trespass on foreign ground.

*

With the extension of their own territory, Rowan and Mayne were in any event preoccupied with local problems. Even with the recent increase in the size of the Metropolitan force, it was impossible to apply the old system of carefully measured beats, and accordingly the main strength was concentrated in the ten 'town' divisions of the inner area, leaving the country districts to be covered by widely-dispersed foot and horse patrols.

The requirements of the 1839 Act put an increasing strain on the slim resources of the Commissioners' Office. Rowan and Mayne were now responsible for a district six times greater than it had

---

[1] W. Melville Lee, *A History of Police in England.*

been ten years earlier and their staff consisted of the indefatigable
Charles Yardley and just four clerks.[1] Thus, early in 1840, probably on Rowan's recommendation, Captain William Hay was
appointed Inspecting Superintendent of the Metropolitan Police at
a salary of £600. His duties were not precisely specified but he
seems to have taken over many of Rowan's routine responsibilities,
though not that for operational policy. In practice he carried out
the functions of the subsequent office of Assistant Commissioner.
His appointment marked the second departure from Peel's cardinal
principles of not employing ex-officers and of 'filling up from
below', but Rowan clearly felt that none of his superintendents,
however experienced as policemen, were suitable candidates for the
new post. Once having been set aside, the original principles were
forgotten and the practice of recruiting from outside the force to
fill new or senior posts became an established procedure, and
a source of much ill-feeling; indeed, before his death fifteen
years later, Hay himself was to be the cause of considerable
friction.

In 1841 Melbourne resigned and the Tories—now re-styled
'Conservatives'—were returned to power under Peel. For Rowan
and Mayne it must have been a consoling change of pilots; and the
new Home Secretary, Sir James Graham, was an uncomplicated
personality and an able administrator. His period of office was to be
marked by perhaps the greatest and, in some ways, the most contentious innovation in the development of the Metropolitan Police.
And like so many such innovations, this one came about through a
curious chain of events.

On 6 April 1842, the body of a murdered girl was found at
Roehampton. The evidence pointed conclusively to a known
criminal named Daniel Good, a fact which the police—although
certainly not the press, who provided a running commentary on
his movements—seemed slow to grasp and slower still to follow up.
The fault lay less with individual policemen than with the cumbrous
system of communications within the force; eventually, ten days
later, Good was arrested in Tonbridge. He was duly tried, convicted, and publicly hanged in front of a large and appreciative
audience.

There followed an inevitable outcry in the press, led by *The Times*

---

[1] There were a further four clerks in the Receiver's Office. In 1840 the
total cost of the Metropolitan Police was £293,948 12s 2d.

in its most pontificating vein, and summed up by the *Weekly Dispatch* with the hypocritical announcement that the police conduct of the case had been 'marked with a looseness and want of decision which proves that unless a decided change is made in the present system, it is idle to expect that it can be an efficient detective force'. As to what kind of change, the paper was careful not to speculate.

The debate about the Good murder case was still at its height when the police were involved in another *cause célèbre*, the pursuit and arrest of a much-convicted criminal, Thomas Cooper, who, before he was eventually captured, shot and killed a police constable and a public-spirited passer-by. This time the press aimed its broadside at a system which could risk the lives of unarmed officers in the single-handed arrest of armed desperadoes. What price now the *Weekly Dispatch*'s talk of 'want of decision'? Rowan and Mayne decided to draw a few dragon's teeth.

*

The General Instruction Book had laid down the principal object of police as the prevention of crime; but it had added (almost as an afterthought) the natural corollary of detection of culprits, where crimes had already been committed, on the logical basis that certainty of detection was in itself a powerful deterrent, and therefore a secondary form of prevention.

The establishment of the New Police had made no allowance for a 'detective' element and Peel's Act would certainly have aroused uncompromising opposition if it had spelled out any such concession to the idea of 'police espionage'. The Popay affair had illustrated the extent—however absurd or unfounded—of public suspicions. Thus, with the passing of the 1839 Act and the disbanding of the Bow Street Runners, the one traditionally accepted form of 'thief-taking' disappeared from the London scene. That the Runners had for many years been little more than a private, and highly distasteful, agency was of less concern to the citizens of the Metropolis than the idea of a proper and publicly accountable alternative.

Now, after the growing press campaign which accompanied the Good and Cooper murders, and fortified by the prospect of a new attitude at the Home Office, Rowan and Mayne presented Graham on 14 June 1842 with a memorandum 'relative to the Detective Powers of the Police'. Since they were both now battle-scarred veterans of the guerilla warfare waged against them in public and private, they proceeded with more than usual care. The 'Detective', as Charles Dickens liked to describe it, consisted of two inspectors and six sergeants,[1] based on Scotland Yard and answerable directly to the Commissioners. Of the founder members, the most interesting is Nicholas Pearce, the senior detective inspector, for he was one of the few survivors of the old Bow Street Foot Patrol and well-versed in the ways of criminals. His junior colleague was John Haynes; and the first six sergeants, drawn from different divisions, were: Thornton, Gerrett, Shaw, Braddick, Goff and Whicher. To these were added shortly afterwards Shackell and Field, who was to become the celebrated Inspector Bucket of *Bleak House* (Whicher was the model for Wilkie Collins's Sergeant Cuff).

Dickens, who had no illusions about the Bow Street Runners and their shady methods, embraced the new Detective Force with enthusiasm and, on a famous occasion in 1850, invited all its members to tea at the editorial offices of *Household Words*, whence we have a delightful picture of the solid citizens who composed this new elite. Indeed, it may well be said that the acceptance of a properly constituted detective branch owes much to the favourable publicity which it received from this odd but influential quarter.[2] Dickens could not have foreseen how events would presently confound his great expectations.

Authority for the establishment of the Detective Force was given by Graham on 20 June, although with a lack of enthusiasm which was understandable. The practice of employing a few selected constables in plain clothes for special duties was not new, but the public, always ready to beat the police with any available stick, saw in it the thin end of a dangerous wedge. Rowan, with his now unfailing instinct for public reaction, kept a low profile and the press was left to draw its own deductions. Police Orders, however, were explicit, to the point of absurdity. The Detective Force was so

---

[1] Melville Lee and others give the figure of three inspectors and nine sergeants, but this is inaccurate; the names of the original team are recorded in Mayne's letter of 23 August to the Home Office.

[2] The year 1841 marked the first appearance of *Punch*, which in its early days treated the police not as a legitimate comic target but as a subject for ridicule and contempt.

circumscribed in its activities—not least in its association with the criminal class, without which the detective function of policing is impossible—that it is surprising that Pearce and his dedicated team were able to operate effectively. The old Bow Street Runners had left a legacy which long survived their overdue disbandment; but Pearce and—after his promotion to Superintendent of F Division—Shackell devised their own methods. There were no spectacular successes in the grand manner of the late nineteenth century, and as yet no scientific aids to detection; but, for all its limitations, the Force gradually acquired a professional expertise and it was not long before its services were in demand outside London.

Inevitably, the creation of the Detective Force aroused much jealousy among the uniformed branch of the police service, partly because of marginally higher rates of pay but also because they tended—quite wrongly—to be thought of as 'Commissioners' men'; and it may have been with this in mind that in 1846 Rowan instituted a system by which two constables in each division were to be trained in detective work and temporarily seconded to plain-clothes duty. Public suspicion and professional jealousy combined to prevent any expansion. 'The strength of the prejudice against the detective force,' wrote Moylan,' can be gauged from the fact that not until 1864 was there any increase in the establishment, and in 1868, when Sir Richard Mayne died, it was just a small section of the Commissioner's Office, fifteen strong in a force of nearly 8,000.' Under Mayne's successor, Henderson, there was a steady increase in strength until the notorious Turf Frauds scandal in 1877; but that, as we shall see, is a very different story.

*

By comparison with what had gone before, the 1840s were quiet years for the Metropolitan Police, although the end of the decade also marked the end of Rowan and Mayne's long and distinguished partnership. During this period, the force continued to expand to keep pace with the growth of the Metropolis, although the original idea of identical 'companies' of 164 men had long since been abandoned. Rowan had explained to the 1834 Committee that the distribution of his resources had been decided 'according to the measurement of the ground and afterwards as experience pointed out'. The population explosion of the mid-nineteenth century and the rise of the property speculator created a very different kind of Metropolis, a growing traffic problem, and a constant strain on police man-power.

It is impossible to be certain, from contemporary Home Office papers, of the basis on which, from time to time, the police establishment for the Metropolis was fixed. The two determining factors —and they have not changed to this day—were Treasury parsimony and the quality of applicants for the service. Wastage from resignations and dismissals was still considerable (the pay structure below the rank of superintendent was still the same as it had been in 1829), but a memorandum from the Commissioners to the Home Office in August 1845 suggests that the rough norm was one policeman to 450 head of population; and a study of annual returns over the next hundred years shows that actual strength varied by about 10 per cent on either side of this figure. There were inevitable exceptions to the norm: the Great Exhibition of 1851; the Hyde Park riots of 1866; the Fenian troubles, which threw a long shadow forward to our own time; even the panic occasioned by the Whitechapel murders of 1888.

There were other calls on the Commissioners' resources. In 1841, it was decided that responsibility for policing dockyards should be assumed by the Metropolitan Police, starting with the London Docks (Rowan's reaction is contained in a letter which perfectly illustrates his placid temperament—raised eyebrows and a soldier's obedience to orders). Woolwich and Deptford yards followed in 1842, Woolwich Arsenal in 1843 and the Royal Dockyards of Chatham, Portsmouth, Devonport and Pembroke much later in 1860. It was a compliment to the reputation of the Metropolitan Police with which the Commissioners could have happily dispensed.

Despite the rising tide of Chartist agitation, there was little disorder in London during this period, and Rowan, mindful of the lesson of Birmingham, avoided any further provincial involvement, much to the relief, no doubt, of his faithful Supt May of A Division. But if the Chartists were to win their war, then the final battleground had, by logic and tradition, to be London. 1848—'the year of revolution'—was the occasion; and Kennington Common the assembly place.

The Chartist leaders, with Victorian courtesy, gave due notice of their intentions. They proposed to organize a giant demonstration at Kennington on 10 April and to march thence upon Parliament to present a petition of working-class rights.

The Government, under its new Liberal leader, Lord John Russell, and its Home Secretary, Sir George Grey, who fifteen years earlier had cut Lord Melbourne down to size after the Coldbath Fields affair, acted swiftly. 150,000 special constables were enrolled, the regular police were detailed to cover all bridges over the river, and a military reserve was assembled on the north bank. With gross constitutional impropriety, the aging Commander-in-Chief, Wellington, was put in charge of the operation; and Charles Rowan who, left to his own devices, would certainly have handled the situation otherwise, must have enjoyed his brief reunion with the old Duke.

The militant leaders, without even sending out reconnaissance patrols, accepted defeat; and in an atmosphere of splendid anticlimax, delivered their monster petition to the House of Commons in three hansom cabs. It was an act of surrender which would have greatly amused the shade of John Wilkes.

*

In March 1848, Charles Rowan was knighted. The fact that his KCB was matched by the simultaneous award of the lower-ranking CB to Mayne was the source of much adverse comment in *The Daily Telegraph*, as ill-informed as it was petty. But Rowan's own CB dated from the year of Waterloo; he was fourteen years older than his colleague, and had been in the service of the Crown since 1797. While the 1829 Act had made no distinction between the two Joint Commissioners, there is no doubt that Rowan was invariably considered as *primus inter pares*. There is no evidence of any jealousy on Mayne's part, and indeed he did not have long to wait, for his own KCB followed the successful conclusion of the Great Exhibition in 1851.

For some time Rowan had been in poor health, and on 5 January 1850 he retired. Two years later he died of cancer in the house of a friend in Park Lane. In its obituary notice of 24 May 1852, *The Times* wrote: 'No individual of any rank or station could be more highly esteemed or loved when living, or more regretted in death.' It was no more than the truth. He had seen the New Police, of which he was the prime moving spirit, grow from a raw body of 1,000 men to a tried and tested force of 5,625. He had survived

years of obstruction and abuse with tact and patience and with that
'perfect command of temper' which he had enjoined upon every
constable under his command. His enemies had been men of a
calibre which only served to enhance his own outstanding qualities.
The Metropolitan Police are his memorial and it is not greatly to
their credit that he is so little honoured by them today.

*

Mayne clearly assumed that, with Rowan's retirement, he would
be left in sole command, but the Home Office decided to maintain
the *status quo* by promoting Capt Hay, albeit designated as Second
Commissioner.[1] It was to prove an unfortunate arrangement, for
Mayne—without the restraining influence of Rowan—could be
stubborn and abrasive, and Hay tactless to the point of disloyalty.
The relationship was soon under fire.

The Great Exhibition of 1851, with its special problems of crowd
control, resulted in the formation of a new temporary Division X,
(later to be made permanent) consisting of 17 inspectors and 1,101
other ranks, under the experienced Supt Pearce. Mayne assumed
responsibility for the arrangements, to the ill-concealed annoyance
of Hay who might reasonably have been given this opportunity of
cutting his teeth in public. There followed an acrimonious exchange
of letters, which was of itself a new departure, for Mayne's instinctive understanding of Rowan's mind had made correspondence
between the two of them unnecessary.

A year later there was further trouble. On the occasion of the
lying-in-state of the Duke of Wellington at the Royal Hospital,
Chelsea, the crowd got out of hand and several people were crushed
to death. Hay thereupon took the extraordinary step of writing to
the *Globe* dissociating himself from any responsibility for the police
arrangements at Chelsea, which drew a justifiably angry letter from
Mayne, and an apology from Hay.

But matters did not end there, and the summer of 1853 found
Hay writing private letters to the Home Office, without reference
to Mayne, in which he criticized various aspects of police organization and made a number of proposals which could only be con-
strued as a deliberate attempt to undermine the authority of his
effective superior. This impossible situation—of which the press,

[1] Hay was succeeded as Inspecting Superintendent by Capt (later Col)
D. W. Labalmondière.

with its persistent criticism of police affairs, seems to have been
unaware—was fortuitously resolved by the death of Hay in August
1855. The Home Office conceded defeat, and in February 1856 a
short Police Act was passed appointing a single Commissioner
(Mayne) and two Assistant Commissioners, Labalmondière and
Capt William Harris of the Hampshire Police, both with the
executive powers of justices. So, to paraphrase Douglas Browne,
the 'King' enjoyed his own at last. He was to reign for thirteen more
years, a law unto himself and impervious to the strident demands
of the press for his resignation. His refusal to do so was as much a
disservice to his own outstanding record as it was to the police
themselves.

*

But in spite of private bickering at the top, the police continued
upon their public occasions in a busy and fast-growing Metropolis.
The unsung heroes of this transitional period are undoubtedly the
divisional superintendents about whom police history is largely
silent, but who, ill-rewarded and grossly overworked, continued to
run their 'manors' in strict accordance with Rowan's simple but
unassailable rules of conduct. By the 1850s every superintendent
had progressed to his office through the hard school of practical
police experience and only on one occasion—to which we shall
return—does there seem to have been any ground for public criticism. Of praise or commendation in Police Orders of the period
there is no trace; Mayne's congratulations to Supt Pearce for his
handling of the crowds at the Great Exhibition were equally
intended as a snub to Hay.

But perhaps the best illustration of the growing popularity of the
police is to be found in another uniquely English institution. For
years, *Punch* had conducted a rude campaign against the force
which differed only from that of the *Weekly Dispatch* by its comparative literacy. Now, in the 1850s, came a change of heart.
'Directions for finding a policeman' is a fair sample:

> 'Look down every area in the street; if you do not by accident
> see one, ring the bell and inquire if the policeman is in the
> kitchen. Repeat this at every door, and you cannot fail even-
> tually to find one.'

Thus there began to emerge a composite picture of the Victorian policeman which was to become, by its affectionate absurdity, a powerful element in maintaining the Queen's Peace. The English are never more law-abiding than when they accept the comic aspect of authority; and they are never more dangerous than when they are alienated by humourless officialdom. *Punch* led the way with its irreverent cartoons of kitchen-consorting constables, never too remote from a surreptitious pot of ale, large of frame, flat of foot, patiently re-directing lost souls, and indulging in a vocabulary of which Dogberry would have been proud.[1] It was a fair travesty—but it did the police no harm. It is impossible to think of any other country in which the satirical pursuit of the law would have actually promoted the standing of its officers.

At the same time, there were other problems which had nothing to do with constables and kitchen-maids. Of these the most important was one which still absorbs the greatest time and man-power of the Metropolitan Police: traffic.

In the early 1850s, private carriages—status symbol of the privileged classes—were a negligible element on the thoroughfares of a Metropolis with a population now of the order of 3,000,000, and many years were to pass before the volume of traffic at street-level compelled the authorities to turn to a second, underground network of communication. But public transport was another matter and had been an increasing problem for two centuries since Evelyn had opened his traffic office in Great Scotland Yard. The licensing of 'hackney coaches' had been introduced less for reasons of administrative control than as a source of revenue and during the eighteenth century the responsibility rested with a board known as the Hackney Coach Office which was designated as an 'Office of Police', but only in its original sense of a department of local government. Traffic control, where it existed at all, was regulated by a small army of 'street keepers' whose chief function seems to have been to keep crossing-places clear of beggars and other public nuisances.

With the passing of the 1829 Act,[2] responsibility for traffic control passed to the New Police for no better reason than that

---

[1] Mayne's Police Orders are full of sharp reminders about 'correct' phraseology. To 'run a man in' was considered especially unconstabulary. The authorized version was to 'take into custody'.

[2] In July 1829 the first London omnibus, the 'Shillibeer', made its appearance.

since they alone were responsible for public tranquillity, they were the logical means of creating order out of chaos. It was not until the 1839 Act that the Commissioners were formally required 'from time to time, and as occasion shall require, to make regulations for the route to be observed by all carts, carriages, horses and persons, and for preventing obstruction of the streets and thoroughfares'; despite which worthy intention, the police have ever since been fighting a losing battle.

The Hackney Carriage Act of 1831 transferred the licensing of all public transport to the Commissioners of Stamps, and a further Act seven years later extended the licensing principle to drivers and conductors under a new office, the Registrar of Public Carriages. Rowan's evidence to the Select Committee that year shows that he, at least, could see which way the wind was blowing; and he was right. In 1843, the Commissioners were required to fix the location of cab ranks; and in 1853, a Public Carriage Branch was formed at Scotland Yard, under an incompetent nonentity named Paschal, to assume the duties of the Registrar of Public Carriages. To the very end of his time, Mayne bitterly resisted every attempt to saddle the police with what he considered to be a purely administrative function of the Home Office, related neither to the prevention of crime nor to the maintenance of law and order; but to no avail. In 1869, the year after his death, a comprehensive Public Carriage Act transferred all licensing functions in respect of public carriages to the Commissioner under powers predictably delegated to him by the Home Secretary. The wheels had indeed come full circle.[1]

By the mid-1850s, a curious fact of life in the Metropolis may have occurred to some of the more elderly citizens: for years there had been little or no mob violence, not even during the days of Chartist agitation. Could it be that police respectability had begun to rub off on Londoners at large?

During the summer of 1855 there came a sharp, if synthetic, reminder that the old Adam was not to be denied. In June Lord Robert Grosvenor introduced his 'Sunday Trading Bill', a piece of

[1] All traffic in the Metropolitan Police District is now regulated by the department of Assistant Commissioner 'B', with a wealth of additional responsibilities which Mayne would have found incomprehensible.

officious and puritanical legislation which would not have disgraced the Lord Protector. Public reaction was at first one of amused contempt and on 24 June there was a small gathering of traders in Hyde Park who jeered the gentry in their fine carriages and then dispersed without incident. But other, less moderate, minds were at work and placards and handbills at once appeared summoning a mass meeting on the following Sunday, 1 July, of the 'Leave-us-alone Club'. 'Come in your best clothes,' said the invitation. 'His Lordship is very particular.'

It was scarcely the language of incitement to riot, and the occasion would probably have passed off without incident, if the Home Secretary, Palmerston, had not instructed Mayne to prohibit the meeting. The press at once accused Mayne of taking the law into his own hands, but the subsequent inquiry established beyond argument that the decision was that of the Home Secretary.

The opposing forces on 1 July tell their own story: 40,000 potential trouble-makers faced by 450 police under Supt Hughes.[1] It was the largest demonstration yet seen in the Metropolis and for that Palmerston was entirely responsible. His decision to ban the meeting established a precedent which was to have repercussions far into the future.

The day started quietly; but as spirits and tempers rose (and boredom, one of the chief ingredients of aggressive behaviour, increased), there were clashes with the police and Supt Hughes ordered a baton-charge in which a few members of the public were knocked down and the police suffered some fifty casualties. A small section of the crowd meanwhile marched upon Lord Grosvenor's house in Park Street where, apart from some choice use of language, they caused no harm and were dispersed with an unnecessary show of force by Supt O'Brien and his reserve body of constables. Seventy-two persons—some of them innocent passers-by—were arrested and crowded into the altogether inadequate cells at Vine Street police station. It had not been one of the Metropolitan Police's more distinguished performances.

None the less, the Government chose to wield a sledge-hammer to crack this particular nut by appointing a Royal Commission to

[1] There was one weapon which Mayne could well have employed to his advantage; but the use of mounted police for crowd control does not seem to have been contemplated until the 1880s.

investigate the conduct of the police. The resulting Report and Evidence filled a massive volume of 546 pages and if even a handful of the 'prosecution' witnesses called had been telling the truth, Hyde Park on that Sunday would have resembled a corpse-stewn battlefield. The entire exercise is a classic commentary on the English preoccupation with the old adage about mountains and mice. In the event, the Commission decided that the majority of the police had shown 'moderation and forbearance', but that 'the superintendent in Hyde Park had lost his head, that certain officers had been guilty of unnecessary violence and that there had been some mismanagement at Vine Street'. Hughes and O'Brien were reprimanded and six constables were dismissed. The Commission seems not to have considered the strong probability that a demonstration by 40,000 people would inevitably have had unfortunate consequences. Mayne's own evidence made no attempt to conceal his lack of interest in the proceedings; and the old Adam went into temporary retirement again.

In 1839 the so-called 'Permissive Act' had allowed counties to form their own police forces. It had not been a success, for three main reasons: first, since no county councils yet existed, the local police authority had been defined as a committee of justices in Quarter Sessions, and to the average county magistrate a policeman meant a parish constable; second, 'optional' Acts of Parliament invite soft options; and third, since the cost of a Metropolitan-style police force was then chargeable entirely on the rates, the idea did not readily commend itself to the ratepayers.

In 1856, when Sir George Grey returned to the Home Office, there existed a notional police force in 24 counties, and an elementary organization in 7 others. In 20 counties there had been no alteration to the traditional partnership of justices and parish constables. Grey, acting on the proposals of Edwin Chadwick, a barrister and friend of Charles Rowan (at the time of the Municipal Corporations Act in 1835 they had together recommended the establishment of a national police force under the Metropolitan Commissioners), introduced the County and Borough Police Act, which made the institution of provincial forces compulsory instead of permissive. This Act contained two important innovations. First, it provided that one quarter of the cost of pay and clothing would be met by central government. Secondly, it appointed Inspectors of Constabulary to report on the standard and efficiency of each provincial force.[1]

This latter provision is of special importance. To this day the Home Secretary has no direct powers over provincial police forces, where the local authority is the Watch Committee in the case of boroughs, and the Standing Joint Committee in the counties. He is responsible for approving the appointment of chief constables and through the Inspectors of Constabulary he can exercise a potentially dangerous form of control through the financial sanction of withholding the Exchequer grant in the event of an adverse annual report.

This system of vicarious control does not apply to the Metropolitan Police District where the Home Secretary is the statutory police authority. But there is no system of independent inspection in the Metropolis. The Commissioner is responsible to Parliament, through the Home Secretary, for the conduct of his office and the efficiency of his force. It is a curiously English arrangement, partly historical in origin, but equally designed to prevent too great a concentration of power in any one pair of hands; but in effect it has conferred immense powers on an anonymous body of permanent Home Office officials answerable only to their Minister. 'Their efforts,' wrote Reith, 'to assert their authority and those of Scotland Yard to resist it reveal a relationship suggestive of a permanent cold war between them.'[2] This may be an exaggerated judgement, but as we shall see, the evidence suggests that it has often been uncomfortably true.

The thirteen years of Mayne's autocratic rule as sole Commissioner are of particular interest since they illustrate in a wide variety of ways, some important and others trivial, the precarious tightrope of public opinion which the police were obliged to walk. Mayne was a strong, some might say headstrong, character and an able lawyer and administrator; but he was not a policeman. Without Rowan's special knowledge of man-management, he was unable to

---

[1] In 1857, 120 provincial forces were reported as being inefficient; in 1875, the number had fallen to 38; and in 1890, all were given a clean bill of health. In 1857 there were 239 police forces in England, including the Metropolitan and City Police. In 1979, the figure is 39 (43 including Wales).

[2] Reith, *op. cit.*

establish that 'kind and conciliating' relationship with his men
which had sustained the New Police through its early tribulations.
Nor, despite the presence of two assistant commissioners, was he
prepared to delegate his authority. Thus there developed a great
gulf between the Commissioner and the men who, as never before,
needed his help in keeping their public equilibrium.

Mayne's increasing remoteness from the real world is illustrated
by the fatuous Police Orders of this period. In 1859, a solemn
instruction was issued forbidding constables to carry umbrellas
when on duty—a pre-Gilbertian charade which invited (and
received) the full weight of *Punch*'s most lethal artillery. Two years
later, the Commissioner was warning his troops against the insidious practice of children who bowled hoops 'in places of public
resort'. And on 11 February 1865, the full majesty of the law was
invoked to prevent the throwing of snowballs in public parks.
Superintendents, more urgently concerned with the new and prevalent crime of garotting, were now instructed to detail constables to
patrol *in pairs* to stop this dangerous excess of juvenile high spirits.
'How much longer,' asked *Judy*, 'is suffering London to put up
with the imbecility of Sir Richard Mayne?'

There is another aspect of Mayne's autocracy which has received
little attention.

The structure of the Metropolitan Police had been based from
the outset on the rigid class divisions of the day. The small hierarchy at the top consisted of 'gentlemen'—a word much used not
only by Peel, but by his Commissioners and the members of subsequent Police Committees. Below this top stratum, there evolved a
police force with the ingrained attitudes of the working class from
which it came and, despite Rowan's constant concern that his men
should conduct themselves without fear or favour ('civil and
attentive to all persons, *of every rank and class*'), increasingly
deferential to authority. Mayne's style of management demanded
deference, and the language of Police Orders during his period of
'monarchy' is that of a Victorian schoolmaster to his dim-witted
pupils. While Rowan's paternalism had held the force together
in the early days, Mayne's remoteness invited a reaction which was
not long in coming.

The working-class attitude to the police was that they were the
paid servants of the privileged, and that their only function was to
be respectful to the squire and his relations and to keep the lower

orders firmly in their proper stations. In this there was more than an element of truth, since most crime had its origins among the latter, even if prostitutes could demand the best prices from the former. *Punch* never tired of poking fun at the deferential police-man, 'always ready to hold a gentleman's horse for 6d'; and despite a century of social change, the image has survived. The modern constable ridicules the idea, but he deceives no one but himself. The Metropolitan Police is still a very Victorian institution.

*

The force continued to grow. In 1862, X Division, the tempor-ary adjunct to the Great Exhibition, was put on a permanent foot-ing and two new Divisions, W and Y, were formed. By 1864, the strength had increased to 7,113; and in that same year the swallow-tail coat and tall beaver hat were replaced by a tunic and the dis-tinctive 'bobby's' helmet. One reason for the change was the fact that the original uniform, which had always been uncomfortable, was now a sartorial anachronism (only a few years earlier the Chelsea Pensioners were still wearing the same uniform that Marl-borough had designed for them in 1703); but the real reason was one of breath-taking ambivalence.

By the mid-1860s, the press campaign against Sir Richard Mayne had become a fully orchestrated assault; even *Punch* found the aging Commissioner arrogant and unfunny. Mayne certainly had his problems, not all of his own making. Pay and conditions of service and the virtual breakdown of the superannuation scheme combined to create serious difficulties in recruiting men of an acceptable calibre. There is no doubt that morale in the force was at a very low ebb and relations with the public—that yardstick by which Charles Rowan had measured the success or failure of the New Police—were strained. In the year 1863 alone, 3 sergeants and no fewer than 212 constables were dismissed for drunkenness on duty. The press chose this moment to compare the Metropolitan Police unfavourably with the Army (probably the only occasion in the entire nineteenth century when the soldiery were paraded as paragons of even modest virtue) and suggested that a little military discipline would be a salutary prescription for the constabulary. Mayne had long since withdrawn from any public debate with the press and thus there is no record of his reaction to this extra-ordinary departure from what had been, throughout his long years of service, the cardinal source of antagonism to the police idea; but it is not difficult to imagine his feelings of anger and disgust. He made no attempt to resist the 'militarization' of his civilian army. Drill parades under Guards sergeants were organized and the new tunic and helmet were crude imitations of the uniform of Regiments of the Line. Only the boots remained uniquely constabulary; and for *Punch*, a whole new world of irreverence opened up.

*

The long reign was nearly over;[1] but it was to end not with a whimper but a bang, and with a sad last curtain for a great public servant.

The campaign for Parliamentary reform in the 1830s had made a small but important breach in the traditional defences of parliamentary privilege, although the slogan of 'no taxation without representation' had yet to be revived.[2] Income tax, first introduced by Pitt in 1799 to finance the war, meant little to a working population still far removed from the mysteries of 'fiscal drag', while property tax meant nothing to a class most of whose worldly wealth was pledged to pawnbrokers. The pressure for further reform was overshadowed by the Chartist troubles.

In 1859, Disraeli had revived the issue without success; a second attempt by Lord John Russell in 1866 resulted only in the fall of the Liberal administration; and in June of that year the radical Reform League decided to take to the streets.

The League, which unlike the old NPU was a responsible organization, announced a public demonstration in Hyde Park. There is little doubt that its intentions were peaceful, but the citizens of the Metropolis had lost none of their taste for trouble-making and here was an opportunity which, unlike Lord Grosvenor's wet little Bill eleven years earlier, gave every promise of a ripe political confrontation.

Spencer Walpole, the new Home Secretary, decided to ban the demonstration. There is no evidence whether, in taking this action, he consulted Mayne, but the Commissioner, weary alike of press,

---

[1] In 1864, Charles Yardley, the original Chief Clerk appointed in 1829, died. With him went Mayne's last link with what must now have seemed to him to be the good old days.

[2] The phrase is attributed to Lord Camden in a speech in the House of Lords in 1765, referring to the American Colonies.

public and politicians, did as he was bidden. His statutory duty was the protection of persons and property and the preservation of law and order. As in the circumstances of another, more celebrated order, his was not to reason why.

Mayne accordingly assembled a force of 3,200 police, and perhaps remembering the action of his old colleague Rowan at Coldbath Fields thirty-three years before, took personal command of the operation. The peaceful procession of Reform Leaguers arrived at Hyde Park Corner. Confronted there by a strong police cordon, it turned and made its way to Trafalgar Square where it contented itself with the resounding oratory of John Bright.

But the London mob had not attached itself to the demonstration to listen to speeches. It had come in search of trouble and when this did not occur, it took the law into its own hands and created it. Park railings were torn down and a pitched battle between rioters and police took place in which Mayne himself was wounded and many policemen were seriously injured. Order was not restored until the Guards were summoned. It was the first time in its history that the Metropolitan Police had needed the intervention of the military to preserve the Queen's Peace.

For Mayne it was a personal humiliation. Predictably he was accused of ruthless abuse of his authority, of 'disgraceful provocation by inviting the support of soldiers', and of nameless crimes against humanity. There is something infinitely sad about the spectacle of the old man sitting on his horse with blood running down his face and with twenty-eight of his men so injured that they were disabled for life, while Walpole received a deputation from the Reform League to whom he expressed his personal regrets for the events of 'Bloody Sunday'. Mayne at once offered his resignation. The one criticism that can be made is that he did not press his request when it was refused; for there was one more humiliation awaiting him.

*

The English have always had an 'Irish problem', and it was now to show its face in the Metropolis.

In 1867 a group of Irish-American militants formed the Fenian organization to promote by violence the cause of Irish Home Rule. After an abortive coup in Chester, the leaders moved to London where two of them, Burke and Casey, were arrested by Detective Inspector Thompson and committed to Clerkenwell prison.

Early in December an anonymous letter was passed to Mayne giving details of a plot to 'spring' the two men, and further evidence reached Scotland Yard from other quarters. Beyond alerting the Prison Governor and marginally strengthening the normal police patrol in the vicinity, Mayne issued no special instructions either to the divisional superintendent or to the Detective Force. What followed began as pure farce and ended in tragedy.

On 12 December, at the exact time indicated by intelligence sources, two men rolled a barrel of gunpowder up against the prison wall, lit the blue paper and retired. The fuse, however, was damp and failed to ignite the powder, so the men returned, collected their barrel, and drove away. This performance was conducted in full view of a police constable who did not think fit even to report the incident. Accordingly, the men repeated the exercise the next afternoon. In the explosion which followed four people were killed, forty were injured and extensive damage was caused to the prison wall and to property in the street. Burke and Casey did not escape. The Governor, at least, had taken the precaution of moving them to another part of the prison. Four conspirators were arrested and, as a small footnote to history, one of them—Michael Barrett—was to have the sombre distinction of being the last criminal to be publicly executed in England.

The Clerkenwell affair created a wave of panic. Londoners were no strangers to mob violence, but terrorism was something new. Thousands of special constables were sworn in, sanction was given for a large increase in the Metropolitan Police, even the regulations for muzzling dogs were reinforced. The air was full of rumours and an Irish accent was something not to advertise in public places. In the event there were—at least for the present—no more incidents.

Mayne accepted full responsibility for the tragic consequences of police ineptness and of his own failure to take the warnings of an impending coup seriously. It was no doubt a further symptom of his declining powers and of his stubborn refusal to delegate, for it is at least arguable that he might have put one of his assistant commissioners in charge of a counter-plan. This time he had only himself to blame for another public humiliation and he again submitted his resignation; and again it was refused. 'We told Mayne,' said Under-Secretary Liddell, 'that he had made a damned fool of himself, but that we weren't going to throw him over after his long public service.' It was a loyal sentiment, but a wrong decision.

Mayne never really recovered from the public obloquy that was heaped upon him throughout the succeeding months, and he died on Boxing Day, 1868, a tired and embittered man. He had stayed too long, not because he enjoyed the taste of power, but because the Metropolitan Police was his life and he could not contemplate the possibility of all his years of work being frustrated by another hand. He was not involved with his men as Rowan had been, but with the building and perfecting of a great experiment in social engineering. If Rowan was the natural counterpart of Henry Fielding, Mayne was the natural heir to Patrick Colquhoun; and each, in his way, was a great public servant.

The tributes after his death were muted, and years later Chief Inspector Cavanagh perhaps came closest to the truth when he wrote of him that he was 'respected, but feared by all the service'. On the day of his death the strength of the Metropolitan Police was 8,963 and he had changed it from 'one of the most valuable modern institutions' into an indispensable buttress of Victorian society. He was not going to be an easy man to follow.

CHAPTER SIX

Scotland Yard and the 'Not-at-Home Office'[1]

'WHO,' ASKED the *Daily Telegraph* on 2 February 1869, 'is Colonel Henderson?' It was a fair question.

The death of Peel's 'sensible lawyer' had started inevitable speculation about his successor. Labalmondière had been appointed Acting Commissioner on 27 December and this perfectly reasonable improvisation aroused the dark suspicions of the *Telegraph* and others that the new occupant of the Metropolitan Police Office would be a military man. Typically, the press chose to ignore the fact that it was a soldier who had been largely responsible for the successful development of London's police, and that only a few years previously they had been campaigning for the introduction of some military discipline into the constabulary ranks.

Bruce, the Home Secretary, wisely paid no attention to this chorus of unsolicited advice. To a deputation, led by a professor, demanding 'demilitarization' of the force, he replied that the police were in no sense whatever a military body and hinted that even academics might benefit from a little discipline. His problem was none the less a real one. Mayne, during his last years, had become increasingly autocratic and sensitive to Home Office interference, while his impersonal style of management had created a growing sense of dissatisfaction among the lower ranks. Bruce explained that he was seeking a man 'best acquainted with the habits of criminals, able to detect crime and protect the public peace', who also had the ability to command an 'army' of nearly 10,000 uniformed men. He does not seem to have considered either of the two Assistant Commissioners as suitably qualified; and finally he

[1] During the twenty years following Mayne's death, *Punch*—with jibes such as this—concentrated most of its fire not on the police but on the politicians. There were plenty of targets; and some very palpable hits.

chose Colonel Edmund Henderson, a regular officer of the Royal
Engineers.

Henderson came very close to matching Bruce's requirements.
There was very little 'military' about him for, after six years as a
soldier, he had been seconded to civil duties, first as Comptroller
of the new convict settlement in Western Australia, and since 1863
as Director of Prisons at the Home Office.[1] Thus he was no
stranger to the criminal classes, although he had no experience of
police administration. He was in almost every way the antithesis of
Richard Mayne, and his seventeen years of office were to be marked
by far-reaching changes, the first demonstration of mutiny in the
ranks, a major police scandal and—towards the end—an abrasive
relationship with the Home Office.

Henderson's style of management is best illustrated by his first
Annual Report covering the year 1869 and a complete departure
from Mayne's laconic approach. He had applied himself with
energy and understanding to the complexities of his new office and
at a very early stage he must have realized that quick action was
needed to reverse the growing sense of disillusionment in the
service. In his Report he advanced the disturbing statistic that, out
of a force of 9,000 men, 'during several hours of the day the actual
duty in the streets of the Metropolis devolves upon some 800
Constables', and that while the population of London had increased
by no less than 50 per cent (to 3,563,410) since 1849 and 1,030
miles of new streets had been added 'to the charge of the Police',
the net available strength of the force had risen by only 1,500. He
urgently needed more men; and his men urgently needed more
money. Constables on the lowest rate were still being paid only
£1 1s 0d a week, while the new and responsible rank of chief
superintendent carried a weekly salary of £8 3s 5d. 'I think,'
reported Henderson cautiously, 'that the sergeants and constables
of the Metropolitan Police Force have a reasonable claim to some
increase of pay . . . A constable on promotion to the rank of sergeant only receives an addition of one shilling a week.'

Because of the length of beats in the outer divisions, it was his
policy, he said, to employ all available Mounted Police in the rural
districts, although he added—perhaps the first such observation—
that they were also useful as an aid to crowd control. Of known

[1] The only other Commissioner to be appointed from the Civil Service
was Sir Harold Scott (1945–1953).

offences committed in the Metropolis during the year, drunkenness (nearly 30 per cent), assault and simple larceny made up 53.4 per cent of the total.

Finally he turned to the detection of crime 'which is, after repression, a most important part of the duty of a Police Force. At the best the Police can only make clean the outside of the platter; the improvement of the morals and manners of the people must be left to higher agencies.' He was under no illusions. 'There are many and great difficulties in the way of a Detective system; it is one viewed with the greatest suspicion and jealousy by the majority of Englishmen.' Nevertheless within four months of taking office he had persuaded Bruce to sanction an increase of the Detective Force to 27 men, and the employment of 180 detectives in the different divisions. 'The development of the Detective system,' he concluded, 'will be an interesting and important duty, to which I am justly alive.' Just how interesting—and disturbing—he was presently to find out.

Throughout his first year, Henderson devoted much of his time to improving the policeman's lot in small but sympathetic ways. In the matter of pay the best concession he could wring out of the obstinate Drummond[1] and the officials at the Home Office was an extra 3s and 1s a week for sergeants and constables respectively.

On 30 March, the following appeared in Police Orders:

BEARDS AND MOUSTACHES

The members of the Metropolitan Police Force are permitted henceforth to wear beards and moustaches.

Hitherto the rules had stipulated side-whiskers or clean-shaven, and the cartoonists leapt upon the new order with abandon ('I likes it,' ran one caption, 'because it gives us a HAIR and looks MILINGTARY.'). A month later, officers were given permission to wear plain clothes when off duty. Progressively, old police stations were modernized or rebuilt and recreation rooms were provided where men off duty could smoke and relax, while the spartan section-houses for single men were modestly improved—hot water, drying-closets, wet canteens, and a much better standard of messing. Concerned at the level of illiteracy in the force, Henderson even

---

[1] Maurice Drummond was appointed Receiver on John Wray's retirement in 1860.

instituted 'schoolmaster sergeants' in each division, although the experiment, brave in intention, proved unworkable in practice and seems to have been discontinued within two or three years.

Weekly rest-days had long been a major problem, not least because they necessitated an augmentation of one-seventh of the force if normal duties were to be carried out in divisions. Henderson dwelt upon this at some length in his Report—'an experiment [which] has been a disappointment to all who watched its effects. 'The constable,' he added, in a phrase straight from Samuel Smiles, 'becomes unhinged and unsettled by constant interruption of duty. The fallacy is that one day's leave is one day's rest.' Instead, he proposed two days' leave in the month, 'one of which to be invariably on a Sunday'. It was a problem which was to come to a head forty years later.

This busy and productive year was also marked by three important developments. The first was a direct result of Henderson's well-argued case for an increase in the strength of his force to meet his growing commitments. Home Office sanction for an additional 1,350 men made it possible not only to revise street patrols but to introduce the 'fixed point' system, by which constables could be located at determined points and thus provide more complete coverage of each divisional area. Science now also began to play its part in the more efficient administration of the Metropolitan Police District. During the summer of 1867 the electric telegraph had been installed at Scotland Yard and in three 'town' divisional headquarters. The experiment had been so successful that by the end of 1869 (in which year the Post Office was made responsible for the system) telegraphy had been extended to cover virtually every division in the district. Peel, the preamble to whose Act had spoken of 'the Want of Connection and Cooperation', would have been much gratified by this modern miracle of communication and Police Orders went to comical lengths to explain the method of operating what must have been, to the simple constabulary of the day, an invention of formidable complexity.

Finally, at Henderson's instigation, a start was made on a Register of Habitual Criminals. It will be remembered that in 1758 Sir John Fielding, activated by the principle of 'quick notice and sudden pursuit', had established a central registry of known criminals on a 'national' basis for the benefit of all magistrates, supported by *Weekly Pursuit*, forerunner of the *Police Gazette*.

With the growth of provincial forces, Henderson decided to revive the idea but on a scale which proved to be too comprehensive and impracticable to be operated by the limited staff available. It was not until after the move to New Scotland Yard and the arrival in 1901 of Edward Henry and his Central Fingerprint Bureau that the modern Criminal Record Office was brought into existence.

Thus, by the end of his first year of office, Henderson had done a great deal towards 'making clean the outside of the platter'. But before we arrive at the first sounds of breaking crockery, it is necessary to retrace our steps to the previous year.

*

As a result of public concern over the apparent shortcomings of the police occasioned by the Clerkenwell explosion, a Departmental Committee was set up at the Home Office to make a confidential Report[1] which was duly submitted on 6 May (Mayne's evidence is a further reflection of his declining powers). The Departmental Report—the first of its kind since the Royal Commission of 1855—was concise, factual and, with one vital exception, constructive. It was to provide the incentive and authority for many of Henderson's reforms.

The Report recognized from the start that a 'police force [now] resembling, both in numbers and distribution, a division of the army, has a complement of superior officers less than that of a single battalion'. (It was tactful enough not to point out that this was due to Mayne's stubborn refusal to delegate.) It accordingly proposed that the Metropolis should be divided into four districts each under a district superintendent. Its further proposal that police divisions should be re-defined to coincide with parish boundaries was not acted upon, and the new system came into force in Police Orders for 27 February 1869 thus:

No. 1 Dist. A. C. Howard, late Bengal Constabulary
No. 2 Dist. Robert Walker, late Chief Supt, A Division
No. 3 Dist. Lt-Col. R. Pearson, late Grenadier Guards
No. 4 Dist. H. Baynes, late Governor, Hants County Prison.

It was hoped that the new organization would make one of the assistant commissioners redundant, but in fact, by 1884, two of the

[1] The printed copy in the library at New Scotland Yard is extensively—and revealingly—annotated (*c.* 1886) by Sir Richard Pennefather who was appointed Receiver in 1883.

district superintendents had disappeared and a third assistant commissioner (in charge of the new Criminal Investigation Department) had been appointed.

The Report next turned to various aspects of conditions of service[1] and administrative improvements. It proposed the introduction of the weekly rest-day which Henderson was to find so contentious; the institution of good-conduct badges which Mayne, for some reason, rejected out of hand; the formation of an enlarged Detective Force into a separate division (a proposal not fully acted upon until the controversial decision to create a separate CID in 1878); an extended use of the telegraph; and the first hint of new and much larger premises for the Metropolitan Police Office. It then came to the problem of pay and pensions.

'As may be expected, this is the most difficult question with which the Committee have had to deal.' Difficult it may have been, but its proper solution was fundamental to every other recommendation in the Report; and the Committee, like others before and since, shirked the issue. 'They do not recommend,' the Report continued, 'any general increase in the pay.' Instead, they hoped that the men would be satisfied with small improvements in allowances; and as a cosmetic exercise they proposed the creation of three separate classes of sergeants and constables and a complicated system of long-service increments by which superintendents would start at the *reduced* salary of £250, rising to £350 after ten years, while constables would be rewarded in princely fashion: after ten years an additional 1s a week; after fifteen years, 1s 6d a week; and after twenty years, 2s a week.

Turning to pensions, the Committee considered the old scale 'excessive, especially having regard to the lax way in which constables were passed for pension'. They duly proposed a new scale starting at £14 after fifteen years' service (less than half the previous figure) and rising to £40 after twenty-eight years (the same as the old maximum for thirty years). How the scheme was to be funded was not touched upon.

Thus, in the most vital area of their Report, the Committee laid up much trouble in store for Edmund Henderson.

*

[1] In his evidence, Dr Farr of the General Register Office stressed the onerous duties of policemen. 'An average constable on night duty walks 16 miles. A constable on a day beat (10 hours) walks 20 miles.'

The first signs of unrest appeared around the middle of October 1872 when a series of protest meetings were held at various stations at which the demand was made for 'the right to confer' and proceedings were orchestrated by an MP named Eykyn, the first, albeit self-appointed, political adviser to the force.

Henderson was quick to counter these early indications of insubordination by announcing that 'the question of pay will immediately be submitted to the Secretary of State'.[1] At the same time he advised the voluntary suspension of all further meetings in order to avoid the distasteful necessity for a compulsory ban.

It is doubtful whether the Home Office has ever moved faster in so delicate an area, for within sixteen days the following pay increases were announced:[2]

Superintendents	£50 p.a.
Inspectors	10s p.w.
Sergeants	5s p.w.
Detective constables	4s p.w.

Pay for the three classes of constable were increased to the following rates:

First class	30s p.w.
Second class	27s p.w.
Third class	24s p.w.

Tours of duty were also made less onerous. Superannuation deductions remained at $2\frac{1}{2}$ per cent, but the Police Order stated that the whole subject of pensions would be discussed as a matter of urgency with the Home Secretary (in the event, there was neither urgency nor discussion).

It seems that, with these proposals, honour would have been satisfied; but, whether on his own initiative or not, Henderson decided to dismiss the chief agitator. From such sparks, unexpected bonfires start; and on the night of Saturday, 16 November, 7 sergeants and 173 men of D, P, E, and T Divisions[3] refused duty. It was, by any standard, a very minor mutiny, but it was the first of

[1] Police Orders, 22 October 1872.

[2] Police Orders, 7 November 1872.

[3] Marylebone, Camberwell, Holborn and Kensington. It was a matter of particular concern that E Division based on Bow Street—the oldest of all police stations—was involved.

its kind and to Henderson, however 'unmilitary' a soldier, mutiny was not to be tolerated.

Accordingly, all the men involved were immediately suspended; and two days later 109 were formally dismissed the service.[1] Had Richard Mayne still been in the saddle, punishment would have been a good deal more exemplary, but Henderson showed that he understood better the quality of mercy. He therefore waited a few days to allow the contagion of guilt to take effect; and on 29 November he reinstated all but a handful of the misguided militants. During that day the penitents were duly re-sworn as constables. The first police 'strike' was over.

In his Report for 1872, Henderson wisely did not exaggerate the importance of the incident and, in a paragraph of true Victorian eloquence, dismissed the whole affair as an aberration of foolish children. 'This occurrence . . . has left nothing behind it but a regret that by the unjustifiable conduct of a few men, a stain should have been left on the honourable annals of the force.' He might well have added that the real culprits were the Home Office and the Treasury.

*

The 1872 mutiny had one curious result. After the predictable press reaction had died down, a new, conciliatory attitude towards the police began to appear in the public prints. The *Telegraph* and the *Weekly Dispatch* even discovered posthumous virtues in Richard Mayne, the man they had for so long subjected to derision and abuse. Police affairs still continued to exercise the leader-writers of Fleet Street (a century later *The Times* was to conduct its own historic detective investigation) but the heat had gone out of the public debate and the police enjoyed the novel experience of being praised rather than pilloried. The new climate of opinion must have encouraged Henderson in carrying forward his many reforms. What he did not know was that, under his very feet, a lethal time-bomb was ticking.

The expansion of the Detective Force in 1869 had created a number of new senior posts. By 1877 the head of the force was Supt Frederick Williamson, with over twenty years' detective service. Of his four chief inspectors, three—Clarke, Palmer and

[1] Police Orders, 20 November 1872.

Druscovitch—were now to be involved in a scandal which made the corrupt practices of the Bow Street Runners seem like minor cases of juvenile delinquency. In this they were joined, indeed led, by Inspector Meiklejohn, a former sergeant in the old Detective Force and incredibly promoted while himself involved in corruption on a grand scale. Clarke and Palmer were officers of long experience while Druscovitch was, by origin, an East European whose knowledge of languages and proven ability had led to accelerated promotion at the age of thirty-seven. All four men were to figure prominently in what has been variously called the Turf Frauds or de Goncourt case.[1]

Sometime during 1872, Meiklejohn had started accepting bribes from a small-time crook named William Kurr, whose speciality was the running of bogus betting establishments. Meiklejohn's part in the association was to act as a listening-post at Scotland Yard and alert Kurr in the event of any suspicions being aroused in the detective department. At first, the sums of money involved were relatively small and Kurr, although an astute operator, had neither the financial means nor the facilities to expand his shady activities; until, in the summer of 1873, he met Harry Benson.

Benson was a confidence trickster of some genius. The son of wealthy parents, he had been brought up in Paris, spoke perfect French, and had the poise and manner of an aristocrat. He also had a very persuasive tongue. Of his apprenticeship in crime little is known, but during 1872, posing as the Comte de Montagu, he succeeded in extracting £1,000 from the Lord Mayor of London for relief work at Châteaudun after the Franco-Prussian War. Even by his own standards it was too wild a fantasy. He was arrested and sent to prison for a year where, in an attempt to commit suicide, he succeeded only in crippling himself. He was released in July 1873.

That might have been the end of Harry Benson; but he was an infinitely resourceful criminal. If he was now, in every sense, a marked man, then why not enlist the support of his potential enemies and involve the guardians of the law themselves in the subversion of the law? It must therefore have been an occasion of rare encouragement to him when he stumbled upon William Kurr and the already deeply compromised Sergeant Meiklejohn. Few men could have expected to be presented with so golden a key.

[1] For a detailed account, see Dilnot, *The Trial of the Detectives*.

Benson removed himself to the Isle of Wight where, in Shanklin, he set himself up in a large house under the assumed name of Yonge. That his movements, as a recently convicted criminal, did not invite the interest of Supt Williamson is curious. They did, however, engage the attention of Chief Inspector Druscovitch; so, *tout simple*, Benson/Yonge decided to compromise Druscovitch. And like all successful criminals, he was in luck.

Early in 1873, Druscovitch had guaranteed a bill of £60 for his brother. When in due course this was presented he was unable to raise the money and the resourceful Meiklejohn suggested that his friend Kurr would be happy to oblige. For Druscovitch it was a harsh dilemma. He was aware of Kurr's reputation and was in fact investigating his activities, but in a moment of desperation rather than deceit he accepted the money, and in so doing sold himself to the devil.

Benson, whose turf frauds had now become big business, next turned his attention to the senior chief inspector. In 1875, Clarke had run to earth two minor members of the gang, to one of whom he wrote an innocent but injudicious letter. Armed with a copy of this, Benson invited Clarke to Shanklin where, according to his later (and uncorroborated) evidence, he persuaded the chief inspector to accept bribes as the price of his silence. It is likely that Clarke's colleague Palmer was also recruited into the conspiracy about this time and Benson could congratulate himself that, at a modest cost, he had bought himself and Kurr virtually complete immunity from investigation. It seems inconceivable that Williamson was unaware of the conduct of so many of his officers, but a hundred years later, in not dissimilar circumstances, it was a question which was again to be asked of Scotland Yard.

Benson now went in search of bigger fish. Under a new alias— Hugh Montgomery—he invented a news-sheet entitled *Sport* which purported to advertise infallible betting systems. But, wrote 'Mr. Montgomery', so great had been his own success that he had been boycotted by the bookmaking fraternity. Accordingly he invited readers to act as his commission agents, by placing bets in their own names on his behalf and with stake money provided by himself.

Copies of *Sport* were mailed to a carefully selected register of names in France accompanied by a letter in translation which explained the 'unwarranted restraints' of the bookmakers' boycott. To the Comtesse de Goncourt, a Parisian lady with more money than sense, it seemed an inviting proposition, and impressed by Mr Montgomery's own apparent infallibility she ventured a flutter of £1,000 on her own account. Predictably, it was 'arranged' for her to win and thus encouraged she increased her own bets until by the autumn of 1876 she had invested over £10,000 for which she held post-dated cheques ('an irritating requirement of English law', explained Mr Montgomery) on the non-existent 'Royal Bank of London'.

Benson now fatally overplayed his hand by suggesting to the Comtesse that she should invest £30,000 with a 'bookmaker' of impeccable honesty. To raise this sum, the foolish but insatiable lady consulted her lawyer who, sensibly suspicious, referred the matter to a London solicitor named Abrahams; and Abrahams went at once to Scotland Yard.

The hunt was on; and at last the truth began to dawn on Williamson. Thus two parallel investigations began. While the senior detectives were detailed to round up their paymasters (Druscovitch, the linguist, was ironically dispatched to arrest Benson in Rotterdam), a confidential inquiry was started into the activities of the detectives themselves. On 13 April 1877, Benson, Kurr and three accomplices stood trial for fraud and forgery. Benson was sentenced to fifteen years' penal servitude,[1] Kurr and two others to ten years, while the fifth defendant received eighteen months' hard labour. Inexplicably, throughout their trial neither Benson and Kurr nor their defence counsel mentioned the involvement of the detective department, but a month later both men, in the hope of some remission of their sentences, made full statements; and on 24 October, on a charge of conspiring to obstruct the course of justice, the trial of Clarke, Palmer, Druscovitch, Meiklejohn and a solicitor named Froggatt began. It was to last nineteen days, the longest trial in the history of the Old Bailey at that date; and it is at least arguable that only a sense of professional loyalty saved a number of other detectives from joining the defendants in the dock.

---

[1] Harry Benson remained incorrigible to the end. Released after serving ten years of his sentence he resumed his fraudulent activities, first in New York (with his old accomplice Kurr) and then as a freelance in Brussels and once more in New York. Jailed for a bravura swindle on Adelina Patti, he made a second—and this time successful—attempt to commit suicide in prison.

Colonel Sir Charles Rowan, KCB. Commissioner 1829–1850

ir Richard Mayne, KCB. Commissioner 1829–1868

Home office

Sir Robert Peel

July 20th 1829

Sanction of Establishment
of Police Consisting of
3 Clerks for Commissioner
2 for the Receiver
and 8 Superintendents
20 Inspectors 88 P.S.s
and 895 Constables with
their Respective Stations.

N.B. Augmentation

Peel's first directive to Rowan and Mayne, 20 July 1829

Peel's Police,
RAW LOBSTERS,
Blue Devils,

Or by whatever other appropriate Name
they may be known.

Notice is hereby given,

That a Subscription has been entered
into, to supply the **PEOPLE** with
STAVES of a superior Effect, either
for Defence or Punishment, which will be
in readiness to be gratuitously distributed
whenever a similar unprovoked, and therefore unmanly and blood-thirsty Attack,
be again made upon Englishmen, by a
Force unknown to the British Constitution, and called into existence by a
Parliament illegally constituted, legislat-
ing for their individual interests, consequently in opposition to the Public good.

———*ooo*———

" Put not your trust in Princes."—DAVID.
" Help yourself, and Heaven will help you."—FRENCH
MOTTO.

10th Nov 1830 Eliz. Soulby, Printer, 91, Gracechurch Street.

A typical anti-police broadsheet, 10 November 1830

The earliest known photograph of a 'Peeler'

Police Constable, 1979

Great Scotland Yard, 1829

New Scotland Yard, 1890

New Scotland Yard, 1967

The Reform Riots, 1837

Red Lion Square demonstration, 1974

The Fenians. 'The Rising Sun', Great Scotland Yard, May 1884

The I.R.A. The Naval and Military Club, December 1974

Sir Robert Mark, GBE, QPM.
Commissioner, 1972-1977

Sir David McNee, QPM.
Commissioner, 1977-

Despite the evidence and perhaps because of Williamson's intervention on his behalf, Clarke, the unsuccessful sinner, was acquitted. He forthwith retired on pension and became a successful publican. The other four men each received the maximum permitted sentence of two years' hard labour. All England was scandalized; and well might it have been asked: *Quis custodiet ipsos custodes?*[1]

*

In his Report for the year 1877, Henderson made only a passing reference to the state of affairs which the trial of the detectives had revealed, not because he considered it a matter of small importance but because a major change of policy had intervened.

Two months before the start of the trial, a Departmental Commission was convened by the Home Secretary to inquire, as well it might, into 'the state, discipline and organization of the Detective Force of the Metropolitan Police'. The commission held its first meeting four days before the trial ended, which may explain why its report made no direct reference to the recent scandal, which was still *sub judice*; and it made a number of fundamental recommendations which, in the opinion of one recent Commissioner, were to do lasting damage to the Metropolitan Police. We shall have occasion to examine this opinion in due course; but in the winter of 1877, under the shadow of Benson and Kurr and with a sudden increase in serious crime, they must have seemed imperative conclusions.

The commission's proposals were to be influenced from an unexpected quarter. At a very early stage, it had been decided that the reorganized branch should be under the control not of a professional policeman but of a criminal lawyer (at once an echo of and a departure from Peel's principle of forty years earlier). To a young barrister named Howard Vincent this was an interesting piece of intelligence, and he proceeded with some haste to Paris to make a study of the highly effective system of centralized detective operations there, which had for so long been viewed with deep suspicion by the citizens of the Metropolis. On his return, he prepared a detailed memorandum for the commission and this document was

---

[1] Writing in 1956, Douglas Browne (*op. cit*) described the affair as 'a net of corruption and deceit happily unique in the history of the Metropolitan Police'. He little knew what lay ahead.

to provide the basis of many of their subsequent recommendations, although curiously Vincent's name occurs nowhere in the final Report which was presented on 25 January 1878.

The main recommendation of the commission—not, in the event, acted upon as such—was that a completely reorganized Detective Branch should be formed and that it should be entirely separated from the uniform police under 'an Assistant Commissioner who should be a lawyer having magisterial experience, ranking next to the Commissioner, *and having charge of the whole force in his absence*'.[1] In effect, the commission were proposing that 'little firm in a firm' of which much was to be heard a century later; indeed, the Report went so far as to say that the men of the Detective Branch 'should, in their respective ranks, take precedence of the uniform or preventive branch of the service' and underlined this new policy of elitism by proposing higher rates of pay for plain-clothes officers.

With the publication of the Report, Vincent at once applied for the new post and his appointment was duly gazetted in Police Orders of 6 March. His status and terms of reference, however, differed significantly from the Committee's recommendations.

In the first place his title was 'Director of Criminal Investigations' (borrowed literally from the French system) and he ranked as an Assistant Commissioner only for purposes of pay. While nominally subordinate to the Commissioner, he was to have *carte blanche* in his own department *with direct access to the Home Secretary*, and was instructed 'not to pay too much attention to what was said of him, either by the Commissioner, or anyone else at Scotland Yard'.

It was an impossible position, and also an anomalous one, since, as a 'Director', Vincent had no statutory powers (he was not, for example, a justice) and no disciplinary authority over his department. Fortunately both he and Henderson were tolerant and sensible men and they seem to have arrived at a reasonable working relationship for six years, until the restless Vincent departed in search of fresh fields to conquer.

The Criminal Investigation Department came into existence a

[1] The copy of the Report in the library at New Scotland Yard is heavily annotated by Henderson, and by James Monro, who succeeded Vincent with the title of Assistant Commissioner (Crime) in 1884. Their comments show how contentious a subject criminal investigation had already become.

month later.[1] The precipitate removal of most of the senior detective officers the previous year led to a major reshuffle, and the establishment of the new CID was accordingly fixed as follows:

At Central Office

  1 Chief Superintendent
  3 Chief Inspectors
  3 First Class Inspectors
 17 Second Class Inspectors

An office staff of six men under Chief Inspector Harris of the Executive Branch.

In Divisions

 15 Inspectors
159 Sergeants
 60 Divisional Patrols
 20 Special Patrols

Mindful of the fact that the 1877 trial might not have purged the ranks of all corrupt practitioners, Vincent put all but twenty specifically named officers on three months' probation.

The new Chief Superintendent was Williamson, and while his experience must have been invaluable to Vincent, he could have considered himself fortunate to be thus promoted after his failure to detect the criminal activities of so many of his senior colleagues. In July, the new establishment was confirmed and the new CID rates of pay came into operation.

It does not seem to have occurred to Henderson, who was lazy, or Vincent, who was headstrong, that the division of the Metropolitan Police into entirely separate preventive and detective branches would cause considerable trouble. The special pay and status of the CID aroused the understandable jealousy of uniform men at the 'sharp end' of policing, while divisional superintendents reacted so strongly to the presence on their ground of police officers over whom they had no authority that it was at once laid down that all reports from detectives in divisions must be submitted through superintendents and that the former must cooperate closely with the latter. None the less, a dangerous precedent had been set.

Vincent was interested in neither tradition nor convention, since both seemed to him to have contributed significantly to police

---

[1] Police Orders, 6 April.

inefficiency, if not worse side-effects. His policy, pursued with indefatigable zeal and occasional lapses into fantasy, was to 'abate the power of felons' so that where prevention failed, detection of crime would provide an increasingly effective second line of defence.[1] He even found time to produce a *Police Code* in 1881. It was in effect a manual of criminal law running to 454 pages and summarizing for the benefit of police constables the application of statute law from 'Abandoned Children' to 'Wrecking', with nine oddly assorted appendices. With subsequent revised editions it became a policeman's bible, although chiefly consulted, one would guess, by earnest seekers after promotion.

One unsuccessful innovation proved short-lived. Convinced that the science of detection required a higher standard of intelligence than that possessed by the average constable, Vincent experimented with the idea of appointing outsiders to CID posts—'gentlemen of good education and social standing' drawn largely from the armed services or possessing special language qualifications. Apart from inevitable opposition among regular members of the CID, the scheme proved conclusively that there was no substitute for basic police training and it was soon discontinued. The experiment also gave colour to Peel's refusal 'to employ gentlemen . . . because I am certain they would be above their work'. When, in 1933, Trenchard revived Vincent's idea, albeit in a very different form, his experiment did not survive the Second World War, and for much the same reasons.

One example of Vincent's alleged excess of zeal in obtaining convictions is illustrated by the Titley case. Titley was a chemist suspected of providing drugs to procure abortions, and a policeman's wife, on the pretence of seeking his assistance, was used to obtain evidence. Titley was duly arrested and convicted, but the case created a public stir and the sinister spectre of the *agent provocateur* was paraded in press and Parliament. It was, in fact, a perfectly legitimate course of police action but an indictment—subsequently quashed—was brought against the officers concerned; and it was left to Sir William Harcourt, one of the wisest of Home Secretaries, to excuse the subterfuge in the Commons with the important dictum that 'the cases in which it is necessary or

[1] The number of arrests by detectives for criminal offences in the Metropolis rose from 13,128 in 1879 to 18,343 in 1884 (*Commissioners' Reports*).

justifiable for the police to resort to artifice of the description practised in this case must be rare indeed. As a rule, the police ought not to set traps for people.'

But the CID had only one *raison d'être*—to catch criminals. Murder has always had a peculiar fascination in the public mind, not only because it is, as defined earlier, the ultimate crime against the person, but because, to the lay observer, it is the classic game of wits, in which the ingenuity of the law is matched against that of the malefactor. Moreover, since murder is often gruesome, it gratifies one of the less attractive of human appetites. It also makes good headlines.

There had been many sensational murders before the coming of the CID—cases like those of Madeleine Smith, Constance Kent, Dr Pritchard, and Dr Palmer, the Rugeley poisoner—but before 1878 was out, the name of Charlie Peace was on everybody's lips and a new anti-hero had been born. Peace was, in fact, no scheming villain, but a ruthless armed burglar, and a month after his arrest in Blackheath (he was hanged in 1879 for a murder committed three years earlier in Sheffield) the CID was involved in the Orrock case, which is the first classic example of patient and inspired detective investigation.

Forensic science was still a thing of the future and pathology in its infancy. Vincent's detectives could rely only on their training and their police instinct. *Punch* thought little of them and listed a number of scenes of unsolved crimes which might usefully engage the attention of the 'Defective Police', while a few years later police-baiting assumed a new, sophisticated gloss with the arrival of the insufferable Sherlock Holmes and his dull-witted butt, Lestrade. The English continued happily to enjoy the literary humiliation of the law by its Marples and Wimseys, and it is not without significance that perhaps the two most celebrated professionals in detective fiction were to be a Belgian and a Frenchman.

Long before then Vincent had gone to the more comfortable security of the House of Commons, leaving as his memorial a powerful, if often controversial, weapon in the continuing war on crime.

*

One reason why Henderson was apparently content to let Vincent have a free hand at the CID may have been his preoccupation with growing problems at the administrative level and with the revival of terrorist activity.

The office of Receiver had evolved out of Peel's determination to ensure good housekeeping in the matter of police finances; and while the force still remained comparatively small, the problem of accountability was little more than an exercise in book-keeping. Indeed, John Wray had found time to pursue outside interests by delegating the routine office work to his chief clerk. By the 1840s, however, Wray was under fire from his Home Office masters. The accusation was not of impropriety but of negligence, and Wray did not like the imputation. 'I confess I am much annoyed by that part which proposes that I should take upon myself the duties of Cashier.'[1] And four years later: 'Educated as a gentleman, a member of the University of Cambridge and afterwards called to the Bar, I should have considered the office of Cashier as degrading to my position.'[2]

The long dialogue concerning responsibility and accountability was to drag on until Wray's retirement in 1860; but by then the guide-lines had been fixed. 'The Receiver was not to be the third, if junior, member of an independent board of police management but an instrument of Home Office control, subordinated by means of the Finance Regulations. Only for a short period had the rates been the sole source of revenue. As the Government subvention became larger so did the Government pipers make sure they called even more of the tune.'[3] It was a recipe for trouble.

Drummond's attitude to the Receiver's function was markedly different from Wray's (a short Act in 1861 had converted his office into a corporation sole) and he considered himself first and last a Home Office man, with the role of watchdog over executive profligacy. For some years, there was an uneasy peace, although the refusal of Drummond and the Home Office officials to improve police pay after the 1868 Report had contributed directly to the 1872 mutiny. But by 1878 there was a state of open warfare between Henderson and the Receiver. Henderson felt that his statutory obligations entitled him to be master in his own house and not subject to divided authority. He was responsible for

[1] Wray to Phillipps, 29 May 1843.
[2] HO 45/OS109, 18 January 1847.
[3] R. M. Morris, 'The Metropolitan Police in the 19th century' (unpublished MS).

maintaining the Queen's Peace in a Metropolis where both the population and the rate of crime were increasing rapidly. To carry out his operational duties, the Metropolitan Police had to be expanded significantly and that was impossible if he was subjected to unreasonable financial restraints. Drummond, an archetypal bureaucrat, had come to assume the character of a Home Office spy in the Commissioner's camp.

By 1878, however, Henderson was on difficult ground. The detective scandal of the previous year had called the whole conduct of the Metropolitan Police Office into question; and when the inquiry into the Detective Branch was set up, the Home Secretary also convened a parallel commission to examine the administration of police accounts.

In his evidence to this commission (no report seems to have been published) Henderson set out his objections to what he called 'dual government'. 'The mistake it seems to me is to make a financial officer an executive officer, or to fancy that a financial officer is to check upon any executive officer' except to ensure that the money had been properly provided and applied. He went on to complain that he was never able to discover the financial state of the Police Fund at any given time. In short, there should be only one person clearly responsible for the *whole* of the police and that person should be the Commissioner.[1]

Drummond categorically disagreed. 'If the Home Secretary is left entirely to the tender mercies [*sic*] of the Commissioner, the Commissioner will, in my opinion, play ducks and drakes with the money which he has to deal with.' He proceeded to turn the knife in the wound. 'The fact that a department like my own ... has been called upon to justify its existence at the suggestion of a Department whose extravagance it controls, and which is notoriously in a state of utter disorganisation, is an incident I believe without parallel in the records of the public service.'[2] This offensive exercise in hyperbole tells us much about the character of Maurice Drummond; and it was one of the opening shots in a confrontation between successive Commissioners and the Home Office which was to become increasingly abrasive over the next twelve years.

*

[1] Morris, *op. cit.*   [2] *Ibid.*

Meanwhile, Henderson had other problems which not even Drummond would have claimed to be the province of the Receiver.

At 9 p.m. on 15 March 1883, a bomb exploded outside a government office opposite the headquarters of A Division in King Street, Westminster, and later the same evening an attack on the offices of *The Times* was only frustrated by an alert watchman. The two incidents marked the beginning of a new and widespread outbreak of Fenianism which was to last sporadically for two years and occasion a public panic even greater than that which followed the Clerkenwell explosion.

During this period there were twenty-two acts of terrorism in the Metropolis, mostly abortive and few resulting in any casualties. The range of targets was impressive, including the Tower, the Houses of Parliament, London Bridge, the Admiralty, and four mainline and underground railway stations. An attempt to blow up Nelson's Column was thwarted by an intrepid constable who defused sixteen cakes of dynamite and laid them neatly, if innocently, on the pavement in Whitehall; while the most daring attack was on Scotland Yard itself where, on the evening of 30 May 1884, a bomb destroyed the unoccupied office of Sergeant (later Chief Inspector) Sweeney, and severely damaged the 'Rising Sun' public house on the corner of Whitehall. Sweeney was philosophical about the incident. 'We could not console ourselves in the same way as the proprietor of the "Rising Sun",' he wrote later. 'Naturally thousands of people flocked to see the effects of the outrage; he charged 3d a head for admitting spectators, and what with this and the increase of custom that accrued to him, he more than recouped himself for the damage done to his premises.'

Henderson was under constant pressure from the Home Office to put a stop to these terrorist activities, and by the autumn of 1884 over 1,000 constables were occupied in guarding public buildings and protecting distinguished persons. The more resourceful Vincent had other ideas, and during the spring of that year he had formed the first anti-terrorist squad, known as the 'Special Irish Branch' of the CID and headed by Chief Inspector Littlechild, who had arrested William Kurr seven years earlier. So successful was this experiment that the following year, when the 'dynamiters' had been rounded up, Vincent's successor, Monro, retained the squad, dropped the word 'Irish', and created what is today that branch of the CID which deals with offences against the security of the state.

It all seemed a far cry from Drummond and the bleatings of the Audit Office.

*

Vincent's successor as head of the CID was James Monro, a former Inspector-General of Police in Bengal, whence were to come no fewer than seven future senior officers of the Metropolitan Police; and a short Act of Parliament corrected the anomaly created by the 1878 Committee by defining his office as that of Assistant Commissioner.[1] Monro's six years at Scotland Yard were to be varied, and often stormy.

*

London had been notably free of civil disturbances ever since the Hyde Park riots of 1866. While this was gratifying for the citizens of the Metropolis, it meant that the police, greatly increased in numbers during the intervening years, were inexperienced in the technique of controlling large and militant crowds. They were now to have their fair share of riot and disorder.

On Monday, 8 February 1886, after giving notice of their intention, a body calling themselves the London United Workmen's Committee held a meeting in Trafalgar Square to protest against the evils of rising unemployment. Aware that their action might provoke trouble from the rival Social Democratic Federation, the LUWC duly gave warning to the Commissioner.[2] Henderson, lulled into a false sense of security by the long years of public tranquillity, was not greatly impressed. A small force of police was stationed in the square and some 563 men were held in reserve in the immediate vicinity. Command was delegated to Robert Walker, one of the two surviving district superintendents, who after nearly fifty years' service should at least have been alive to the possibility of serious trouble; but he was now seventy-four and quite unfitted to handle the situation. Arriving at the meeting in civilian clothes,

---

[1] The same Act also authorized the appointment of another Assistant Commissioner to handle 'civil business'.

[2] By chance, or possibly by intent, the meeting coincided with the arrival of the weak and totally inexperienced Hugh Childers at the Home Office.

he was soon caught up in the crowd where he lost not only control but also the contents of both his trouser pockets.

The two rival demonstrations proceeded without incident, but when the speakers had had their say the mob, numbering some 5,000, decided to take matters into their own hands and within seconds a peaceful demonstration became an ugly riot, as the crowd surged down Pall Mall bent on mayhem. All semblance of police control broke down. Henderson was not at his office, Walker was stranded in Trafalgar Square, and the police reserve ordered to Pall Mall was wrongly directed to the Mall. After a brief pause for inflammatory speech-making in Hyde Park, the rioters made tracks for Oxford Street to indulge in more violence and looting; but where the full might of the Metropolitan Police Office had failed, one man showed now what resolution and discipline could achieve. At Marylebone police station, Inspector Cuthbert was parading his evening relief of one sergeant and fifteen constables, when news reached him of the approaching mob. He at once led his men to Oxford Street where without hesitation he launched a baton-charge. The rioters broke and ran, and some semblance of law and order returned to the ravaged streets. During the following two days, there were constant rumours of further trouble which Henderson did nothing to allay by warning shopkeepers and property-owners to take elaborate precautions. In the event, nothing happened, and Henderson found himself in the uncomfortable position of a defeated general deserted by his natural allies.

Childers, concerned for his own political skin, acted with less charity than Bruce and Liddell had shown to Mayne in similar circumstances. Within a week he appointed a committee, most improperly chaired by himself, to inquire into the disturbances of 8 February 'and the conduct of the Police Authorities in relation thereto' (the unsubtle implication of the wording did not escape Henderson). On 22 February the committee reported in uncompromising terms and concluded 'by a strong expression of opinion that the administration and organisation of the Metropolitan Police Force require to be thoroughly investigated; and we hope that this investigation will take place without delay'.[1]

Henderson gave his evidence and, preferring to avoid the ignominy of inevitable dismissal, resigned the following day. He

[1] The Report did not avail Childers. Within five months he had followed Gladstone out of office.

had been a good, if not great, Commissioner who scarcely deserved to pay so harsh a price for a single dereliction of duty. He had rendered great service to the force during a difficult period of consolidation. He was well-liked by his men and not least by the cab-drivers of London who on his departure presented him with a replica of a hansom cab in silver. Perhaps, like Mayne, he had stayed too long and this had resulted in growing tension with Drummond's successor, Pennefather, and more especially with the Home Office officials.

At the date of his resignation, the strength of the Metropolitan Police had grown to 13,115, including a Criminal Investigation Department of 313.[1] Ahead lay four troubled years.

*

It was widely assumed that Monro, the head of the CID, would be the new Commissioner. He had practical experience and had shown unusual administrative ability; but Childers had other ideas. Having, in a sense, contrived Henderson's resignation, he now saddled the police and, indeed, the Home Office with an intractable successor, the very speed of whose appointment suggests something more than lack of judgement on Childers's part. 'The place was offered to [General] Sir Charles Warren, a well-known officer of Engineers, whose talent for administration had been proved in Bechuanaland and who now relinquished the Governorship of the Red Sea Littoral.'[2] It is difficult to imagine a more improbable qualification for a Commissioner of Police of the Metropolis.

Warren was to set something of a record at Scotland Yard. During his 2½-year reign, he succeeded in alienating simultaneously the new Home Secretary, Matthews; the Permanent Under-Secretary, Lushington; the Receiver, Pennefather; and his own Assistant Commissioner, Monro. This versatility ensured some memorable passages of arms, but it did not do the Metropolitan Police much good.

The trouble lay as much with Childers as with Warren, for the latter had been plainly given to understand that he was being summoned, like some colonial missionary to the archbishopric itself, to reorganize and reinspire a demoralized public institution.

[1] The clerical staff consisted of 17 in the Commissioner's Office (with 6 temporary copyists) and 12 in the Receiver's Office.
[2] W. Melville Lee, *op. cit.*

This was palpably untrue and the public records give no hint of the real reason for Childers's choice. If he felt that the Metropolitan Police needed the firm smack of military government, it was a very curious proposition for a Liberal Home Secretary to advance. Warren took office on 29 March, but before he had fully settled into his chair, he found that he had a new Conservative master at the Home Office, Henry Matthews.

It is tempting to dwell upon Warren's commissionership, for it represented the culmination of all those latent stresses which had been building up virtually since the retirement of Charles Rowan in 1850. But the fact of the matter is that Warren's years at Scotland Yard are no more than a historical hiccough. And he was at least as much sinned against as sinning.

He was an abrasive character, arrogant, opinionated, and determined to have his own way. He was first and last a soldier, and he did not like civil servants. In his view, they were political toadies who merely obstructed his direct relationship with the Secretary of State and the conduct of his office. In this he may have been wiser than he knew, for Robert Anderson, who became an assistant commissioner on Monro's resignation, felt that Lushington, the Permanent Under-Secretary, had been inclined to apply 'blisters to wounds rather than plasters'. The cemeteries of Whitehall have long been reverently stocked with the graves of feuding soldiers and civilians.

More importantly, Warren was not a policeman; and this brought him into conflict with the professional, Monro, for whom he had little time and less sympathy. So little was Warren interested in crime, not the least of his statutory obligations, that in neither of his two Annual Reports is the word so much as mentioned. It may have suited Warren; but not Monro, who resigned in August 1888.

*

Despite his constant bickering with Matthews and his officials at the Home Office and his lack of sympathy with Monro, Warren was not idle in his concern for improvements in police organization to which Robert Anderson, not one of his most devoted disciples, later paid tribute.[1] Most of his reforms can be seen, on reflection, to have been in the area of command and control, and his apparent

---

[1] Anderson, *The Lighter Side of my Official Life.*

indifference towards the rank and file, symptomatic of his military origins, was the cause of widespread disaffection. It was one of the unfortunate defects of Warren's character that whenever he applied oil to the administrative wheels he succeeded in introducing even more grit into the machinery.

His first action was to revive the virtually defunct district command structure by appointing four Chief Constables.[1] The Mounted Branch was reorganized under an Assistant Chief Constable and, for the first time, trained in riot control duties. Subdivisional inspectors were posted to divisions to provide relief for superintendents and 330 men were made up to inspector and sergeant in order to reduce the hours of duty of these ranks from twelve to eight hours. The quality of boots, for so long a source of public merriment and police complaint, was improved. Harder and handier truncheons were introduced. And Police Orders of the period, while silent on pay and pensions, are discursive on the subject of saddlery and smoke abatement.[2]

Statistics of crime for the year 1887, when the strength of the Metropolitan Police had risen to 14,081 and the cost to £1,302,492, showed an encouraging fall,[3] and for a while it seemed that Warren might be spared the kind of outbreak of civil disorder which had precipitated the resignation of his predecessor. But it was not to be.

During the late summer of 1887, many of London's vagrant population began to take up residence in Trafalgar Square. It was not so much a manifestation of the modern 'sit-in' as a kind of urban gypsy encampment. Charitable citizens, moved by this spectacle of squalor, provided bread-vans and soup-kitchens and soon the Square became an unofficial welfare centre. For a time the police were not disposed to interfere, but soon questions were being asked in the House, if only because the presence of this growing army of squatters in the heart of the Metropolis was a disagreeable advertisement for the Government's lack of social

[1] Howard, the old Superintendent of No. 1 District, and three ex-officers of the Army.

[2] There was one small but important concession to civil rights. In 1887 the police were given permission for the first time to vote in parliamentary elections, a right extended in 1893 to municipal elections.

[3] One statistic in Warren's Report reflects the change in social standards. In 1831, apprehensions for drunkenness and assault had been 31,353, or 20.57 per 1,000 of population. In 1887 the figure had fallen to 20,658, or 3.77 per 1,000 of population.

conscience. Nothing was done; and Warren was slow to recognize
the likelihood that a peaceful 'occupation' might quickly turn into
public disorder.

It was not long before political agitators were at work, with
banners, processions and much inflammatory oratory, until
Trafalgar Square was in a state of virtually permanent occupation
by an increasingly volatile mob. It was an intolerable as well as a
dangerous situation, and at last Warren moved. Early in October,
with the hesitant agreement of Matthews, he issued an order
banning all public meetings in the Square. It was widely ignored.
At once there were more questions in the House, and the perennial
issues of the right of assembly and freedom of speech which had
continued to exercise Parliament since the affair of John Wilkes
were debated with varying degrees of legal and historical accuracy
(no one seems to have remembered the Coldbath Fields inquiry).
Meanwhile, on the streets matters went from bad to worse.

On 8 November[1] Warren at last shamed Matthews into taking
decisive action and as a result a notice was issued stating that 'until
further intimation no further meetings will be allowed to assemble
in Trafalgar Square'. And this time the Commissioner was determined that the order would be enforced. The *Pall Mall Gazette*
was incensed. Referring to Warren as 'this soldier in jackboots', it
went on: 'It is a usurpation of the most insolent kind. Sir Charles
Warren has no more right in law to forbid the holding of public
meetings in Trafalgar Square than he has to close St. Paul's
Cathedral.'[2] But by now Warren was in the mood, if he could, to
close St Paul's. So far as he was concerned, where discipline was
involved there was not much difference between the natives of
Bechuanaland and the natives of Bethnal Green; and when a mass
meeting in the Square was announced for Sunday, 13 November,
he issued a final notice banning all organized processions from the
area.

The battle of Trafalgar Square was the most serious public con-

---

[1] On 2 November, Warren had written: 'It appears that the Commissioner of Police and the Secretary of State take a totally different view of
the state of affairs.' It was not surprising, for they were totally different—
and incompatible—men.

[2] This, from the same journal which had greeted Warren's appointment
the previous year with an eloquent description of 'a stern, just, incorrupt-
ible, religious man, a kind of belated Ironside [*sic*], born in a century
which has but scant sympathy with his Puritan ideals'.

frontation which the Metropolitan Police had faced in the sixty years of its existence. Over 2,000 men had cordoned off the area and as many again were held in strategic reserve at key points. They had been under severe strain for weeks and were now in no mood to trifle with the militants, and throughout the day a pitched battle continued, as large crowds of rioters attempted to force an entry into the Square (for the first time mounted police were used to support the foot constables). By mid-afternoon the defences had been breached at several points and Warren was obliged to call on a squadron of Life Guards and two companies of Foot Guards, while a magistrate, armed with the Riot Act, rode up Whitehall with a cavalry escort. In the event, there was no military intervention, but it was the first time since 1855 that soldiers had been called out in aid of the civil power. By 6 p.m. the situation was under control and even through, by good fortune, there had been no fatalities, Charing Cross Hospital had assumed the appearance of a casualty clearing-station. Sporadic rioting continued until the end of the month (23 November even saw 2,000 hooligans brawling inside Westminster Abbey) and it was not until 2 December that order was finally restored. By then it was time to take stock.

The police, provoked to the limit of their endurance, had emerged with much credit, and there was general public approval of their conduct and of their success in restoring a proper tranquillity to the heart of the Metropolis. Warren was unrepentant. He had done no more than his statutory duty, and the weak and often ambivalent support he had received from Matthews served only to widen the already unbridgeable gap between him and the Home Secretary. Meanwhile the constitutional lawyers took over, and for months a war of words was waged in Parliament and in the courts while learned—and some not so learned—luminaries argued the legal issues of freedom of assembly and the preservation of law and order (in a debate in March 1888, an MP made the charming observation that 'it was bad taste of the people of London to parade their insolent starvation in the face of the rich and trading portions of the town. They should have starved in their garrets.'). In the event Warren carried the day and the ban was extended until October 1888.[1]

[1] The powers of the Commissioner of Police in regard to public meetings and processions are now laid down by the Public Order Act 1936, and defined in Metropolitan Police General Orders, Sec. 49.

Warren's Report for 1887 dismissed the whole affair in a single, laconic sentence: 'During the Autumn attempts were made by unruly mobs to riot in the streets and Trafalgar Square, which proceedings were successfully coped with by the Police.' There seems little doubt that by now he had become obsessive about his relationship with the Home Office and there is equally little doubt that both Lushington, a devious man, and Pennefather, an aggressive one, encouraged Matthews to resist the Commissioner's determination to be sole master in his own house. More seriously, Warren—for much the same reasons—also fell out with Monro, the Assistant Commissioner in charge of the CID. The CID had always tended to be a law unto itself and Monro persisted in keeping open a direct and private channel with the Secretary of State and in dealing with the Home Office without reference to his statutory superior. Whatever Warren's faults, it was an impossible and provocative situation, and when, in August,[1] he decided to put a stop to it, Monro resigned and was replaced by Robert Anderson, who was chosen by no less than a Committee of the Cabinet and was probably the only suitable Daniel prepared to enter the lion's den of Scotland Yard.

Within four months, Warren himself had resigned. At the time it was widely thought that the issue which brought about his decision was the public concern over the Jack the Ripper murders which horrified—and fascinated—the citizens of the Metropolis during the months of October and November. But the true reason was a final collision with the Home Secretary over statutory control which prompted Warren to publish a caustic article in *Murray's Magazine* in which he defined the powers and duties of the Commissioner, criticized the attitude of the Home Secretary and his officials towards the police, and even challenged the Secretary of State's right to apply the regulations of the Official Secrets Act to himself or to any member of the force. It is scarcely conceivable that he took this step without fully accepting its implications. It was, in fact, a melodramatic act of resignation; and on 1 December 1888 he stepped down. Lushington could add a second scalp to his bureaucratic belt.

It is difficult to assess Charles Warren's true influence on the

---

[1] The same month (13 August) saw the passing of the Local Government Act which created the first County Councils including, significantly, the LCC.

history of the Metropolitan Police. He was unfortunate in the officials with whom he had to deal and he was not very clever in dealing with them. He was respected, if not liked, by his men, and their view of him is best summed up by a police sergeant, Thomas Dodd, who wrote a few years later: 'He was a hard man, but then he had a very hard responsibility.' After his resignation, which was widely regretted by both press and public, he returned to Army life, served without much distinction in the South African war, and, as if to give a mellow touch to an abrasive public life, joined Baden-Powell in 1908 to help form the Scout Movement.

*

Matthews did not make the same mistake as Childers; instead, he made a different one. He appointed James Monro as Commissioner.

On the evidence, Monro was an obvious choice. He had practical experience. He had shown, by his resignation, that he was not a 'Commissioner's man'. And he was not a soldier. But if Matthews thought that, by appointing a policeman who had enjoyed private access to his office, he would acquire a well-trained poodle, he was very wrong. Poodles have a habit of becoming terriers when let off the leash.

It did not take Monro long to discover that the view of the Home Office from the Commissioner's chair was very different from the one he had grown accustomed to at the CID, and that Matthews and Lushington in tandem were still the thorny obstacle that Warren had tried unsuccessfully to negotiate. Monro himself was a curiously contradictory character, part crusader, part parish priest, at once extrovert and introvert; and it was typical of his unpredictability that, after his resignation (a third scalp for Lushington), he departed to establish a medical mission in Bengal.

Above all, he was a professional policeman and his men were devoted to him. A present Home Office official has dismissed him as an 'ineffective ass'. He was not. He did much in his short time to establish police service as a professional career rather than a form of casual employment and he understood, as Rowan and Mayne had done, that without public acceptance the police were powerless. Some years later he wrote: 'The police are not the representatives of an arbitrary and despotic power. They are simply a disciplined body of men engaged in protecting "masses" as well as "classes" from any infringements on the part of those who are not law-abiding.' Henry Fielding would have liked that.

His nineteen months as Commissioner were marked by a sharp decline in crime statistics and by comparative peace and tranquillity in the Metropolis. There were demonstrations by the growing army of unemployed (the last decade of the nineteenth century was to be an unexpected—and largely forgotten—period of recession) and in the autumn of 1889 there was a major dock strike. Monro handled these problems with tact and efficiency, but he was constantly stretched for man-power and, like his two predecessors, his real battle was not on the streets of the Metropolis but in Whitehall. The issue for which he fought—and felt himself defeated—was police pensions.

The subject had been a major grievance ever since the formation of the force. The 1839 Act had established a superannuation fund and a scale of pensions which were purely discretionary and not payable under the age of sixty except on medical grounds, but the revenue to maintain the fund was never sufficient and by 1856 the capital was exhausted. Parliamentary authority was then granted for any deficiency to be met out of the Police Fund. In 1862, the pension scale was altered—in effect, reduced—to two-thirds of earnings after 28 years, two-fifths after 20 years, and three-tenths after 15 years. The discretionary principle remained.

In 1875, after much agitation, a Select Committee was set up to re-examine the whole state of police pensions. Two years later it recommended that pensions should be awarded as a matter of *right* after 25 years' service although the minimum age limit was retained. It also recommended that pensions should be a charge on the rates and it was on this issue that a Bill, introduced in 1882 (so slowly do the mills of bureaucracy grind), foundered. By 1889, when Monro had succeeded Warren, feeling in the force was running high.

A fight with the Home Office over the pensions issue greatly appealed to the crusader in Monro and he waged unrelenting warfare against the citadels of bureaucratic power, much to the gratification of his men and, one suspects, his own ego. Matthews even suspected him of deliberate subversion, and Anderson tells an amusing story of an occasion when he was asked privately by the Home Office to monitor a meeting of superintendents called by Monro to discuss new pension scales.[1]

[1] Anderson, *op. cit.*

By the spring of 1890, parliamentary draftsmen were at work on a new Bill and two wiser and more tactful men than Matthews and Lushington might sensibly have taken Monro into their confidence. But they did not do so; and Monro, convinced—wrongly as it proved—that the Home Office proposals would not meet his minimum demands, suddenly resigned. The parish priest in him had proved more decisive than the crusader.

*

It had been a critical period for the Metropolitan Police. After fifty-seven years of stability, three Commissioners had resigned within four years. The old order had changed and out of the smoke of battle had emerged, however surprisingly, a new kind of professionalism.

At the date of his resignation, Monro was presiding over a force of 14,995 men. But despite this expansion, the Metropolitan Police Office was still housed in Whitehall Place and Great Scotland Yard where the Receiver had year by year acquired every inch of available accommodation, and where offices, stairs and corridors were cluttered with a growing mountain of files and documents. The decision to move had been taken in 1886 and a site had been acquired on the newly-constructed Embankment. Monro did not survive to see the completion of this enterprise; but he did give it a name: New Scotland Yard.

CHAPTER SEVEN

New Scotland Yard

DURING HENDERSON'S commissionership, the expansion of the force and the pressure on accommodation in and around Great Scotland Yard—not least because of the loading of functions on the Metropolitan Police Office which had little to do with its proper role—had created a serious problem. Indeed, a modern industrial psychologist might argue that the frictions of the 1880s were due in part to the intolerable working conditions in what *The Times*, with a condescension born of the cloistered corridors of Printing House Square, described as 'a dingy collection of mean buildings' and 'a state of what, outside Scotland Yard, would be called hopeless confusion'. The solution was reached not without dust and heat, and by way of an interlude of Gilbertian absurdity.

In 1860, work had been started on the Victoria Embankment, which necessitated a massive exercise in land clearance and reclamation. Thus, when the new roadway between Westminster Bridge and Blackfriars was opened in 1868, it left a derelict and unsightly rectangle of swamp in the very shadow of Parliament; and so until the soil had dried and settled it remained, to London's shame and *Punch*'s sly delight; until the arrival, in 1875, of Colonel J. H. Mapleson.

The Colonel's grandiose vision was the building on this prime, if muddy, site of a National Opera House which would up-stage Covent Garden and even vie with the splendours of the Opéra in Paris. On 16 December, amid much pomp and circumstance, the Duke of Edinburgh laid the foundation stone. Thereafter there was no pomp but some embarrassing circumstances. Francis Fowler's elaborate design soon drained away Mapleson's limited subscription income and despite his optimistic forecast in *The Times* that £10,000 would complete the project, there were no more benevolent patrons of the arts to pay for the roof, and Mapleson's Grand National Opera House expired without even the last sad notes of a dying swan,[1] but with a mournful load of unpaid debts.

Henderson, meanwhile, had been waiting in the wings. Here was the perfect situation for the new headquarters which he so desperately needed; and on 16 April 1878 he addressed himself on the subject to the Home Office. He was not, after the Turf Frauds scandal, in the strongest position to press his claim and there is reason to think from the public records that he did not even receive a reply. But he was a persistent man; how persistent may be judged by the fact that it took him eight more years—indeed, until a few months before his resignation in 1886—to persuade the tight-fisted triumvirate of Childers, Lushington and Pennefather to accept his advice. By then they had to pay £186,000 for the land and its derelict building which could have been acquired for £25,000 six years earlier.[2] So much for good housekeeping.

It was thought that the Police Surveyor, Butler, would be put in charge of the project, but Matthews, who had by then succeeded Childers at the Home Office, decided that a major building on so prestigious a site required an architect of the highest public reputation; and accordingly he commissioned Norman Shaw.

Shaw was a curious choice. He was certainly eminent, a Royal Academician, and something of a cult figure. But his work had been concentrated first on neo-Gothic churches and subsequently on imposing country mansions of which Chesters and Bryanston[3] are the two most impressive examples. In London he had designed a number of town houses on Chelsea Embankment and suitably patrician offices for banks and insurance companies; but New Scotland Yard was the only public building to which he applied his Pre-Raphaelite talent, and it was to become one of the most celebrated, if controversial, landmarks in the Metropolis. It was also to prove quite inadequate to house the fast-growing Metropolitan Police Office, a fact to which Charles Warren, with shrewd if caustic foresight, drew attention when he saw the plans.

[1] The *Daily Telegraph* had earlier revealed that the house would open with a performance of *L'elisir d'amore*, which would have greatly flattered the shade of Donizetti.

[2] Butler to Drummond, 16 December 1880.

[3] 'The palatial expression of nobleness' says the *Dictionary of National Biography*, 'has nowhere in the 19th century been given such distinction as at Bryanston', which was Shaw's first commission to follow the opening of New Scotland Yard in 1890.

The central building of New Scotland Yard was a work *sui generis*. Shaw, who had once observed that 'the mind of an artist should be closed to all but his own intuitive judgement', did not enjoy his first public commission and was exasperated by having to accept continual interference from Whitehall committees and a succession of unwanted Job's comforters; but from his basic architectural concept he refused to depart, despite Warren's view that he was building a monument to the past rather than the future. The result was part mediaeval fortress, part French château, and quintessentially Victorian. A. P. Herbert neatly described it as 'a very constabulary kind of castle'.[1] Rank and status were reverently restricted to the two lower floors, aptly faced in granite quarried by Dartmoor convicts, and Shaw's concession to the proper dignity of public architecture ended at the Commissioner's turret office overlooking the river. Above that, by a simple inversion of the country-house principle, the lesser orders ascended in a maze of random rooms and corridors to the roof, and the present Reception Officer of New Scotland Yard recalls working many years later in a remote attic with a large water tank for company. The Superintendent of A Division at nearby Cannon Row must have watched the progress of events with some trepidation; and rightly so, for it was not long before this large and hungry neighbour began to swallow his surplus accommodation.[2]

The move to the new building was completed in December 1890, with the exception of the two unwanted waifs, the Public Carriage and Lost Property Offices, which remained at Great Scotland Yard until the following spring when they succeeded in storming the new citadel and laying claim, at least in part, to the accommodation allotted to them by Shaw. Since then they have always been the first two departments to be, so to speak, boarded out, chiefly because they bear a constant traffic of visitors whose business has little to do with the more serious duties of the Metropolitan Police Office.[3]

*

[1] By a macabre chance, the CID was put early to work, when preliminary excavation revealed the dismembered body of a young girl. The murder was never solved.

[2] In December 1890, the staff of the Metropolitan Police Office in fact only numbered 164.

[3] In 1891 the Lost Property Office handled, among a fascinating variety of articles, 14,212 umbrellas, four sets of dentures, and a stuffed badger.

Meanwhile events of a very different kind had been taking place. Monro's sudden resignation has been assumed to have taken everyone by surprise; but this cannot be so. His decision to go, submitted on 12 June—despite the knowledge that the Police Pensions Bill was to be published on the 17th—took effect from 21 June. Within forty-eight hours Matthews had appointed his successor, which, given the Home Secretary's indecisive nature and the history of the four previous years, scarcely looks like an unpremeditated act of impulse. Matthews was well aware of the growing discontent in the force and indeed had even suspected Monro's motives. It therefore seems, from the timetable of events, that he had taken precautionary measures; and this time he could not afford to be wrong.

The new Commissioner was Colonel Sir Edward Bradford, a distinguished cavalry officer and veteran of the Indian Mutiny.[1] His qualities of leadership and—unusual in a senior soldier of Victoria's army—his administrative ability led to his being seconded in 1874 to the Indian political service, and since 1887 he had been head of the political and secret departments of the India Office in London. Thus, by the summer of 1890, he was well-known in the corridors of Whitehall. In choosing him, Matthews took a calculated risk. There was a strong feeling among the rank and file that Monro had been victimized for his support of their grievances[2] and Bradford's appointment was considered by many to be provocative. But the situation needed a man of decision, and Bradford's known qualities, not so unlike those of Charles Rowan, ensured that at least he would not be another Warren. He did not have to wait long to demonstrate those qualities.

Pensions were not the sole grievance of the Metropolitan—nor, indeed, of the provincial—Police. There had been no increase in rates of pay since the trouble in 1872; and a hard core of militants, encouraged by outside agitators, was pressing once more for the 'right to confer', and for the formation of a police union. These men were a small but vocal minority for whom pay and conditions of service were no more than important factors in achieving their political ends.

---

[1] In the tradition of a true Henty hero, his left arm had been amputated —without anaesthetic—after an encounter with a tiger.

[2] In several divisions the men went so far as to organize a collection on his behalf.

By 23 June, the day on which Bradford took office, the terms of the proposed Pensions Bill were already known and had met with general approval. That same afternoon the militants decided to act and there was trouble when a sergeant and a constable in M Division (Southwark) were suspended for disobedience to orders. By early evening, delegates from seven divisions had gathered in Bow Street—the now traditional rallying-point of dissident opinion —and there was a noisy demonstration. Bradford, although barely installed at Whitehall Place, was quick to counter these signs of indiscipline and at once instructed superintendents to ban any further meetings. There was a pause while both sides considered the next move.

On 28 June a petition was delivered to the Commissioner's office on behalf of the rank and file (a similar petition was signed by inspectors). It was moderate in tone and—since the Pensions Bill had largely pre-empted this particular grievance—dwelt instead on the question of pay, leave and hours of duty. Since for the first time the matter of comparability was raised, the form of this petition is interesting: 'We, the undersigned, most respectfully ask that our weekly pay may be increased to the labour market value, which is at the present time at least 15 per cent higher than we are receiving. Besides being underpaid as compared with ordinary workmen, our conditions of living and abode are different and more expensive than those of workmen.' The signatories did not suggest that they were 'a special case' but only that there was a distinction, in social terms, between policemen and labourers. Peel's wrong-headed preference for 'a three shillings a day man' to 'a five shilling a day man' was coming home to roost. Wisely, the petition did not mention the wider political issue or the right to confer; and on 1 July Bradford replied that he would give sympathetic consideration to the men's views.

But the militancy remained. Perhaps too hastily, Bradford transferred one of the leading trouble-makers from E Division and on Saturday, 5 July, he refused to meet a delegation on the reasonable grounds that since there was no legally authorized negotiating body, the delegation was not representative of anyone. That evening, 130 men at Bow Street refused duty until an inspector undertook to refer their demands, including the right to form a union, to higher authority. Bradford at once showed a firmness which Henderson, in similar circumstances, had not, and the following day the thirty-nine ring-leaders were paraded individually before him at Bow Street. Each was informed that his action had made him liable to prosecution, that he was unfit to be a policeman; and each was summarily dismissed. The remaining ninety-one men were transferred to other divisions.

Bradford's action effectively defused the situation. The following day, professional agitators took over briefly, in search of some political advantage. There were brave invocations to social revolution and from the security of a public house in Long Acre the former constables sent a telegram to the Home Secretary threatening a general police strike, an empty gesture which even Matthews could afford to ignore. It was an occasion which the riotous English enjoy and by evening they were duly rioting in Bow Street, and there was a pitched battle with mounted police supported presently by two troops of Life Guards. By midnight, order had been restored.

The troubled summer of 1890 was to prove the beginning of perhaps the most tranquil period in the history of the Metropolitan Police. After the stormy 1880s, there followed a decade of consolidation and modest reform. In one important regard, these years are a milestone, for they mark the emergence of the police, both in the Metropolis and in the provinces, as a fully-fledged public service. 'There was,' writes Critchley, 'a spirit of change that was converting a job into a vocation.' In London responsibility for irksome duties like smoke abatement and the inspection of common lodging-houses was transferred to the new municipal authority, and to their principal purpose of crime prevention the police were now able to add a new kind of social service to the public. That special relationship by which Charles Rowan had laid such store was fast becoming a reality. Bradford himself understood the need for what he called 'a period of recuperation' after the years of stress and above all a healing of old wounds caused by civil war with Whitehall.[1] In a way, Norman Shaw's baronial hall seemed to symbolize the new spirit of solid respectability.

The Police Act became law on 14 August 1890. It did not meet the demands of the men in full (the economic climate ruled out the

[1] With the fall of Salisbury's Government in 1892, Henry Matthews departed from the Home Office. He was succeeded by Herbert Asquith, his first ministerial appointment, in Gladstone's last administration.

augmentation of the force which alone would have made possible an extension of leave and weekly rest-days, and the agitation for a police union was quietly dropped), but it did provide modest pay increases and, more significantly, it established a wholly new system of pensions, properly funded and administered.

The Act, which applied to all police forces in England and Wales (itself a sign of the times), allowed police authorities a measure of flexibility within a prescribed maximum and minimum. In the Metropolitan Police, the rules were laid down as follows:

1. All members of the force were given the legal right to a pension, without medical certificate, after twenty-five years' service and without age qualification.

2. If, after fifteen years' service, a man was discharged on medical grounds, he was entitled to a modified pension.

3. If, before completing fifteen years' service, a man was discharged on medical grounds, the Commissioner, at his discretion, could grant him a gratuity.

4. If, at any time, a man was medically discharged through injuries received in the execution of his duty, he was entitled to a modified pension.

5. The widows and children of police officers dying from whatever cause during their service were covered by a system of pensions or gratuities.

6. The maximum rates of pension were: two-thirds pay after twenty-six years, or three-fifths pay after twenty-five years. The rates for men discharged before completing twenty-five years were scaled down *pro rata*.

To fund this superannuation scheme an Exchequer grant of £300,000 was authorized, divided equally between the Metropolitan Police and provincial forces,[1] and the Act laid down that any shortfall was to be met out of police revenues.

It was by any standard a generous scheme, even if its cash value was dependent on police pay maintaining its level in the labour market; and if these were indeed the terms included in the draft Bill, it is difficult to understand why Monro chose this issue over which to resign. In his subsequent writings he never referred to the subject again.

[1] The Local Taxation (Customs and Excise) Act 1890. With unconscious irony the source of revenue was the excise duty on beer and spirits.

Bradford at once set about mending fences. He could safely assume that Matthews and his officials would avoid any further risk of confrontation and in turn he accepted without protest that the establishment of the force had of necessity to be restricted virtually to its existing size. The one small, if ominous, cloud to appear on the horizon was the recommendation of a Royal Commission in 1894 that the police of the Metropolis should come under the control of the new municipal authority. The argument of the London County Council was that, unlike the other counties with their standing joint committees established under the 1888 Act, the ratepayers of the capital had no direct control of the police force to whose cost they contributed so substantially. It was an argument which has since been rehearsed many times, and the government answer has remained the same: namely that, precisely because London *is* the capital city,[1] there are exceptional reasons, both national and 'imperial', for control of the Metropolitan Police to be vested in the Home Secretary. No such argument justified the continuing independence of the City of London Police.

Bradford was quick to take advantage of the new climate of opinion created by the Police Act, and within a year of taking office he had personally visited every station in his District and had listened courteously to the men's problems. It was something that not even Charles Rowan had done and it was yet another indication of slowly changing attitudes both towards and within the service. The results may be seen in successive Commissioner's Reports during the period. Each year new police stations were built and others improved; accommodation was modernized; beats were altered and communications extended; lighter-weight uniforms were provided for summer wear; sport and recreation were encouraged, despite the limited leisure time available.

Bradford also managed to make a virtue out of necessity. With the establishment of the force pegged, other than for exceptional reasons, he could afford to be more selective in his recruiting policy. To take the year 1896 at random, total wastage from all causes—retirement, resignations and dismissals (at 59, the lowest yet recorded)—was down to 805 all ranks. For over sixty years, as the force grew, successive Commissioners had been obliged to accept a high proportion of applicants in whom brawn was more

---

[1] No less to the point, the then County of London represented only one-sixth of the Metropolitan Police District.

noticeable than brain and whose level of illiteracy[1] was a constant cause for concern, except to the editors of *Punch* and *Judy*. Now Bradford could at least aim at higher standards even if the pay structure still lagged behind the labour market. And early in 1893 he found support from an unexpected quarter.

*

The previous year, one John Kempster, reflecting upon the virtual isolation of the police service from the rest of society, decided to start a journal. 'I saw,' he explained later, 'that they [the police] needed a paper that would ventilate their troubles, advocate their interests, and assist their better education.' And on 2 January 1893 there appeared the first issue of the *Police Review and Parade Gossip: The Organ of the British Constabulary* (weekly, at six shillings a year, post free).

It was an event to which too little attention has been paid. Not only did Kempster address himself to the police service on a *national* basis, but he provided a forum which would have been unthinkable before the 1890 Act. What Charles Warren's reaction would have been requires no imagination.

In his first leader, Kempster wrote: 'It seems hardly creditable that there should hitherto have been no newspaper of metropolitan or national rank specially devoted to the entertainment or instruction of policemen, or to the advocacy of their interests . . . The policeman is not to be regarded as a mere chattel or machine: he is a man and a citizen.' And he proceeded to set the tone. 'Our first number partakes somewhat of the holiday nature of the season.' 'Gossip Notes' administered an imperial snub to Arthur Conan Doyle, and contained a jolly account of the E Division (Bow Street) Annual Ball—'the great hall filled by a brilliant gathering of dancers, ladies and gentlemen in well-balanced numbers [*sic*]'.

Within a month, the idea had caught on. 'Now that we have our own "society" newspaper . . .' wrote one reader, while a constable from Wandsworth promised: 'I shall certainly push it all in my power.' Soon the correspondence columns were busy, the letters at first cautiously anonymous but presently over open signatures.

---

[1] This largely explains the almost total absence of 'constabulary' archive material from the early years.

Kempster, primarily concerned to entertain and instruct,[1] was quick to allay the suspicions of higher authority by printing each week an adulatory profile of a chief officer of police, starting with Bradford. He was to prove over the years a good friend of the service, (though not of the Establishment) and today the *Police Review*, with a circulation of 34,000, is the most influential organ of comment and opinion in police journalism.

It was a quiet decade in the Metropolis, reflecting the long Victorian sunset. In this Bradford was more fortunate than his predecessors, but much of the credit for the climate of comparative tranquillity belonged to the police themselves. In the divisions, superintendents more than ever were absolute lords of their 'manors', and senior officers at New Scotland Yard wisely interfered as little as possible in the conduct of routine duties, even though district chief constables found occasion to complain to the Commissioner that they were under-worked.

Under Robert Anderson the CID, now 800 strong, had grown in both numbers and experience, although in the process the division between uniform and detective branches—initiated by Vincent and sustained by Monro—remained a continuing source of discontent. In 1896, criminal offences in the Metropolis fell to 18,536, the lowest figure yet recorded, and convictions rose by 18 per cent. It was an equation that was soon to be reversed. And in a period which saw the appearance of the first great 'theatrical' attorneys, there were many celebrated cases which illustrate the hazardous minefield through which the executive arm of the law has had to pick its way: Neill Cream, the compulsive poisoner who, despite persistent efforts to incriminate himself, failed to engage the interest of the CID until he had murdered seven women; Fowler and Milsom, the Muswell Hill murderers, who were brought to justice by a classic example of patient detective investigation; and Adolf Beck, whose melancholy fate was to cast a long shadow forward to our own time. His case has a special place in police history.

In 1877 a man calling himself 'Lord Willoughby' fraudulently

---

[1] The 'Nutshell News' column must have puzzled many of his readers, with items like: 'The Emperor of Bokhara is visiting Russia'; or, with a nod towards John Boyd Dunlop: 'An omnibus with pneumatic tyres is running in Glasgow.'

divested a woman of a considerable quantity of jewellery by passing her a bogus cheque. He was in due course arrested and, in the improbable name of John Smith, sentenced to penal servitude. In 1884, he was released on licence. The date is important.

In 1885, Adolf Beck, a Norwegian citizen, arrived in London from Peru where he had been engaged in various business enterprises. For ten years—the time-gap again is important—he lived a somewhat tenuous existence first at the Covent Garden Hotel and then at a hotel in the Strand. By the summer of 1895 he was living in Victoria Street where, on 20 December, he was confronted by a Mme Meissonier who, in the presence of a police constable, accused him of being the man who had defrauded her of money and jewellery. Beck was taken into custody.

The details of the charge strongly recalled the case of John Smith in 1877. At a series of identity parades ten out of twenty-three victims of similar frauds confirmed that Beck was the swindler. A hand-writing 'expert' compared Beck's specimens with those of Smith and declared them to be identical.[1] And the police constable who had arrested Smith *eighteen years earlier* emerged from retirement to identify positively that he and Beck were one and the same person.

Beck was sent for trial, found guilty of obtaining money under false pretences, and sentenced to seven years' penal servitude. The proceedings were a travesty of justice, since Beck's defending counsel was forbidden to raise the issue of mistaken identity or to point out the not immaterial fact that throughout the whole period of the Smith affair, the defendant had been in South America. In the eyes of the Common Serjeant and of Mr Horace Avory, the prosecuting counsel, the fact that Beck was Smith was not in dispute. In Portland Prison he was even given Smith's old number.

Through his lawyer, Dutton, Beck continued to protest his innocence and petitioned repeatedly for a rehearing of his case. Then, in 1898, evidence emerged—conclusive in the matter of identity—that Smith, a Jew, was circumcised while Beck was not. Incredibly, the Home Office, on the grounds that Beck in his own person had been properly convicted of fraud, refused a re-trial and graciously noted the establishment of Beck's true identity by

---

[1] E. R. Watson: *The Trial of Adolf Beck*, which contains many specimens of both Smith's and Beck's handwriting which in no way resemble each other.

giving him a new prison number. In 1901 he was released on licence. It was by no means the end of his story.

Three years later, five women complained, over a period of two months, that they had been defrauded of money and jewellery. In each case the circumstances were so similar to those of the frauds for which Beck had been convicted in 1896 that he was remanded in custody. All five complainants identified him. No one noticed—or remembered—that to one victim the swindler had introduced himself as 'Lord Willoughby', the 1877 alias of John Smith. And even the Home Office accepted that Beck was not Smith, while concealing the evidence in its possession.

Beck stood trial for the second time on 27 June and was again found guilty. But—and it was the one stroke of fortune to befall this unfortunate man—the trial judge, Mr Justice Grantham, had some residual doubts about the case and postponed sentence. Ten days later a William Thomas was arrested in the act of pawning some items of jewellery which he had obtained by what was now an immediately recognizable form of fraud. His letter to one of his victims was shown to be in the same hand as the incriminatory documents of 1877, 1895 and 1904. For John Smith, alias 'Lord Willoughby', it was the end of the road.

On 19 July Beck was released from prison. He was given a free pardon and, grudgingly, a sum of £5,000 in compensation. He died in 1909, a broken and dissolute man. After his release, a committee published its findings. The police were exonerated of any blame for wrongful arrest, although Anderson and Bradford had certainly been seriously at fault in refusing Beck's lawyer access to John Smith's records. The Home Office and the prison authorities were sharply rebuked for their conduct, and the Common Serjeant was criticized for his mishandling of the first trial. It was small comfort to Adolf Beck.

The Beck case is important not only because of the light it throws on the judicial procedures and Home Office attitudes of the day, but because it raises in a particularly dramatic way the critical issue of positive identification in criminal proceedings. At the inquiry after Beck's final release, the Master of the Rolls commented on the unreliability of evidence as to identity based on personal impressions, 'unless supported by other facts'. At the time of Beck's first trial scientific aids such as anthropometry and the analysis of blood samples already existed, and three years before he stood trial for the second time the one infallible means of identification had been introduced. But none of these aids was applied. It was Beck's fate to be the victim of an arrogant, perverse and wilful determination to see that justice was not done. He was by no means the last man to pay a harsh price for the fallibility of human judgement.

The end of the century is a convenient point at which to take stock.

In 1800, when the Metropolis was in a state of anarchy, Patrick Colquhoun had estimated that the preservation of law and order in a capital city with a population of 1,000,000 effectively devolved upon the 117 peace officers at the public offices and the 80 permanent officers of the Marine Police, and that the only means of countering public disorder was military intervention. Prevention of crime was no more than a pious objective and the 'new science of police' was little understood.

Within thirty years Peel's Act had brought the Metropolitan Police into existence, and by 1830 the force consisted of 3,314 men covering an area of 100 square miles and organized into seventeen divisions at an annual cost of £207,481.

By 1900 the population of the Metropolitan Police District had grown to 6,576,648 and covered an area of 700 square miles. The force, organized into twenty-one land divisions and the Thames Division, totalled 15,847 men at an annual cost of £1,635,270. Since the Municipal Corporations Act of 1835, the 178 boroughs of England and Wales had been required to create police forces on the Metropolitan pattern, while the Acts of 1839 and 1856 had extended the process to the counties, at first on a voluntary and then on a compulsory basis.

It was a period of unprecedented social and political change, of vast urban growth and scientific advance. In 1800, the country was fighting for its life. A hundred years later it was involved in a punitive expedition which had become a disastrous war. The electric telegraph had replaced the 'running man' as a means of rapid communication; the locomotive had superseded the stage-coach. The very pace of crime itself had accelerated; and the last decade of the century had seen the appearance of the motor-car and had brought a new dimension to urban traffic problems.[1]

[1] The initial speed limit of 4 m.p.h. was increased, in 1896, to the horrendous figure of 14 m.p.h. In 1900 the statistics for street accidents in

Yet in a curiously English way, much was unchanged. The London disease remained; and the Metropolitan Police, despite its growth in numbers, its new distinctive uniform, and its right to grow all manner of whiskers, was still a kind of urban peasantry, largely illiterate, grossly underpaid, and balanced precariously on the tightrope of public opinion. That it existed at all was due solely to the devoted efforts of Rowan and Mayne in its infant years, and to the long line of superintendents, who, for all their faults, had followed the basic principles laid down in the General Instruction Book of 1829. There had been dramas and scandals, and there were many more to come. But the tiny seed planted by Henry Fielding had taken root and grown. The private dream had become a public institution.

In 1901, Robert Anderson retired as head of the CID. His reason, according to his own account, was 'a strong desire for a more restful life', but it is possible that his decision was hastened by an increasing disenchantment with the Commissioner. Like Mayne and Henderson before him, Bradford had stayed too long. The deceptive calm which followed the 1890 mutiny encouraged him to adopt a passive attitude to events and the man of action had become the lotus-eater for whom it was always tomorrow afternoon. But now, with the end of the South African war and a growing army of unemployed organizing street-collections throughout the capital, Bradford became obsessed by the spectre of those public disorders which had caused the downfall of Henderson. Rather than risk a confrontation, he chose to let matters drift, and the feeling of insecurity rubbed off on his subordinates and on his men.

The Home Secretary, Ritchie, could read the signs and in seeking a replacement for Anderson he sensibly looked for a man who would be capable of succeeding Bradford at short notice. He turned once more to the Indian Police service.

Edward Henry was a professional with long experience in Bengal and later in South Africa. His appointment was therefore a reversion to the system of checks and balances which had produced characters as different—and as temperamental—as Warren and Monro. But Henry was not only a man of outstanding calibre; he also brought with him to Scotland Yard an innovation which was

the Metropolis were: 158 killed, 8,010 injured. Seventy-five years later deaths and injuries totalled 64,918.

to revolutionize the whole science of identification and detection and which would, at a stroke, have saved Adolf Beck from the malice and ignorance of his persecutors.

The use of finger prints as evidence of identity is as old as pre-literate society itself, but not until the nineteenth century does it seem to have had any application in the context of criminal proceedings. The reason is partly a lack of scientific expertise but also, if more cynically, a lack of concern with the ethics of innocence or guilt. Tyburn accepted its daily diet of victims without asking any questions.

The study of scientific means of establishing positive, rather than visual, identification in criminal cases followed two different tracks. In France, Alphonse Bertillon introduced in 1880 his anthropometric system, based on the measurement of certain individual bone structures and physical features which do not change after adolescence, and used in conjunction with photography, itself an imprecise method of identification. *Bertillonage*, as it came to be called, was slow, complicated, and by no means infallible. Its chief weakness was the obvious fact that it was only a comparative system and valueless except in cases of previously convicted offenders or of habitual criminals. But in the absence of any other scientific method, it filled a vacuum and it was used by Scotland Yard during the 1880s, with little enthusiasm and less success. It also met with strong reservations in the courts. In Paris, the system prospered.

There was, however, another scientific method. In Bengal (the origin of so much police innovation) Sir William Herschel, an Indian civil servant, had studied the individual characteristics of finger and palm prints and in 1858 had developed a system of recording such prints as a means of preventing corruption and personation in documents admitted to the Register of Admissions. Like many pioneers, he was ahead of his time, and his conviction that he had stumbled upon a method of identification with wide implications in the criminal field was quietly buried by the bureaucracy in Calcutta.

But not in London. There, Herschel's work was noted by Francis Galton, a student of genetics; and Galton, the scientist, took over from Herschel, the civil servant.

Galton's signal contributions to the science of dactyloscopy were his systematic study of individual ridge patterns in digital prints (he put the odds against the occurrence of identical prints in any two persons at 1 in 64,000 million), and his discovery of the law of 'persistence' which confirmed that the patterns of prints remain unchanged in every individual from birth to death. Thus he developed what had been for Herschel an administrative convenience into a positive, though not yet infallible, means of identification; and while *bertillonage* was only applicable in the case of convicted felons, Galton's research provided the police with a new and vital weapon at actual scenes of crime. What his system lacked was a simple and effective means of classification.

In 1892 Galton published his findings and the following year the new Home Secretary, Asquith, set up a committee to consider the best means available for identifying habitual criminals. The committee was impressed by Galton's evidence but doubtful of its acceptance in criminal proceedings; and in due course it recommended the introduction of a compromise system based chiefly on Bertillon and to a much lesser degree on Galton. Thus, in a sense, it was to be Adolf Beck's misfortune that he was not a habitual criminal, for the system then would have established his undoubted innocence of the crime for which he was convicted.

*

Meanwhile in Bengal Edward Henry was applying himself to the one underlying weakness of both the Herschel and Galton systems —the lack of a simple primary means of classification, without which the science of dactyloscopy was virtually unworkable as a practical method of positive identification. By 1898 he had arrived at an ingenious—and infallible—series of mathematical formulae which eliminated those problems to which the 1894 Committee had objected. His findings were published in 1900 in his classic study *Classification and Uses of Fingerprints.*[1]

By 1899 it was clear that the *bertillonage* experiment was a failure for in that year there were fewer than 450 'recognitions' by anthropometry. A second committee was accordingly appointed under Lord Belper to examine the whole problem of identification. By a fortunate coincidence Henry was on leave in London at this moment and had been invited to address the British Association at

[1] For a clear and concise exposition of a highly complicated subject, see also Frederick R. Cherrill, *The Finger Print System at Scotland Yard* (HMSO).

Dover on his practical experience of finger-printing in India. So great an impression did he make upon his audience that, when the Belper Committee met the following year, he was called before it. His evidence remains a model of how to explain a highly technical subject to a group of sceptical laymen. No one could any longer doubt that his system, and especially his method of classification, was a significant advance on Bertillon and, within certain limits, potentially infallible.[1] Not only was it indispensable in maintaining accurate criminal records but, as we have seen, it was a completely novel aid to detection at scenes of crime. The time would come when it would even be used to carry out identification by elimination on a massive scale.[2]

The Belper Committee duly recommended the immediate adoption of Henry's system. To his credit, Galton, far from feeling that his thunder had been stolen, strongly supported its findings. And in 1901, on the retirement of Sir Robert Anderson, Henry was appointed Assistant Commissioner 'C' at New Scotland Yard.

*

He took over on 31 May (Bradford, increasingly isolated in his turret office, seems barely to have noticed his arrival beyond the customary announcement in Police Orders for that date) and at once set about the formidable task of creating what was virtually an entirely new department—the Central Finger Print Bureau. But that, he realized, was not enough. Finger prints were not, by themselves, a magic formula for detecting offenders, but only a scientific means of identification (in his 1904 Report he referred to them for the first time as 'corroborative evidence') and accordingly he remodelled the cumbersome Register of Habitual Criminals, adapted it to his new system of finger-printing, and created the Criminal Record Office (CRO).

The second half of 1901 was necessarily a transitional period, while the recommendations of the Belper Committee were implemented. Henry chose three experienced CID officers to supervise

---

[1] In fact, it was not until the passing of the Criminal Justice Act in 1948 that finger prints alone were accepted as sufficient proof of a previous conviction (section 38).

[2] The first classic example was the case of June Devaney in May 1948, when virtually the entire male population of Blackburn was finger-printed in order to establish the identity of the murderer, Peter Griffiths.

the new Bureau,[1] and the relevant section of Bradford's report for that year (clearly written by Henry) noted that, of 503 'recognitions', 410 were attributable to anthropometry and 93 to finger prints. It was the last reference to *bertillonage* and Henry confidently predicted that the new system would show 'a threefold increase' during the following year. In the event, 1902 recorded 1,722 finger-print identifications; 1903 (by which time 60,000 sets of prints had been registered[2]) showed 3,642; and 1904 showed 5,155. Henry could report that this figure was 'ten times larger than the highest figures secured by the anthropometric system'. As a footnote to history, the first conviction directly attributable to Henry's Bureau was in 1902 when Harry Jackson, a professional burglar, obligingly left a perfect palm print on some wet paint at the scene of the crime; while the Farrow murders in March 1905, and the subsequent arrest and conviction of the Stratton brothers, are the first classic example of dactyloscopy—in this case a thumb print on a cash box—working in conjunction with the new register of habitual criminals to provide 'corroborative evidence' of guilt. From now on, no criminal could feel safe from the results of his own negligence.

*

On 4 March 1903, Bradford retired. An exchange of letters with the Home Office a month earlier suggests that had he not chosen to jump, he would certainly have been pushed; and the following day the heir-apparent, Henry, was appointed Commissioner.[3] He was to prove one of the five outstanding occupants of that office.

Thirteen years earlier Bradford had set out to mend fences. Henry was at once faced by the need for radical change, for by 1903 the force was seriously under strength (a situation imposed on Bradford after the 1890 Police Act but one which he made no

[1] Their names deserve to be recorded: Stedman, Stockley Collins, and Hunt.

[2] At the date of Henry's resignation as Commissioner in 1918, the register of prints stood at 283,000. In 1978, it had grown to 2,500,000, representing no less than 25,000,000 single prints.

[3] He was succeeded as Assistant Commissioner 'C' by Melville (later Sir Melville) Macnaghten who had been Chief Constable, CID, since 1890.

attempt to rectify during his last years) and morale was low. To
the twin problems of quantity and quality Henry now addressed
himself. Within six months he had obtained Home Office sanction
for an additional 1,600 men and the money for four new section-
houses and additional married quarters. The processions which
had been so great a cause for concern to Bradford were disposed of
by the simple method of regulating street-collections; and regular
visits to divisions by the new Commissioner revived the flagging
spirits of the rank and file.

Quality was another matter. Henry was quick to realize that the
policing of the Metropolis in the new mechanical age required
different techniques and a professional expertise such as he had
introduced into the CID, and that the day of the Victorian Dogberry had vanished with the changing social and political climate
of the new century.[1]

For over seventy years no attempt of any kind had been made to
train police recruits. It might be thought that Rowan, the Shorncliffe veteran, would have made this the cornerstone of efficiency,
but during the early struggle for survival and the years of high
wastage, there was time only for elementary drill. There were no
qualified instructors and few men with adequate standards of
education. A constable was therefore left to learn his trade on the
beat—and that, despite all modern refinements, still remains the
unrivalled training-ground.

Early in 1902, with the establishment of his Finger Print
Bureau, Henry started a small training-school for detectives at
New Scotland Yard. It was used largely as a means of testing the
suitability of applicants for the CID, but also for refresher courses
in new techniques. On 17 July Henry sent a memorandum to
Bradford proposing the extension of his successful experiment to
recruits for the uniform branch. There is no trace of any comment
or reply, for by then Bradford was unable or unwilling to support
so novel a proposition; and it was not until May 1907 that the first
Police Training School was opened at Peel House in Westminster.
It was perhaps the most far-reaching of all Henry's reforms, for at
last it was possible to institute a system of selection, to set a proper
minimum standard of education, and to equip suitable recruits
with a knowledge of their work beyond the bare bones of the

[1] It is from Henry's time that the oldest surviving Metropolitan Police
pensioners date.

General Instruction Book. Now, as the force continued to grow, Henry could begin to match quality to quantity.[1]

The growth of the force had been marked elsewhere during that year, when Scotland House was opened on the south side of New Scotland Yard and linked to it by a bridge spanning a public right of way. As Warren had foreseen, Shaw's building was quite inadequate for its purpose, especially with the introduction of space-consuming departments like the Finger Print Bureau and the CRO, but despite years of discussion, work on the new extension was not started until 1905. By then Shaw had virtually retired and was disinclined in any event to involve himself again with Whitehall committees. Accordingly, the work was entrusted to the police surveyor, Butler, who, with less space at his disposal, wisely elected to match Shaw's design with an identical, if slightly truncated, building; and in March the Receiver (still Pennefather and still independent of the Commissioner's Office) moved in with his staff and six assorted police departments.

*

But the old Adam was already at work again.

The English have an infinite capacity for melodrama, not least when they are persuaded—whether by politicians or the press—that liberties are being taken with personal liberty itself. In 1887, the public uproar over the wrongful arrest of the virginal Miss Cass on a charge of soliciting had even brought about the defeat of the Government. Now, in May 1906, the arrest of the far-from-virginal Mme D'Angely set in train a concerted assault upon the methods and conduct of the Metropolitan Police, the absurdity of which was equalled only by its viciousness.

Briefly, on the night of 1 May a Frenchwoman calling herself Eva D'Angely was arrested in Regent Street for 'riotous and indecent behaviour'. She was, in fact, a common prostitute, but a consummate actress with a well-rehearsed cover story and a convenient 'husband'; and the charge against her was dismissed by the magistrate's court.

Once again, as in the past, a small spark ignited a bonfire of indignation, fuelled by mindless prejudice and wild assumptions.

---

[1] Recruit training and the detective training school were transferred to the Hendon complex shortly after the Second World War. Today Peel House houses the offices of the Secretariat.

It was Henry's misfortune that early in 1906 a Liberal Government had been returned with a massive majority, and history had shown, from the days of Melbourne and Duncannon, that the police were a prime target for so-called 'Liberal progressives'. Now the Government took the extraordinary—and provocative—step of setting up a Royal Commission (the first since 1855) to inquire into the handling of 'street offences'—prostitution, drunken and disorderly behaviour, and betting. The decision was provocative since the terms of reference restricted the inquiry solely to the conduct of the Metropolitan Police. Henry must have been sorely tempted to treat the matter as an issue of confidence.

The Commission did not report until two years later. Within days of its first meeting, it was inundated with letters and postcards alleging police perjury, corruption and brutality, 'often in language both intemperate and illiterate'. From this distasteful midden, it chose nineteen oddly assorted cases of alleged police misconduct (Mme D'Angely was asked to travel from Paris, expenses paid, to give evidence, an invitation which she prudently ignored).

The Commission sat for sixty-four days over a period of eleven months (which scarcely suggests any great sense of urgency) and heard evidence both for and against the police. The minutes of those meetings, which fill 1,258 printed pages, are revealing in two senses: they show increasing impatience on the part of the Commission with the long succession of 'prosecution' witnesses and with the threadbare quality of most of their evidence; and they provide a striking commentary on the social *mores* of Edwardian London.

In its Report the Commission exonerated the Metropolitan Police as a whole of virtually every charge of corruption and malpractice and declared that, far from harassing street offenders, uniform constables were even, in Rowan's memorable phrase, 'kind and conciliating' towards many of them. There had been only nine instances of reprehensible conduct, but—and it was perhaps the first public acknowledgement of the fact—policemen were, it accepted, as subject *as any other citizen* to the frailties of human nature. 'The Metropolitan Police Force,' the Report concluded, 'is entitled to the confidence of all classes of the community.'

It was a resounding vindication, firmly reinforced by *The Times* on 1 July 1908. Above all—and this has not been said before—it was a tribute to the Commissioner, for the result was a reflection of his own pursuit of higher standards in a service which had for so long been vulnerable to public criticism.[1] Much remained to be done and old prejudices die hard.

*

'The police service the Edwardians inherited,' writes Critchley, 'was leaderless and lacked inspiration; the men were groping for a sense of unity and means of corporate expression; the nature of police work, more demanding than ever before, called for higher qualities.'[2] This was especially true in the Metropolis where the Victorian caste system had maintained a strict division between leaders and led. The men no longer took this for granted, and a recently retired police sergeant, Thomas Payne, giving evidence before the 1908 Select Committee on weekly rest-days, spoke his mind. Asked for his views on the command structure of the Metropolitan Police, he replied: 'I am at a loss to understand what earthly good the [District] Chief Constables are. I think the duties could be easily performed by the Superintendents.' Henry understood the problem, but the Home Office, where even at this date no police department yet existed, did not.

The search for some kind of trade union remained a vague but insistent aspiration; but the immediate concern of the men, grossly overworked throughout the country, was for some respite from their intolerable hours of duty in a society which elsewhere accepted the virtues of regulated leisure. They were to find a resolute champion in John Kempster.

The files of the *Police Review* over a long period illustrate how strongly policemen felt on this issue; and while allowing for the vagaries of human nature, it is not difficult to see why. 'Even convicts,' wrote one correspondent, 'are given time for recreation.' Sometimes the letters demonstrate a nice sense of logic. Thus 'Albino', writing on 22 June 1906, complained that while some fortunate men were given two days off in seven to play cricket ('a useless pastime'), no time was allowed for practising swimming

---

[1] The institution of the King's Medal for acts of gallantry or particularly meritorious service, gazetted in Police Orders of 15 July 1909, owed much to Henry's initiative. He himself headed the list of the nine first recipients in the Metropolitan Police in November that year.

[3] Critchley, *op. cit.*

('a valuable skill by which members may be enabled to save lives').

Kempster conducted a vigorous campaign inside and outside Parliament, and although he probably did not know it at the time, he was the first man to express the corporate view of a dissatisfied police service without recourse to the self-defeating militancy which had marked the mutinies of 1872 and 1890 (the men's gratitude was shown by the organizing of a testimonial fund on his behalf). His efforts were rewarded by the setting-up of a Select Committee on 13 May 1908 to consider the feasibility of allowing the rank and file one rest-day in seven, the same proposition which Colonel Henderson had found so intractable nearly forty years before.

Predictably, the opposition to what was no more than a matter of common justice and wise management came from the Home Office which took refuge behind the hackneyed barricade of 'guardianship of the public purse'. An official spokesman did his neat sums and declared that in the Metropolis alone the granting of a weekly rest-day would require an augmentation of 8.904 per cent (i.e. 1,386 men) at a cost of £174,264 a year. To the suggestion that a contented service might be a more efficient service he had no answer. It was left to others—Henry, Kempster, doctors, and police officers of every rank—to demonstrate the social consequences of treating public servants like figures in a balance-sheet; for, as one writer to the *Police Review* observed, 'Even cows have time off for milking.'

'The policeman,' Kempster had written, 'is not to be regarded as a mere chattel or machine.' To this novel idea and to the unconventional wisdom of a cloud of witnesses, the Select Committee bowed; and two years later the Police Forces (Weekly Rest-Day) Act became law.[1] What few people noticed—for it lay outside the Committee's terms of reference—was another, deeper undercurrent. Witness after witness had demonstrated, sometimes unconsciously, the absence of any formal machinery for airing legitimate grievances. Without John Kempster there would have been no 1910 Act; but there were very few Kempsters and the

---

[1] It was the first parliamentary measure to be introduced by the new and energetic Home Secretary, Winston Churchill. The following year, he went to the Admiralty; and there is little doubt that the Royal Navy's gain was the police service's lasting loss.

Police Review was widely held by the Establishment to be an organ of subversion. In the eyes (and words) of many of the men, what passed for 'leadership' more closely resembled 'tyranny'. The police service could only wait for some initiative from the Home Office. They waited in vain until, eight years later, they were literally to take the law into their own hands.

The slow march of the Metropolitan Police towards a proper acceptance of their status in society took place against a background of social and political transformation. Just as the conventional image of eighteenth-century London concealed a paradox, so too did that of the Edwardian years; and for the old, comfortable sense of security, there were not many years left.

The chief symbol of change was the motor-car, and its very novelty posed serious problems for the police. In 1899, Bradford had reported that 'this class of vehicle does not appear to find favour with the general public'. The public soon began to change its mind. In 1905 there were still only 19 cabs and 241 motor-buses; but by 1910—a year that was to be notorious in other ways—there were 6,397 motor-cabs and 1,200 motor-buses. Horse-power had acquired a new meaning.

But the true social significance of the motor-car lay in the private sector. For over seventy years, the attitude of London policemen towards the gentry had been 'civil and attentive' to the point of deference; even the wilder excesses of young bloods were treated with a tolerance not shown to less privileged offenders. It was a relationship much resented by the lower orders, not least for its implication that crime is an activity exclusive to the working class. Now, as the hansom-cabs trotted into the past, the new engines of progress began to redress the balance in a very English way.

The arrival of the motor-vehicle resulted in a predictable spate of legislation, some of it necessary but most of it irrelevant; and it is the duty of the police to carry out the law of the land. For many years private cars were to be within reach of only the more affluent members of society; *ergo*, the police—however deferential —found themselves having to deal with, in every sense, a new class of offender, and suddenly *Punch* discovered a whole new world of comedy. But not everyone thought it funny. An Act of 1903 increased the speed limit to 20 m.p.h., and to ensure that the law was observed the police instituted the speed-trap. Even motorists who were unaware of Harcourt's dictum after the Titley case thought that this was cheating; and from this early confrontation there grew a sullen conviction among motorists that they were prime targets for police persecution. The conviction remains.

The motor-car was also to become a prime target for criminals. There is no record of the first case of 'taking and driving away', and even as recently as 1934 Sir John Moyland could quaintly plead: 'If people would give up stealing *bicycles*, one-sixth of London's crime would disappear.' But in the Commissioner's Report for 1971, a new word made its appearance: 'autocrime' (i.e. taking of or stealing from cars and bicycles). In 1977 the total number of such cases *reported* was no less than 174,479.

*

These were also years of growing political unrest. It was to take many forms—the first concerted campaign for Women's Suffrage ('the most unlikely thing since Aphra Behn', said Max Beerbohm); a sharp increase in the activity of anarchists, most of them undesirable immigrants from Eastern Europe; and widespread industrial militancy. For the Metropolitan Police they were dangerous and difficult times.

The Women's Freedom League, or 'suffragette' movement, was formed in 1908 with the principal object of winning voting rights.[1] What started as a legitimate political campaign soon got out of hand and the police found themselves involved in a kind of public disorder for which there was no precedent. A pensioner who joined the force in 1905 ruefully recalls his experience: 'You wouldn't credit what some of them got up to. One of them harpies was a bigger handful than a couple of drunken Paddies and I remember when I went to arrest a young chit for using abusive language to passers-by, she nearly bit my ear off.' In such situations, it was not easy for young constables to observe Queensberry rules. Few of them did. And the movement—like many others before—died of a surfeit of militancy.

Anarchy was another matter. Since the Fenian troubles of the previous century, the Irish had gone to ground. Their place had been taken in the 1890s by a variety of continental cranks who imported their alien ideas of revolution into London, and one of

[1] In the event, women did not get the vote until the Equal Franchise Act of 1928.

whom succeeded in blowing himself to bits while on his way to flatten the Observatory at Greenwich.

Political refugees were not a new phenomenon. Some, like the Huguenots in the seventeenth century, left a lasting mark on the culture and prosperity of their adopted country. But by the twentieth century the word 'refugee' had become largely a euphemism for a new breed of political extremist from Eastern Europe. In 1905 an Aliens Bill was introduced which gave the Home Secretary wide powers to limit entry and to deport undesirables, and Special Branch was busy as never before. Anarchist activity continued sporadically until it reached its climax in 1909 and 1910 with the Tottenham 'hue and cry' and the Houndsditch murders which led to the celebrated siege of Sidney Street.

Violence in pursuit of political ends was not new to the Metropolis; but anarchism, organized by armed revolutionaries to overthrow a democratic system, was not to be tolerated. The English do not like alien thugs who murder policemen in the execution of their duty; they do not particularly like aliens; and above all, they do not like those who bite the hand that feeds them. From these troubled times the Metropolitan Police emerged with their reputation enhanced and with the genuine respect and admiration of the public. It was not long before the pendulum swung again.

Anarchism was not the only expression of political trouble. The rise of the Labour movement was accompanied by growing trade-union militancy and from 1910 onwards the country was racked by a series of major strikes—miners, dockers, railwaymen, even East End tailors (ironically protesting against the sweated labour of precisely those foreigners whose extremist elements had provided so great a threat to public order and the rule of law).

Most of the industrial action was confined to the provinces—Hull, Liverpool, Salford, Sheffield and, notably, Tonypandy in the Rhondda Valley. This, however, was small comfort to the Metropolitan Police who were called upon to provide assistance to inadequate local forces, and an immediate casualty of these calls on Henry's resources was the virtual suspension of the newly-introduced weekly rest-day.

The Tonypandy riots were to find a place beside the 'Tolpuddle Six' and Peterloo in Labour's book of martyrs; and they were to dog Churchill throughout his political life. His crime was to have acted in preserving law and order with a firmness not notable among Home Secretaries before or since, and the myth of brutal suppression by the army has died hard. Not one shot was fired. Not a sword was drawn. The sole military victory was in a football match between soldiers and strikers, reported with straight-faced formality on 15 November by General Macready, commanding the reserve force which the local magistrates had requested. From London came 100 mounted and 700 foot constables to reinforce the Glamorgan police, and, far from inciting him to heroic counter-measures, Churchill advised the Chief Constable, while acting vigorously against serious riots, 'to go gently in small matters'. It must have given Henry particular satisfaction that Macready in his final report said that 'for tactful, firm, good-tempered handling of an angry mob so as to prevent, if possible, resort to force, the Metropolitan Police Officer stands out far beyond his country comrades'.

*

Amid all the sound and fury of the social unrest of 1910, one still, small name should not go unrecorded: that of Dr Hawley Crippen. There was nothing exceptional about his case, except that a *crime passionel* is, by definition, an unusual form of murder in an English context. He was a very composed little man, and it is said that when, at his trial, portions of the skin of his murdered wife were handed round in a soup-plate for the inspection of the court, he alone of those present showed a lively professional interest. But he has a special place in police history; for his eventual arrest was to show that the long arm of the law had become very long indeed. The dénouement is well-known. Crippen and his mistress, Ethel le Neve, unconvincingly disguised as his son, took passage for Canada from Antwerp in the *Montrose*. The alert Captain Kendall sent a radiogram to Scotland Yard and Chief Inspector Walter Dew sailed from Liverpool on the *Laurentic* to intercept his quarry. The meeting, off Father Point, has something of Stanley and Livingstone.

'Good-morning, Dr Crippen,' said the detective. 'I am Chief Inspector Dew.'

'Good-morning, Mr Dew,' said Dr Crippen, courteous and composed as ever.

And to Henry's Finger Print Bureau, science had added a new and formidable dimension.

On 18 December 1913, the following appeared in Police Orders:

> It has come to the knowledge of the Commissioner that attempts have been made to induce members of the Metropolitan Police to join a Federation or Union. He desires to point out that membership of such an Association is prohibited by Standing Orders and that any man serving who violates these Orders or incites others to violate them renders himself liable to disciplinary proceedings which may result in his dismissal from the Force.

This order had a curious history. In August 1909, an inspector at Gerald Road Police Station, John Syme, was involved in minor disciplinary proceedings. It was a trivial affair; but Syme was a difficult, aggressive man and his superiors handled him with considerable ineptness. Thus a matter which should have been swiftly disposed of was allowed to become a major issue. An inquiry led to Syme's suspension pending the findings of a disciplinary board, but this served only to sharpen his insubordinate behaviour and when the Commissioner intervened with an offer to reinstate him in a lower rank, Syme appealed over his head to the Home Secretary. Summoned once again before the disciplinary board on 29 January 1910, he was summarily dismissed the service.

By now Syme had become the victim of persecution mania and he embarked on a long vendetta against Henry and Wodehouse, the Assistant Commissioner 'A', in which he was aided and abetted by left-wing agitators and by an absurdly over-zealous John Kempster. There was support, too, from militants in the Metropolitan Police itself, disenchanted by the suspension of their hard-won weekly rest-day; and at some date during 1912, Syme began organizing what was later to be called the National Union of Police and Prison Officers, confined originally to the Metropolitan Police District. It was to the activities of this illegal association that Henry's order of 1913 was directed. He could not have foreseen that five years later Syme's ineffective crusade would be instrumental in bringing about his own downfall.[1]

[1] Syme continued his private vendetta for many years, even after the establishment of the Police Federation in 1919. An inquiry in 1924 largely

By 1914, an additional assistant commissioner had been appointed and Central Office was divided into four police departments, A, B, C, and D, which in essence carried out the same functions as they do today. By early summer the strength of the force had risen to 22,048 which made it possible at last fully to implement the provisions of the Weekly Rest-Day Act. On 4 August the nation went to war.

vindicated his sense of grievance and in 1931 he received a modest sum in compensation from the Government. He died in 1945 after being committed to Broadmoor as a certified lunatic.

CHAPTER EIGHT

Desborough and after

NOT FOR a century had Britain been involved in a major European conflict. In that time the Metropolis had been transformed. The population had multiplied seven times; the peripheral fields and villages had been swallowed in a vast and growing urban development; and where parish constables and dilapidated watchmen had presided effortlessly over the decline into social anarchy there was now a force of 22,000 uniformed, disciplined, if still imperfect, policemen. As the lights went out over Europe, London took stock.

'Over by Christmas' was the measure of public euphoria; but the Government was under no such illusion. The Defence of the Realm Act (DORA), introduced within six days of the declaration of war, was probably the most far-reaching measure ever placed before Parliament, ranging over every aspect of national life and public security. Even the canine population was covered by four solemn regulations.

In the Metropolis the burden of giving effect to the flood of new legislation fell squarely on a police force weakened by the demands of the armed services. In August, 1,019 naval and military reservists were recalled to the colours. Under the Police Constables (Naval and Military Services) Act of 18 September, 2,826 men enlisted. In all, 4,027 members of the Metropolitan Police served in the armed forces during the war; 864 were killed or wounded in action and 377 won medals for gallantry in the field. It is a proud record which serves to sharpen the discreditable conduct of those mutinous members of the force who four years later were to break their statutory oath in pursuit of political ends.

The drain on Metropolitan Police man-power was increased by the withdrawal of a further 1,000 men to strengthen the dockyard contingents and to protect military establishments; and—a crowning irony—350 experienced *policemen* were seconded for duty as drill instructors for the raw recruits of the new *soldiery*. That about-face would surely have made Charles Rowan smile.

The gaps were filled by the recall of 1,200 police pensioners; by the enrolment of over 30,000 special constables under the 1831 Act; and, inevitably, by the suspension of the weekly rest-day. In December 1914, the old fortnightly system was reintroduced, and by the end of 1915 the *status quo* had largely been restored.

In 1915, the Metropolitan Police suffered its first 'home' casualties when a regular constable and a 'special' were killed in an air-raid.[1]

*

At the outbreak of war, the pay of Metropolitan Police constables was in the range of 30s to 42s a week, according to length of service. It was still, as it had been for over eighty years, a labourer's wage, and as the inevitable spiral of inflation began and the pay of industrial workers moved ahead, the police experienced increasing hardship and in many cases destitution.[2]

Henry made repeated representations to the Home Office to improve the pay and conditions of his men, but apart from a derisory increase in allowances and a modest bonus specifically restricted to 'the duration of hostilities', the basic scale remained unchanged.

The pay situation was only a contributory factor in Henry's greater cause for concern. Despite his unequivocal warning in 1913, John Syme's embryo Police Union had continued to grow in numbers and influence, although its activities and membership were carefully concealed from higher authority. By 1916, the leaders of the Union, who included militant outsiders and three Labour members of Parliament, had dropped the pilot, for Syme's personal vendetta against Henry had brought him several prison sentences for criminal libel and for disturbing the peace and he had become an embarrassment to his former colleagues. His only

---

[1] Between 1914 and 1918 there were 32 air-raids on the Metropolitan Police District. On 16 February 1918 a bomb destroyed the North-East Wing of the Chelsea Pensioners' retreat at the Royal Hospital, with casualties. By an extraordinary coincidence, the same wing was destroyed by a V2 rocket on 3 January 1945.

[2] In evidence before the 1919 Committee it was stated that during the war years the cost of living increased by 133 per cent; or, if the figure was adjusted to take account of food rationing, by 151 per cent.

remaining champion was John Kempster who pursued his cause with tedious persistence in the columns of the *Police Review*.

Henry was well aware that the true object of the Union was political control of the Metropolitan Police and that the Home Office's obdurate refusal to meet the men's justifiable grievance over pay was precisely the ammunition which the militants needed; for, ran their argument, without the industrial muscle of a proper negotiating body, the pay and conditions of service of the Metropolitan Police were at the mercy of ministerial whim. Their tactical error was to ignore the Promissory Oaths Act of 1868 which rendered a police constable liable to disciplinary action for any refusal to obey orders. Such a refusal—call it 'strike' or 'mutiny'—was the only ultimate sanction.

By 1917, the decline in morale was so marked and the clandestine activities of the Union so widespread that Henry addressed himself in unequivocal terms about the gravity of the situation to Sir George Cave, a Home Secretary who for ineffectiveness compares unfavourably even with Henry Matthews. Cave dismissed Henry's warning with the airy conviction that patriotic policemen would not endanger the safety of the realm, but in February of the following year, a month before the great German offensive, he called a meeting to consider, with no great sense of urgency, the matter of pay, and to put the government actuaries to work on a plan for widows' pensions submitted by the compassionate Henry. But it was too late. The Union executive, determined on confrontation, deployed its troops for action.

*

It was a long, hot summer. In France, the tide had turned and the Allies stood poised for the final and decisive blow. At home, the Executive Committee laid its plans. That it should have chosen so critical a moment to hold the Metropolis to ransom seems, in the retrospect of history, inconceivable. That the then occupant of 10 Downing Street was the second most devious prime minister of modern times was, in the short term, to be its good fortune.

War or no war, August was still the close season in Whitehall. While work proceeded in leisurely fashion on a new formula for pay and conditions, divisional superintendents reported at a series of weekly meetings that all was quiet on the Metropolitan front; and, suitably reassured, Henry went on holiday to Ireland (a curious choice) and the Home Secretary to his country estate. For the Union executive it was the signal to act.

On 25 August, a Police Constable Thiel was dismissed for union activities at Hammersmith police station and for attempting to subvert members of the Manchester constabulary. Since he was the provincial organizer of the Union, it is fair to assume that his conduct was deliberately provocative, for by the date of his dismissal the new proposals for pay and for widows' pensions were common knowledge; and pay, as we have seen, was not the Union's real objective.

On Wednesday, 28 August, the Central Committee forwarded an ultimatum to the Commissioner—knowing perfectly well that he was on holiday—demanding full union recognition, the immediate reinstatement of Thiel, and substantial increases in pay and pensions. A reply was required by midnight on the following day. The ultimatum was worded in terms so insolent and contained demands so unacceptable as to invite instant rejection. It was duly rejected by Wodehouse, the acting Commissioner; and by noon on the Friday, 6,000 men were out on strike.

At this point the Prime Minister, Lloyd George, panicked. His apologists have claimed that his chief concern was lest, at this crucial point of the war, police disaffection might spread to the armed forces. In the event his actions played into the hands of the mutineers and created the far more serious situation which was to arise a year later. Now, on the afternoon of 30 August, his only consideration was to buy off the strike.

Troops were posted outside government offices and the special constabulary was called out. Jan Smuts, an unelected member of the Cabinet, was absurdly co-opted as a kind of honorary Home Secretary pending Cave's return from Somerset. A Union deputation attempted without success to see Smuts on the Friday afternoon and by midnight virtually every uniform constable in the Metropolitan and City forces was on strike.[1] Lloyd George intervened.

By Saturday morning, Henry had returned. Without consultation, Lloyd George—through an intermediary, Charles Duncan, a left-wing MP and (more importantly) President of the illegal Police Union—invited a delegation of strikers to Downing Street,

[1] For a racy account see Reynolds and Judge, *The Night the Police went on Strike.*

at which meeting he, Cave, Henry and (still irrelevantly) Smuts were present. The Prime Minister promised immediate and substantial pay concessions and the reinstatement of Thiel. On the critical issue of union recognition he made the Delphic observation that this was unacceptable 'in war-time', but that a form of representative body would be set up at once with direct access to the Commissioner on all matters other than disciplinary. The strikers took him at his word and they might be forgiven (it is the only credit due to them) for not knowing that with David Lloyd George words were part of a very flexible political language.

At 3 p.m. the strikers' delegation left, satisfied that they had won the day. An hour later they were followed by Sir Edward Henry who had been given no option but to resign ('jettisoned' was his own description to the Desborough Committee). Lloyd George had not even the grace to wield the axe himself but delegated the formal deed of execution to Cave. To be fair to him, Cave felt obliged to offer his own resignation; but one scapegoat was enough for the Prime Minister and in due course the Home Secretary, absolved of all blame, was elevated to the peerage.

Henry's dismissal was a shabby reward[1] for a dedicated public servant who had guided the Metropolitan Police through a long and difficult period of growth and development. He was undoubtedly the most distinguished Commissioner since Mayne and had won, to a degree that Mayne had not, the admiration and respect of his men. He was the first policeman's policeman and it might be said that he paid the penalty for his popularity, as subsequent events were soon to prove.

*

By Sunday morning, the police were back on the streets of the Metropolis. During the previous evening the Cabinet, after long argument, had persuaded General Macready (of Tonypandy fame) to relinquish his post as Adjutant-General and, 'in the national interest', to take over at Scotland Yard. Police Orders for Sunday, 1 September, set out the price of Lloyd George's deal with the strikers. The main details were as follows:

[1] The subsequent award of a baronetcy was as much an insult as an honour.

1. An increase in basic pay for constables of 13s a week, thus creating a new scale of 43s to 55s.[1]

2. A pension of 10s a week for widows.

3. A minimum pension of £1 15s 4d after twenty-six years' service.

4. The establishment of an organization to represent the interests of the men.[2]

The sting, as Henry had warned, was in the tail.

Macready was a new version of an old recipe—the military man summoned to put a militant house in order. On the evening of his appointment, as he wrote later, he 'left Downing Street in a very sad frame of mind', but it was a mind of very decided cast. He despised Lloyd George; he disliked politicians; he thought little of Henry and less of his immediate subordinates; and he was saddled with a potentially explosive time-bomb in the shape of the strike settlement terms. But he was a man for all seasons and before he departed twenty months later to take command of British troops in Ireland, the future of the Metropolitan Police—and indeed of the whole police service—had been transformed. He was not, in fact, the catalyst but rather the necessary re-agent.

*

The new Police Representative Board showed all the signs of hasty improvisation. In setting it up, Cave stipulated that it should be 'independent of and unassociated with any other body', but he also agreed that men could, if they wished, join the Union, while refusing recognition of the Union itself. It was not even a compromise. It was a licence for chaos and an invitation to disaster. It achieved both.

The Board was elected on 2 December, and when it met the Commissioner at New Scotland Yard a fortnight later, Macready predictably found himself confronted by what was, in effect, a duly constituted group of union extremists. He would have nothing to do with them and both sides took to the trenches. If it was to be war, then the militants had picked a formidable opponent.

*

[1] In addition there was a war bonus of 12s a week and an allowance of 2s 6d for each child of school age.

[2] PC Thiel had already been reinstated despite the strong and valid opposition of Henry.

By the spring of 1919, the real war was over. Lloyd George was at Versailles and Cave had given way at the Home Office to Edward Shortt. The deadlock which had followed the Cabinet's hasty action after the 1918 mutiny in the Metropolis was no nearer solution and this was the fault neither of the Union nor of Macready, but of the Home Office. The Executive Committee's claim that Lloyd George's 'pledge' of formal recognition after the war ended should now be honoured was countered by the Home Secretary's denial that any such undertaking had been given. Since no minutes of the crucial meeting were taken, the truth will never be known, but Lloyd George's political record is a matter of history. Of his virtues, a passion for the truth was not the most notable.

In March, a decision was taken at last to set up a committee under Lord Desborough 'to consider and report whether any and what changes should be made in the method of recruiting for, the conditions of service of, and the rates of pay, pensions, and allowances of the police forces of England, Wales and Scotland'.

The Desborough Committee, and the 1919 Act which it fathered, together represent the greatest single milestone in the history not only of the Metropolitan Police but of the entire police service of the country. It was the first such committee to treat the problem on a national basis and to accept the imperative logic that the police institution had now become as essential a constituent of the safety of the realm in its own sphere as the armed services were in theirs. It understood, as no previous committee or Royal Commission had done, that only a radical reassessment of the policeman's place in society would satisfy that overwhelming majority of the rank and file whose allegiance to union militancy was born not of conviction but of desperation. And time was of the essence, for the Executive Committee, concerned only with the politics of power, was already planning industrial action on a national scale.

Wisely, Desborough decided to divide his Report into two parts, the first concentrating on matters of immediate concern and chiefly designed to spike the Union's guns. By the middle of May his committee had made its main recommendations to the Home Secretary. On the basis of these, work started on drafting a Police Bill and by 29 May the Government had announced that legislation was in hand to forbid policemen from belonging to a trade union; that a new form of representative machinery would be incorporated in the Bill; and that any policeman who went on strike would be instantly—and irrevocably—dismissed. The challenge to the Union was unequivocal.

The first part of the Desborough Report was published on 1 July.[1] On the matter of pay and conditions, it recommended standardization throughout the country on the following scale:

1. For constables, a starting rate, retrospective to 1 April 1919, of 70s a week, rising by annual increments of 2s a week to 90s after 10 years' service, with further small increments after 17 and 22 years.[2]

2. An eight-hour day, and overtime at the basic hourly rate.

3. The abolition of war bonus and child allowance.

4. Comparable adjustments to pension scales.

5. Free rent, or an allowance in lieu.

'In future,' notes Critchley, 'the constable was to be a semi-professional man.'[3]

Next, the Metropolitan Representative Board was to be scrapped and replaced by a national Police Federation organized into branch boards and representing all ranks up to and including chief inspector (similar machinery for higher ranks was to follow later); and in pursuance of the 'national' concept, there was to be an advisory Police Council consisting of police authorities and delegates of all ranks under the chairmanship of the Home Secretary or one of his principal officers. Thus, through an ingenious English compromise, the police were given the right to confer *outside* the context of conventional trade unionism.

Finally, the cost of these far-reaching reforms was to be met by transferring to the Exchequer half the total cost of the police

---

[1] The second part of the Report appeared on 1 January 1920. This dealt largely with details of organization and administration, particularly in the provinces. Perhaps its most important recommendation was the creation of a Police Department in the Home Office, to act as both channel and filter for the increasingly complex management of police business.

[2] The Report provided the following interesting comparative weekly rates of pay:

A Newcastle tram driver	65s.
A Liverpool carter	72s.
A Birmingham road scavenger	61s.
A London labourer (unskilled)	68s.

These jobs carried neither pensions nor fringe benefits.

[3] Critchley, *op. cit.*

service, hitherto restricted only to pay and clothing. It was a neat formula for robbing taxpayer Peter to pay ratepayer Paul, the oldest of all fiscal devices.

*

Macready, unlike provincial chief officers, was quick to play his hand. A Special Order on 30 May, printed in menacingly large type, spoke of 'a movement on foot to induce the Metropolitan Police to again withdraw from their duty to the State' and repeated that any such action would result in instant and final dismissal. The following day a Sergeant Hayes (later to become an MP) announced that a national strike ballot in pursuit of union recognition had resulted in a vote of ten to one in favour. Macready was unimpressed; and Police Orders for that same day contained the following unequivocal statement, as valid today[1] as then: 'It is impossible to grant recognition of a Union among men . . . who, from the nature of their duty to the State, must hold themselves aloof from anything savouring of political bias.'

A week later the Commissioner carried the war into the enemy's camp by calling a meeting—craftily referred to as a 'parade'—of 2,600 men at the Queen's Hall. Macready was a born communicator and his talk to the assembled company was frank and humorous, not least in the field of self-criticism. He rehearsed the old arguments, explained the Desborough proposals, and invited his audience to reflect upon the nature of the Commissioner's office. Towards the end, he indulged in a little rhetorical speculation. 'Now I think it has been said: "Why should not a policeman be put in as a Commissioner?" ' He then referred to 'our old friend Mr Olive' and explained the different problems facing a district chief constable and himself. 'I only say,' he added prophetically, 'that the day *may* come when you may have a Commissioner who comes from the ranks.'[2]

[1] 'On such a fundamental issue as the preservation of law and order, the withdrawal of labour would be incompatible with the responsibilities of the police service and contrary to the interests of the nation.' (*Report of the Edmund-Davies Committee*, July 1978)

[2] James Olive, then a district chief constable and subsequently Deputy Commissioner, was the first constable to achieve so high a rank. He retired with a knighthood in 1925 after no less than fifty-three years' service. Nearly forty years were to pass before Macready's prophecy became a reality, with the appointment of Joseph Simpson.

Macready's talk was greeted with acclamation and he withdrew, carrying with him most of the Union Executive's clothes.

*

The Police Bill was introduced on 8 July, and the report stage was due to be reached on 31 July. In London, Macready and his senior officers were confident that the Desborough recommendations had been received with overwhelming approval and that support for strike action would be unenthusiastic. Chief Constables in the provinces were less certain, for the new militancy was a novel experience and progress towards a national[1] concept of a police service had yet to achieve the momentum which Desborough was to provide.

The Union Executive, with time running out, repeated its demand to Lloyd George to honour his earlier promise. It received no reply. A year before—in very different circumstances—it had achieved a sort of victory by direct action. It now turned again to the weapon of last resort, and on 31 July it called a national strike.[2]

*

The 1919 strike was a classic example of the wrong-headed pursuit of an already lost cause. In the Metropolis, out of a total strength of 19,004, only 1,083 men (including one inspector and 28 sergeants) refused duty. All were summarily dismissed; none was reinstated. But whereas the 1918 mutiny had been widely reported as 'good-humoured' (an English euphemism for public demonstrations in which no actual violence takes place), the temper on 31 July was different. There were several cases of intimidation, and even physical violence at King's Cross and subsequently at four other police stations. But Macready's firmness and leadership and the wise counsels of Desborough prevailed; and by 9 August the Commissioner could report that life was back to normal. At the

---

[1] The idea of full-scale nationalization of the police had been raised in evidence to the Desborough Committee but firmly rejected. It was to be revived many times, most recently by Dr A. L. Goodhart in his minority report after the 1960–2 Royal Commission.

[2] July was not a month of unrelieved tension in the Metropolis. Police Orders for 15 July, dealing with the celebrations to mark the signing of the Peace Treaty, contained this pleasing little item: 'The Public are cautioned against the use of squirts, ticklers or other articles likely to cause annoyance.'

critical moment the great majority of Metropolitan policemen, of whom he had spoken so warmly in 1911, had justified his faith in them.

In the provinces, the strike had an uglier face, although—except on Merseyside—support for the Union soon collapsed. In Liverpool and Birkenhead, over half the men refused duty. There was serious rioting and looting, and public order was only restored by the intervention of troops and by bayonet charges in the streets.

By the end of August it was all over. The Police Union, defeated and discredited, had ceased to exist. It had never enjoyed the confidence of the men whom it claimed to represent; but more importantly, it had never received the public support without which industrial militancy is doomed to failure. The melancholy figure of John Syme serves only to show that the English are very careful of the powers they are prepared to delegate to the office of constable.

*

To the energetic Macready, union problems were only a distraction from the more urgent task of post-war reconstruction. Henry's departure had been followed by the retirement or resignation of a considerable number of senior officers, among them Wodehouse. Macready used the opportunity to carry out a preliminary reorganization during the autumn of 1918. Predictably— apart from Supt Olive, promoted to Chief Constable—the newcomers were soldiers, who in the event did not make particularly distinguished policemen (with one exception, they never did). As AC 'A', in place of Wodehouse, Macready chose Brigadier-General Horwood, formerly Provost-Marshal in France, whose practical experience extended to a brief spell in charge of the North Eastern Railway Police. To assist him, and particularly to reorganize the Mounted Branch,[1] Macready appointed—in the new rank of Deputy Assistant Commissioner—Lt-Col. Percy Laurie of the Royal Scots Greys, who brought with him his old Trumpet-Major, George Scorey, later to achieve some sort of immortality at the Wembley Cup Final of 1923.[2]

[1] Since then the strength of the Mounted Branch has remained around the 200 mark.

[2] Thus, years later, PC Scorey in conversation with the author: 'During the General Strike I was on duty in Kentish Town when a woman comes

In October the Commissioner's Chief Clerk, unchanged in status since Charles Yardley ninety years earlier, was upgraded to Secretary, a civil rank confirmed in 1931 with the status of an assistant commissioner; while a month later, for no good reason, AC 'C' was redesignated Director of Criminal Investigations, Vincent's old title, and Special Branch was put under separate management, an experiment which did not work and which ended in 1921 when, after a clash of personalities between Horwood and Sir Basil Thompson, the old CID organization was restored.

It may be convenient here to summarize the changing senior rank structure of the Metropolitan Police.

After Henderson's District Superintendents were replaced by Chief Constables in 1886, there were no further changes in rank until the arrival of Macready and the appointment of the first Deputy Assistant Commissioners. At the same time AC 'A' was made *ex officio* Deputy Commissioner, until James Olive's confirmation in that post in 1922, ranking *primus inter pares* with the four Assistant Commissioners. This structure continued until 1946[1] when the title of Deputy Assistant Commissioner was changed to Commander and (to salve the wounded dignity of provincial chief officers) that of Chief Constable to Deputy Commander. After the Oaksey Report of 1949, Superintendents were up-graded to Chief Superintendents, a rank that had existed briefly in the 1860s. And finally, in 1969, Commanders reverted to their old title of Deputy Assistant Commissioner, while Deputy Commanders and the new Chief Superintendents were designated Commanders, in charge of divisions, and of branches at Central Office.

*

It was now the turn of the ladies.

Back in 1907, Henry had employed a Miss Macdougal, in a purely unofficial capacity, to take statements from girls involved in sexual assaults. The idea found favour with the Home Office, but before it could be pursued on a larger scale, war broke out.

up and says, "You're that Wembley man, aren't you?", and gives me a shilling.'

[1] Trenchard's reforms included the new ranks of Station and Junior Station Inspector, both of which lapsed with the demise of the Metropolitan Police College in 1939.

War also brought its own brand of social problems at home, and towards the end of 1914 the Women's Auxiliary Service recruited a vigilante organization to assist with the care of refugees and to protect girls from the attentions of the brutal and licentious soldiery. These volunteers, although wearing a uniform—illegal and of singular inelegance—had no official status; but their work did not escape the attention of Henry and in 1918 he obtained Home Office approval for an officially recognized number of patrols to be known as the Women's Police Service, under a 'Superintendent', Mrs Sophia Stanley. These worthy ladies were viewed with hostility, not only by policemen but by a public not yet converted to the cause of feminism. They had neither status nor powers— they were, in the words of one police pensioner, 'a bloody nuisance since we spent much of our time seeing they came to no harm'— but in 1919 Macready, ever the chauvinist, absorbed them into the Metropolitan Police.[1] It was a tiny triumph for feminism; and it was to be an arch-feminist who saved them from extinction.

In 1920, the Baird Committee was invited to consider the suitability of women for police duties. They found few friends; indeed, a rude magistrate pronounced in evidence that women wanting to join the police 'have sterilised any maiden modesty they may have had'. Thus, unloved and unwanted, they were a leading candidate for execution when the Geddes Axe fell in 1922; but a resolute rearguard action, led by Nancy Astor, preserved a small group of 20 (2 inspectors, 3 sergeants and 15 constables, the latter on a basic wage of 64s a week) and these, released from their disability by the Sex Disqualification (Removal) Act of 1919,[2] were duly sworn in as constables in April 1923 and posted to divisions. For eight years, during which they were ignored by the Commissioner and disparaged by the Police Federation, their highest rank remained that of inspector, until the appointment of Miss Dorothy Peto as Staff Officer in 1930. The following year Miss Peto was promoted to Superintendent by Trenchard and the issue of Women's Police Regulations by the Home Office provided the formal *imprimatur* on their status and conditions of service as a duly constituted part

---

[1] The original nucleus of the Women's Police was 110. In 1930, the number was 47, and in 1939 still only 136. By 1977 the strength had risen to 1,433. (*Commissioner's Report*, 1977)

[2] The earlier Police Acts had laid down that only 'fit men' could be sworn in as constables.

of the Metropolitan Police. The slow process of integration was
finally completed in 1974 when policewomen were given equal pay
and the same opportunities for promotion and specialization as the
rest of the force, even to providing a decorative addition to the
Mounted Branch. Horwood would have strongly disapproved; but
not Nancy Astor.

What the future course of the Metropolitan Police might have been
if Macready's reputation as a trouble-shooter had not taken him to
Ireland to preside over the delicate process of military disengage-
ment is a matter for conjecture. In the second of his two Annual
Reports, he spoke of the marked improvement in the discipline and
efficiency of the force after the 1919 Police Act, and the men had
come to recognize that his bark was a good deal worse than his bite.
He had thought of himself at first as little more than a politicians'
back-stop but the job, and its challenge, grew on him and in later
years he wrote: 'When the smoke cleared away, I found myself
enjoying the view.' In his short time at the Yard he introduced a
number of innovations. He was the first man seriously to tackle the
problem of traffic control; to create a Press Bureau; to see the
importance of wireless as a weapon in the war against crime; and
to recognize the need for greater mobility in the age of the motor-
car. As a first step he formed a small team of eight detectives,
equipped with two formidable Crossley tenders and designed at
first simply as a means of transporting men quickly to scenes of
crime.[1]

But like every other soldier-turned-policeman, Macready had a
blind spot. While (unusually) three of his four district chief
constables were promoted from the ranks, senior posts at Scotland
Yard were filled from his own profession, and indifferently filled
at that. The fault lay as much with the system as with Macready,
but when in April 1920 he made the appointment of Horwood as
his successor virtually a condition of his accepting command in
Ireland, he did a great disservice to the Metropolitan Police.

The social revolution of the 1920s would have taxed the abilities

*

[1] This was the nucleus of what the press christened the 'Flying Squad',
the first of those specialist groups that were to become so significant a
feature of police methods after the Second World War.

of a far wiser and stronger man than General Horwood; and he was neither wise nor strong. He inherited a contented force from Macready, but by the time of his retirement eight years later relations between the police on the one hand and the press and public on the other had reached their lowest point for half a century. Charles Daly, who worked for a short time as a clerk in the Commissioner's office, remembers Horwood: 'He was an unattractive man who mistook arrogance for leadership. I never saw him smile or return a courtesy, and his attitude towards his job seemed to be one of distasteful necessity.' There could be no better evidence of this than the flat, impersonal Annual Reports which by their very anonymity reflect the character of their author. In the force, he was known as "the Chocolate Soldier"; and that is sufficient comment.

The high hopes which marked the victory celebrations were soon proved to be a false dawn. By 1922 unemployment was growing fast and there were all the symptoms of a major economic crisis. In the political field, the climate of unrest was marked by industrial trouble, a fresh outbreak of Irish terrorism, and a new threat to public security in the shape of growing communist influence. It was not, after all, to be so brave a new world.

The cuts in public expenditure proposed by the 1922 Geddes Committee included a reduction in police wages. Horwood seems not to have put up any resistance, but the Police Federation—in what was one of the first tests of its effectiveness—argued strongly that any such action would be a clear breach of the Desborough recommendations and of the 1919 Act. The Government, fearful of any recurrence of police militancy, backed down and decided instead to take its tribute in kind rather than in cash. In July, the Commissioner was instructed to suspend further recruitment and to reduce his uniform strength by 5 per cent (or roughly 1,000 men).[1] On 22 July Horwood wrote to the Home Office in protest; but his tin trumpet gave forth an uncertain sound and his letter received a decent Whitehall burial. The damage, however, had been done. Once more the Metropolitan Police felt themselves to be at risk.

*

[1] As recently as the previous year, a new division (Z) had been formed to cover the county borough of Croydon, and No. 4 District, south of the river, had been reorganized accordingly.

But they had also put themselves at risk. In what is almost a laconic aside in his 1923 Report, Horwood referred to 'attacks made upon the Police by some of the less reputable journals' [*and by several of some repute*]. 'The writers,' he continued, 'seem to be obsessed with the idea that blackmail and the acceptance of bribes are not uncommon, and that the higher authorities neglect to deal with offenders ... Nothing could be more unfair and exasperating to the members of the Force.'

Nothing, he might have added, could more seriously influence the public attitude towards the force at this critical time. And it is important to pause here and consider the implications of Horwood's remarks.

The damage had been started in March 1878 when Vincent had been appointed Director of Criminal Investigations, ostensibly to allay public disquiet after the Turf Frauds scandal. From then on the CID had become in effect a separate police institution, divorced from the uniform branch and treated by successive Commissioners —even by Henry—as a privileged elite, whose plain clothes could cover, in the interests of crime detection, a multitude of sins. It is impossible to know with any certainty the extent of police corruption during the fifty years after the CID was formed; corruption is difficult to define. But it is beyond argument that by the summer of 1922 the CID had become a thoroughly venal private army.

*

Nor was the uniform branch without its troubles, which—with a series of scandals involving public figures—came not single spies but in battalions. The newspapers were full of charges and countercharges of wrongful arrest, perjury and intimidation, very few of them substantiated and all reflecting the decay of public morality.[1] The force needed, as never before, some striking success with which to re-establish public confidence; and that, in its most literal sense, was now close at hand.

During 1925, Horwood's acute shortage of man-power was un-expectedly resolved by the decision progressively to transfer back to the Admiralty and the War Department the responsibility for

---

[1] In 1923 Horwood narrowly escaped death from poisoning when he ate some chocolates sent to him through the post by a lunatic named Tatam. Eleven years earlier an attempt to assassinate Henry had been made by an aggrieved cab-driver.

policing their own establishments. Over a period of eight months this released 1,326 Metropolitan policemen, and by March 1926 the Commissioner could report that his effective strength was only 181 below establishment. It was a providential windfall; for at midnight on 3 May 1926, the leaders of the TUC called a General Strike.

The causes need not concern us here, nor the long-term effects. It is fashionable to dismiss the strike as an ill-conceived attempt by organized labour to usurp the authority of the State. That is an over-simplification. Not since the Chartist riots of the 1840s had the country come closer to revolution. That the crisis lasted for only nine days was due to trade union incompetence, panic in the Labour Party, and the essentially English instinct that the umpire's decision is final. But it was a close run thing, handled with considerable skill by Baldwin and the Home Secretary, Joynson-Hicks.

One false step would have had disastrous consequences. The strike leaders, with an eye to the history books, counted on provoking military intervention; but Baldwin was not Palmerston, and while soldiers were deployed to guard key installations, their presence was carefully muted. The maintenance of law and order and the protection of essential services were firmly and properly left to the police. There was an irony in this, for the police mutinies were still fresh in the public memory and it is fascinating to speculate what course events might have taken if the campaign for a Police Union, affiliated to the TUC, had been successful.

After the first shock, the public rather enjoyed themselves. In the Metropolis 60,000 special constables were enrolled.[1] They were reinforced by an organization called the Civil Constabulary Reserve, and the general public, from City stockbrokers to unemployed labourers, volunteered in their hundreds to keep the lifelines of the Metropolis open. Frank Flood, then a constable on traffic control at Oxford Circus, had his problems: 'I was in greater danger from amateur bus-drivers than ever I was from bloody-minded strikers.' He finished in Charing Cross Hospital with a broken leg.

It was clear from the outset that the strike leaders had seriously

---

[1] Horwood, in a brief reference to the strike in his Annual Report for 1926, oddly referred to them as 'this honorary force'. And he ended with this profound observation: 'The experience gained during the strike was most useful.'

misjudged not only the climate of public opinion but also the temper of their own men; and if they believed that the under-current of the mutinies of 1918 and 1919 still ran strong, they were much mistaken. It takes two to make a fight and one side—the police—was not disposed to exchange punches. Except in the dock area, where strikers tried to interfere with food convoys in the early days, there was little violence and the English genius for improvisation ensured that life went on with the minimum of dis-location. Macready, who returned briefly as chief staff officer to the Commandant of the 'Specials', noted with amusement that, as at Tonypandy, the football field again proved an irresistible safety-valve for would-be revolutionaries.

By 6 May, men had begun to go back to work in large numbers, and by the 9th more than 3,000 trains were running again. Ramsay MacDonald and his opposition colleagues, fearful of the political consequences, were seeking a face-saving formula and it was only during the last two days, as the strike petered out, that communists and other extreme left-wing militants attempted to achieve by violence what trade union leaders had signally failed to secure by mass intimidation. But it was too late; and by 12 May the strike was over.

It was, above all, a bloodless victory for the police and for that 'perfect command of temper' which Charles Rowan had enjoined upon every constable. *The Times* rhapsodized about the 'tact, patience, impartiality, and impeccable conduct' of the Metropolitan Police and the auxiliary forces, and forthwith launched an appeal to which a grateful public subscribed no less than £250,000. It seemed for once that the citizens of the Metropolis really did think that their policemen were wonderful.

*

There are no prizes for guessing that the public's euphoria was short-lived. There is no logical reason why this should have been so, for in the immediate aftermath of the General Strike there were no great issues to whet the public appetite; but the times were out of joint and there were many historical precedents to show that at such moments the police were easy game for self-appointed keepers of the public's uneasy conscience. The press—neither for the first nor the last time—has much to answer for. No complaint or alleged misdemeanour, however trivial or ill-founded, escaped the eye of editors alert to the Fleet Street dictum that good news does not sell newspapers. Horwood made no attempt to counter-attack, either directly or through his Press Bureau (his successor was to prove of sterner stuff); and thus the scene was set for the two *causes célèbres* which rocked the country in 1928; one—like the affairs of Miss Cass and Mme D'Angely—demonstrating to a farcical degree the English genius for confusing liberty with licence; the other a genuine scandal which was to dog the Metro-politan Police for forty years.

*

On 23 April, Sir Leo Money, appropriately an economist of repute, and a Miss Irene Savidge were arrested in Hyde Park by two young constables for an alleged offence against section 24 of the Parks Regulation Act, an obscure measure with which the accused had reasonably enough not familiarized themselves. Not so the two constables. On 2 May the charge was dismissed by the magistrate at Marlborough Street who rejected the police evidence and awarded costs against them.[1] There a matter of profound un-importance might have ended.

But to one Labour MP at least, here was a handy stick with which to beat both the police and the government; and on 7 May a question was asked in the House suggesting serious misconduct on the part of the police. Joynson-Hicks had no alternative but to refer the matter to the Director of Public Prosecutions[2] who invited the Commissioner to investigate the allegations. Miss Savidge agreed to make a statement and was duly interviewed at great length at Scotland Yard by Chief Inspector Collins, a mild and courteous man. What occurred during that meeting will never be known for certain, but Miss Savidge's version—or, to be more precise, three different versions—were enough to stoke the fires of public indignation. By now the witch-hunters were in full cry and to the charge of police perjury were now added allegations of police brutality. On 17 May the matter was again raised in the House, and in an attempt finally to silence criticism the Home Secretary

[1] Money rode his luck, for a year later he was convicted of assaulting a young lady in a railway carriage.
[2] This office had been created in 1879 as a temporary experiment but lapsed five years later. It was revived in 1908 on a statutory basis under the Prosecution of Offences Act with greatly increased powers.

appointed a tribunal of three under Sir Eldon Bankes to investigate the whole affair thoroughly. It reported on 11 July and, by a majority of two to one, exonerated the police of every allegation of misconduct, the Labour member of the committee, for transparently political reasons, dissenting from the findings both in substance and in detail.

Accordingly the public clamour continued until, on 22 August, the Government, in what looks in retrospect like an act of desperation, appointed a Royal Commission. As an example of the use of a sledge-hammer to crack a nut and of the triumph of prejudice over reason, the terms of reference of this Commission deserve to be recorded:

> To consider the general powers and duties of police in England and Wales in the investigation of crimes and offences, including the functions of the Director of Public Prosecutions and the police respectively; to inquire into the practice followed in interrogating or taking statements from persons interviewed in the course of the investigation of crime; and to report whether, in their opinion, such powers and duties are properly exercised and discharged, with due regard to the rights and liberties of the subject, the interests of Justice, and the observance of the Judges' Rules both in the letter and the spirit; and to make any recommendations necessary in respect of such powers and duties and their proper exercise and discharge.

It seemed a far cry from the immodest bench in Hyde Park.

*

Meanwhile in another part of the forest more serious matters were afoot.

In the degenerate society of post-war London, there had appeared a new expression of the pursuit of pleasure—the nightclub. These clubs, always expensive and often disreputable, flouted the licensing laws, invited prostitution, and by 1924 had become a serious problem for the police. By then it was estimated that there were over 200 in the West End area alone, covered by C Division with headquarters at Vine Street. Most of the proprietors were foreigners of very doubtful repute, but the acknowledged *doyenne* was Mrs Kate Meyrick who presided over Proctors in Gerrard Street and the Silver Slipper in Regent Street. Despite two sojourns in Holloway Prison, Mrs Meyrick continued to prosper.

Early in 1928, Scotland Yard received a series of anonymous letters alleging police involvement in the night-club racket and naming a Sergeant Goddard. Goddard was station-sergeant at Vine Street and six years earlier had been detailed by his superintendent to take charge of what today would be called a vice squad with the task of cleaning up the West End. That he had signally failed to do so does not seem to have attracted the attention of his superiors; but now some interesting questions were being asked and Fred Wensley, Chief Constable of the CID, decided to take a closer look at Goddard. He did not much like what he saw.

Goddard's police pay was £6 a week, but he owned a £2,000 house in Streatham and an expensive Chrysler car, and was living in a manner to which Metropolitan Police sergeants were not normally accustomed. In September—three weeks after the Royal Commission was set up to consider the implications of the Savidge affair—another anonymous letter suggested that an examination of two safe deposits at Selfridges (in Goddard's name) and in Pall Mall (in the name of Joseph Eagles), might be revealing. They were. The Selfridges safe contained £471 and that in Pall Mall, £12,000. The notes were traced to Mrs Meyrick, to Luigi Ribuffi, another night-club proprietor, and to a Mrs Gadda, a brothel-keeper, who prudently removed herself to Belgium.

On 23 October, unable to offer any acceptable explanation, Goddard was suspended and a month later dismissed the service. On 24 November, he was arrested and charged with conspiring to pervert the course of justice; and in January 1929 he stood trial at the Old Bailey with Mrs Meyrick and Ribuffi. He was convicted, fined £2,000 with costs, and sentenced to eighteen months' hard labour. Kate Meyrick and Ribuffi were each given fifteen months' hard labour. The reader may feel some sympathy for poor Druscovitch who fifty years earlier had been rewarded with two years in prison for a £60 indiscretion.

*

It had been a disastrous year for the Metropolitan Police. The Savidge and Goddard affairs, with their implications of perjury, ill-treatment, and corruption—played *fortissimo* by the press—had severely shaken public confidence in the force. And at this critical moment, Horwood decided to retire. It is true that he had given notice of his intention several months earlier, but the terms of reference of the Royal Commission, let alone the Goddard scandal, might have encouraged a different man to stay and fight it out for the sake of his unhappy force. He retired on 7 November. He had been an inept Commissioner. Nothing so ill became him as the manner of his going.

CHAPTER NINE

The Dove and the Hawk

THERE WAS a marked reluctance to assume Horwood's uncomfortable mantle. At least eight possible candidates politely declined the honour, including two Assistant Commissioners, which says little either for their ambition or their courage. For the police it was a crisis of confidence; for Joynson-Hicks it was a crisis of judgement.

Early in July, a private notice question was asked in the House by Ramsay MacDonald. Was it true that General Horwood had decided to retire and that the new Commissioner would be Lord Byng of Vimy?[1] The Home Secretary replied that this was so. It was the signal for an all-too-familiar parade of those parliamentary prejudices which had pursued the Metropolitan Police for a hundred years, led in this instance, on the Labour side, by Montague and Lansbury. Was this not government by subterfuge? Or a sinister extension of the principle of 'militarization'? Or a perpetuation of an unacceptable caste system? Joynson-Hicks was not a man to be moved by such arguments. Lord Byng, he replied, had agreed to assume this new responsibility on the understanding that he would 'resign at 24 hours' notice if he should prove to be unsuitable'. His decision, said the Home Secretary, was 'the acceptance of a very stern call to duty'.

Fleet Street at once took up the cudgels. The Tory press, led by the *Telegraph*, warmly approved the appointment of this old and respected public servant, while the *Morning Post* commented sharply on 'the petty spirit of Parliamentary questions'. The radical *Daily News* thought otherwise:

> We regard with the utmost misgiving the appointment of another soldier, utterly inexperienced in this essentially civilian job, . . . at a very critical juncture in the affairs of the Metropolitan Police.

[1] 'How old is Lord Byng?' asked a Mr Emanuel Shinwell. 'Sixty-five,' replied the Home Secretary.

It was left to the *Evening Standard* to touch the heart of the matter:

> To speak bluntly, the appointment bears every mark of having been decided in a panic. The public is inclined to think that if the Police Force cannot itself produce men of the requisite calibre, then it requires reform from this point of view.

The arrival on the scene of one such reformer was not far distant.

*

Lord Byng took over the office of Commissioner on 8 November 1928. He was a remarkable man, reflecting the virtues of the Victorian age into which he had been born (his grandfather, the Earl of Stafford, had commanded a brigade at Waterloo) and yet alive to the mechanical revolution of his own time (he had been one of the few convinced advocates of tank warfare). After commanding the Third Army in France during the last two critical years of the war, he had been the most successful and universally respected of all governor-generals of Canada. In 1928 he was living in peaceful retirement at his house in Essex; he was also a sick man.

Byng was under no illusions. His overriding task, as he put it, was to 're-inspire' a force disillusioned by recent events, and by restoring their professional pride to recreate the measure of public confidence which they had enjoyed after the General Strike. His priceless asset was an ability, shared by Charles Rowan a century before, to command respect and affection at every level. He also had a puckish sense of humour which was to stand him in good stead during a period when there was not much to laugh about; and even his Labour critics, when they came to power in 1929, found his personality irresistible. Howgrave-Graham, the Secretary at Scotland Yard, has left an amusing and affectionate picture of Byng at work.[1] Two things in particular were anathema to him— paper-work and the telephone—and he avoided the one and ignored the other. He was not, like his successor, a man for dramatic decisions but rather an initiator of policy who delegated authority to his subordinates and trusted them to get on with the job. It was not his fault that he inherited an undistinguished group of senior officers and it was a measure of his personal influence throughout

[1] H. M. Howgrave-Graham, *Light and Shade at Scotland Yard.*

the force that when, on medical advice, he was obliged to spend the winter months in the south of France, the machine continued to work well despite the fact that his Deputy Commissioner was Admiral Sir Charles Royds whose sole claim to any vestigial distinction as a policeman is the fact that he is the only former senior naval officer to have held high rank in the Metropolitan force.

So much of the credit for police reform has been attributed to Trenchard that Byng's own contribution has been largely ignored. Where Trenchard took the citadels of Whitehall (and even Buckingham Palace) by storm, Byng relied on gentle persuasion. His three years of office were marked by permanent economic crisis and he was obliged to work within a constantly shrinking straitjacket. A small but typical example was the proposal to reduce or even abolish the Mounted Branch which Byng, the old cavalry-man,[1] resisted on grounds not of sentiment but of practical policy. Harry Freeman recalls an occasion at Rochester Row:

> One morning Lord Byng visited our stables. We duly 'stood to our horses' and he walked round chatting to the men and asking all sorts of unexpected questions. Then he turned to the Inspector and asked if there were any former Hussars present. It so happened that there were three of us and soon the Commissioner was happily yarning away, until his driver managed to drag him off to another engagement.

This was Byng's way. He had accepted the command of a force whose civilian origins were not to be confused with military imperatives. His 20,000 men—a trivial number compared with the great Army he had led in France—needed firm but sympathetic handling. Given the situation which Byng inherited, Trenchard would have fallen at the first fence; Byng, even if he pecked on landing, kept his balance—and his sense of humour.

Byng's achievement—properly acknowledged in Trenchard's first Annual Report—was to set in train a fundamental reconstruction of the police function in the Metropolis despite his own poor health and a constant demand for economies which would have disheartened a less resilient man; for Byng's gentle manner concealed a resolute mind.

[1] He had commanded the 10th Hussars from 1902 to 1904.

His prescription contained three main ingredients, each a
corollary of the other: a determined effort to improve public
relations, a reallocation of existing resources and **duties** designed
to make policing more efficient and more interesting for the man
on the beat, and the creation of a whole new range of support
services to help fight the modern criminal by more modern
methods. And it is interesting to reflect that, for all their appearance of novelty, Byng's reforms were simply a re-statement of
those cardinal principles of policing laid down a century before by
Rowan and Mayne, and even earlier by John Fielding. Methods
may change, but not principles.

Byng's first step was to rebuild the bridges between police and
public after the misfortunes of 1928. To do this he needed above all
the cooperation of Fleet Street (something that Horwood had never
understood) and thus he arranged a meeting with Lord Riddell and
leading newspaper proprietors. There were, he admitted, black
sheep in his flock, and their activities, a legitimate matter of public
concern, would be punished with the utmost severity. For the rest,
he asked only for a sense of proportion and an end to the daily
barrage of abuse and innuendo based on little more than gossip and
rumour. He reminded them of Birkenhead's words in the debate
on the Savidge affair: 'There is no finer, no more honourable, no
more honest and no more courageous force of men in the world.
To say, as a result of the reactions and repercussions of a case like
this, that the public are losing faith in the Police, these, my Lords,
are the murmurings of imbecility.' Riddell and his colleagues
accepted the logic of the Commissioner's argument. The sniping
stopped and for nearly three years the press left the police in peace.

Byng next addressed himself to his men. He was constantly out
and about his parish visiting police stations, chatting to the rank
and file, offering encouragement and listening to problems. 'He
made us feel,' said one long-serving constable, 'that we were in the
finest job in the world.' To get the best out of his limited resources,
Byng revised divisional boundaries and reorganized beats so that
they were constantly changed (to the chagrin of petty criminals)
and linked by bicycle and motor patrols. Most significantly, he
swallowed his personal dislike of the telephone and started the
police-box system, with immediate success.[1] 'Time,' he remarked,

[1] Police telephone boxes had first been introduced in Sunderland a few
years previously.

'is always on the side of the criminal. We must give the criminal less time.' Now the man on the beat was no longer an isolated outpost but linked, when necessary, to a source of quick reinforcement. The slow and wasteful fixed point system, with its itinerant sergeants and bored constables, was already obsolete.

This preoccupation with John Fielding's policy of 'quick pursuit' was extended to Scotland Yard itself. The Flying Squad, virtually neglected since its introduction by Macready ten years earlier, was now greatly strengthened and developed with the addition of 'Q' cars and even bogus commercial vehicles, which would have much offended the tender conscience of Sir William Harcourt. To Byng the justification was simple. Crime is a form of war against society and therefore the criminal must be fought with every available weapon within the law. He carried this military simile into the Yard itself by setting up the first Information Room to act as a communications centre linked to a fleet of wireless cars.

Although Byng's main concern was to create a new spirit among his men and to provide them with the best available tools with which to do the job, he could only proceed at the pace allowed by the economic situation. Nor was crime his sole preoccupation. By 1930, the motor-car had become as great a social problem as it was a social necessity, particularly in a Metropolis designed for a more sedate age. In 1931, casualties from road accidents in the Metropolitan Police District numbered 1,326 killed and 54,300 injured and traffic control, expensive in man-power, was putting an increasing strain on B Dept at the Yard and in divisions.

The Road Traffic Act of 1930 introduced the Highway Code and pedestrian crossings.[1] It also, incongruously, abolished the speed limit and resulted in an explosion of traffic offences. The motorist glowered resentfully at the policeman.

Byng's reaction was typical. A pedantic application of laws which few people any longer understood could only undermine the bridges he had built and waste thousands of precious man-hours in magistrates' courts. He chose instead to educate the public by forming traffic patrols—the 'courtesy cops'—with instructions to proceed only in cases of dangerous driving and other serious offences, while relying on avuncular warnings where minor or technical breaches of the law were involved. It was an original idea,

---

[1] The first traffic signals came into action in Oxford Street in July 1931.

but wanton drivers and foolish pedestrians soon put paid to it. And it remains a pleasant irony that it was a man brought up in the old cavalry tradition who should have done so much to encourage what Patrick Colquhoun had called 'the new science of police'.

*

All these changes took place against a bleak background as the country stumbled towards financial disaster. But meanwhile, in May 1929, the Metropolitan Police celebrated its centenary (albeit a little prematurely) with a review of 10,000 all ranks in Hyde Park by the Prince of Wales, followed by a march-past in the Mall in which every branch of the force was represented, including— perhaps rather furtively—a detachment of Special Branch.

The infant which, a hundred years before, faced a harsh and uncertain future had grown to man's estate in a world no less harsh and uncertain. It had survived forty-two commissions, committees and inquiries; indifferent leadership; frequent attacks; and a number of self-inflicted wounds. Yet the force had been slow to adapt to the social revolution which had taken place, in spite of Desborough and a more sophisticated attitude to the prevention and detection of crime. It remained an ultra-conservative, artisan institution, still wedded to a hierarchical structure indifferent to Peel's principle that the force should be 'filled up from below'. The police service, with its lack of incentives, still attracted brawn rather than brains.[1]

A few months before the centenary celebrations, Lord Lee's Commission had issued its report on police powers and procedure. Its terms of reference had included the whole of England and Wales, but the reader patient enough to study the complicated and often arcane evidence is left with the inescapable feeling that once more it is the Metropolitan Police who were in the dock. In its general conclusions the Commission differed little from that of 1908,

---

[1] In 1931, there were 42,000 applications to join the force, by far the greatest number in any one year. But this was only a reflection of the massive level of unemployment. Of these applicants, 80 per cent had received no education beyond elementary schooling. Howgrave-Graham quotes this answer to a general knowledge question: 'The Battle of Trafalgar was fought in 1066 on and around the ground which is now called Trafalgar Square. It was a victory for the English against Oliver Cromwell and his men.' Apocryphal, surely; exaggerated, no.

accepting that the mere assumption of a uniform did not make
saints out of sinners and quoting Stephen's nineteenth-century
dictum that a policeman, in the view of the common law, is 'only
a person paid to perform, as a matter of duty, acts which if he were
so minded he might have done voluntarily'. In the Commission's
opinion, the vast majority of the police service was fair, honest and
efficient in its dealings with the public.

In ranging over so wide a field, however, the Commission
stepped outside its brief in two important respects. The first was
an implied—and deserved—rebuke to the politicians:

> Many complaints which have reached us have proved . . . to be
> in effect directed not against the police themselves, but against
> the laws which the police are called upon to enforce. In our view,
> the attempt to enforce obsolete laws, or laws manifestly out of
> harmony with public opinion, will always be liable to expose the
> police to temptations and to react upon their morale and
> efficiency.

It was high time that a body with the authority of a Royal
Commission reminded Parliament that the police do not make
laws, and that bad or imprecise laws cannot be enforced; and that
it is an axiom that democratic government depends on public
consent.

The second departure from the Commission's terms of reference
was of more specific concern to the police service—so much so
that Trenchard was to quote it virtually verbatim in his celebrated Annual Report for 1932. This dealt with a problem which
had existed with growing urgency since Peel's Act: how was a
police service now numbering over 60,000 men in England and
Wales to generate its own properly qualified command structure?
The Commission concluded with these words, which were to be
the subject of much heart-searching and angry argument:

> We should therefore regard as inimical to the public interest any
> system which limited appointments to the higher posts to those
> who had entered the police as constables and we are of the
> opinion that such posts should be filled by the best men avail-
> able, irrespective of the source whence they are drawn.

Since, in the hundred years to 1929, only six Metropolitan
Police constables had risen above the rank of superintendent, this

was begging the question; nor were the implications of the Commission's view lost on an increasingly sensitive Police Federation. And it was, as Critchley suggests,[1] to conciliate the Federation that a very different kind of kite was flown. In the autumn of 1929 a sub-committee of the Police Council was appointed under Arthur (later Sir Arthur) Dixon, who had been Secretary to the Desborough Committee and then the first head of the new Police Department at the Home Office, to examine a workable scheme for creating within the police service a future command structure drawn from its own resources. The sub-committee duly reported in March 1930.

It proposed the establishment of a National Police College,[2] with a two-year course in general and police subjects for men who had served for at least five years and who had passed the examination for promotion to sergeant. So far, so good; but from that point on, the Dixon scheme lost its way. How were entrants to be selected? And how was subsequent promotion to be monitored? Any hope of acceptance by the Federation—wedded to the lowest common denominator—was dashed by Dixon's further recommendation that eventually graduation from the College was to be a necessary condition for promotion to the highest ranks. 'The proposal,' declared the Federation, 'would cause serious discontent which would far outweigh any benefits.' The fact that it produced no evidence that this would happen suggests that what the Federation meant was that if no discontent existed, it would be necessary to create it.

Byng did not much care for the Dixon scheme which he felt confused means with ends; but the strongest opposition came from local authorities who objected to what they considered an unwarranted additional charge on ratepayers.[3] All the arguments, however, were swiftly overtaken by events. When, in 1931, the full force of the economic blizzard struck the country, the Dixon scheme, which, with all its imperfections, was the first

[1] Critchley, *op. cit.*

[2] The word 'College' was always to invite comparison with Sandhurst, even at the modern Bramshill (see p. 261). But future inspectors and future subalterns are very different animals.

[3] If every police authority, irrespective of size, had been required to contribute the same sum, the annual 'burden' on each would have been £468.

rational attempt to solve an inescapable problem, was frozen to death.

Towards the end of March Byng's health had so deteriorated that he asked to be relieved of his duties as soon as a successor could be appointed. He was nearly 70 and he had given his country incomparable service. His farewell present was therefore singularly inappropriate. On 31 July a committee, which had been set up in February under Sir George May, recommended immediate economies in the public sector which made the Geddes axe look like a blunt instrument. The proposals of the May Committee included wage and salary cuts ranging up to 20 per cent. The figure for the police was 12½ per cent, reduced a month later to 10 per cent, to be implemented in two annual stages of 5 per cent. While the Police Federation was staging a carefully muted protest demonstration at the Albert Hall, the country was shaken by the mutiny of some 500 naval ratings at Invergordon. It was an insult to national pride which served more than anything else to underline the magnitude of the financial crisis. The first casualty was the gold standard.

The Government held its breath. Would the police stand firm or would financial disaster be compounded by social conflict? The police held firm. They had had enough of mutinies and they knew the price of indiscipline. The knowledge that there are 3,000,000 unemployed in the dole queues concentrates a man's mind wonderfully. But the good sense and moderation of the Metropolitan Police at this crucial time is above all a tribute to Byng's example and leadership. He retired to his home in Essex on 9 September 1931. And *The Times* had this to say:

> Scotland Yard's gain is nothing less than the complete restoration of public confidence in the police force and the force's recovery in confidence in itself. Lord Byng has set the police officer of all ranks a professional standard . . . and he has given an impetus to internal reforms by which London and his successors will profit.

Like Richard Mayne, he was going to be a difficult man to follow.

The 'impetus to internal reforms' which Byng provided had an unexpected effect. The Labour Government which, in opposition,

had so strongly criticized his appointment, now accepted the need
to find a military man to succeed him. In March, on the advice of
Sir John Anderson, Permanent Under-Secretary at the Home
Office, MacDonald sent for Lord Trenchard.

'The militarist we want, of course, is you,' said MacDonald.

'The militarist you are not getting is me,' replied Trenchard.

Trenchard's life had been devoted to a single, all-consuming
passion—the Royal Air Force. He had been its mid-wife, father-
confessor, propagandist and defender of the faith; and like many
formidable men, he had made some formidable enemies. He had
retired in December 1929 to devote his time to private interests
and from the vantage-point of the House of Lords, to watch over
the future of the service which he had done so much to create.
The prospect of becoming a policeman appealed to him not at all.

Anderson at the Home Office played his cards shrewdly.
Trenchard, an obstinate man, was not one to be moved by flattery
or appeals to sentiment. The police, explained Anderson, were
going through a difficult time, despite the quiet revolution which
Byng had worked. They needed firm leadership and the Royal
Commission had underlined the necessity for radical reforms
which would invite strong opposition both inside and outside the
force. It was a situation tailor-made for Trenchard who had spent
a lifetime slaying the dragons of entrenched conservatism. But
Trenchard remained adamant.[1] Wisely Anderson bided his time,
although he could not have foreseen the dramatic sequence of
events which finally broke Trenchard's resistance.

On 23 August, faced by imminent national bankruptcy and a
hopelessly divided Cabinet, MacDonald resigned. At the King's
request, he agreed to continue in office at the head of an all-party
National Government. It was an act of personal courage which
impressed Trenchard and was greatly to influence his decision
when, in October, following Byng's long-delayed retirement, he
was again offered the commissionership.[2] Even then it was to take
a personal appeal from the King finally to resolve the *impasse*; and

---

[1] As a last-ditch alternative, the Government seem to have had in mind
General Sir Walter Braithwaite. It was fortunate for the Metropolitan
Police that he was not appointed, for in October he went instead to the
Royal Hospital, Chelsea, where he proved to be one of the least memorable
Governors in the history of that august institution.

[2] Andrew Boyle, *Trenchard*.

from this unique departure from precedent there was to grow a special relationship between the Commissioner's office and Buckingham Palace for which there is no other parallel.

*

Trenchard assumed his duties on 2 November. The four years during which he held office were to be more stimulating and controversial than any other period in the history of the Metropolitan Police except, perhaps, Sir Robert Mark's commissionership forty years later. And by November, events had added some very sharp nails to an already uncomfortable bed.

The Home Secretary in MacDonald's Coalition Government was Herbert Samuel whose first action was to make the police a special case by limiting the May Committee's pay cut to 5 per cent, the balance to be recovered from administrative economies, a decision which he announced in the Commons on 29 September in a form calculated to arouse the maximum controversy. The Police Federation, however, was not to be so easily placated, despite the manifest injustice to other public servants, and campaigned noisily against even the reduced cut as if Desborough had acquired the status of immutable Holy Writ. It was against this background that Trenchard took the stage.

MacDonald had promised him a free hand. 'Even if it means turning the force upside down?' 'If that's necessary, we'll support you,' replied MacDonald. Trenchard took him at his word.

It is still debated among policemen, old and new, whether Trenchard was the salvation or the scourge of the force. There had been no one like him before—certainly not Warren. not even Macready—and there has been no one like him since. He was the complete antithesis to Byng, autocratic, intolerant, but determined to be his own man and to have his own way. In this he was lucky, for, having waited so long to hook their big fish, ministers—with the exception of the Chancellor, Chamberlain, who detested Trenchard (and showed it)—were afraid lest, if they offended him, he would snap the line and escape. There was also his special relationship with Buckingham Palace. Looking at his whole achievement, crowded into four years,[1] he must be judged not only by the two (in the event, short-lived) reforms by which he is

---

[1] He described himself as 'an old man in a hurry'. In fact, he was only fifty-eight when he went to Scotland Yard.

chiefly remembered, but by the legacy of improved conditions and social amenities which he left his men and by the technical advances for which he was responsible. By these and many other standards he was a great man; whether he was a great policeman is more debatable. To the end there was only one real love in his life; but he allowed more than a little of that devotion to rub off on the Metropolitan Police, even if this was not always apparent to the man on the beat.

*

Trenchard's arrival had the effect not of a new broom, but of a seismic disturbance. He questioned, probed, hectored, and bullied. A constabulary wag described him as the only man he had met who would never take 'yes' for an answer. Yet with his sharp brain and eye for detail went a curious inability to communicate clearly, with the result that he was often incoherent in conversation and unintelligible when dictating.[1] Translating the Commissioner into English became a positive art among his secretarial staff.

Among Trenchard's papers there is a note, written at a later date, in which he identified the areas for action:[2]

I found that the state of discipline in the force was not good. There was a great deal of discontent with the conditions of service.

The Police Federation was holding 480 meetings a year and this had been going on for some twelve years. The Police Act of 1919 only sanctioned *twelve* meetings a year of one day each.

Many police constables were still patrolling the beats which were laid down by Sir Robert Peel a hundred years before.[3]

The Statistical Branch, if it could be called such, did not show where crime was most prevalent and was completely out of date.

There was no map-room.

There was no scientific laboratory.

There was no welfare officer.

[1] Howgrave-Graham (*op. cit.*) quotes some remarkable examples of Trenchard gibberish.

[2] Boyle, *op. cit.*

[3] Not so. The original beats were defined by Charles Rowan. By 1931 the geography of London had so changed that none of these beats remained.

The facilities for sport and recreation were completely inadequate.

The police section-houses ... were appalling, the married quarters even worse.

There was a very large proportion of constables compared with officers.

There was too much corruption.

There was too much tipping.

To this formidable catalogue Trenchard at once addressed himself with all the energy at his command.

*

He began with the higher command structure which, by a random process of evolution, had grown into a ramshackle, lop-sided affair with ill-defined and often overlapping responsibilities. It was also, Trenchard decided, indolent and complacent. It did not remain so for long.

His first step was to separate purely 'police' functions form what was known as 'civil business'. Under this reorganization there emerged four police departments with the following broad areas of responsibility: 'A'—administration and operational control of the uniform branch; 'B'—traffic; 'C'—crime; 'D'—organization, including training and recruitment. Aware of the short-comings of his assistant commissioners, Trenchard brought in Col. Maurice Drummond, who had served under him at the Air Ministry, as his personal staff officer—'part watch-dog, part heel-snapper' was his description. On the civil side, the Secretariat was greatly strengthened, while a new department—'L'—was created to take over the growing volume of legal work from Wontners, the firm of solicitors which had been appointed in 1887 to handle police affairs. Finance and related matters remained the province of the Receiver, John Moylan, who still retained the direct and separate relationship with Home Office officials which had proved so contentious since the time of John Wray. Trenchard, with MacDonald's unconditional backing, could afford to humour Moylan. Reading between the lines of his record of the period, Moylan was not amused.[1]

Further down the scale, the district chief constables were given

[1] Moylan, *op. cit.*

more muscle by the appointment of additional senior staff and their vaguely-defined supervisory role was given substance and purpose. A year later a further link in the command structure was provided by the addition of Chief Inspectors (Crime) in divisions. Well might the *Daily Express* report: 'The monthly reorganisation of the Metropolitan Police will take place weekly in future.'

*

Next Trenchard turned to the most critical area of his task—the men themselves.

The pay cut, despite Samuel's pledge to bypass the second stage, had done much to prejudice what *The Times* had called 'the force's recovery of confidence in itself'. Trenchard's first impression was that morale was low, discipline slack, and standards of conduct in both the uniform and plain-clothes branches a matter for serious concern. His first visits to police stations confirmed this view, although it must be said that his brusque and cavalier manner did little to endear him to the men. It did not take him long to decide that most of the trouble was due to the militant activities of the Police Federation.

Trenchard did not care for the Federation as a matter of principle (the antipathy was entirely mutual). Syndicalism seemed to him entirely inappropriate in a disciplined, uniformed body of men, whether civilian or military in origin, and he had all the evidence he needed to show that the London branch boards had been allowed a latitude in their activities which went far beyond the terms of reference laid down in the 1919 Police Act. Representation of grievances through the proper channels he would accept. Insubordination and challenges to authority he would not. Thus, while the staff at Scotland Yard were put urgently to work implementing Byng's plans for the revision of boundaries, beats, and duties,[1] Trenchard decided to take a leaf out of Macready's book and draw a few teeth. A month after taking office, he called a meeting of 3,000 men, representative of all ranks, at the Queen's Hall.

There was nothing of Macready's bluff good-humour about his short address to the men. They were, he told them, the servants of the public, and the public was getting unsatisfactory service. There were too many restrictive practices and too much dishonesty.

---

[1] The changes took place two months later, on 3 January 1932.

Above all, he was not prepared to tolerate the disruptive activities of the branch boards or their practice of using the press as a forum for mischievous propaganda. Urgent and major reforms were necessary and these would be announced in due time; there was also much that needed to be done to improve living and working conditions and to make the police service a profession to be proud of. He would do his part; he expected the men to do theirs.

He left his audience in no doubt that he meant business. It cannot be said that he and they parted on the best of terms.

*

The district officers were quickly put to work. Police Regulations were enforced to the letter. Uniform constables were seconded for plain-clothes duty. The Federation objected. The Special Constabulary was given practical training by attachment to divisions. The Federation objected. The mood was such that branch boards would have viewed with hostility and suspicion even a major improvement in pay and conditions. Trenchard was not to be deflected from his basic strategy, least of all by a body whose motives he suspected and whose activities he deplored; and early in 1932 he began work on a detailed analysis of the sickness at the heart of the Metropolitan Police and of a long-term programme of reforms. Fifteen months later his findings, and his proposals, were presented in his report for the year 1932.

He reduced the problem to a simple equation: age versus youth. 'There are,' he wrote, 'at the present time about 8,400 constables [*half the uniform strength*] who are already beyond the promotion zone and have little incentive to effort during their remaining years of service except their own sense of duty.' The average service of some 4,000 of these men was seventeen years and their attitude to the job was simply to soldier on until their pensionable date.[1] Their sense of duty was conditioned by a beckoning star which warned them that excessive zeal could bring expensive retribution. It was a situation which only a long-term reform could solve. But it was the other half of the equation which caused Trenchard greater concern. Despite the considerable improvement in pay which Desborough had introduced, the police service had

---

[1] A group photograph of S Division taken in 1931 is revealing. Of the 128 men, only 6 are wearing war medals. The others are therefore either the elderly or the very young.

still failed to attract young men of good education and ambition
from whom future leaders might be found outside the guide-lines
laid down by Peel and the artisan traditions of the Victorian era.
Whence was to come a future command structure from within the
service itself? How were youth and experience to be equated? And
how might Macready's rhetorical question one day be answered?

Trenchard worked tirelessly—and secretly—on a solution to
these problems. His so-called 'Police Book' was discussed only
with two or three close associates, and with the King, who took a
personal interest in 'my police'. It was not until the summer that
Trenchard showed his first draft to Samuel; and in September
1932, Samuel suddenly resigned on an entirely different matter of
Liberal principle.

His departure had two important results. First, the decision to
suspend the second stage of cuts in police pay was rescinded.[1] It
had always been an indefensible expedient and Trenchard rode the
storm without much difficulty. Secondly, the new Home Secretary
was Sir John Gilmour who was a devoted disciple of Trenchard.
Thus, despite much Cabinet apprehension, the grand design went
ahead.

*

By sheer force of logic and persuasion Trenchard carried with
him a Cabinet concerned not so much with the wisdom of his
proposals as with their divisive implications and, inevitably, their
financial cost. He had the unqualified support of the King; and he
took the unusual step of consulting the most influential editors in
Fleet Street in advance. Thus, by the spring of 1933, he felt sure
of his ground.

Timing was vital. His Annual Report was due to be published
on 3 May. It was agreed that a White Paper should follow a week
later and, before the end of the month, the parliamentary Bill
which would give effect to his proposals.

Trenchard's Report for 1932[2] is a milestone in Metropolitan
Police history comparable with Desborough. Howgrave-Graham
and his 'interpreters' did a thorough job and the result was the
first, and still perhaps the most important, examination of the
whole status, function, and future of the police service in London

[1] Remarkably, the 5 per cent cut was not restored until 1940.
[2] Cmd. 4294

It is not possible here to analyse in detail the arguments advanced by Trenchard or the radical nature of his proposals. A former Commissioner has suggested that Trenchard did not understand the true police function. The reader may care to consult the 1933 Report, and, even more significantly, Chapter 3 of the 1934 Report,[1] and judge for himself.

Trenchard's underlying concern was to rejuvenate an aging, disillusioned force by the introduction of young blood and—in the longer term—a new system of command structure which did not rely simply on the arithmetic of long service and good conduct. His first proposition was the Metropolitan Police College at Hendon.

A great deal of nonsense has been talked about Hendon—and still is. In the five short years of its existence, only 197 students passed through its doors. Two of them were to become Commissioners of the Police of the Metropolis, thus gratifying the shade of Macready. Many others went on to senior posts in the Metropolitan Police or as provincial Chief Constables and similar appointments overseas. It was an imaginative idea; and it foundered on the twin rocks of police and political prejudice.

Trenchard had carefully studied the abortive Dixon scheme. The resistance of local authorities to the establishment of a National College seemed less important to him than the inherent weakness of the scheme itself—the qualification of a minimum of five years' service before a man was eligible to apply for entry. If a subaltern could be fitted to exercise command at twenty, why not also a policeman? It was a false analogy, but it was central to Trenchard's philosophy.

The Hendon plan was a radical break with tradition. There were two categories of entry: from within the force by competitive examination or, in exceptional cases, by special recommendation; and direct from universities or colleges by examination or existing academic qualifications. Initially, the course lasted fifteen months, later increased to two years. It was not particularly demanding and has been described by a non-alumnus as 'by modern standards, derisory. It can be summed up not unfairly by the ancient dictum that CAT spells cat.'[2] This misses the point. Hendon was designed as a testing ground of character, not of scholastic ability. Even cats have character.

[1] Cmd. 4562   [2] Sir Robert Mark, *In the Office of Constable.*

For those who insisted—and still insist—that Hendon was a blatant attempt to impose an officer class on the Metropolitan Police, it is salutary to remember that of the 32 students who attended the first course in May 1934, 20 came from the force itself and only 12 from outside; while the 28 on the second course in September consisted of 20 serving policemen and 8 outsiders.

The press, with obvious exceptions, approved of the Hendon scheme (Trenchard had already been promised support in the most influential organs of opinion). There the consensus ended. 'It is an entirely Fascist development,' thundered the young Aneurin Bevan in the Commons, designed 'to make the police force more amenable to the orders of the Carlton Club and Downing Street'. The *Police Review* was even sillier: 'It is "class" legislation with a vengeance. In practice the plan will mean that the higher ranks of the Force will be filled in the main by young men who enter college directly from public school and university.'[1] In practice the plan meant nothing of the sort; and if, even by that narrow definition, it had succeeded in producing the leadership that the force so desperately lacked, then it would have amply justified itself. As for the force itself, Hendon immediately became a dirty word. The Federation soon saw to that.

*

Trenchard's second major proposal was an extension of his concern to introduce young blood into an ageing force and to attract a new type of recruit. It clearly owed much to the 'short-service' commission idea which he had initiated at Cranwell and its failure reflects Trenchard's inability to distinguish between the very different nature of service in the armed forces and the police.

The 'short-service engagement', described in detail in the 1933 Report and the White Paper, was duly incorporated in the new Metropolitan Police Bill. It proposed that up to 5,000 men—one quarter of the uniform strength—should be recruited over a ten-year period. They would serve for ten years and would then retire with a gratuity of one month's pay for each completed year of service (it was in fact an 'Irishman's gratuity' since the men had to contribute 5 per cent of their annual pay towards it). Short-service men could resign at any time but they could not transfer to ordinary service after completing their engagement.

[1] *Police Review*, 19 May 1933.

It was a thoroughly muddled concept. The old guard did not take kindly to the newcomers, and the twin objectives of a less elderly image and better promotion prospects for 'career constables' proved largely illusory. Trenchard had repeatedly dodged the most obvious issue—the built-in absurdity of losing young men at the very point when they had gained valuable experience. In practice, many short-service recruits did a limited stint in the Metropolis and, armed with impeccable credentials, departed to good jobs in provincial forces. It was left to Trenchard's successor to give the scheme a quiet burial in 1939. It had proved, if nothing else, that the ghost of Robert Peel was not easily to be laid.

The 1933 Metropolitan Police Act dealt with other matters of domestic rather than public interest. Predictably, the Federation was high on the list and one section of the Act was designed to clip its wings. Membership was restricted to inspectors, sergeants and constables; Hendon students graduating as junior station inspectors were forbidden to join; official time spent on branch board meetings was strictly regulated; and restrictions were placed on the circulation of minutes and resolutions. There was to be no more mischief-making in Fleet Street.

Another section dealt with a reduction in the compulsory retirement age of senior officers. The object was virtuous, but since the problem of finding suitable material for promotion to the highest ranks had not been solved, it was largely academic.

Finally, the Act dealt with an old custom of the trade—the 'gratuities' system—under which policemen could be employed in their spare time by private persons on direct payment. It was a practice to which Trenchard strongly objected. 'Moonlighting' in plain clothes as a means of supplementing wages, although itself contrary to regulations, was one matter; but private employment in uniform outside hours of duty was open to serious abuse and, in a comparable context, 'militated against good order and military discipline'. In future 'the legitimate requirements of all the employers concerned will be met by the supply of such police as are necessary, on payment to the Police Fund at the approved rates'. Such was the new law; and who shall say how many half-crowns continued to pass from hand to hand?

By the end of 1933, Trenchard felt that he had cauterized the most obvious wounds. What remained was a matter of applying anti-septics; and on 13 March 1934 he wrote at great length to MacDonald, setting out what he had done or set in train, and asking to be relieved of his duties. MacDonald might have felt his request to be irresistible; but for a second time, Trenchard found himself trapped by the royal imperative. The King wished him to stay. And so he stayed.

By one of those recurring paradoxes of police history, Trenchard's last eighteen months—when the 'old man' was no longer in a hurry—were the most hectic and fruitful of his commissionership. By the end it could fairly be said that he had indeed 'turned the force upside down'. Moreover, his programme of reforms and innovations was carried through in the face of bitter opposition from Home Office mandarins reminiscent of the days of Lushington, and now orchestrated by Dixon and his deputy, Newsam, of the Police Department. Anderson had long since left to govern Bengal. His successor, Russell Scott, was a time-serving nonentity; and Trenchard had a simple way with nonentities. He by-passed them. Gilmour was his man and Gilmour could speak for him in Cabinet. To the Home Secretary's doubts about the cost to public funds, Trenchard's reply was short and sharp: 'The Government will provide the funds if you dun them hard enough.' Thus encouraged, Gilmour proved more than a match for the Chancellor, Chamberlain.

It is not possible to dwell here in detail on the long calendar of Trenchard's legacy, but a summary will show that it falls into three main areas: the quality of life in the police service; the improvement of training methods and facilities; and the modernization of both preventive and detective policing.

Almost without exception, the force was still living and working in buildings dating from Victorian times, with amenities wretched even by the standards of an urban peasantry. Police stations were gloomy monuments to a world of austerity—'lock-ups for drunkards' in Trenchard's phrase. 4,000 single constables lived in 115 section-houses which Trenchard described in a letter to Gilmour as 'a disgrace to civilization'. 'It is hard,' he went on, 'to raise the status of the decent man if we do this sort of thing to them.' Married quarters were an even greater disgrace. Modest improvements had been made in Bradford's time, but cosmetic solutions were not Trenchard's way; and brushing aside objections of cost, he went ahead with an elaborate programme to provide his men with the best that even limited money could buy: 'Nice things,' he said in a revealing aside, 'make nice people.' And to ensure that his message was clearly understood, he appointed a Welfare Officer in A Dept.

Next he turned to recreation. In 1919, Col. Laurie had established a training centre for the Mounted Branch and a sports ground and clubhouse for the Metropolitan Police Athletic Association at Imber Court near Thames Ditton. This catered for No. 1 District, but by the end of 1934 Trenchard had provided similar recreation facilities for the remaining three districts. This involved killing another sacred cow.

By long tradition, the force had raised money for charitable and recreational ends by door-to-door selling of tickets for various police functions. Trenchard liked this practice no more than the 'gratuity' system, since non-contributors might feel (sometimes with good reason) that they would incur police displeasure; nor, as with the Provident Fund, were true and proper accounts kept. If, in Trenchard's view, a begging-bowl was necessary, then there were less demeaning and questionable ways of handing it round. Ticket-selling was therefore stopped and Trenchard turned instead to the business community, supplemented by an appeal for donations from the general public, and by the end of 1933 he had raised some £30,000 which was used to create a Commissioner's Fund[1] to be applied for recreational and charitable purposes. The men were also encouraged to make their own contribution to sports facilities by a small weekly subscription. This break with precedent was not popular; and that, to Trenchard, was enough to prove his point.

Finally he turned to the problem of Scotland Yard itself where, as a result of the expansion of support services and the addition of new departments, 'the staff are crowded together like warehouse clerks in a Christmas rush'.[2] Despite the appropriation of the Cannon Row section-house and the transfer of the Public Carriage and Lost Property Offices and the Receiver's stores to Lambeth, working conditions remained intolerable. Trenchard's proposal for a complete removal to a new site was rejected and it was not until a

---

[1] The Fund stood at £40,000 in 1978. It is administered by a board of trustees at New Scotland Yard.

[2] *Commissioner's Report, 1935.*

few weeks before his retirement that approval was given for the
construction of a new block to the north of Norman Shaw's
building. It was completed very conveniently for Lord Mountbatten
to move in with his Combined Operations HQ in 1940.[1]

The opening of the Police College at Hendon in May 1934 provided the space and incentive to develop specialist training facilities (there was even room for the new No. 2 District sports
ground), and within a year Trenchard had established a Wireless
School, a Driving School, and a Detective School, while work had
started on a new Peel House which had long since outgrown the
premises in Regency Street where Henry had set up the first centre
for recruit training. Even after the closing of the College, Hendon
remained, as it does today under its new name of Peel Centre, the
breeding-ground for the men and methods of the Metropolitan
Police.

Social welfare and thorough training were essential prerequisites
for an efficient police force, but both were necessarily long-term
in their effects. The maintenance of the Queen's Peace was another
matter, constant, inescapable, omnipresent. The preamble to
Peel's 1829 Act had spoken of 'the Want of Connection' between
parish authorities. Trenchard, unconsciously perhaps, fastened
onto this phrase and most of his operational reforms were designed
to provide realistic information and to improve communications.
His first step was to create a Statistical Department which recorded
all crimes in the Metropolitan Police District under two main
headings: 'preventable' and 'detectable'. The measure of success of
police operations lay in the figures for preventable crime such as
burglary and theft, and the statistics for the two years from July
1933 to July 1935 showed a fall of 19.6 per cent. Figures, however,
have no virtue in a vacuum, so Trenchard instituted the Daily
Crime Telegram and map rooms at Scotland Yard and in divisions
which provided an up-to-date visual record of the incidence of
crime by category and location. Thus his commanders in the
field could identify at any moment how and where the enemy
was operating and so deploy their own troops to the best advantage.

Pursuing the same theme, Trenchard entirely redesigned Byng's
experimental Information Room, linking it to radio cars in fifty-two

[1] For six months the author occupied the office allocated to the head of
the Flying Squad.

'wireless areas' under a newly-appointed Wireless Officer.[1] Within the technical limitations of the time, this provided unique defensive cover for the Metropolis. It was a far cry from the Bow Street Runners and the Horse Patrol, but the natural extension of Colquhoun's 'new science of Police'. And it was to science that Trenchard turned for his final reform.

Since the introduction of Henry's Finger Print Bureau in 1901, detective policing in the Metropolis had relied on the traditional— and, let it be said, still fundamental—system of patient investigation and intuition. Medical jurisprudence, long established abroad and already in existence in a few provincial forces, had made little headway in London, not least because of the conservative attitude of the judiciary. Scotland Yard had thus to rely on Home Office or even private pathologists and chemists. This was not to Trenchard's taste, and on 10 April 1935 the Metropolitan Police Forensic Laboratory was opened at Hendon under Dr James Davidson of Edinburgh University.[2] The wheel had come full circle.

*

Reflecting upon Trenchard's magisterial term of office, two question marks remain.

In all his four Annual Reports and in his considerable correspondence, there is not one single reference to the pay and pensions of his men. He could—and did—fight like a tiger for money for projects like Hendon and for new section-houses and sports grounds. So great was his influence in high places that, despite Dixon and Newsam, he could have carried the day. He seems to have distanced himself from the rank and file as if they were socially inferior to the 'young eagles' of the RAF.

His second—and more serious—failure was in his handling of the CID; for here Trenchard, the man of decision, showed an uncharacteristic irresolution. In his letter to MacDonald on 13 March 1934, he claimed that 'the state of jealous rivalry . . .

[1] In July 1937, Trenchard's successor introduced the '999' dialling system. It was an inspired stroke of public relations for it involved the public themselves in the war on crime and underlined the historical principle that 'the police are the people and the people are the police'.

[1] Today the Metropolitan Police Forensic Laboratory is the only one under the direct control of a police force. All forensic laboratories in provincial forces are subject to Home Office direction.

which has so long existed between the CID and the uniform branch is gradually being put to an end, and the two branches integrated into one harmonious whole'. He was deceiving only himself; indeed many of his reforms went far towards widening a rift which had existed for sixty years. He was constantly alive to the extent of CID corruption and his correspondence with Gilmour during 1934 is a curious commentary on his intellectual cowardice. The man who could talk with kings seemed frightened of corrupt constables.

*

He resigned on Armistice Day, 1935. He had recommended as his successor Air Vice-Marshal Sir Philip Game, who had been a senior staff officer with him at the Air Ministry and subsequently Governor of New South Wales. The one condition that he laid down was that there should be no interference with his two central reforms, the Police College at Hendon and the short-service engagement. But by 1939 both these monuments had been dismantled. Game did nothing to save them, and Trenchard never forgave him for what he called his 'treachery'.

CHAPTER TEN

From Peace to War

TRENCHARD'S DEPARTURE was greeted with mixed feelings. Even the left-wing press, which had campaigned against his major reforms as undemocratic and class-oriented, saluted a man who had practised what he preached and who had done so much for the quality of life in the service. The Government was sorry to see him go, for in the political climate of the day he represented a source of strength and stability. The Home Office officials were, if not gratified, at least relieved. Towards the end, relations between Whitehall and Scotland Yard had become dangerously strained, and Trenchard's contempt for traditional channels had left a trail of bruised egos.

The attitude in the force is more difficult to define. The Federation lit bonfires of celebration. For four years the branch boards had been treated as a not particularly necessary evil and their members had been given clearly to understand that the Commissioner, while disposed to tolerate their existence, was not prepared to accept defiance of his authority. The men wept few tears. As has been suggested, Trenchard's relationship with them *as men* was always at arm's length, aloof, even abrasive. Very few knew or understood what he had achieved, in the face of hostile opposition from other quarters, to improve their condition and contribute to their welfare, for these reforms would take some years to take effect. They did know that he had suspended the old gratuity and ticket-selling practices, and that he had created the 'Hendon' idea; and this rankled. It is difficult to find one single policeman of his time who remembers him today with affection or gratitude. At best he earned respect for his integrity and a kind of reverent awe for his sheer stature as a man.

Philip Game was much closer to Byng than Trenchard, although without Byng's charisma. Four years of reforming zeal had left ministers and mandarins confused and the force, in Trenchard's words, 'very sulky'. It was a time for taking stock; and, by a curious conjunction of events, Trenchard's going was marked by the arrival of Baldwin at Downing Street, and Sir John Simon at the Home Office. Thus at the end of 1935 the Metropolitan Police found itself under entirely new management, and much of the heat went out of the kitchen.

One of Game's first moves was to re-establish diplomatic relations with the Federation. In fact he was scarcely more accommodating than Trenchard, but by meeting the branch board representatives and listening patiently to their long-winded arguments, he gave the impression of impartiality and sweet reason. When, in 1937, he began to dismantle Trenchard's two most controversial reforms, the Federation congratulated itself on having forced his hand. In this they were quite wrong. Game certainly took note of the hostile attitude of the force toward Hendon and the short-service engagement, but his own objections to both schemes were based on other, more serious, grounds. At the Home Office, Dixon and Newsam assumed the role of devil's advocates with enthusiasm.

So far as Hendon was concerned, there were two problems which Trenchard, in his determination to get his project off the ground, had not properly considered. The minimum age limit of twenty for outside entrants was too high to attract the best material, for whom time was an essential element in choosing a career to match their talents. Secondly, the post-war structure of the force, and the extension of the qualifying period for full pension rights to thirty years after the Desborough report[1] meant that, short of arbitrary dismissals at the top, the promotion prospects of Trenchard's 'young men' would be increasingly slim. It was an actuarial fact of life which made nonsense of the whole purpose of Hendon.

Nor did the short-service engagement, designed by Trenchard to 'rejuvenate' the force, commend itself to Game, partly because it was unpopular but much more certainly because it was a rather indifferent conjuror's trick which succeeded only in producing a few hundred rabbits out of the hat to the cost of London's ratepayers and the advantage of provincial police forces. If youth was Trenchard's purpose, it is strange that he never considered the idea of police cadets which was to prove so notable an innovation twenty years later.

In 1938, Game put his proposals for the immediate future of

---

[1] Police Pensions Act 1921.

Hendon to Simon at the Home Office. These were as follows: entry by competitive examination should be suspended; all candidates should do twelve months' service as constables on the beat before acceptance; and, in the last resort, the College should be temporarily closed until the promotion log-jam showed signs of movement.

Thoughtfully, if perhaps unwisely, Game gave his predecessor advance notice of his intentions and incurred an outburst of Olympian wrath for his pains. Trenchard accused Game of disloyalty (which was untrue) and of surrendering to Home Office pressure (which was nearer the mark), but short of making a public fool of himself, he was no longer in a position to influence decisions. The College which he had fathered was now an orphan child.

When, after a leisurely period of deliberation, Simon made up his mind, very little of the original Hendon scheme remained. Game's first two proposals were accepted. Direct entry was restricted to six or less a year and all such applicants were required to do a preliminary year's service as uniform constables. The upper age limit for entrants from the force itself was increased to thirty and the new ranks of station inspector and junior station inspector were abolished, while admission to the College was opened to provincial forces. These radical changes did much to silence criticism from the federated ranks, but to the end Hendon, for all its modest scale, remained an object of suspicion and jealousy.

The new plan was never put into operation, for on the outbreak of war the College was closed. It had always been viewed with hostility by the Left and with the return of a Labour government in 1945 a very different kind of scheme for the higher training of the police service was introduced on a national scale. Hendon therefore remains something of an enigma. It never had a real chance to prove itself. Most of those graduates who went on to greater things (and not all did) would probably have risen to the top whatever the system; but it was a brave experiment and a monument to a considerable man, who could never have imagined the petty— and not so petty—feuds and vendettas which his brain-child would breed in the Metropolitan Police thirty years later.

*

The four peacetime years of Game's commissionership were, in administrative terms, a season of calm weather. Trenchard's imaginative programme in the field of housing and welfare had mortgaged most, if not all, available financial resources and, under a more congenial leader, the force which Trenchard had described as 'very sulky' recovered its temper. There is a certain irony in this revival of morale—and for this reason. Nowhere has it been remarked (and it is a remarkable fact) that in the twenty years between the Desborough award and 1939, the basic pay scale of the Metropolitan Police remained unchanged. In practice, it had actually been reduced three times—twice by compulsory increases in pension contributions (which amounted to reductions in gross pay) and once by the 10 per cent cut ordained by the May Committee. Here was a fertile field for the Federation to exploit, but apart from one half-hearted claim in 1937 there seems to have been a curious conspiracy of silence. In none of the branch board minutes nor in the Commissioner's annual reports is the subject mentioned. Such forbearance was not to be repeated in the postwar years.

On the streets of the Metropolis, however, things were not always so calm. In the autumn of 1933, Trenchard had expressed his concern to Gilmour about the activities of Sir Oswald Mosley's British Union of Fascists and in particular the doubtful legality of the wearing of uniforms by political extremists. The Home Office, blind to the spectacle of unbridled nationalism across the Channel, dismissed Trenchard's anxiety as, in Dixon's words, 'an error of judgement'. Nor did Trenchard get any clear directive when he demonstrated the growing strain on his limited resources in keeping Fascists and Communists apart, or when, mindful of the government attitude to Henderson and Warren in the 1880s, he asked for a definition of the Commissioner's statutory powers in maintaining public order. Peace at any price, it seems, was not the sole prerogative of Baldwin's successor.

Game partially succeeded where Trenchard had failed, for by the end of 1935 the confrontations of Right and Left had become a serious matter of public concern. Jack Lea, a mounted constable at Hackney, was kept busy: 'Ridley Road was our evening's entertainment. The mob called us "Laurie's Cossacks" and when they got nasty we just rode in and thumped them.' At last the Government moved. The Public Order Act of 1936 prohibited 'the wearing of uniforms in connection with political objects and the maintenance by private persons of associations of military or similar character' and it further defined the Commissioner's powers in regulating or, at his discretion, forbidding public meetings and processions. To this extent it reaffirmed his independence of outside interference in the discharge of his operational role; and—by inference—his accountability.[1] The Blackshirts did not take kindly to statutory restraint, and Jack Lea was still kept busy.

As the dogs of war began to bay, an old adversary reappeared to cry havoc in the Metropolis. For many years the Irish had occupied themselves with their private and domestic feuds. Now, for no particular reason other than the pleasure of causing pain, the IRA returned to London and during the early months of 1939 there were seventeen bombing incidents in the West End and at main railway terminals. The pattern was a crude copy of the Fenian troubles of the 1880s and was equally ineffective. The citizens of the Metropolis—and their police—were soon to be confronted by a much more formidable test of their character and courage.

*

It is not possible within the scope of this book to describe in detail the record of the Metropolitan Police in the Second World War, nor to consider the wider context of the whole police service of the country; for, out of the refiner's fire, there was to emerge a new concept of the police function which acknowledged for the first time in over a century that law and order are indivisible and that crime—by no means the sole preoccupation of a police institution—cannot be contained within county boundaries. Throughout the 1930s—by way of the proposal for a National Police College and the even more radical recommendations of the Detective Committee in 1938[2]—there had been a gradual movement towards the principle of 'common services' and the sharing of technical resources. The 'nationalization' lobby found few friends, but the experience of the war years showed that a system which tolerated 183 separate police forces in England and Wales was a financial folly and an administrative absurdity.[3] The process of rationalization

---

[1] 'I have been discussing amendment of the 1936 Act. The general consensus is to leave it as it is.' Merlyn Rees, *Parliamentary Debate*, 4 August 1978.
[2] See Critchley, *op. cit.*
[3] The three smallest police forces were: Liberty of Peterborough—10; Tiverton—11; Clitheroe—15.

was to take several years, and not the least of its by-products was to bring to Scotland Yard perhaps the most outstanding of all Commissioners of Police.

＊

In 1935, the Home Office had begun work on a pilot survey of the organization of civil defence, including 'questions relative to the duties of the Police in the event of war'. The Committee appointed to consider these matters proceeded with little sense of urgency until the Munich crisis in 1938 set the alarm bells ringing. There followed a year of feverish activity.

The strategy of civil defence assumed—on the pattern of Guernica—immediate and massive air attacks, with London as the main target. Central to the defence plan were the police, for war does not override the maintenance of law and order; indeed, the flood of Defence Regulations put a heavy burden on the force which was responsible for ensuring their observance; and because of their existing communications network the police became the agency for coordinating the warning system and the fire, rescue, and ARP services.[1]

During 1939, there had been a review of police man-power requirements in the event of war, since plainly the regular force would not be anything like large enough to handle its additional—and largely unprecedented—responsibilities (in September 1939 its strength was 18,428, i.e. 930 under establishment). Accordingly three reserves were formed: the First Reserve, consisting of pensioners who volunteered for re-engagement; the Second Reserve, consisting of special constables enlisted on a full-time paid basis; and the Third—or Police War—Reserve recruited for war service only.[2] By 5 September, when all three reserves had been mobilized, the respective strengths were 2,737, 5,380, and 18,868. It was in total by far the largest regular and auxiliary constabulary in the history of the Metropolis.

Among their first duties the police were involved in rounding up

---

[1] To decentralize control, England and Wales were divided into eleven regions each under a commissioner, an unconsciously ironic echo of Cromwell's 'little poor invention'.

[2] In addition, these categories were supplemented by a considerable number of part-time special constables and by a newly-formed Women's Auxiliary Police Corps.

and registering aliens and in organizing the exodus of 100,000 evacuees to a countryside which viewed their arrival with an apprehension usually reserved for an invading army. The enforcement of Defence Regulations and the supervision of air-raid precautions kept both uniform and plain-clothes branches busy, and 'Put out that light!' (expletive deleted) was the common currency of the new nightly 'watch and ward'. Security became a national obsession —kite-flying, pigeons, and fireworks were matters of particular moment—and Special Branch was substantially increased in size. The Metropolis braced itself for its ordeal by fire.

But the bombers did not come. This unexpected breathing-space (which the enemy may have had cause to regret) provided an opportunity to give essential training to the thousands of War Reserve auxiliaries whose expertise did not yet match their enthusiasm. Indeed, towards the end of the year a number of 'specials' were stood down subject to immediate recall in an emergency, while those regulars whose obligations as reservists had been deferred on the outbreak of war were released to join the colours.[1]

*

The first bomb to fall in the Metropolitan Police District was at Addington on 19 June 1940, during one of the many daylight attacks on airfields in southern England, and through the long, hot summer the Battle of Britain was fought out in the skies above the Home Counties; but it was not until the night of Saturday, 7 September, that the enemy switched his attack to London with the first concentrated night raid. The 'Blitz' had begun.

The first phase was to last with little respite until July of the following year. During this period alone there were more than 1,000 'alerts'. Civilian casualties by the summer of 1941 were of the order of 23,000 killed and 40,000 injured, and if much of the destruction was concentrated in the East End and the City, no part of the capital escaped without its honourable scars.[2] The English, when roused, are a formidable people, whether in the cockpit of

---

[1] The police service remained a 'reserved' occupation until 1941 when, to meet the demand for aircrew, regulars were allowed to volunteer for the RAF as pilots and observers. Early in 1942, regulars and auxiliaries under the age of twenty-five and thirty respectively were permitted to join the other services.

[2] See Howgrave-Graham, *The Metropolitan Police at War*.

war or in defence of their ancient liberties; and the same breed of
citizen that had reviled Peel's 'New Police' a century earlier now
looked upon them as a very present help in trouble. Charles Rowan
would have been justly proud; for the police were at the heart of the
battle (on 11 May 1941 a direct hit on Scotland Yard deposited
several tons of masonry and the best part of a million registry cards
in the Commissioner's office from the floor above) and their
patience, courage, and 'perfect command of temper' had an incal-
culable effect on civilian morale. Of no other section of the community could it be more truly said that this was their finest hour.[1]

*

As Hitler turned to attack Russia and the Luftwaffe was committed to operations on the Eastern Front, there was a long lull.
During 1942 there were only six minor raids on the Metropolis,
and between January 1943 and April 1944 a further seventy-five
(this was the period of the so-called 'Baedeker raids'). Although
they did not compare in severity with the Blitz, they caused re-
newed disruption and, in five incidents, including the Bethnal
Green tragedy, substantial casualties. None the less, this period of
comparative calm saw the return of many evacuees and a sharp
reduction in the strength of both regulars[2] and auxiliaries, as casualties, wastage, and the man-power demands of the armed services
whittled the numbers down. But for London, the play was not
over. The last and most dramatic act was still to come.

*

The first V1 missile, or 'flying-bomb', landed on 12 June 1944;
the last at Waltham Cross on 28 March 1945. In all, 2,341 flying-
bombs fell in the Metropolitan Police District, mostly concentrated in the period of ten weeks to the end of August, the main
target areas being the south and south-east of the capital. Their
effect would have been substantially greater and the weight of
attack perhaps insupportable but for RAF counter-strikes and the
overrunning of many launching-sites by the Allied armies.

---

[1] Figures for crime, so far as the statistics go, showed a marked decline,
even if the cynics argued that professional rogues had only traded their
civilian suits for service uniforms. The new name of the game was 'Black
Market'.
[2] Recruiting for the regular force had been suspended in 1942.

But there was one more engine of destruction in the German armoury, perhaps the most sinister of all, for its ultimate design was as a vehicle for the atomic warheads which by 1945 the enemy was within measurable distance of perfecting. The first V2 rocket fell at Chiswick during the early evening of 8 September 1944, the second at Epping less than a minute later. Between then and 30 March 1945, 513 rockets fell in the Metropolitan Police District.[1] It proved to be the gambler's final throw. On 10 April the sirens sounded for the last time.

The missile attack created a new dimension of terror for the war-weary citizens of London and new problems for the police and the civil defence organization, for by its random nature the attack succeeded in dispersing the available resources of the fire and rescue services, and launchings were timed to cause the maximum disruption. Thus for nearly ten months London was in a state of virtually permanent alert (V2 rockets arrived without warning) and Government concern was demonstrated by the evacuation of 276,000 citizens after the first flying-bomb attack. It was a close call, but once again the police, despite their reduced numbers, were equal to their last and greatest challenge.

*

With the return of peace the Metropolitan Police could count the cost. 'In all,' wrote Howgrave-Graham, 'nearly 1,900 cases of damage to police buildings were reported and 124 of these were serious.' Casualties among regulars and auxiliaries amounted to 208 killed and 1,942 injured, which in view of the constant involvement of the force throughout these years is little short of miraculous. Between them they won 276 honours and awards for gallantry during air-raids, including 82 George Medals (astonishingly, no police officer received the George Cross).[2] Of the regulars who joined the services, 490 were killed in action, three-quarters of them in the RAF. 101 were decorated or mentioned in despatches; and the civil staff had equal cause for pride.

[1] Casualties from V1 and V2 missiles totalled 7,988 killed and 20,783 seriously injured, a much higher ratio per incident than in conventional air-raids. It is worth recording that the city of Antwerp, in easier range, received 8,696 flying-bombs and 1,610 rockets (Churchill, *History of the Second World War*, Vol VI).

[2] Three police horses were awarded the Dickin Medal for bravery during air-raids.

With the end of the war in Europe, the pensioners and auxiliaries returned to cultivate their gardens. When, after ten years in office, Sir Philip Game resigned on 31 May 1945, the regular strength of the Metropolitan Police stood at 12,231, the lowest figure for over sixty years.

Interlude: Change and Decay

The end of the war left a Metropolis disfigured, a people strained by years of austerity, and a nation close to bankruptcy. It was in no way a parallel with 1918 when, despite the sacrifice and the cost, men and women looked hopefully to the future. Now, in 1945, the prospect was bleak and the national temper cynical; for one single second on the morning of 6 August had determined that nothing would ever be the same again.

The Bomb changed everything. If this seems an extravagant premise on which to base the problems and dilemmas which were to face the Metropolitan Police in the post-war years, then it is important to turn aside and briefly consider the implications. What has Hiroshima to do with Grosvenor Square? Or Notting Hill? Or Grunwick? Fair questions.

It is no part of this book to dabble in the muddy pond of geo-politics; but the Hiroshima bomb produced an 'ideological' fall-out no less devastating than the explosion itself and more dangerous and persistent than any nuclear physicist would have contemplated. It created a new world of super-powers and it contributed to the destruction of the greatest empire of modern times. It is these two momentous events which, however improbably, were to transform the British way of life and create, by way of an unprecedented social revolution, a crisis of conscience. Ten days before Hiroshima the Attlee government took office, the first Labour administration with the majority and mandate to create a socialist state in a country long wedded to the inevitability of gradualness. Any Metropolitan policeman, of whatever political persuasion, should have had cause for concern, for law and order have never been central to the radical tradition and the belief that a police institution is an affront to proletarian aspirations dies hard. Peel had discovered this and so, to their cost, had Rowan and Mayne. In 1948, Bevan had referred to the Labour Party as 'the party of compassion'. Thirty years later, on 2 September, in a speech dealing with juvenile delinquency and the increase in crime due to a lack of parental discipline and the decline in moral standards, Lord Justice Lawton had this to say: 'If and when a new Edward Gibbon comes to write the *Decline and Fall of the British Empire*, he might well entitle the last chapter "The Age of Compassionate Fools".' It is not difficult to suggest a number of equally apposite and less temperate alternatives.

*

All power corrupts; but it corrupts only those who enjoy the experience of being corrupted. Never was this to be more true than during the post-war years. The new society, with its vision of a synthetic Utopia, its appeal to materialism, its tolerance of indiscipline, and its politics of envy, has much to answer for; both in its equivocal attitude to law and order and in its tacit acceptance that the distinction between liberty and licence is no more than a pleasant dialectical exercise at university high tables. The age of 'angry young men' took no account of the silent—and equally angry—majority; and in this moral confrontation, the police were to be sorely tried; not all were themselves to escape contamination.

These were to be the 'permissive' years, a typically English euphemism for the devaluation of moral standards and justified by civil libertarians as the cult of virtue through the tolerance of vice. There had been nothing comparable since the eighteenth century when the wise and troubled Patrick Colquhoun had written: 'Evil will always drive out good, unless good takes up arms to defend itself.'[1] Indeed, London in the post-war period had much in common with Rome in the years before the fall of the Western Empire: a city stifled by bureaucracy, decadent, corrupt, happily feasting on borrowed bread and circuses, its churches empty and its prelates marching from Aldermaston to Trafalgar Square. It spawned its own language: the 'spiv'; the 'fellow traveller' (or more precisely, the communist without the courage of his convictions); the 'beautiful' people; the 'trip'; 'demo'; 'aggro'. And the police, holding that narrow line between anarchy and order, were charmingly labelled 'pigs' and 'fuzz'. It took a Scottish crofter's grandson, with Robert Peel's badge in his button-hole, to sum it all up: 'You've never had it so good.'

*

[1] Colquhoun, *op. cit.*

There are very few Metropolitan policemen of the post-war period who would not find that a more offensive—and provocative —commentary on the temper of our times than all the radical invitations to public indiscipline put together; for consider some of the manifestations of this new Jerusalem.

The traitors—Fuchs, Nunn May, Pontecorvo, Burgess and Maclean, Philby—a new breed of men dedicated to the subversion of the very society in which they had prospered; the Anti-Vietnam demonstrators who abused civil liberty to an extent that would have shamed John Wilkes; the militant trade unionists who defied the law and challenged the law to defy them; the urban guerillas who sought by terror to overthrow an ancient, if yet imperfect, order of democracy; the immigrant tidal wave, born of the dissolution of empire, which was to create for the police the most intractable of all their problems. Hence Grosvenor Square and Grunwick and Notting Hill.

To be sure, the criminal was never to have had it so good, as the bleak statistics of successive Commissioner's Reports rehearse year by year. Typical of the new morality was the growth of two flourishing industries, virtually unknown in pre-war days: drugs and pornography,[1] whose financial possibilities were presently to prove irresistible to a small but greedy handful of detective officers themselves. In such a climate of decadence, Socrates, convicted of corrupting the young, would have been thought a folk-hero.

Yet in the sombre calendar of the years ahead, two other growth industries dominate all the rest: crimes of violence[2] and juvenile delinquency. Neither was new. Both were to achieve levels which would have astonished the Fieldings and even Charles Dickens. Of the two, juvenile crime was, and is, the most serious of all post-war developments. There has always been vandalism; but how many of Lord Byng's police telephone-boxes would have survived for a single week today? There has always been hooliganism; but how many railway carriages were reduced to rubble by football followers

[1] To the permissive catalogue, Judge Lawton's 'compassionate fools' added the liberalization of abortion and homosexuality.

[2] In 1956, a Royal Commission recommended the abolition of capital punishment (briefly suspended for an experimental period in 1948), but instead the Homicide Act of 1957 divided the crime of murder into two categories: capital and non-capital. The death penalty was eventually abolished by the Wilson government in 1965. The last two murderers to be executed were Allen and Evans in 1964.

forty years ago? This has nothing to do with Pascal's view of human nature. It has everything to do with the collapse of authority, both domestic and public. In no other city is it possible to find a parallel statistic to the fact that, during a sixteen-month period, of those arrested for taking and driving away a motor vehicle, seventy-one were under the age of twelve.

*

Such was the world in which the Metropolitan Police was now to find itself involved; short of men, short of leadership, vulnerable as always to political attack, slow to assert its public image. On 26 May 1977, *The Times* published a leader under the heading: *The Anger of the Police*. They had good cause to be angry.

The Disorderly Society

IN NOVEMBER 1944, the Home Secretary, Herbert Morrison, sent for Sir Harold Scott. 'Can you ride a horse?' he asked. It was an unusual way of inviting a man to become Commissioner of Police of the Metropolis.

Scott was an archetypal civil servant. His career had started in 1911 in that section of the Home Office which dealt with Metropolitan Police affairs (eight years before Arthur Dixon and the formation of the Police Department) and he was later chairman of the Prison Commissioners for seven years. In 1944 he was Permanent Secretary at the Ministry of Aircraft Production.

There is no formal record of the reasons for Morrison's choice. With three exceptions—Mayne, Monro and Henry—the post of Commissioner had always been filled by a senior officer of the armed services and it could well have been argued that during the post-war period of reconstruction the force needed, as never before, a man of the stature of Trenchard. There was no shortage of candidates. According to Scott, Morrison explained that he wanted to emphasize the civilian character of the police (he himself was a policeman's son)[1] and that 'in the changed conditions of a post-war world the work of the Commissioner would call rather for experience of administration in a big civil department than experience in the military field'.[2] There is, however, an equally plausible explanation. At the Home Office, Sir Arthur Dixon was not far from retirement. To his deputy, Frank Newsam, Scott—a far more senior member of the Establishment—appeared a strong candidate for the succession . . . unless he could be enticed away by a more challenging prospect. And what prospect more challenging than the commissionership of the Metropolitan Police? If this theory is

---

[1] The Police Federation acquired a cordial dislike for Morrison, an arrogant man who treated the Joint Central Committee with something less than brotherly love.

[2] Sir Harold Scott, *Scotland Yard*.

right, it worked to perfection; for Scott became an administrative robot (if never an accomplished horseman), and Newsam the power behind the Home Office throne. Whatever the true answer may be, Scott's appointment broke once and for all the tradition of a service chief at New Scotland Yard, and in that sense was to make possible the fulfilment of Macready's prophecy; and with one exception— Sir David McNee—all Scott's successors were to be promoted from the office of Deputy Commissioner. But that, as we shall see, is another story.

*

Scott took over from Game on 1 June 1945. The Annual Report for his first full year opens with these words: 'The year 1946 has been a difficult year for the Metropolitan Police. Crime is far above the pre-war level and traffic has returned to the London streets on a pre-war scale, while the strength of the Regular Force is lower than it has been for sixty years.' Before his resignation in 1953, he was to present six more Reports. Give or take a change of emphasis here or a different phrase there, each begins with the same melancholy message.

There were many reasons for this continuing situation, some of them ancient, some modern. Just as police pay had fallen well behind that of industrial workers during the First World War, so now the pattern had repeated itself. Even the extra benefits which Desborough had introduced began to lose their special attraction as the welfare state assumed the role of Dutch uncle to the nation at large. The Police Act of 1946[1] provided modest increases in the pay-scale but they were little more than hollow gestures; and one increase which the Commissioner could have done without was the addition of forty-seven squares miles to an already overstrained Metropolitan Police District.

A more serious problem and a direct legacy of the war was the housing shortage. And this, even more than inadequate pay, was a

[1] One of the main purposes of the Act was to give statutory authority for the compulsory amalgamation of provincial forces, a process which had started on a voluntary basis during the war. By the end of 1947, the 183 police forces in England and Wales had been reduced to 131; in 1960 there were still 125; and it was not until after the Royal Commission of 1960–2 and the 1964 Police Act that the total was reduced to the present figure of forty-three.

deterrent to recruiting and a major reason for premature retirement. 'My wife and children,' recalls a former constable with—in 1945—fourteen years' service, 'had been evacuated to Dorset at the time of the buzz-bombs. Our home in Bermondsey had been blitzed. It was impossible to find decent accommodation in London and since she could not join me, my only alternative was to chuck it in and join her.'

The war had effectively brought Trenchard's building programme to a halt and bomb damage had seriously reduced the number of available section-houses and married quarters. The police were by no means alone in their problem, but Scott's last Report is revealing. Even in 1952, there were still 1,487 Metropolitan policemen without official quarters, despite a marked improvement in the rate of rebuilding and new construction in districts as far removed as Putney and Limehouse, Kensington and Edmonton. But in this year only five local councils—all Conservative-controlled—provided the Receiver with rented accommodation. Most councils operated a 'points' system for the homeless and this left young constables a long way down the list. In the social priorities of post-war London, the police did not rate very high.

Crime was another matter, for criminals are not greatly concerned with the problems of police pay and conditions, provided that both are unattractive; and this is an appropriate point at which to reflect briefly on the problem of statistical evidence.

'Crime' is a conveniently generic term for all acts punishable by law, from the indictable extreme of murder to the non-indictable aberration of obstructing the highway. All breaches of the law are matters of police concern and all are prodigal of the most expensive of commodities, time; but the true measure of criminality in society is indictable offences. These are the reflection of deliberate lawlessness, and they are often a commentary on the state of the law itself.

The published statistics of indictable crime in the Metropolis are complicated by the fact that there are two different classifications: Home Office and Commissioner's Office, the former with sixty-five categories and the latter with six (not, in effect, as disparate as they may seem). Secondly, there is a danger of distortion by using broad *percentage* variations. For example, 'autocrime'—much of it petty pilfering for which the victim is largely to blame—now represents one-third of all indictable offences. Were the present figure to be doubled—as well it might—the statistical balance, in percentage terms, would change significantly. Thus the true yardstick is one of numerical growth, and of the nature and 'quality' of that growth. The Metropolitan measure of our disorderly society in the post-war years may be illustrated by some awesome figures:

	1938	1946	1977
Known indictable crime	95,280	127,796	568,972
Arrests for indictable crime (aged 20 and under)	8,614	10,367	55,828
Known crimes of violence	1,679	2,155	25,793
Autocrime	20,177	17,212	174,479[1]

By any yardstick, statistical or otherwise, these figures should give food for thought to even the most convinced libertarian.

Scott was faced by the uncomfortable truth that history repeats itself. All major wars have been followed by periods of social disturbance, and just as Colquhoun had remarked upon the extravagant tastes of the under-privileged, so—to the surprise of sociologists—the affluent society encouraged rather than inhibited crime. This was not a new phenomenon. The Royal Commission of 1839 had gravely reported that 'in the great mass of cases [crime] arises from the temptation of obtaining property with a less degree of labour than by regular industry'. A witty Bow Street magistrate of our own day, sentencing an habitual thief, put it more bluntly: 'It seems to me that for a long time you have been living immorally on the earnings of others.' Even if Scott's estimate of 20,000 deserters living off their wits in the Metropolis tended to distort the statistics, there was no escaping the simple truth that crime was paying increasingly handsome dividends at increasingly diminished risk.

To combat this rising tide of lawlessness, Scott needed an arithmetical miracle. Instead he found himself having to solve the old schoolboy's conundrum of taps filling a bath without a plug.

Recruiting for the regular force was resumed on 1 January 1946, but simultaneously the 'freezing' order was lifted and this resulted in the departure of 2,682 men, the largest proportion of whom were regulars who had been retained in the service far beyond pension-

[1] Parking and meter offences (not included in this figure) are non-indictable. They are dealt with under the fixed penalty and ticket systems and in 1977 totalled 1,989,922. Only half the fines were recovered.

able age. The total strength of 14,453 was only made possible by the readiness of auxiliaries to extend their service for a limited period.

During 1946, 3,316 regulars and auxiliaries left the force on superannuation or for other causes; 1,413 rejoined on demobilization; 1,775 new regulars were recruited.[1] In the battle between taps and waste-pipe, the waste-pipe was already winning, and it is not difficult to identify the reasons. Apart from normal wastage, an unexpectedly large number of men who had joined the armed services during the war elected not to resume their police careers on demobilization, and for this pay and conditions were only partly responsible. The national mood was changing and with it the national attitude to public service. The intake of new recruits, although large enough to warrant the opening of a second training-centre at Hendon, was far below Scott's expectations, and here the reasons were reversed. While some ex-servicemen were attracted by the prospect of a career which had something in common with their war-time experience, full employment provided formidable competition in other less exacting fields. Pay was not always the prime consideration (one present Assistant Commissioner felt himself to be 'royally rewarded' at £5 5s od a week with pension and other benefits); housing and 'unsocial' hours in the new world of the five-day week were the chief deterrents. At the end of 1946, the force was 5,565 below establishment. In 1979, the shortfall was still 4,432.

*

It did not need a prophet new-inspired to foresee that peace would bring revolutionary changes in society and that the police service would have to adapt itself to deal with problems at present unpredictable but wholly novel; and in 1944 a Postwar Reconstruction Committee consisting of representatives of the Home Office and chief officers of police was set up to examine both short- and long-term policy. It duly produced four reports ranging over every aspect of the service from the employment of policewomen to new building projects, from the traditional beat system to the senior command structure. We need here concern ourselves only with the

[1] Virtually all the highest posts at the Yard and in divisions in 1978 were filled by men of this immediate post-war vintage.

first report, presented in March 1947 and dealing with the higher training for the police service in England and Wales.[1]

It will be remembered that in 1929 the Dixon Committee had proposed the establishment of a National Police College, a promising embryo aborted by a suspicious Federation and by parsimonious local authorities. In its place, Trenchard had fathered his controversial college at Hendon, an unloved child which had died in infancy on the outbreak of war.

The purpose of both conceptions was the same in substance, if not in form: to create a seed-bed in which the police service could generate its own future leadership from within its own ranks and through a system broadly acceptable to all parties involved; in other words, the ultimate fulfilment of Peel's cardinal principle.

The war had shown that the old order of an absurdly fragmented police service, tenuously held together by the Home Office, was as out-dated as the eighteenth-century parochial system; and the advent of a Labour government ensured that Hendon, with its implications—however mistaken—of privilege and class, would never be revived. The 1944 Committee accordingly recommended the establishment of a National Police College,[2] open to the whole service and to serving officers only. The object should be 'to broaden the outlook, improve the professional knowledge, and stimulate the energies of men who have reached or are reaching the middle and higher ranks of the service'. It was a brave statement of intent. Only the police themselves could make it work, for this time there was no opposition either from the Federation or from local authorities.

The College opened in June 1948 at Ryton-on-Dunsmore, symbolically located almost exactly at the centre of the country and housed, for want of any ready alternative, in a drab industrial hostel. That it did not founder within its first year is a tribute to the English genius for survival and to the belief of its authors that, if it did founder, the police service would wither on the vine. 'We felt,' wrote one of the original staff, 'that we had to invent something half way between a university and an assault course, like teaching a Commando that Aristotle is good for the soul.' The first curriculum included short courses to prepare sergeants for

[1] Cmd. 7070

[2] Renamed in 1979—wrongly and inaccurately—the Police Staff College.

promotion to inspector; inspectors and chief inspectors to superintendent; and superintendents to the highest appointments. The basic weakness was the same one which had so exercised Trenchard; the average age of sergeants selected for the first courses was thirty-seven, and it needs no great talent for arithmetic to see that this was simply perpetuating a root evil of the service.[1]

But the service was learning fast, and the College survived. In 1960 it moved to Bramshill, a magnificent Jacobean house in Hampshire, around which has grown a complete police university. It should be known as 'Colquhoun College' for it is the first practical expression of 'the new science of police'; but the service has never been strong on history.

Bramshill[2] now caters for the whole range of studies which policing demands in an increasingly complex society. If it may seem at times to take itself unduly seriously, it is properly aware of the gravity of the problems which will face its students when they return to translate theory into practice. Above all, it provides a forum in which men of widely differing experience can learn from each other, and it has done much to break down the inferiority complex which provincial forces have long felt towards the Metropolitan Police and which the Metropolitan Police has done little to discourage.

The College is administered by the Home Office as a central service, financed out of the Home Office common services fund and managed by a Board of Governors representative of every branch of the police service and of local authorities. It is a not inexpensive institution and it would still do well to forget the existence of Sandhurst.

There are six courses. The first—or Special—course is for young officers selected by a system similar to the Civil Service 'extended interview' and consisting of three four-month terms. On successful completion of the course, students are entitled to promotion to the rank of sergeant and, after one year's satisfactory service in that rank, to further promotion to inspector. Two new

[1] Attitudes change slowly. Thus, thirty years later, a Metropolitan Police sergeant with twenty years' service: 'How can you make a Superintendent at 36? He hasn't any experience of people.'

[2] See T. G. Lamford, 'The Police College, Bramshill', *Police Studies*, Vol. I, No. 1.

(1979) Inspectors' Courses[1] train officers of that rank for the responsibilities of middle management. The two Command Courses are designed to prepare superintendents for the special responsibilities of divisional and departmental command; and to equip selected senior officers for the highest posts in the service. Finally there is a three-month Overseas Command Course. A later innovation has been the granting of Bramshill scholarships to young sergeants and inspectors who have graduated at the College to enable them to study for university degrees in a subject of their choice—a simple inversion of Trenchard's original idea. In the words of the Commandant, 'police officers must be encouraged to gain a better knowledge of the community which they serve and protect. To hold high rank in the Police Service of a democratic state is to be confronted with a need to wield effectively the techniques of management, the skills of communication and the arts of leadership.'[2]

Bramshill is an imaginative concept, but it is only as good as the material on which it can draw. This was the problem which Trenchard was the first to grasp. It is a problem which still remains.

*

While the Postwar Committee was beavering away at its formidable brief, Scott was surveying his own Metropolitan battlefield with a detachment born of many years in the cloistered corridors of Whitehall. Morrison's idea of a civilian administrator to run an essentially civilian institution had been at least original, but it ignored the prime need for leadership at a time when that priceless quality was central to the rebuilding of the Metropolitan Police; and for all his intellectual talents, Scott was not a leader. It was not his fault that he was not a policeman. His task would have been made easier if he had inherited a strong and energetic team of senior officers, but in this he was no more fortunate than his predecessors. And Scott's own account of his stewardship,[3] even if written by another hand, reads like a set of variations on the theme: 'All rowed fast but none faster than "stroke".'

---

[1] A four-week regionally-based course for all newly-appointed inspectors, followed by a six-month 'junior command' course at the College for senior inspectors and chief inspectors.

[2] Lamford, *op. cit.*   [3] Scott, *op. cit.*

The regeneration of the Metropolitan Police in the immediate post-war period looks at first sight like a classic example of Parkinson's Law in action. By the end of 1946 the Receiver had succeeded in dislodging Combined Operations HQ from the new North Building and this was now occupied in the main by C Dept, including the CRO, the Finger Print and Photographic branches, and—briefly—the Forensic Laboratory. But at Central Office, if not in divisions, the taps were soon handsomely winning the battle over the waste-pipe; and the overflow—Lost Property Office, Public Carriage Office, Receiver's stores, and sundry non-operational personnel—had long since moved across the river to Lambeth. By 1948 the civil staff[1] had grown to 1,492, appreciably greater than Rowan's entire *uniform* resources 120 years earlier. This was in some part a reflection of the new bureaucracy, but more properly it represented a deliberate attempt to replace police officers by civilians in as many non-constabulary functions as possible, both clerical and technical, including such areas as the CRO, Finger Print branch, and what came to be known as 'the Lambeth Walk'. Indeed, a working-party under the ubiquitous, but now retired, Sir Arthur Dixon was put to work to study the best use and distribution of available police man-power, and in 1952 the mountain, having laboured prodigiously, produced a mouse amounting to 212 police officers freed from the shackles of an office desk. But Scott's Report for 1946 includes one small and interesting contribution to the vexed matter of man-power: 'During the year, as an experimental measure, six Labrador dogs have been purchased and trained for work with officers in the outer suburbs of the district. Their role is purely detective and not offensive.'

By 1948, it had become clear to a government in the flush of social and economic euphoria that it had the makings of a national crisis on its hands. In the Metropolis, the continuing shortage of police in an increasingly disorderly society was creating a situation which only a major blood transfusion could resolve. In January, the *Telegraph* wrote: 'The Government may enjoy the view from Olympus, but it is only a short and rocky road from there to the Styx.' And in March, Chuter Ede, a wise and realistic Home

---

[1] The civil staff of the Metropolitan Police, though similarly graded, do not rank as part of the Civil Service as their cost is not borne exclusively out of Exchequer funds.

Secretary, wrote to Scott: 'I understand your difficulty and have made urgent representations to my colleagues.'

On 12 May Lord Oaksey was invited to chair a committee to consider police conditions of service in the United Kingdom. Its terms of reference were virtually unlimited and it presented its Report in two parts, the first in April 1949, exactly thirty years after Desborough's celebrated findings. The ghost of Desborough haunts every page of Oaksey. He is quoted again and again, not only as statutory evidence but as a kind of Delphic oracle whose prophetic vision was as apposite to the present as to the past, and whose clinical diagnosis was as valid now as then.

Predictably, pay was at the heart of the Oaksey inquiry. At the date of the committee's first meeting, the basic pay of a Metropolitan Police constable was £5 5s od a week. The evidence presented to the committee—by both the Metropolitan and provincial forces—is a fascinating commentary on the English genius for ambivalence. Jointly and separately the Police Federation and the Association of Chief Constables arrived at a basic weekly wage of £7. Local authority associations, paymasters as to half the cost, insisted that there should be no increase in basic rates, but a modest acceleration in annual increments so that a constable might reach his maximum level earlier. As for the Home Office, Oaksey commented drily: 'The witnesses who spoke on [their] behalf did not seek to influence our views on whether police pay should, or should not, be altered.'

Inevitably, the final decision was a compromise. After some actuarial juggling with figures to arrive at the value of pension rights and other benefits, the following proposed new scale was accepted. Constables started at a figure of £330 a year (the committee recommended scrapping the 'weekly wage' basis of payment) rising undramatically to £420 after twenty-two years' service. Sergeants started at £445. The special problems and the additional cost of living in the Metropolis were marked by an extra 'London allowance' of £10 a year, later doubled to £20.

To provide better negotiating machinery for the future, Oaksey recommended replacing Desborough's Police Council by a more fully representative body. A new non-statutory Police Council for Great Britain duly came into existence in 1953 consisting of three panels (chief officers, superintendents, and federated ranks) each with a staff side and an official side, the whole Council presided over by an independent chairman. Provision was made for referring disputes to a panel of three arbitrators appointed by the Prime Minister. Excluded from the Council's terms of reference were such matters as discipline and promotion. The new Council[1] was re-constituted as a statutory body under the 1964 Police Act (and further under the 1969 Police Act) and at the same time Desborough's original Council was replaced by a Police Advisory Board, thus inserting, as it were, a small Pelion *under* an already over-blown Ossa.

The ironic result of the Oaksey award was the largest decline in the strength of the Metropolitan Police since 1945. 'Experience in 1950,' wrote Scott, 'suggests that [the recommendations] have been ineffective either in attracting sufficient suitable candidates or in arresting wastage.' An uncomfortable truth was beginning to dawn. 'We shall continue our efforts to attract and retain men in the Service, but it is difficult to combat the attraction of civil life with its shorter hours of work, free week-ends and Bank Holidays, and absence of shift and night-duty.' It was a situation which boded ill for the future, even if, by a further irony, it was accompanied by the first significant fall in the statistics of indictable crime. 'I think,' comments a sergeant of the time, 'that villains almost felt sorry for the police.'

*

There is a grim parenthesis to Scott's years as Commissioner, for they included some of the most bizarre and brutal crimes in the calendar of murder. It is a curious fact that, since the early 1950s, murderers seem no longer to have been remembered by name. Who, for example, can recall the ruthless killers of three police officers at Shepherd's Bush in 1966? Or any of the IRA terrorists? The reason is not so much public acceptance of violent death as a natural feature of the disorderly society, as the abolition of capital punishment and with it the forensic drama of the court-room. There was an historical parallel; for whereas Tyburn was a place of public entertainment, transportation for life rated no more than

---

[1] The Police Council has never found much favour with the rank and file who tend to view it as little more than a talking-shop. There has been constant friction between the official and staff sides, culminating in a walkout by the Federation in 1976.

an entry in the Newgate Calendar. It is the gallows that are remembered, not the penitentiary.

The post-war decade was marked by an unprecedented increase in the use of firearms by criminals and by rapid advances in the field of forensic science and police technology. The classic cases, from that of Neville Heath in 1946 to Christie and Evans' charnel-house in Rillington Place in 1953, demonstrate an extraordinary diversity of motive and method: the shooting of Alec Antiquis, an innocent victim of a smash-and-grab raid, in 1947; the killing of PC Edgar in 1948;[1] the paranoiac Haigh who in 1949 surpassed even Neill Cream in his efforts to incriminate himself; the curious case of Stanley Setty later in that year; the murder of PC Miles by Bentley and Craig in November 1952. Whatever its shortcomings in other fields, the CID had become a formidable adversary for the violent criminal.

*

Scott's field of manoeuvre was severely limited by his meagre resources and the growing appetite for lawlessness. But there were encouraging advances on the credit side.

For centuries, criminals had traded very profitably on the greed and gullibility of their fellow creatures, as the Comtesse de Goncourt had learned to her cost. In the heady atmosphere of post-war London, fools and their money were parted with increasing abandon and in March 1946 Scott formed the Fraud Squad (C.6) or, to give it its full title, the Metropolitan and City Police Company Fraud branch. This very specialized team was soon kept busy and in its first year dealt with 290 cases. It has a special place in the development of the Metropolitan Police for two reasons. First, it was the prototype for inter-force cooperation in handling specific forms of crime. Secondly, it revived a delightfully Gilbertian situation which went back over a century to Lord John Russell's ultimatum to the City Fathers.

The Police Act of 1839 had given Metropolitan constables the power 'to execute their office within the royal palaces of Her Majesty and ten miles thereof'. All warrants were addressed to

---

[1] The murderer, Donald Thomas's, death sentence was commuted to life imprisonment during the suspension of capital punishment (see footnote on (p. 253). During this seven-month period, seventeen convicted murderers were reprieved.

'each and all of the Constables of the Metropolitan Police'. Not so the City Police who, as an act of penance for the sins of their Fathers, were forbidden to operate outside the City limits. Thus, while Metropolitan officers had powers of arrest within the City, their City colleagues had no such reciprocal rights beyond their boundaries. Accordingly, by a neat English compromise, five City Police officers were sworn in as Metropolitan constables and it was not until the 1964 Police Act that this anomaly was regularized.

In 1949 a new uniform was introduced, with open-neck jacket, collar and tie, and a lightweight tunic for summer wear. There was some argument about replacing the traditional helmet by a peaked cap, but this was not pursued; nor was a Federation proposal that the wearing of numerals on epaulettes should be discontinued. The reason for these changes—apart from comfort—was partly to bring the police into line with the armed services and partly to give a more modern look to what Rowan had described as 'a civilian livery'.

In two specific areas, there was good progress. By 1952 Scott could report growing success in recruiting policewomen and by the end of that year the strength had increased to 388 and authority had been given for an establishment of 458. By then women officers were serving in the CID and in 98 of the 175 stations in the MPD.

These were dog-days, too. In 1952 there were seventy Alsatians and Labradors on duty or in training[1] and their success-rate in assisting in arrests was notable enough for Scott to include a special Appendix to his 1951 Report describing the adventures of such canine sleuths as dog 'Dante' and dog 'Prince'. There had been nothing like it since Rin-tin-tin.

There were two further developments of particular importance during 1951. Three years earlier, in an effort to make the best use of his limited man-power, the Chief Constable of Aberdeen had introduced a scheme known as 'team-policing'. This involved the abolition of conventional beats and the division of the city into districts, each policed by teams of varying size (usually about six constables) and each in the charge of a sergeant provided with a

---

[1] By 1977 the strength of the Dog Section was 360, including dogs specially trained in detecting drugs and explosives. During that year officers of the Section were responsible for 8,910 arrests. (*Commissioner's Report for 1977*).

two-way radio car so that districts could be covered with the maximum flexibility. The results were immediately encouraging, not least in breaking the boredom of routine patrolling and delegating more responsibility to the man on the ground. With its then conventional disdain for provincial innovations, the Metropolitan Police was slow to react to the Aberdeen scheme; but in January 1951 Scott introduced a similar system in four sub-divisions in the MPD. With something less than good grace he duly reported that the experiment was not only a success, but—which was perhaps more important—that it had the full support of his hard-pressed men. Since then team-policing, as we shall see, has been, in one form or another, the basis of all subsequent methods of crime prevention in the Metropolis.

The second significant innovation in 1951 also owed its origin to a provincial experiment. Before the war, many forces had used youngsters as messengers and office-boys. They wore no uniform, naturally had no constabulary powers, and were paid pin-money; but it was a useful way of catching them young and giving them a practical demonstration that 'cops and robbers' was not just a game. From 1946 onwards a number of provincial forces went an important step further by forming cadres of Police Cadets, aged between sixteen and eighteen, provided with uniform and a modest wage, and employed on simple duties at police stations. The idea was an immediate success and a strong incentive for boys of the right quality to make a career in the police service.

Once more the Metropolitan Police, whose man-power shortage was by far the most critical, dragged its feet; and it was not until 1951 that Scott sought Home Office permission to establish his own Police Cadet Corps. 'The response,' he reported somewhat naively, 'was enthusiastic.' Within two weeks there were over 1,000 applications and eventually 175 (with a waiting list of 302) were accepted for training at a special four-week course at Hendon, after which they were posted to the Yard and to districts and divisions. There they were given further practical training in simple police duties before their call-up for national service, whence a remarkably high proportion returned in due course to join the regular force. There is little doubt that the development of the Police Cadet Corps has proved an indispensable source of good material for the regular force; and in his Report for 1977 Sir David McNee was to voice his proper concern at the Government's decision to restrict the strength to 600 (400 below the training capacity available at Hendon) despite the fact that in that year there had been a record number of 4,698 applications to join and that the number of cadets attested represented one-fifth of the annual intake.

Scott, not the most imaginative of men, never liked the idea of police cadets which he seems to have equated with a breakaway Boy Scout movement. Nor, during the early years of the experiment, was there much enthusiasm from the Federation. Even in 1961, the Joint Central Committee 'revealed its deep suspicion of the Metropolitan scheme' and reported rather prissily that 'the new system brings the young man into the police service as soon as he leaves school and deprives him of close and intimate contact with the public during the period when his character and personality are being moulded'.[1] It did not add that for many other youngsters their closest and most intimate contact with the public took the form of juvenile delinquency.

*

In August 1953, Scott resigned. He is a difficult man to assess. He inherited formidable problems, many of them entirely novel and in the social climate of the time capable of solution only by the most resolute action; and, as we have seen from his tentative acceptance of provincial innovation, he lacked resolution and the humility which makes great men out of the merely good. He was a prisoner of his background and he proved, if nothing else, that Commissioners of the Metropolitan Police require something more than 'a fugitive and cloistered virtue'. He was succeeded by his deputy, Sir John Nott-Bower, whose limited virtues were both fugitive and cloistered.

*

Nott-Bower was the 'safe' Tory reaction to Morrison's thinly-veiled attempt to play politics with the police. He was by definition a professional, for like so many previous Commissioners he had spent over twenty years in the Indian Police Service before coming to Scotland Yard as a chief constable in 1933 (his father had been Commissioner of the City of London Police at the time of Sidney

[1] Anthony Judge, *The First Fifty Years* (*The Story of the Police Federation*).

Street). Thereafter he progressed by way of Deputy Assistant Commissioner to AC 'A' during the war years, and then Deputy Commissioner.

He had a good brain and all the social graces, and was an expert horseman (as the Mounted Branch discovered to their advantage) and a devoted bridge-player (as his staff discovered to their cost). Above all, he was excessively idle. There has grown up around him in the force a kind of demonology and an unenviable reputation. With all their problems, the Metropolitan Police deserved something better—even Maxwell-Fyfe, the Home Secretary who appointed him, became exasperated—and it was only by an instinctive act of self-preservation that they were saved from an identical fate some years later.

Of the nineteen holders of the office of Commissioner, Nott-Bower is the least memorable. He was not, like Warren and Trenchard, combative. He was not, like Rowan and Henry, creative. He was not, like Mayne and Mark, decisive. If he has any counterpart, it was Bradford during his last anonymous years. And the 1950s were anything but anonymous years. A superintendent who knew him well has summed him up with the sympathy of one professional for another: 'He was a nice man when what we needed was a bit of a bastard.'

Nott-Bower's period of office was not one of innovation. The crime figures which, in Scott's last two years had begun to decline, now started to escalate again, at first slowly but presently, in Peel's phrase, 'at a frightfully rapid pace'. Central to this new manifestation of the disorderly society were crimes of violence, juvenile delinquency and a climate of public indiscipline which stretched the resources of the Metropolitan Police to breaking-point. In May 1955 *The Times* expressed a view which was to be repeated frequently, and with growing justification, in the years ahead: 'The British people, in their attitude to civilized standards, are fast becoming ungovernable.' Any reader of *The Times* with a sense of history would have remembered the Gordon Riots; and any reader who feared for the future of democratic government would have had due cause, with the explosion of civil disorder which followed the Suez crisis.

To say that Nott-Bower fiddled while London burned would be an exaggeration; but his constabulary 'fire-brigade' remained stubbornly short of men and hose-pipes. Since the Oaksey award in

1949 there had been a series of modest pay increases, squeezed out of a reluctant Home Office by the Federation and by the inexorable pressure of events; but by 1958, the police had reverted almost to a pre-Desborough status in relation to the national level of wages. There had been changes at the Yard: a Research and Planning Branch (not before time); a central organization to deal with the growing problem of London's traffic; a new exercise in inter-force cooperation which was to become known as the Metropolitan and Provincial Crime Branch (C.9). But the Metropolitan Police needed something a good deal more effective than casual therapy. It needed a strong and resolute leader, and a Home Secretary who would fight his political battles for him with equal resolution. By one of those striking dispensations of history it got both.

On 31 August 1958, Nott-Bower retired. He was succeeded by his deputy, Joseph Simpson; and there followed ten eventful years.

CHAPTER TWELVE

The Commissioned Constable

'THE DAY may come when you may have a Commissioner who comes from the ranks.' On 1 September 1958, Macready's words came true.

Joseph Simpson was educated at Oundle and Manchester University. He joined the Metropolitan Police as a constable in 1931, and in 1934 entered the first course at Hendon by competitive examination. In 1936, he became an instructor. In 1937 he was called to the Bar, and in the same year was appointed Assistant Chief Constable of Lincolnshire. After war service as a Regional Police Staff Officer, he was successively Chief Constable of Northumberland and Surrey, returning to the Metropolitan Police in 1956 as AC 'B' in charge of traffic. In 1957 he became Deputy.

It is proper to record Simpson's service in some detail for not only was he the first Commissioner to rise from the ranks, but by the time he succeeded Nott-Bower he had a breadth of practical experience at that date unique among Commissioners of the Metropolitan Police. He was the automatic choice of the new Home Secretary, R. A. Butler, who was resolved, after the experience of Scott and Nott-Bower, to provide the Metropolitan Police with a leader rather than an administrator, and with a professional policeman rather than a police professional.

Butler chose wisely. Joe Simpson was a shy, reserved man whose intellectual capacity lacked only that gift of communication which was to be the signal talent a decade later of Robert Mark. His total commitment to his men and to his uniquely demanding office was reflected in a stubborn refusal to delegate responsibility, and, as a result, it could well be said that he worked himself to death. Two small glosses tell us more about the private man than the outward austerity of his public *persona*.

Every year, throughout his ten years of office, he made time to visit an old pensioner of Q Division who had been his guide, philosopher and friend as a young constable in 1931. And two days before he took office as Commissioner, he wrote thus to a former colleague in the Surrey Constabulary:

> Although I'm only thirty miles from my old office at Mount Browne, I might be on a different planet. So much *paper*! So much *talk*! I want to do away with all the paper and half the talk. Then we may get back to the fact that a police force consists of *policemen*!

*

When Simpson took office in September 1958, the strength of the force was 16,661 and that of the civil staff 3,487. Infinitely slowly, the taps were beginning to beat the waste-pipe, although the gain was minimal when set against the growing lawlessness in the Metropolis. Simpson's Report for that year, during which he had been Commissioner for only four months, is notable in several ways. The style is both novel and individual, with a directness that looks back to Trenchard and forward to Mark. There are none of Horwood's platitudes nor Scott's counsels of despair, but rather the clinical diagnosis of a specialist and—most unusually—practical suggestions for curing the spreading epidemic. Here, for the first time, we find a Commissioner with the temerity to remind Parliament that it cannot abdicate its sovereign responsibilities; for example, his suggestion that repeal or amendment of the antique laws covering betting and gaming would release a large part of his limited uniform force for more effective deployment in the prevention of serious crime. Here, too, we find the first mention of 'hooliganism' and, in his account of the week-long disturbances in Notting Hill, the first reference to those racial problems which have become so much a part of the language of law and order.

If a man may be judged by the company he keeps, then a Commissioner can tell us much about himself by the quality and character of his immediate subordinates. It is important here to be clear about the constitutional position. The six top posts in the Metropolitan Police are Crown appointments made on the advice of the Home Secretary, who is under no statutory obligation to consult the Commissioner. It is a potentially dangerous form of patronage, for there is absolutely nothing—other than the certainty of public retribution—to stop a Secretary of State from appointing three bus-conductors and three Methodist ministers of whatever impeccable virtue. It was the curious conviction of some senior police officers, who should have known better, that these top appointments lay within the Commissioner's gift which caused so much animosity towards the end of Simpson's term of office.

Within a few months of taking over, Simpson had reshuffled the pack; and since Butler gave him a free hand, the 'court cards' were an interesting commentary on the style of the new regime. The Deputy Commissioner was Alexander Robertson, formerly AC 'A', who had won a DCM with the Scots Guards and whose parade-ground manner belied a shrewd and decisive brain. AC 'A', AC 'B', and AC 'D' were all products of Hendon: Douglas Webb, who had taken part in the centenary parade in 1929, himself a very young constable, his father at the head of a divisional contingent; John Waldron, whom Simpson had persuaded to relinquish the post of Chief Constable of Berkshire; and Tom Mahir who had been awarded a George Medal during the Blitz, and was a sick man. The one inexplicable appointment, which Simpson inherited from Nott-Bower, was that of Richard Jackson, a lawyer from the office of the DPP who had come to Scotland Yard as Secretary and in 1953 had been translated to AC 'C' in charge of the perennially sensitive area of crime. The pattern was becoming clear.

Simpson did not have to wait long to discover that the office of Commissioner was no sinecure. Life began quietly with an overdue reorganization of the Special Constabulary which tied what Horwood had called 'this honorary force' more closely into the regular divisional organization. But it was not long before storm clouds began to gather.

Since 1956 there had been several incidents involving provincial chief constables—in Cardiganshire, Worcester, Brighton and Nottingham—which resulted in the dismissal, premature retirement, or (in the case of Worcester) conviction and sentencing of the officers concerned. In 1957 allegations were made that a Thurso boy had been assaulted by a policeman (a complaint barely supported by a subsequent inquiry). Public anxiety over these revelations was compounded by the statutory inability of members of Parliament to question the Home Secretary about matters relating to the conduct of provincial chief officers.

If the Metropolitan Police thought they would remain unscathed, they were soon to be rudely disillusioned, even if the ultimate flash-point was to be a matter so trivial as to make the affairs of Mme d'Angely and Miss Savidge, by comparison, issues

of profound constitutional importance. During 1959, there had
been two cases of, respectively, alleged police brutality and 'planting' incriminating evidence which were, five years later, to be
revived as a private vendetta against Simpson and a public attack
upon the credibility of the Home Secretary. But before that, in
December 1958, a Christmas pantomime had been staged.

One morning, the actor Brian Rix was stopped by PC Eastmond
for speeding on Putney Heath. A civil servant called Garratt, who
was driving behind the police car, pulled up and, for no apparent
reason, involved himself in the argument. There followed allegations of assault on both sides and when Garratt was taken to the
police station, the inspector refused to accept the charge. Garratt
was duly released and proceeded to bring an action for damages
against Eastmond for assault and battery and against the police for
false imprisonment. The case, however, did not come to court and
was settled by the payment, without admission of liability, of £300
to the plaintiff from the Police Fund. No disciplinary action was
taken against Eastmond. And there the matter might have rested.

But if Butler and Simpson had reflected for a moment on past
history, they might have remembered that bonfires can be started
by a single spark. A year after the Rix incident, the case was
debated in the House and questions were asked as to why, if Eastmond was innocent, £300 of public money had been paid to
Garratt; and why, if he was guilty, no disciplinary action had been
taken against him. As the debate developed, members quickly
forgot the original roadside argument on Putney Heath. Once again
a Home Secretary found himself with the pack baying at his heels,
the issue no longer the rights of a private individual, not even the
wider question of police accountability, but—as Critchley says[1]—'a
redefinition, acceptable to Parliament, of the constitutional position
of the police in the State'. For probably the only time in his life,
Brian Rix must have found himself reading a script without a single
funny line.

Butler bowed before the storm, and in January 1960 the fifth
Royal Commission in the history of the police was appointed,
under the chairmanship of Sir Henry Willink, QC, who had been
a member of Churchill's war-time Cabinet. By one of those recurring ironies, the Commission, although convened because of an

---

[1] Critchley, *op. cit.*

incident in the Metropolitan Police District, was to involve itself almost exclusively with provincial affairs. It was to conduct the most searching examination ever made into the police service in England and Wales; it was to make the most far-reaching recommendations; and the Police Act of 1964, which followed upon those recommendations, was to be the most important measure in its field since Peel's Act of 1829. In his letter to a former colleague in 1958, Joseph Simpson had also said: 'There will have to be many changes, even revolutionary changes.' He was wiser than he knew.

*

The terms of reference of the Royal Commission included: the constitution and functions of local police authorities; the status and accountability of all members of police forces; relations between the police and the public; and 'the broad principles' which should determine the level of police pay (the latter included almost as an afterthought at the instigation of James Callaghan, who had been engaged as a 'consultant' by the Police Federation four years previously).[1]

As with Desborough and Oaksey, it was agreed to give priority to the question of pay, and the Commission's recommendations were duly published in November as Part I of its Report.[2] In fact, to the embarrassment of the Government, the indignation of local authorities, and the satisfaction of the police, the Commission went far beyond 'broad principles', by proposing specific scales of pay and increments which represented easily the greatest percentage increase in the history of the service to that date; and, unlike Oaksey, Willink virtually discounted the notional value of benefits in cash or kind.

In its Introduction, the Report stated: 'We do not think that anyone acquainted with the facts can be satisfied with the state of law and order in Great Britain in 1960. Society has, in our opinion, a duty not to leave untried any measure which may lead not only to the detection, but above all to the prevention of crime.' It was a sentiment straight out of Robert Peel's book and it is still equally valid, word for word. There were no easy answers, but central to the war on crime were the number and quality of the troops. Thus

---

[1] When Callaghan became Home Secretary in 1967, the Federation were to find him a good deal less than sympathetic to their cause.

[2] Cmnd. 1222

the Commission concluded: 'The evidence we have heard and the information we have obtained in the course of our visits convince us that police pay is at present inadequate either to inspire in the police and the community a sense of fair treatment, or to attract to the service as a whole and retain in it, enough recruits of the right standard.'

The old scale for constables had been £510 a year rising to a maximum of £695, after nine years' service. There were no long-service increments. Under the Willink recommendations the starting rate for a constable was fixed at £600 a year rising to £910, also after nine years, but with further supplements of £30 a year after seventeen and twenty-two years' service respectively. The Federation, always hostile to the idea of pay differentials, opposed any increase in the 'London allowance' which remained at £20. Willink also recommended a triennial review related to the wage structure in eighteen basic industries, later changed by negotiation to a review every two years.

The Government had no alternative but to accept the new proposals. Police and public alike were delighted. Local authority representatives on the official side of the Police Council, who had bitterly opposed any kind of increase, were horrified but powerless to resist; and they little knew that the Royal Commission had by no means finished with them. Unlike the unexpected sequel to the Oaksey award, the Willink proposals resulted in a sharp improvement in the recruiting rate, and at the time of Simpson's death in 1968 the establishment of the Metropolitan Police had been increased by a third to 25,417 and the effective strength had risen to 20,112. These were not the only figures to have risen. So, even more dramatically, had those of crime.

*

Part II of the Royal Commission's Report was presented in May 1962.[1] Since the 1829 Act had clearly defined the constitutional position of the Metropolitan Police as subordinate to the control of the Home Secretary, the arguments were concentrated almost entirely on the relationship between Whitehall and provincial police authorities and on the vexed question of accountability to Parliament. As such, these arguments do not lie within the compass

[1] Cmnd. 1728

of this book except in one important respect, which was of equal concern to the Metropolitan force. This was what might be called the 'nationalization lobby', formidably represented in a dissenting memorandum by Dr A. L. Goodhart. The Commission as a whole was not greatly influenced by the opinion that a national police service might result in a police state under a French-style Minister of the Interior, observing with impeccable logic that 'to place the police under the control of a well-disposed government would be neither constitutionally objectionable nor politically dangerous; and if an ill-disposed government were to come into office, it would without doubt seize control of the police however they might be organized'. Goodhart, however, went much further by exploding a number of historical myths and even challenging the sanctity of *Fisher* v. *Oldham Corporation*. What neither side thought fit to consider was the likelihood that for 'imperial' reasons, if none else, a nationalized police service would inevitably be Metropolitan-dominated.

In the event the Commission chose the course of political realism rather than administrative expediency, but not without proposing far-reaching reforms which, so far as local authorities were concerned, offered naught for their comfort. Its recommendations included greatly increased powers for the Home Secretary over local authorities and over chief constables, making them in effect as accountable to Parliament as the Metropolitan Commissioner. 'The problem of controlling the police,' it observed bluntly, 'can be restated as the problem of controlling chief constables.' It further recommended a considerable strengthening of the inspectorate, including the appointment of a Chief Inspector of Constabulary who would act as adviser on provincial police matters to the Home Secretary and supervise a Research and Planning Department at the Home Office. The Commission also recommended that the process of reducing the number of provincial forces by amalgamation or disbandment should be vigorously pursued, and that the composition of watch committees and standing joint committees should be brought into line, consisting of magistrates and councillors in the proportion of one to two.

On a more domestic level, the Commission addressed itself among other things to the question of police cadets, of recruiting methods, of housing conditions, and of the need to make the police service a more attractive career for men of higher educational attainments. When, finally, it came to the matter of relations between the police and the public—especially (with a backward glance at Brian Rix) the motoring public—it seems to have decided that enough was enough and that it had made as many radical recommendations as any legislature could sensibly digest. Except in isolated instances, it reported, the police enjoyed the respect and support of the public, as the reaction to its interim Report confirmed, and, with three members dissenting, proposed that apart from some minor procedural improvements there should be no further action to establish an independent system of investigating complaints against the police. It was an issue, however, with strong political overtones and when, fourteen years later, a Labour government introduced an independent Police Complaints Board under the 1976 Police Act, it was to precipitate the resignation of the Commissioner, Sir Robert Mark.

Butler at once made the Government's position clear. While accepting the general recommendations of the Commission, in no circumstances would he introduce legislation to nationalize the police. The subsequent debate in the House cut across party lines, and also demonstrated some very curious attitudes towards the constitutional position of a police service in a democratic society. Those members who quoted Peel as a witness for the defence against nationalization forgot—or did not know—that he had been its first and most convinced supporter; and in keeping with historical precedent, it was the Tories who argued most strongly for a national police service. No one was happy about the proposals for investigating complaints against the police.

The Police Act which followed the Willink report became law in June 1964. It repealed in whole or in part seventy measures touching in greater or lesser degree on the police service, including Peel's 1829 Act. It was the first statutory instrument since the formation of the Metropolitan Police to 're-define the constitutional position of the police in the State'. 'For the first time in the history of the police,' writes Critchley, 'the Bill attempted to define the respective functions of the Home Secretary, police authorities and chief constables.'[1] To this extent it did not greatly involve the Metropolitan force where the constitutional position had not been in argument. But the eventual Act ranged much

[1] Critchley, *op. cit.*

wider, to include the future of the whole service in a complex, modern society.

In particular it went far towards the development of a 'national' as opposed to a 'nationalized' police institution by giving statutory backing to the new concept of common services, the Police College, provincial forensic science laboratories, and communications in the widest sense; and, as we have seen, the old negotiating machinery which had been cobbled together by Desborough was put on a statutory, if never very happy, basis. The historical autonomy of local authorities, reaching far back to the mediaeval partnership of justices and constables, was swept away; indeed, the powers of a constable were extended beyond his own local boundaries to give him legal status throughout England and Wales, something that has never been contemplated under even the most draconian Continental system. Finally, the Bill made provision for a chief officer of police to invite an officer of another force to investigate a public complaint within his own, and directed that in the event of conclusive evidence of a criminal offence, the charge should then be referred to the DPP. This procedure was soon to be severely tested in the Metropolitan Police District.

The 1964 Police Act is a milestone comparable to that of 1919 and, as subsequently amended, remains the statutory authority for our entire present police system. But while Parliament was sitting in judgement on these weighty affairs, life had not stood still for Joseph Simpson in his Metropolitan parish.

*

The disorders of the 1950s seem in retrospect like a comparatively innocent dress rehearsal for the state of permanent confrontation with which Simpson and his men—as yet without the moral encouragement of Willink's award—were now faced. The Aldermaston marchers had largely been led by middle-aged Pied Pipers, shepherded by patient policemen who listened to the speeches and wished themselves elsewhere, enjoying their own Bank Holiday break.

Now the rats took over. Whereas the pioneers of nuclear protest had relied on peaceful persuasion, a new movement of young extremists, calling itself the Committee of 100, chose instead the politics of violence and by provoking the police, sought like the demonstrators of the 1880s to defeat the forces of law and order by sheer numbers. From April 1961 until the autumn of that year there were repeated clashes, in Trafalgar Square, in Whitehall, on the Embankment, in Grosvenor Square, and at American airfields outside London. Significantly, there were no similar scenes outside the Russian Embassy. And to this eruption of disorder was added a new dimension in the shape of the television camera which, however innocently, provided the militants with massive publicity. The disease was contagious, for violence breeds violence, and to political disorder was added an outbreak of mindless hooliganism in London and in coastal resorts.

The strain on Simpson and his inadequate uniform resources was continuous and immense. There are many men who recall being on duty or on stand-by for as much as 112 hours a week. The scale and ferocity of many of these demonstrations was a novel experience, and A.8 branch at the Yard had not yet acquired its present expertise in organizing counter-measures. Communications were often unreliable, there was no system of strategic reserve, and men were sometimes on duty for hours on end without a proper meal. By the time of the pitched battle in Red Lion Square in June 1974, things were very different and, as it was to prove, the subject of bitter controversy.

Preserving law and order on the streets of the Metropolis was one preoccupation; but there were other no less pressing demands, and to these Simpson addressed himself with characteristic energy. There were still, as he argued in a memorandum in February 1960, too many constabulary grades engaged in work which could equally well be done by civil staff. Wherever possible, policemen should be employed solely on duties for which they alone were qualified by training and by statute. 'We shall not recruit or retain young men in the police force by making clerks out of constables,' he wrote; and he carried his argument onto the streets of London.

He turned first to the problem of traffic, the post-war growth of which was matched only by the growth of organized crime. Under Scott, a Central Traffic Squad of 100 men had been formed to control the main areas of congestion, and Simpson expanded this nucleus into what has today become a Traffic Division of some 1,300 men under B Dept—a highly professional team of specialists. Traffic policing is a way of life. 'This suits me,' said a patrol-car driver with twenty years' service, threading his way through a crowded Kilburn. 'I've not wanted promotion. Since most motorists are mad, it's a bit like working in a lunatic asylum. Very rewarding.'

But traffic is not all movement. Of equal concern to Simpson was the thrombosis of uncontrolled parking and the wasted man-hours of uniform time in bringing offenders to book and attending the last rites in court. His answer was the introduction of traffic wardens and the fixed penalty system (parking meters came earlier). The scheme started with 39 wardens, now increased to 1,500. They are members of the civil staff with no police powers, under the operational control of AC 'B' (B.7), but responsible to the Receiver for pay and discipline, and it has been estimated that they represent a saving in terms of time and money of three divisions of uniform police. Even if they have done nothing to reduce the temperature of the motoring public, for that they bear no special blame.

By 1960, organized crime had assumed not only a new dimension but also a new sophistication,[1] since technology is a game at which two can play. It was still true that most indictable offences were committed locally by criminals operating on their own, but increasingly the war was being fought by professional gangs which, if they still found the Metropolis the richest field for plunder, removed themselves and their loot as far and as fast as possible from the scenes of crime. Simpson could only counter these activities with his existing resources. To a larger and better-equipped Flying Squad (C.8) he added the first embryo version of the Robbery Squad and, in the same year, two important new branches of the CID—Criminal Intelligence (C.11) and Stolen Vehicles' Investigation (C.10), both reflecting the military axiom of 'know your enemy'. And the military metaphor was underlined by a concept which was to become central to CID operations—the 'target' criminal. 'It was,' explains a detective superintendent, 'the start of a new game—super-cops against super-robbers.'

Meanwhile some interesting developments were taking place in the hierarchy at the Yard. In 1961, Robertson retired and Douglas Webb became Deputy Commissioner, while his place as AC 'A' was taken by another Hendon graduate, Ranulph ('Rasher') Bacon. Two years later, Jackson at last stepped down after ten unremark-

---

[1] The classic example of a crime planned on the scale of a commando raid was to be the Great Train Robbery on 8 August 1963.

able years as AC 'C', and in the consequent reshuffle Waldron moved to 'A', Andrew Way was promoted to 'B', Bacon took over 'C', and Mahir remained at 'D'. 'At last,' remarked a contemporary drily, 'it was "game, set, and match" to Hendon.' And so it was to remain for nearly four years, until an unexpected cuckoo arrived in the nest, with predictable but disturbing results.

There is no evidence that Simpson was wedded to a policy of 'Hendonization', or that Butler was unduly influenced by any such pressure. Arguably, the men appointed were at least as experienced as any contenders without the Hendon cachet, and further, with the departure of Jackson, the Metropolitan Police, for the first time in its history, found itself under the exclusive direction of professional policemen, even if inter-departmental liaison was largely non-existent. The force had long since ceased to think of Hendon as anything more than an exploded myth from the receding world of Trenchard, and the younger generation of policemen probably did not even notice that the 'cream' had risen to the top of the cup. The new Police College had set the pattern for the future and Simpson was a confirmed advocate of Bramshill, an attitude by no means universally shared.

But not all was sweetness and light. Promotion to senior rank below assistant commissioner was a matter for the Commissioner to decide. Within this middle-management range there was a group who believed—without the slightest justification—that they were entitled to preferential treatment and that Simpson had been divinely appointed to lead them to the promised land. They were sadly mistaken. Simpson was no Moses and he was well aware that Hendon had produced at least as many bad policemen as good; indeed, to take the year 1963 alone, not one promotion from superintendent came from within the magic circle.

Other than a minimum retiring age, there is no statutory limit to a Commissioner's term of office, but by the 1960s there had emerged a conventional wisdom which held that five years was as long as any man could reasonably carry the burden imposed by modern pressures. Thus the dissidents bided their time, confident that when Simpson retired in 1963 his successor would not only be a Hendonite but a man in sympathy with their quite unwarranted claims to advancement. Once more they were sadly mistaken. Simpson did not retire in 1963 (if he had done so, he might well have survived to enjoy that 'unhoped serene which men call age').

He was a dedicated policeman, and Butler knew the measure of his man; so he soldiered on. The dissidents were dismayed, and one of them boasted to a chief superintendent that they would 'have Joe out of his chair by Christmas'. Simpson must have been well aware of this situation but he had more serious problems on his mind; and when the bullet was fired it was not an envious Casca who pulled the trigger, but the Labour MP for East Islington.

In February 1964, during the Committee stage of the Police Bill, Eric (now Lord) Fletcher resurrected the two incidents of alleged misconduct by the police in 1959. (The time-lapse, not once remarked upon in the subsequent inquiry, is very material. Furthermore, by 1964, Butler had been replaced at the Home Office by Henry Brooke, a good and honourable man so dogged by ill-fortune that, in the words of a senior police officer, 'if he had kept a goldfish it would probably have died by drowning'.)

Fletcher told the Standing Committee that in 1959 he had asked Butler for an independent investigation 'because I did not trust the impartiality of a Police investigation'. He went on:

> Nevertheless he [Butler] ordered a Police investigation. An investigation was made and the Report confirmed what I had said. Now what happened to that Report? It was suppressed. It was not sent to the Home Secretary. [*It was*.][1] Someone at Scotland Yard said, 'We cannot let this go to the Home Office because this will reveal merely another scandal in the Metropolitan Police.' After all, perhaps someone was shortly due for a knighthood. Therefore, the report was deliberately destroyed [*it was not*][2] and someone else in the police was ordered to produce a white-washing report . . .[3]

When pressed by another member of the Committee as to the evidence on which he based these allegations, Fletcher gave a very interesting reply:

> The evidence I have consists of statements of these facts by a number of senior superintendents or ex-superintendents in the Metropolitan Police Force.[4]

The argument continued in Committee until 26 March, when Brooke announced the setting-up of an inquiry under Mr W. L.

---

[1] Hansard, 13 February 1964, cols. 714, and 741   [2] *Ibid.*   [3] *Ibid.*
[4] See p. 8 of the Mars-Jones Report.

Mars-Jones, QC. For the first time in all the long history of police-baiting, the Home Office and a Commissioner found themselves facing the same firing-squad.

Mars-Jones reported in December.[1] He had called sixty-nine witnesses ranging from Simpson and Cunningham (Permanent Under-Secretary at the Home Office), by way of Fletcher and the aggrieved parties, to police constables. The report gives the impression of some perplexity on the part of the Chairman, and of considerable personal animosity between police officers. Plainly Mars-Jones was unaware of the private vendetta which lay at the root of the whole affair. At Christmas, Joseph Simpson was still firmly in his chair.

During his exchanges with Brooke, Fletcher had referred to a letter from a 'senior Police Officer', drawing his attention to an article in the *Sunday Telegraph* on 24 November 1963 in which he (Fletcher) was reported to have asked the Home Secretary 'for certain information concerning Detective Sergeant Challenor' in respect of an incident in July of that year. 'This incident,' continued the police officer, 'bears a striking resemblance to one of the cases I brought to your notice when I was in correspondence with you in the early part of 1961.' There was certainly some unpleasant woodworm at work in the upper timbers of the Metropolitan Police.

The Challenor affair was to become a *cause célèbre* as considerable as that of Sergeant Goddard, although for different reasons. The circumstances were briefly thus.

Challenor, after distinguished war service during which he won the Military Medal, joined the Metropolitan Police in 1947. He soon showed himself to be an officer of exceptional ability and the reports of his superiors spoke of his 'zeal and industry'. In due course he applied for transfer from uniform duty to the CID and was posted to West End Central police station. There James (now Sir James) Starritt, then Chief Superintendent of C Division, remembers him as a man with a dedicated sense of mission to bring criminals to justice and a positive obsession with work. He was a difficult, abrasive character with a strong, if not always beneficial, influence over some of his younger colleagues. By the beginning

---

[1] Cmnd. 2526. A copy was circulated by Simpson, without comment, to all officers of the rank of superintendent and above.

of 1963, the strain of working long hours was apparent and his superintendent had restricted him to normal shift duties.

On 11 July 1963, the King and Queen of the Hellenes arrived in London on a State visit, an occasion ripe for political protest. Despite specific orders to the contrary, Challenor joined the crowd outside Claridges where he arrested a man for causing a public disturbance. At Savile Row, the prisoner was charged with being in possession of an offensive weapon, namely part of a brick, which he in turn claimed had been planted on him by Challenor. A not-unfamiliar fuse had been lit.

An investigation into charge and counter-charge was set in train and in February 1964—at precisely the moment that Eric Fletcher was priming his own political fowling-piece—the DPP instituted proceedings against Challenor and three police constables for conspiracy to pervert the course of justice. At the subsequent trial in June, Challenor was found to be insane and therefore unfit to plead. The three constables were convicted and sentenced to terms of imprisonment, while the defendant was acquitted and paid a sum of £500 in compensation for false imprisonment, malicious prosecution, and assault. It had proved to be an expensive brick.

Predictably the decision to prosecute the four police officers led to a scramble to get on the band-wagon. In May ten other cases involving twenty-nine complaints against Challenor and other officers were investigated by a chief superintendent of the Metropolitan Police (the 1964 Act was not yet law), but the DPP decided that none of them on the evidence warranted criminal proceedings. If justice seemed to have been done, it was still not the end of the affair; for in June, the new Act came into operation.

As if testing the temperature of the water, on 2 July the Home Secretary invited the Chief Constable of Wolverhampton to review the Challenor investigation, and on 31 July, under section 32 of the new Act, he set up an inquiry under Mr A. E. James, QC, 'to consider the circumstances in which it was possible for Detective Sergeant Challenor to continue on duty when he appeared to have been affected by the onset of mental illness'. James did not submit his Report until over a year later.[1] In his findings, he exonerated both police and medical officers of any blame for failing

---

[1] Cmnd. 2735

to identify the deterioration in Challenor's mental condition, and dismissed allegations of corruption as unfounded and largely actuated by malice. Simpson's resentment at what he felt to be a deliberate and well-orchestrated attempt to discredit the good name of the Metropolitan Police by imputing to the force as a whole the frailties of a few is illustrated by a long and moving passage on 'Complaints and Morale' in his 1965 Report. He sought no special privilege in law for his men, but he would not have them treated as if their uniform deprived them of the rights of any other citizens. 'An accused police officer is entitled to the same benefit of the burden of proof in disciplinary enquiries as he or any member of the public is in the case of a criminal prosecution.'

The Challenor affair—although not of itself a very special case— has a significance quite outside its purely criminal context. First, it illustrates more clearly than ever before the 'referee' function of the DPP in deciding or rejecting the issue of criminality in cases of public complaint against the police (Simpson quotes some revealing figures resulting from the Challenor publicity). Secondly, it was the first demonstration of the 1964 Police Act in action, particularly section 49 which defines the procedure to be adopted by a chief officer in the event of a complaint which may involve criminal proceedings. Although Challenor is now forgotten (and it should be remembered that he never stood trial), he personifies in a very real sense the historic dilemma which Juvenal posed nineteen centuries ago: *Quis custodiet ipsos custodes?*

*

There followed a comparative calm after the storm and Simpson could concentrate, despite a persistent counterpoint of protests and demonstrations, on a programme of modernization and reform which reflected, in a way that Trenchard's had not, a true understanding of the police function. He had no time to lose, for his 1965 Report opens with these words: 'I regret to say that 1964 has proved to be the worst year of the century for crime.'

Simpson's priorities were unusual but logical. He started with his men, on the principle that 'without a contented force the public cannot be given the protection to which they are entitled nor will there exist between police and public that mutual trust and respect which is itself a vital element in the war on crime'. He referred again and again to 'contentment'. His men must be properly rewarded, but money alone did not make an efficient police force. The job had to be made more interesting, and responsibility must be delegated increasingly to the men on the ground. The section-patrol system of policing with its emphasis on the motor-car, which had been introduced in Scott's time when the man-power shortage was at its most critical, seemed to Simpson a total negation of the principle that a policeman should be—and should be *seen* to be—a member of his community, in keeping with the ancient office of constable, and that the uniform man on the beat should be trained to deal not only with routine incidents but with all 'beat' crime. He therefore started two experiments—in New Addington and Banstead—which were to be the genesis of an entirely new system; and to these we will return.

The impetus of Simpson's programme of innovation was virtually halted in its tracks by the passing of the London Government Act 1963, which created the Greater London Council and re-drew the map of the Metropolis. It provided a field-day for the bureaucrats and a nightmare for the Commissioner, for the creation of new boroughs necessitated a complete reorganization of the Metropolitan Police District—the first since Trenchard's time in 1933—to conform to the new local authority boundaries and adding, with the Borough of Havering, forty-seven square miles of the Essex Constabulary area.[1] When the Act came into force in 1965, the MPD had been turned upside down, with enough anomalies and absurdities to provoke Simpson, a man not easily exasperated, into writing to a friend: 'I feel like issuing an Order to all ranks that if they can't find their police station, they should apply to the Lost Property Office.'

*

Simpson now returned to his priorities. By the end of 1964 he could report a surplus of married accommodation for the first time since the war; a total of forty-nine either new or refurbished section-houses; and plans for modern catering and canteen services. The Research and Planning Branch was put to work with D Dept on a complete review of future training and of the re-development of the Hendon complex as a central establishment for

---

[1] The result is now to be seen in the curious conglomerate of 'K' District stretching from East Ham to Upminster, with headquarters at Romford.

promoting the efficiency of the force in an increasingly complex and disorderly society. By the end of the year there were not many men under his command who had not seen or met their Commissioner, and in his tours of the Metropolitan battlefield he seems to have combined the energy of Trenchard and the humanity of Byng. To all ranks he was known as 'Joe', which would have pleased Rowan as much as it would have shocked Warren or Horwood.

Next he turned from his constant theme of 'contentment' to the hard realities of policing: the fight against crime and the preservation of law and order.[1] In a specialist age, it is not long before criminals begin to follow the fashion, and Simpson was quick to grasp the problem. The pattern had been set by Macready with the original Flying Squad which had been little more than an acknowledgement that wheels move faster than feet. There had been no further specialization until thirty years later with the creation of the Fraud Squad and, for rather different reasons, the Murder Squad. Serious crime is the province of C.1 Branch[2] at Scotland Yard, although the diversity of criminal activity is now such that there is no room for elitism or narrow definitions. Crime, like peace, is indivisible. In the 1960s, however, two areas, symptomatic of the new morality, had grown to such proportions that Simpson moved against them with the creation of the Drug Squad and the Obscene Publications Squad. It is a supreme irony that these two squads were shortly to be the centre of a public scandal on a scale which was to make the Turf Frauds affair a century earlier seem like a minor aberration.

But not only is crime indivisible. It does not conform neatly to county boundaries; nor is it a purely Metropolitan phenomenon. A bank raid in Barking may as easily be planned in Brighton as drug-smuggling in Dagenham may be organized in Droitwich.

For some years, provincial chief constables, aware of the mobility of criminals, had pooled their resources with those of neighbouring

---

[1] During 1964 the first computer was installed in the Receiver's Office at Tintagel House across the river from the Yard. Initially it handled such matters as pay and criminal statistics but early in 1965 the 'modus operandi' records were transferred to it on an experimental basis. 'Modus operandi' is the standard reference to those professional criminals whose method of operating follows a similar or identical pattern.

[2] In 1979, C.1 consists of seven very specialist squads.

forces and had set up small teams of very experienced detective officers who would concentrate on the apprehension of travelling criminals engaged in serious crime. The Research and Planning Branch at the Home Office, established in the late 1950s, studied the results of these *ad hoc* teams and duly recommended that the experiment should be adopted throughout England and Wales. Thus there came into existence one of the most imaginative and successful exercises in cooperative policing—the Regional Crime Squads, corresponding to the nine police regions of England and Wales and with an initial establishment of 600 (now increased to around 1,000). The responsibility for inter-squad liaison and assessing and advising on the progress of operations was vested in a National Co-ordinator who, although based in London, is independent of the Commissioner and may be appointed from any of the forty-three police forces.[1]

The Metropolitan Police District is covered by No. 9 Regional Crime Squad consisting chiefly of Metropolitan officers with the addition of detectives from the City police and Home Counties forces. The squad comes under the general supervision of AC 'C' (C.8 and 12) and was originally organized into ten branches, four (known as the 'inner ring') operating near the centre of the MPD and six (the 'outer ring') on the periphery.[2] The terms of reference of the squads are broadly as follows:

1. To concentrate on the detection and apprehension of persons actively engaged in the commission of serious crimes, especially those covering more than one force.

2. To provide mobile and organized detective experience to assist local officers in the investigation of large-scale crime.

3. To keep 'watch and ward' on the activities of professional and travelling criminals.

4. To act as an intelligence agency providing specialist information about prominent criminals and patterns of crime.[3]

[1] In June 1967, the Home Secretary appointed an Inspector of Constabulary (Crime) among whose duties is, so to speak, the co-ordination of the Co-ordinator.

[2] It now (1979) consists of four branch squads: NE (Barkingside), NW (West Hendon), SE (Brockley), and SW (Mitcham).

[3] J. C. Bliss: 'Regional Crime Squads—Operation and Working Methods' (an Internal Paper). John Bliss was the first National Co-ordinator, appointed in 1964.

By the very nature of their work, Regional Crime Squads are kept free from routine case loads. They may best be defined as providing strategic support for locally-based detective officers, and their already sophisticated equipment and special techniques are under constant review by the Home Office Research and Planning Branch. Since their formation they have achieved striking successes in the battle against what John Bliss, the complete professional, called 'good-class criminals'; a classic example of their expertise was Operation 'Julie' (so-called after a woman detective member of the squad) which in 1977 broke the largest known international LSD[1]-traffic organization. 'Julie' was master-minded from an unassuming office in Wiltshire, ranged from Wales across Europe and as far afield as America and Canada, and cost—at a conservative estimate—£400,000.

*

'A good relationship between the members of the Force and the general public leads to contentment and efficiency within the Force and the converse is equally true.' Early in 1965, Simpson turned again to the experiment he had started during the previous year in Surrey to make, as he put it, 'the best use of limited resources'.

The system which he introduced bore an extraordinary resemblance to the 'Shorncliffe experiment' which Charles Rowan had studied under Sir John Moore nearly two centuries earlier and which had so greatly influenced the shaping of the 'New Police'. In essence, it was a return to first principles: small, well-equipped teams with responsibility delegated to the constable himself and working under junior officers—in this case inspectors—at section-station level. Communication was provided by personal radio ('bat-phones', in police jargon), at first in short supply but presently to become standard equipment for all foot patrols. What might Rowan (or even Sir John Moore) have achieved with 'bat-phones'!

Simpson called this new idea 'unit-beat' policing, and wherever possible constables worked a 'home beat' within the locality where

---

[1] LSD is an abbreviation not of a chemical compound but of the 'League of Spiritual Discovery', an organization of drug-addicts set up by an American psychiatrist, Dr Tim Leary, who received a thirty-year prison sentence for his pains.

they lived. Perhaps unconsciously, Simpson in his pursuit of first principles had gone back even further—to the mediaeval drawing-board and to the image of the village constable. He had, after all, been chief officer of two county constabularies.

There were inevitable problems. The introduction of unit-beats was largely conditioned by available man-power and by the boundary changes under the 1963 Act; and it could only be fully effective in the outer, less urbanized divisions. There were also teething troubles. 'For the first week,' recalls a constable, 'every time I switched on my bat-phone, I got what sounded like Radio Luxembourg.' But Simpson's instinctive understanding of the police function paid a double dividend. The public were happy to see the return of the local 'bobby'; and the men were pleased to be, as one of them said, 'proper policemen again'. Contentment is all.

*

Simpson pressed on. The monolithic structure of the force still owed too much to its Victorian origins and to inter-depart-mental jealousies. The lines of command were strictly vertical, and despite Simpson's delegation of responsibility for 'beat' crime to uniform constables, the CID remained a private world of its own, with all the inherent dangers which that implied. For all his professionalism, Simpson seems not to have sensed that the theory of setting a thief to catch a thief was increasingly becoming an insidious and practical reality. In military terms his inability—or refusal—to delegate to his senior officers meant that instead of concentrating on long-term strategy he was too much involved in commanding platoons. The strain began to tell.

Nevertheless, the next major innovation owed everything to his Deputy, Douglas Webb. This was the formation, on 1 April 1965, of the Special Patrol Group, the first successful experiment in 'bush-fire' policing and in providing A.8 Branch with something it had long lacked—a tactical reserve. The primary function of the SPG, which originally consisted of 100 volunteer uniform officers, was mobile preventive patrolling, especially in areas where there were localized outbreaks of crime. Its further assignments included large-scale searches, escort duties, and stand-by support in the preservation of law and order; and its effectiveness was so marked and immediate that Simpson, at first a doubtful disciple of Webb's plan, was quick to recommend its extension to the other three districts.[1] Predictably, the existence of the SPG gave rise to some dark suspicions; that it was in some way a sinister extension of the perennially 'mysterious' Special Branch or that its name suggested a para-military role comparable to the military function of the Special Air Service—so much so that, in his Report for 1977, Sir David McNee was to write: 'A myth has been fostered by some elements of the media that the SPG is a specially trained and equipped riot squad. This is without foundation.' Its role, he went on, is what it has always been—to provide a mobile reserve which can be deployed quickly in support of divisional or headquarters officers.

As 1965 drew to a close, something rare and encouraging had become apparent. Simpson's practical and positive approach to the maintenance of the Queen's Peace had met with a degree of response from the corridors of Whitehall which no previous Commissioner had enjoyed. For more than a century the relationship had been soured by a 'them and us' attitude for which both sides had, at different times and for different reasons, been responsible. Ineffective Commissioners had been brow-beaten by arrogant mandarins, and sensible civil servants had been driven to despair by abrasive Commissioners. Inevitably, as in all such confrontations, the victims had been the ordinary citizen and the ordinary policeman. Battles may be planned by generals; in the end they are fought by private soldiers. The highest casualties are in the trenches.

Simpson knew this, and in his dealings with the Home Office he never pressed his view beyond what politicians would call 'the art of the possible'. He emphasized this in another private letter in which he wrote: 'You have to live with the System, because in the long run the System has to win.' As a result, he achieved something far beyond peaceful co-existence and, within the cash limits which a now endemic financial stringency was to impose, a significant part of his material requirements. It was a virtuoso performance, greeted by the Home Office with respectful applause.

Recruiting continued to exceed wastage, and by the summer of 1966 the strength of the force was 18,776 (the London allowance

---

[1] The Special Patrol Group now covers the whole MPD, with a still modest strength of 204 men, based on six operational centres.

was increased to £50 in April); the SPG was improving its performance and expertise;[1] and the unit-beat system, despite a
continuing shortage of bat-phones, had been extended to twenty-
three sub-divisions. At Hendon, 'leadership' courses had been
introduced to complement the more limited facilities for higher
training at Bramshill. Contentment was beginning to pay handsome dividends.[2]

During the year, there were important changes in the command
structure at the Yard. Early in 1966, Douglas Webb retired as
Deputy Commissioner, and the occasion was noted by Simpson in
these curiously guarded terms: 'It was with the deepest regret that
I heard [*sic*] at the end of the year of the inability of the Deputy
Commissioner, Mr. Douglas Webb, CVO, OBE, to continue on
duty.' The reason given was 'for health reasons', but a more likely
explanation reflects a streak of insensitivity in Simpson's character
born of an excessive remoteness, not of malice.

After the state funeral of Sir Winston Churchill, John Waldron,
who as AC 'A' had been responsible for the police arrangements,
was made a KCVO, a preferment within the sole discretion of the
Sovereign. For the New Year's Honours List, Simpson was
invited to recommend another senior colleague for a knighthood.
Ranulph Bacon, then AC 'C', was within a few months of retirement and it is reasonable to think that Simpson put his name
forward on the basis that Webb would inevitably be similarly
rewarded at the end of his service. It does not seem to have
occurred to him that Webb might be embarrassed by finding
himself as *primus inter impares*, with two 'Ks' as assistant commissioners. He was certainly in poor health, but Simpson's decision
undoubtedly hastened his premature retirement; and with him
went one of the outstanding policemen of his time.

Bacon succeeded Webb until his own retirement a few months
later, when he in turn was succeeded by Waldron as Deputy
Commissioner; and Bacon's office as AC 'C' was filled by Peter
Brodie, educated at Harrow, who had spent much of the war with
Waldron in Ceylon and who had progressed by way of Chief

---

[1] A prime 'scalp' was the arrest of Roberts, one of the Shepherd's Bush
murderers.
[2] Simpson was not the only virtuoso. During the World Cup of 1966,
the force provided a team of two sergeants and nine constables as interpreters at Wembley Stadium.

Constable of Warwickshire to the Inspectorate of Constabulary. It was still 'game, set and match' to Hendon.

In all the history of the Metropolitan Police, there has probably not been a year like 1967.

At 6 a.m. on Wednesday, 8 March, after a move spread over twenty-three days, the Metropolitan Police Office became fully operational in its imposing new premises on Broadway and Victoria Street. The decision to move had been announced by Henry Brooke as far back as May 1964 and the site chosen was already being developed as a speculative office block. Work had only just started, and thus it was possible by some ingenious re-planning to convert the design into a purpose-built police head-quarters capable of accommodating virtually every department, including that of the Receiver, under one roof (there was still no room at the inn for the now traditional waifs and strays).

With childish delight, the new Public Relations Office issued a string of facts and figures—a gross floor area (including lavatories) of over 11 acres, $1\frac{1}{2}$ miles of corridors, 13 lifts, 4,240 windows, 662 offices, 7 drawing offices, 3 libraries, 10 conference rooms . . . and so on. It was clinical, air-conditioned, impersonal, and not at all to the liking of the old guard accustomed to the planned con-fusion of the Embankment complex. 'There,' reflects a veteran, 'no one could ever find my office. Now I can't find anyone else's.' But the new building was efficient, not least in its modern com-munications facilities, its 'selective vertical document conveyors' and its single-floor accommodation for space-intensive depart-ments like CRO, Finger Prints, and Photographic.

As if to mark the final break with Norman Shaw and the Victorian era, the year provided the largest increase in strength since 1947—to a total of 20,078, with 6,782 civil staff—and the first decrease in indictable crime since 1954.[1] With the delivery of more bat-phones and 'Panda' cars, the unit-beat system at station level was extended to all outer divisions and special anti-crime teams were formed at larger commands. With the new sophisti-cated communications facilities, a Central Traffic Control was set up at Broadway and the fixed penalty system for parking offences was applied throughout the MPD. A further pay increase—the

[1] In spite of Simpson's continuing advocacy, the strength of the Special Patrol Group was still only 130.

second since Willink—raised the scale for constables to £815–
£1,255. The first phase of the re-development of Hendon was
started; and even rusty police dogs were sent for refresher training.
It was a year of formidable progress and activity, and in everything
Simpson's hand was to be seen. He even took time off to report on
a mass meeting of 'Flower People' in pursuit of legalizing cannabis.
'No speeches were made,' Simpson noted, 'but poetry, mostly
incomprehensible, was recited.'

'I have often wondered,' wrote Simpson, 'whether the Force was
in the era of rapid development, relying too much on self-gener-
ated ideas for its progress, and whether an examination from
without was required.' He was too modest to say that virtually
every idea had been Simpson-generated, but he was certainly the
first Commissioner to suggest that it might be salutary for the
Metropolitan Police to see themselves as others saw them. The
outcome was the appointment of a team of management consultants 'to investigate in the broadest possible way, the distribution
of functions and responsibilities within the Metropolitan Police'.

By far the most radical interim proposal of the team, duly
adopted on 1 April 1968, was the merging of the Receiver's office
with that of the Commissioner.

Ever since the appointment of John Wray in 1829, the Receiver
had enjoyed (a word not always strictly true) an entirely separate
status from that of the Commissioner, with direct responsibility
and access to the Secretary of State. It was an arrangement which,
as we have seen, caused considerable friction, not only during
Wray's term of office, but notably during the 1880s. In the 1930s
Trenchard and Sir John Moylan were barely on speaking terms.
It did not take the team of consultants long to determine that,
while they had much to learn about the police function, here was
an administrative absurdity which owed everything to entrenched
attitudes from the past and nothing to managerial techniques of the
present.

The revolutionary change has been lucidly explained by the
present Receiver, Mr R. A. James:[1] 'Although the statutory functions of the Receiver have remained unchanged—for example he is
still responsible directly to the Home Secretary as guardian of the

[1] R. A. James, *The Changing Role of the Office of Receiver*. An address to
the Institution of Professional Civil Servants, 23 February 1978.

Metropolitan Police finances and owner of all Metropolitan Police property—there is now one office and one staff with the Receiver being directly responsible to the Commissioner in respect of his functions as the Chief Administrative Officer of the force and as head of the unified Metropolitan Police civil staff',[1] ranking 'pari passu' with the Deputy Commissioner.

In the process of reorganization, the Receiver's Office became responsible for six departments: E—the former Secretariat, dealing with all civil personnel matters; F—finance; G—general administration; Architects; Engineers; and later Catering. James gives some interesting comparisons of the growth of the administrative function during the ten years since 1968. The level of expenditure rose from £78,000,000 to £314,000,000 (the current value of police property is equivalent to that controlled by one of the largest property companies); there are now more than 280 different civil staff grades organized into 10 associations and unions; in 1968 there was a single computer shared with the Home Office, and there are now twenty-four, apart from the Police National Computer at Hendon; then there were 663 bat-phones, now over 7,000; technical support has revolutionized the whole concept of detective policing. It is a far, far cry from John Wray in his office at 4 Whitehall Place with a staff of two clerks.

The team of consultants returned to the drawing-board and it was not until the following year that it presented its final report. Meanwhile Simpson did not wait upon events. A 'Scenes of Crime' branch was formed consisting of civilian technical staff specially trained in finger prints, photography and forensic science while two new squads were added to C Dept to deal with the growing traffic of crime in philately and works of art. One member of the latter squad was mildly surprised. 'I didn't know a Botticelli from my backside.' He soon did; and now—in a civilian capacity—is one of the world's leading authorities on art forgery.

1968 started with an explosion of football hooliganism and a growing climate of public disorder. The 'protest industry' was in full cry—Biafra, Vietnam, Rhodesia, Ukraine, anti-Apartheid, Czecho-Slovakia,[2] student demonstrations, student sit-ins. A solitary protester even progressed down Whitehall bearing a

---

[1] By 1978, the civil staff had grown to 15,000 full and part time members.

[2] On this occasion, the Trotskyists and Maoists were conspicuous by their absence. The field was largely left to Czech emigrés.

banner with that strange, if here not readily explicit, device: 'Excelsior!' The climax came on Sunday, 17 March, when the committee of the Vietnam Solidarity Campaign launched a full-scale assault on the United States Embassy in Grosvenor Square. It was by far the most violent demonstration yet seen in the Metropolis, and in something approaching a pitched battle 145 policemen were injured. The television cameras provided a visual commentary. The public was deeply shocked. The civil libertarians uttered cries of indignation. And three days later, Joseph Simpson died of a heart attack.

He had been unwell for some time, but had refused to take life more quietly. He was the first Commissioner since Richard Mayne to die in office and it is not unlikely that the battle of Grosvenor Square proved to be the ultimate breaking-point. He had brought greater distinction to his lonely office than any man since Charles Rowan and it is perhaps as well that he did not survive to see the humiliation of the CID or the years of terrorism on the streets of London. He was a great policeman and a devoted public servant.

His sudden death took the Home Secretary, James Callaghan, by surprise, for much of the work which he had initiated was not yet completed. But before we turn to the events which followed, it is necessary to put the clock back to a significant decision which had been taken a year earlier.

CHAPTER THIRTEEN

Odd Man In

TOWARDS THE end of 1966, Tom Mahir's continuing ill-health precipitated his retirement.[1] He had occupied the office of AC 'D' virtually throughout Simpson's commissionership and for most of that time his department had been, in the words of one of his contemporaries, 'the dumping-ground of the Yard; if in doubt, give it to 'D'. Thus, for example, while the Mounted Branch was the responsibility of 'A' Dept, dogs were Mahir's concern, on the principle that 'A is for 'orses, D is for dogs'. His impending departure touched off some agitated speculation among the senior officers of the force. It did not last long; and the answer, when it came, was greeted with incredulity.

In December the Home Secretary, Roy Jenkins, sent for Robert Mark. 'I have decided,' he said, 'to appoint you an assistant com-missioner in the Metropolitan Police.' Mark, no innocent in the matter of police politics, got the signal loud and clear. 'Have you,' he asked, 'consulted the Commissioner and does he agree?' After a lengthy silence, Jenkins replied carefully: 'He has loyally promised to abide by my decision.'[2] And so it was that a lively cat was put among some very nervous pigeons.

Robert Mark had joined the Manchester City Police in 1937. By 1956, after war service, he was a chief superintendent, having taken out an inexpensive insurance policy for the future by attending a three-week course at the new Police College at Ryton—'wholly without value of any kind, but providing me with the label I wanted'—and thus armed, he applied for a number of posts as chief officer, succeeding at the seventh and last attempt, Leicester.

---

[1] Mahir left two memorials: the Convalescent Home at Hove; and the Cadet Corps which, like much else under Nott-Bower, had lost all sense of purpose and direction. The Corps was completely reorganized by Mahir in October 1960 and under his guidance progressed from a training-ground for tea-boys to an academy for future constables.

[2] Mark, *op. cit.*

He took up his appointment there on 1 January 1957. He was young; he was experienced; he was almost excessively articulate; he was ambitious; and during his ten years as Chief Constable he was to impose a new and highly personal style of policing on the 500-strong force of that solid and prosperous city. He was also, like all innovators, to make some formidable enemies, not least Edward Dodd, then Chief Constable of neighbouring Birmingham and later Chief Inspector of Constabulary.[1]

He was still only forty-nine and enjoying the comparative luxury of life on the Willink salary scale when, in his own words (and those of P. G. Wodehouse), fate sneaked up behind him and struck him smartly behind the ear with a stuffed eelskin; and, ironically, the agent of his ill-fortune was Roy Jenkins who, in pursuit of rationalization, had decided to amalgamate the county and borough police forces of Leicestershire. As head of the numerically stronger force, the new job went to the Chief Constable of the county; and Robert Mark was out in the cold.

How he came to be saved from one exposure to frostbite only to be translated to another has long been a subject for speculation. A little detective work may throw some light on the argument.

During 1966, Mark had lunch with Jenkins and shortly afterwards was invited by the Home Office to be the police member of the Standing Advisory Council on the Penal System. Nine days later the super-spy, George Blake, was 'sprung' from Wormwood Scrubs. Lord Mountbatten was appointed to head an inquiry into prison security and Mark was seconded to the committee as assessor. It proved to be the marriage of two very similar minds. By early December, after an interlude at Dartmoor enlivened by the escape of the dangerous Frank Mitchell, later 'silenced' ('no one knows where his body is although legend has it that he is now part of a motorway flyover'), the Mountbatten Report was published. Robert Mark's contribution figured prominently.

Jenkins has implied[2] that Mark's appointment to the Yard was a *coup de théâtre* entirely of his (Jenkins's) devising, but if that is true, it was a deliberately provocative, and therefore uncharacteristic, act. When Mark became redundant, there were influential voices raised in Leicester on his behalf, but none more influential

[1] It is at least arguable that if Dodd, a close friend of Simpson, had not died in September 1966, Mark would not have come to Scotland Yard.

[2] *The Observer*, 8 October 1978.

than that of Mountbatten who had seen some of the qualities of
this very unusual policeman at first hand; and to be influenced by
Mountbatten was much more characteristic of Jenkins.

There was another and unexpected lobby at work. Since the
final Hendon 'takeover' in 1963, a comfortable assumption had
taken root that, despite the Crown prerogative, the line of succession was assured within the existing hierarchy. Simpson, the
patrician, would ensure the advancement of his pro-consuls; all
was going to be for the best in the best of all possible worlds.
There was only one problem. The Home Office was determined
that no such self-perpetuation of the species by natural selection
should occur. When the news of Robert Mark's appointment was
announced, a fearful truth dawned on the pro-consuls. He was not
coming just to run Tom Mahir's Cadet Corps, or even his dogs.
Here was a probable Commissioner-designate.

*

In a letter to Mark, Simpson had made it very clear that his
appointment would not be welcomed by the Metropolitan Police.
He did not explain whether this was on personal grounds or
because a Home Secretary had had the temerity to impose a
provincial peasant on the Praetorian Guard. In either sense, it was
a curious way of honouring his promise to Jenkins, and so far as the
rank and file were concerned there was no surprise; for generations,
Whitehall Caligulas had been making consuls out of horses. A
sergeant at Gerald Road telephoned a friend at Leicester. 'He's a
copper,' he was told, 'and he won't stand for having men buggered
about.' The word soon got around.

Mark has described his chilly reception at the Yard in some
detail in his autobiography,[1] although there are those who disagree
with his account and believe that he had not troubled to do his
homework. He had come, in military terms, from a small, very
personal command no bigger than a battalion to the General Staff
of an Army Corps in which the senior officers had grown up under
a system where joint consultation had long been subservient to
private ambition. A present deputy assistant commissioner has
summed up the sterile philosophy of the command structure of the
Metropolitan Police in a bleak phrase which still colours attitudes

[1] Mark, *op. cit.*

within the force today: 'You are only as good as your last mistake.' As a prescription for managerial inertia, that could hardly be bettered.

In fact, Simpson's attitude and the hostility of his colleagues suited Mark very well. He had inherited Mahir's 'dumping-ground' and a large part of his little empire consisted of civil staff. Since no one took the trouble to define his function or question his decisions, he simply applied the lessons of thirty years of practical policing; and the hive began to buzz. A small but typical example was his attitude to 'assessment', a time-honoured Metropolitan system by which a police officer was required to pay for any articles of equipment lost in the course of duty. In Mark's view, a constable had only one irreplaceable asset which he could lose—his life. Beside this, a torch or a pair of gloves were trivia; and he laid down that no assessment of less value than £50 was to be charged against an officer unless 'wrongdoing or negligence' could be proved.

*

The team of management consultants had started work a month or so before Mark's arrival at the Yard. The main recommendation of its interim report had been the radical alteration in the status and function of the Receiver's Office, but at the same time it had trodden rather more gingerly through the minefield of the four Police Departments. The consultants shirked any major reorganization in this sensitive area; such as, for example, re-defining the status and duties of the Deputy Commissioner. They did, however, transfer some of the accumulated debris of the years from D Dept, chiefly to the Receiver's Office, and nominated AC 'D' as third in line in the police pecking-order at Scotland Yard.[1] The remaining recommendations of the consultants were not to be implemented until after Simpson's death, but the grace and favour bestowed upon the office of AC 'D' ensured that Mark would not long be left to enjoy the view. There was a quick, instinctive reaction. Andrew Way was moved sideways to 'A'; Mark took over Traffic— 'B'; Brodie remained at 'C'; and John Hill—the last of the Hendon-ites—was appointed to 'D'. It was to prove the final act in a game

[1] This surprising departure may well have been an approving nod in the direction of Robert Mark, rather than an attempt to evaluate the comparative importance of different police functions.

of 'Beggar my Neighbour' which had lasted too long and was beginning to play to empty houses.

Simpson's death was not only the end of an era; it was also the start of a revolution: within the Yard, within the force, and on the streets of the Metropolis. The ten years which followed were to be so full of incident and so critical for the future that they are best considered not in strictly chronological terms, but rather as a series of separate actions and reactions. For example, by yet another historical irony, they were to reflect the two faces of the Criminal Investigation Department—the corruption of the few set against the devotion to duty of the many. And by a strange coincidence, it was almost exactly 100 years since an identical set of circumstances had given rise to that sickness at the heart of the Metropolitan Police against which Mark was to move with a sharp scalpel and a ruthless conviction that cancer is not incurable. First, however, he needed to progress from general practitioner to consultant surgeon.

*

Eight days after Simpson's death, Callaghan, who had exchanged chairs with Jenkins after the devaluation crisis of the previous November, summoned Mark to tell him that he was a possible candidate for the succession. A less astute man would have jumped at the opportunity, but Mark, still suffering from frostbite, was well aware—even if Callaghan and his Permanent Under-Secretary, Philip Allen, were not—that his appointment would result in a mutiny among the ivory towers of Scotland Yard a great deal more disastrous than that of the rank and file in 1918. He gave his reasons, and politely declined the honour. 'Well,' said Callaghan, decisive as ever, 'what would you do in my shoes?' Mark, alive to even greater dangers from some quarters of the provincial police, suggested that the rational choice was the Deputy Commissioner, if only on a care and maintenance basis. A week later Callaghan sent for him again. 'I've decided to take your advice. Waldron is to be appointed for two years[1] [*by which time he would be sixty*]. You are forthwith deputy commissioner.' The general practitioner was on his way.

[1] There were to be two subsequent extensions, each of one year.

Waldron, who had never wanted to leave the comparatively quiet pastures of Berkshire in the first place, would not have thanked Robert Mark if he had been privy to these curious consultations. He was not the stuff of which Commissioners are made and he resented the obvious implication that he was merely a caretaker. There thus followed four years which Mark has described as the most unpleasant of his life, partly because, as Deputy Commissioner, he had virtually no authority over the four Police Departments, partly because some of his colleagues in those departments knew this, and partly because he was, through no fault of his own, Callaghan's man, not Waldron's.[1] No man's land can be a lonely and dangerous place when the bullets are flying; so Mark kept his head down and only fired back at sitting targets. One such target had been sitting there for nearly 100 years, clearly visible, increasingly ominous, and for far too long ignored. It was this time-bomb which was soon to rock the Metropolitan Police to its foundations and, in so doing, bring Robert Mark in from the cold. For the moment, we will leave it ticking.

*

The management consultants had submitted their final report to the Home Office a month before Simpson's death. Their proposals—which Callaghan accepted virtually in their entirety—were concerned with administrative changes. They would have been brave men indeed if they had commented in necessary detail on the operational defects at Scotland Yard, and in any event operational control of the Metropolitan Police was not within the statutory powers of the Home Secretary. Fate, however, was waiting in the wings, armed with a regular arsenal of stuffed eelskins; and of danger all unconscious, Waldron proceeded with the administrative changes.

The chief of these was the replacement of districts by an Area Inspectorate of four Commanders (later regraded as Deputy Assistant Commissioners). There was no change of territory, and the new title was a misnomer since alone among the police forces

[1] At senior staff meetings, Waldron delegated the chair to Mark and himself sat to one side. If the purpose was to embarrass Mark, its true effect was to diminish Waldron.

of England and Wales the Metropolitan Police is not subject to 'inspection'.[1]

Next, the consultants proposed the setting up of a Management Services Department, working to the Deputy Commissioner, which would combine the functions of the former Research and Development and O and M Departments. It was a sensible attempt to provide a mangerial link with the parallel department at the Home Office and, perhaps unconsciously, to impose a proper discipline on the autonomous police departments. It was also a rational corollary to the new status and function of the Receiver's Office.

The report then looked at the monolithic structure of the force as a whole, virtually unchanged for over 100 years, and recommended that 'there were too many levels in the structure which could only lead to bottlenecks'. It was the understatement of the year. They therefore suggested that district (area) commands should be eliminated and replaced by eight 'super' divisions each with eight subdivisions. 'The Force,' commented Waldron with the air of a man who has suddenly discovered that the earth is round, 'has suffered in the past from too heavy a hand from above.' It was accepted, however, that the recent reorganization of the MPD under the London Government Act had been both costly and time-consuming and that another radical upheaval was not to be contemplated. But 'eight by eight', as the proposal came to be known, was put into cold storage until it emerged again some eight years later under the name RUFUS (Review of Force Structure).

Simpson did not survive to see the final results of his own labours (he had accepted the intrusion of the management consultants with neither enthusiasm nor antipathy). Thus the move of the recruit training school from Peel House to Hendon in May 1968 set the seal on his policy of bringing together in a single complex all the different strands of training and of technical development within the Metropolitan Police.[2] Peel Centre remains today as Simpson's memorial.

*

[1] For a brief period in 1967, Jim Starritt had been appointed to the post of Inspector to the Force.

[2] 1968 also saw the introduction of the Graduate Entry Scheme, which linked entry through the ranks to Bramshill and thus helped to bridge the gap left by the demise of Trenchard's college.

When Mark took over as Deputy Commissioner, he was already well aware of a dangerously anomalous situation peculiar to the Metropolitan Police and to no other force. As Deputy he was the *de facto* disciplinary authority, except—and it was a vital exception —if an allegation against a police officer amounted to crime. In all such cases, the responsibility for investigation was vested in AC 'C' who in turn was accountable only to the Commissioner himself. The historical origin of this procedure went back to the creation of the CID under Vincent in 1878 after the Turf Frauds scandal and the decision effectively to separate the preventive and detective branches of the Metropolitan Police. The inevitable result was a 'them and us' situation in which the uniform branch deeply resented the implication of inferiority, and the CID demonstrated with growing arrogance their contempt for their less-privileged colleagues. Far more seriously, the autonomy of the CID and their jealously-guarded right to be their own judge and jury led inevitably to an assumption that in the war against criminals any means— even a resort to crime itself—justified the ends; and from there it was a short step to what Mark has called 'institutionalized' corruption.

From its earliest days corruption had been rife in the CID. It had long been common knowledge throughout the force but only publicly advertised when a man like Goddard—actually a uniform sergeant—became the victim of his own excessive greed. Trenchard, for example while deluding himself that he had stopped the rot, had constantly shirked the issue. Detectives played the game according to their own rules, confident that neither their superiors nor the courts would accept the evidence of known or convicted criminals; and by 1969 a whole grey area of the CID had literally become a law unto itself.

The answer, Mark recognized, lay in the system by which all complaints involving alleged crime were investigated exclusively by a CID long skilled in the art of cosmetic surgery. To his suggestion that *all* disciplinary proceedings should be the province of the Deputy, Waldron turned a deaf ear. Even the Home Office, increasingly concerned at the growing tension in the force and alone having the authority to issue a directive to the Commissioner, hesitated to act. And on Saturday, 29 November, the time-bomb exploded.

That morning *The Times* revealed that the previous evening it had handed to Scotland Yard 'disturbing evidence of bribery and corruption among certain London detectives'. The story, by two young journalists, went on to name three men—Det. Sgt Symonds of Camberwell, Det. Insp. Robson of C.9 Branch at the Yard and Det. Sgt Harris, a Metropolitan CID officer seconded to No. 6 Regional Crime Squad in Brighton—as having taken large sums of money 'in exchange for dropping charges, for being lenient with evidence offered in court and for allowing a criminal to work unhindered'. Across 100 years the ghosts of Meiklejohn and Druscovitch were casting long shadows as the article went on to suggest that these cases might well not be isolated, and that there was enough suspicion to justify a full inquiry. The conduct of that inquiry, when it was duly set up, more than justified the suspicion. It also revealed a ruthless determination by the CID to ensure that justice was neither done nor seen to be done. *The Times*, explaining its reasons for printing the story within hours of submitting its evidence to the Yard, bluntly stated that it had done so because it had no confidence in the Yard's ability—or willingness—to conduct a full and impartial investigation into the behaviour of its own detective officers. Waldron ignored the damning implication of this indictment, nor did it occur to him that a newspaper of the standing of *The Times* would hardly have risked its reputation unless it was certain of its facts.

It is possible here only to outline the course of events.[1] The fuse which ignited the time-bomb was lit by pure chance. A year earlier *The Times* had enlisted the services of a 'retired' burglar named Brennan to cooperate in a series of articles on the art of housebreaking. The project proved too expensive (and too risky) and was dropped. Instead the paper published a single feature with Brennan acting as a very 'professional' consultant.

In the autumn of 1969, Brennan re-surfaced. He had a young friend in need of advice. Would *The Times* see him? On 27 October the 'young friend' went to Printing House Square. He turned out to be a man named Michael Perry, with a lengthy criminal record— and (if true) a very disturbing story; for it seemed he was in double trouble. He had been framed on two serious charges, and he was being blackmailed, as the price for 'safe conduct', from two

[1] For a detailed account of the *Times* inquiry and the subsequent cases involving the Drug Squad and the Obscene Publications Squad, see Cox, Shirley, and Short, *The Fall of Scotland Yard*.

different quarters—his local detective sergeant (Symonds) and the Yard (Robson and Harris). Moreover, he alleged, he was not alone in attracting the corrupt attentions of CID officers in his neighbourhood. There existed, it seemed, a standard practice which amounted to something like the periodical payment of club subscriptions.

To the two journalists, Lloyd and Mounter, the alternatives were simple. If the story was an invention, it was a blank cartridge; if it was true, it was highly explosive. They decided to test it by what can best be described as audio-visual means—tape recordings and photography. By the end of the investigation, Perry had become a kind of mobile recording-studio and the tapes a unique testament to the new techniques of investigative journalism. 'If I had had my way,' says a chief superintendent, 'I would have asked Lloyd and Mounter to give an illustrated lecture to every subsequent detective-training course.'

At the trial of Robson and Harris which opened on 26 January 1972, (they had been suspended on full pay over *two* years previously), defence counsel, James Comyn, based his case on two counts; one, an attempt to discredit the tapes, the other, an old (and itself discredited) argument that the traffic in pursuit of criminals was a one-way street involving paying out, not raking in. The jury was unimpressed; and Robson was sent down for seven years, Harris for six.

This left John Symonds, whose relations with Perry had been a great deal closer and had extended far outside the Metropolitan Police District. Indeed it was the involvement of another villain, MacDonald, and the patient investigations of a parallel provincial inquiry which brought Symonds within measurable distance of the bar of justice. On committal, he was allowed bail in the modest sum of £500—a figure some way below the profits he had made out of his private enterprise—and shortly before the date fixed for his trial (12 April) he bought a caravan, sold his house, and absconded with his woman-friend. He has not been seen since, and it is at least arguable (since his passport was not surrendered) that the System decided that it would be convenient to ensure that he did not stand trial. He had made it very clear that, if he stood in the dock, he would produce a telephone directory of 'bent' policemen. Whereever he may be, he should be remembered for two classic statements recorded during the *Times* inquiry. To Perry he said:

'We've got more villains in our game than you've got in yours, you know.' And—even more memorably: 'I know people everywhere. *Because I'm in a little firm in a firm.*' It was a phrase which was to have a significance which John Symonds did not foresee. It ensured that Robert Mark would be Waldron's successor as Commissioner.

*

The *Times* revelations caused—as they were intended to do—a sensation, not only because of the nature of the allegations but even more because of the exceptional methods of investigation to which Lloyd and Mounter had resorted. The immediate reaction of the Establishment at the Yard was to close ranks and to counter-attack by attempting to discredit the article as another piece of irresponsible journalism. But not even Waldron, with his professional sense of loyalty to his own men, could sweep the *Times* evidence under the carpet, and after a preliminary report from Detective Chief Superintendent Lambert on 1 December, he ordered an internal investigation. The fact that this investigation was at first concentrated on Lloyd, Mounter and Perry is indicative of the ingrained attitude of the System and it was not until 4 December that Robson, Harris and Symonds were suspended (the *Times* article had also referred anonymously to two other CID officers). 'Nowhere,' says a lawyer, 'was the legal privilege of the "right of silence" more clearly demonstrated at that time than at the Yard.'

But the Yard was not a law unto itself. Laws are made by Parliament to whom the Home Secretary, as the Metropolitan Police authority, is accountable. Faced by a cross-fire of Parliamentary questions, Callaghan acted; and on 9 December the Home Office issued this statement: 'The Home Secretary, at the request of the Commissioner of Police of the Metropolis, has agreed that in view of the wide public interest someone independent should be associated with the investigation of allegations recently published in *The Times* about the conduct of police officers.' It was an odd form of words, not least because it implied that the Home Secretary's hand had been forced, not by clear allegations of criminality in the one force for which he was solely responsible, but by the Commissioner and by that most convenient safety-net, 'public interest'. It was also unusual since, even under the 1964 Act, the Metropolitan Police alone remained insulated against 'outside inspection'. A little piece of history was about to be made; and the System went to battle-stations.

Callaghan's choice was Frank Williamson, Inspector of Constabulary (Crime), and therefore no longer a member of the police service. He had been a senior detective officer in Manchester whence he had gone to be Chief Constable of Carlisle and, in the final reorganization, Chief Constable of Cumbria, before joining the inspectorate. He was a very 'provincial' policeman who had no great love for the Met. and a low opinion of the integrity of their CID. Callaghan denied him the muscle that he needed by defining his investigatory function as 'advisory', and Williamson accordingly insisted that he must have a team of provincial officers to counter the inevitable antagonism of the Yard. He was not only wise; he was also to stumble on the fact that the most incriminating evidence, certainly in the case of Symonds, was to be provided by events outside the MPD.

There are two views of Williamson. First, that he brought with him a built-in distrust of the Met. which became an obsession; second, that the Met., contemptuous of provincial interference, slammed the door in his face. The truth is largely irrelevant, except for one crucial decision.

In effect, because of the refusal of the Yard to accept outside interference in its 'private' affairs, two separate investigations were conducted: Williamson's and Lambert's. The Byzantine implications of this situation are brilliantly described in *The Fall of Scotland Yard*.[1] By the spring of 1970, Williamson and Lambert had moved their 'joint' inquiry teams to Tintagel House in Lambeth, largely to escape the hostile atmosphere at the Yard, and by then they had achieved a close working relationship. Suddenly, on 26 May 1970—six months after the parallel inquiries had started—Lambert was replaced by Detective Chief Superintendent William Moody. The Yard had decided that love at first sight was a dangerous portent of the marriage of true minds.

Moody was head of the Obscene Publications Squad. When, in May 1970, he took over the *Times* inquiry, no one—at least, it may be hoped no one—was aware that he was himself already deeply involved in corruption in Soho on a scale which made the operations of Robson, Harris and Symonds seem like those of amateurs

---

[1] Cox, Shirley and Short, *op. cit.*

in a highly professional field. The appointment of Moody to the Met. investigation must have been the last straw for Callaghan's watchdog. 'Although Williamson could have had no precise idea in the summer of 1970 of what Moody was up to in Soho . . . his gut feeling was one of revulsion.'[1] As policemen, he and Moody were worlds apart—the Cromwellian Puritan and the man on the make. At the end of 1971, Williamson was 'so fed up with banging his head against a brick wall' that he resigned from the inspectorate.

*

Four months after the suspension of the three CID officers, the scene changed to another part of the forest, with a new cast of actors—the Drug Squad, formed in the late 1960s by Simpson, and by April 1970 consisting of some twenty officers.

Drug-peddling has a history half as old as time, but it was not until after the Second World War that clandestine traffic became a major industry and a social menace. The peddlers were, for the most part, Asians, Levantines and West Indians, their stock-in-trade heroin, LSD, and cannabis, and they operated in an area ill-defined by law and moral precept. One thing was beyond argument. Whatever the cost in human degradation, it was a highly profitable trade. Not only the peddlers knew this; so did the detective agents of law enforcement. It was a situation which invited dangerous liaisons, but, unlike the circumstances in which men like Symonds had operated, there was a significant difference. Since most traffic in dangerous drugs involved smuggling from abroad, the 'little firm in a firm' was not the only or even the most important law-enforcement agency. The prime surveillance of illicit smuggling was in the hands of HM Customs and Excise, and this was to prove a new and disturbing element in the progressive disintegration of the CID's credibility, to say nothing of its debauched standards of conduct; for it was Customs men who were soon to come very close to answering Juvenal's question: *Quis custodiet . . .?*

In the twilight world of dope-peddling, the Drug Squad was in its element. Although nominally accountable to the Commander

[1] *Ibid.*

in charge of serious crime (C.1), it developed its own highly original techniques, so secretive that it became virtually 'a firm within a firm within a firm'. These techniques took several forms such as: setting up deals on their own account, paying informants to set up deals which they then bust, even aiding and abetting the smuggling of drugs as *agents provocateurs* in pursuit of the chief operators in drug distribution (it was this which brought the Drug Squad into conflict with the Customs and with provincial police).

When eventually six members of the squad stood trial in September 1973, they were charged with conspiracy to pervert the course of justice and five of them with perjury. All six were acquitted on the first charge and three detectives were found guilty on the second and sentenced to prison.

*

The Drug Squad affair, with all its attendant court cases and sordid implications, served to heighten the public disquiet about the state of affairs in the Metropolitan CID;[1] and this disquiet, to say nothing of growing concern at the Home Office and Customs and Excise, was reflected in a virtual declaration of war between the Yard and Whitehall. Customs, in particular, were fully aware of the activities of the Drug Squad and their relationship with the chief operators in drug-trafficking, but at the Yard the System once again pulled up the drawbridge. 'The hierarchies in both law-enforcement institutions went into battle for their respective sides, refereed uneasily by an appalled Home Office.'[2]

Waldron played his cards with an ineptitude and a degree of obstructionism which would have fully justified the Home Secretary in removing him from office. Mark, his deputy, was in his own words 'emasculated' by the System. Much has been said of the attitude of the CID (and the worst was yet to come), but in the last analysis the ultimate responsibility lay with the Commissioner. He was well aware that the Home Office had a detailed dossier on the questionable activities of the Drug Squad. He was

[1] There had also been famous victories for the other, 'acceptable' face of CID activities; notably the long and patient investigations which destroyed the ruthless Richardson and Kray gangs in 1968 and 1969. The names of Gerry Macarthur and 'Nipper' Read should be recorded.

[2] Cox, Shirley and Short, *op. cit.*

soon to have the evidence at the trial of Basil Sands, one of the Squads prime contacts, which began on 9 June 1971. Yet until then he had taken little action beyond setting up another internal inquiry within the Yard.

The Sands trial at last forced Waldron's hand. Two days after it started, the existing Drug Squad was virtually broken up and its members were posted to other duties (one of them, Prichard, who was subsequently to be jailed for perjury, was actually promoted to detective sergeant); and on 20 July, the day after the Sands verdict, the Yard announced that an investigation into allegations made at the trial would be conducted by Lancashire detectives under their Assistant Chief Constable, Harold Prescott. For the first time in its history the Metropolitan Police was subjected to outside investigation by a provincial team armed with all those powers under section 49 of the 1964 Act which Callaghan had denied Williamson. It was a humiliating moment for the force and a devastating comment on Waldron's refusal—or inability—to put his own house in order.

*

Throughout these proceedings, Waldron had virtually ignored the existence of Mark, but in the autumn the two men were to become closely and, as it proved, dramatically involved. AC 'C', Peter Brodie, had gone to a meeting of Interpol and then on leave. At a routine conference during his absence, Waldron expressed his concern at the increasing number of suspensions in the force. 'It must,' he concluded plaintively, 'be lack of supervision.' 'Not so,' replied Mark, and went on to insist that the answer lay in 'the thoroughly unsatisfactory way in which the CID investigates allegations of crime against its own members.' 'Then,' said Waldron with a breath-taking disregard for the facts of life at the Yard, 'why don't you do something about it?' Mark did.[1]

He put to work Jim Starritt, AC 'A', and two of his senior officers, and within ten days they had produced a plan for creating a new supra-departmental branch composed of specially-selected officers drawn from both uniform and CID branches and working

---

[1] Mark's version is disputed by several of those also present.

directly to the Deputy Commissioner. A.10,[1] as it came to be called, was to deal directly with *all* allegations of crime against members of the force, and the CID would only be involved in such investigations if required so to assist by the Deputy Commissioner. It was the turn of the office of AC 'C' to be 'emasculated'. More importantly, it was the first practical move in nearly 100 years to put into bankruptcy 'the little firm in a firm' of which Symonds had boasted to Perry. That 'the little firm' is still modestly solvent today is a tribute—if that is the word—to the resilience of the darker side of human nature.

The Starritt plan was approved by Waldron (he could scarcely do otherwise) and received with enthusiasm by the Home Office and the Home Secretary, Maudling; and with his foundation-stone well and truly laid, Mark departed on a lecture-tour of America. He was not there long, for towards the end of October he was summoned back to London by the Home Office. The specific reason, or reasons, for his sudden recall have not been explained, but a week after his return he was sent for by Maudling and without preamble was offered the commissionership of the Metropolitan Police. He accepted, subject to being given authority 'to switch assistant commissioners from one department to another'; and on 3 November the formal announcement was made.

There are still those who express surprise, although only a political innocent could have failed to notice the white smoke signals rising from the Vatican chimney at Broadway. The Home Office decision had been taken in principle months before; all that remained was the question of timing. Even then the date of Waldron's retirement was delayed until 16 April 1972 and the resulting atmosphere of 'interregnum' was embarrassing for Mark and bad for morale in the force. The immediate effect of the Home Office announcement resulted in a number of changes in 'C' Dept. The resignation of Peter Brodie was followed in quick succession by the retirement of three deputy assistant commissioners.[2] The CID, under no illusions about Mark's intentions, took to the trenches; and the uniform branch settled back comfortably to await the arrival of the new surgeon at the operating-table.

*

[1] A.10 formally came into existence on 1 May 1972 under Commander (now DAC) Ray Anning.

[2] See p. 84 of Mark's Report for 1972.

The early months of 1972 brought into sharp focus the reasons for Maudling's decision and the need for quick executive action. The Robson–Harris trial had started at the end of January and some five weeks later the verdict coincided with the disappearance of Symonds and Prescott's investigation into the activities of the Drug Squad.[1] But the really explosive event occurred on 27 February when the *Sunday People* revealed that Commander Kenneth Drury, head of the Flying Squad, had recently spent a holiday in Cyprus as the guest of James Humphreys, the most celebrated and successful of Soho pornographers. That his success was entirely due to the protection extended to him by officers, both junior and senior, of the Obscene Publications Squad and the Flying Squad provided a new dimension to the scale of corruption now prevalent in the CID. It was no longer the routine misconduct of a 'bent' detective and a small-time crook in Peckham. Larger, greedier snouts were in the gravy-bowl; and the price of gravy had risen very sharply indeed. How sharply, we shall presently see.

*

Mark took over from Waldron on 17 April. During the interregnum he had not been idle and now, with public speculation at its height as a result of the spate of scandals and revelations since the New Year, he took up a well-sharpened surgeon's knife.

He began by forming a Policy Committee which included the six top policemen and the three senior civilians at the Yard. This was to be his General Staff, armed with an executive authority hitherto unknown in the Metropolitan Police. It was a clear declaration of intent—some might even say a declaration of war—and it was swiftly followed by action which, in the medical world, would be described as 'heroic' surgery.

Following a meeting with the relevant staff associations on 23 April—St George's Day and a *Sunday*—Mark summoned the press and announced his decisions. They may be summarized thus:

    1. All detectives (about 2,300 out of a total of 3,200) serving in divisions would forthwith come under the command of uniform

---

[1] 5 February saw the violent 'Bloody Sunday' demonstration in Whitehall.

divisional commanders[1] for all purposes, including discipline.

2. The four Area Detective Commanders at the Yard were to be deployed to the offices of the four uniform DACs in charge of Areas and thus effectively removed from the cosy privacy of C Dept.

3. The investigation of *all* complaints against police officers, including allegations of crime, would be vested in Ray Anning's new A.10 Branch, working directly to the Deputy Commissioner.

4. The responsibility for enforcing pornography laws would be transferred from C Dept to A Dept.

5. There would in future be a routine interchange between CID and uniform officers on a regular basis.

The ranks of Tuscany—uniform officers, Home Office, most of the press, and even the Federation—could scarce forbear to cheer. The cancer had not been cured, but at least the surgeon had plainly identified where it lay and how he proposed to excise it; and a few days later Mark called in the representatives of the CID and told them that in the last analysis he would return every detective to uniform duty, rather than tolerate the existing stigma on the force. A century earlier, Henderson had said that the Metropolitan Police could only keep the outside of the platter clean. Now the whole plate was being disinfected.

Since that lively spring of 1972, there has continued an equally lively debate within the force. There are those who insist that Mark's decisions were the culmination of his years of anger and frustration at his treatment since he came from Leicester in 1967; that he was at heart a provincial chief constable who shared Williamson's distrust of the Metropolitan Police; that he was a 'uniform die-hard'; even that he believed that the image of Mark was more important than the image of the Met. The answer is more simple. Robert Mark was first and last a *policeman*. He was not greatly concerned in the distinction between a uniform and plain clothes, beyond the fact that both branches had a statutory obligation to enforce the law and that neither branch had a divine

---

[1] In 1972 there were twenty-three land divisions. A further division (AD) was added in November 1974 to cover Heathrow Airport.

right to abuse the office of constable. It was no bad qualification for a Commissioner of Police of the Metropolis; and if he was in due course to become obsessive about the world in which he lived, it was an honourable obsession.

CHAPTER FOURTEEN

From Mark to McNee

WITH MARK thus occupied in his operating theatre at New Scotland Yard, we will return to Soho; for it was there, on a scale of which he was still only dimly, if instinctively, aware, that the cancer of corruption had reached a point at which the whole structure of law enforcement was at risk. When, five years later, fifteen officers (some forty more had been investigated but not proceeded against) stood trial at the Old Bailey, Mr Justice Mars-Jones estimated that the payments made by pornographers over the years to their police protectors amounted to £100,000. He did not attempt to put a figure on benefits in kind.

The story of Commander Drury's holiday in Cyprus with Humphreys was by no means the first indication that there was something rotten in the state of Soho; indeed, the Flying Squad were comparatively new passengers on a gravy-train for which tickets were carefully controlled. A few detectives from West End Central police station—Challenor's old stamping-ground—had managed to climb aboard, but the chief operators—and beneficiaries—were members of the Obscene Publications Squad, a part of C.1 Branch at the Yard and led by the same Det. Chief Supt William Moody who had so inexplicably replaced Lambert on the *Times* inquiry in May 1970.

About that time Fleet Street, and in particular the *Sunday People* and *The Sunday Times*, had started to take a close interest in the activities—and the apparent immunity—of James Humphreys and his associates in the murky world of pornographic literature and blue films. It was big business. In 1971 Raymond Palmer of *The Observer* estimated that in the West End alone turnover was of the order of £3,000,000 while Humphreys on his own admission put his profit over a period of three years at £216,000.[1]

---

[1] Cox, Shirley and Short, *op. cit.*

Humphreys had embarked on a singularly unsuccessful life of crime as a teenager and it was not until he met the notorious Bernie Silver in 1969 that he acquired a key to the pornographic treasure-chest and—the essential passport to immunity—an introduction to Silver's influential friends in the CID.

The obscenity laws, and particularly those referring to pornography, had for over a century been even more ill-defined than the legislation dealing with drug-trafficking (there had recently been the twin fiascos of criminal proceedings against the publishers of *Lady Chatterley's Lover* and *Fanny Hill*), but the penalties for trading in 'hard porn' were severe enough to invite the best available protection; and there is no better protection for a breaker of the law than an enforcer of the law. Nor is there any better inducement than a fat cheque-book. The cheque-books were very fat indeed.

For example (and the examples are tedious in their extent and enormity): Moody received £4,000 for 'licensing' the opening of a shop in Rupert Street and an additional £6,000 for opening three further shops in Soho. Money on a scale which would have amazed Druscovitch passed from hand to hand; weekly payments, monthly payments, four-figure 'sweeteners', the high life, the low life, senior officers making their own market, juniors dragged— often unwillingly—into the rich swill-bin. Moody, at least, has a place in history for having received a payment of £14,000 from Ronald Mason (a pornographer on the level of Humphreys), possibly the largest single bribe ever paid to a senior officer of the Metropolitan Police.

But for the cosy conspiracy in Soho time was running out, and it is a measure of the arrogance of 'the little firm in a firm' that none of those with their hands in the till seems to have realized exactly why Mark, the uniform 'provincial', had been summoned by Maudling to wield his surgeon's knife.

In March 1972, Prescott's team investigating the Drug Squad submitted its report to the DPP. In May it was announced that on the evidence provided there were no grounds for criminal proceedings. Mark was unconvinced; and as a result of allegations made during the trial for conspiracy of the Salah family in the previous September, he set up a third inquiry led first by a uniform officer, Chief Inspector Faulkner, and subsequently by DCS Gordon Mees. The sprats had come and gone; now it was the turn of the sharks, and it was in November that the Faulkner–Mees team hooked its fish.

But Prichard and his two colleagues were still small fry compared with the real killer-whales—the Obscene Publications Squad and the Flying Squad; and against them Peter Brodie had already made an adroit move. He had started with the paymasters; and to pursue Bernie Silver and James Humphreys and his associates, he had chosen DCS Albert Wickstead, head of the Serious Crimes Squad (set up two years earlier to tackle the Richardson and Kray gangs) which operated from the comparative obscurity of Limehouse. Wickstead had one cardinal virtue. He did not care for criminals—at *any* price.

The appearance of the Serious Crimes Squad on the Soho scene caused as much concern among the CID brethren as it did among the villains themselves, and unsuccessful attempts were made to get Wickstead to stick to his Limehouse patch and leave the West End to the Flying Squad. Progress was slow and the eventual breakthrough unexpected, when in October the former lover of Humphreys' wife was savagely beaten up by a group of his gang. The game was nearly up. First Silver made a hasty exit to Spain, followed by Humphreys who, with an unconsciously ironic sense of history, chose Rotterdam for his bolt-hole, as Harry Benson had done a century before. There he was run to earth by two of Wickstead's officers, duly extradited, and in November sentenced to eight years in prison for causing grievous bodily harm. Most of his associates had already been rounded up by the Serious Crimes Squad and charged with possessing obscene material for gain. For Moody and his men, the well had run dry. Their turn was soon to come.

There still remained Bernie Silver. Towards the end of December he had been ingeniously lured back to London and on 29 December he was arrested outside his Knightsbridge flat. Nine months later he was charged (with several of his associates) with living off immoral earnings during a period of eighteen years, and on 18 December 1974 he was fined £30,000 and sent to prison for six years. Their mission accomplished, Wickstead and his squad returned to their East End parish.

*

By the spring of 1973 it was Mark's turn to play a trump card. In April, he appointed Gilbert Kelland, now AC 'C', but then a DAC with the Area Inspectorate, to investigate the allegations of bribery and corruption among the Yard squads operating in the West End. It was a distasteful assignment, for professionals can take no pleasure in putting their own colleagues under the microscope; but following on Mark's appointment of Faulkner and Mees to investigate the Drug Squad, it was the clearest possible evidence of his determination to bring the CID under control and to stamp out a century of tolerated, if not actually condoned, malpractice.

Kelland divided his forces (all uniform officers) into two teams concentrating respectively on the Obscene Publications Squad and the Flying Squad. The material evidence began to accumulate, first in a letter from Humphreys in Holland to Deputy Commissioner Jim Starritt, then in two diaries in Humphreys' hand which Wickstead's men had unearthed. These and other sources provided the kind of telephone directory of 'bent' policemen which Symonds had earlier threatened to produce, but—given their origins—they were not of themselves conclusive, not even when Humphreys made a long statement to one of the investigating team in prison after his conviction. The 'song' recital continued. Kelland's men checked and cross-checked, even travelling to America and the Continent to take independent statements which gave substance to their growing dossier of information. 'They [also] talked to serving and retired police officers in the Met. whose confirmation of the original Humphreys claims in itself gave them greater credence.'[1]

Kelland's investigation lasted nearly three years. During that time a procession of suspect officers from commander to constable had retired, or had been suspended, or dismissed the force. The reaction in the Metropolitan Police varied between that of the old guard of the CID who interpreted Mark's draconian policy as a private vendetta (it does not seem to have occurred to this faction that at the time no more than 50 detective officers out of over 3,000 were subject to inquiry[2]), and that of the overwhelming majority

---

[1] Cox, Shirley and Short, *op. cit.*

[2] Mark was later to express a curious kind of pride in the fact that during his term of office 487 Metropolitan Police officers were dismissed or required to resign from the force.

of men (including most of the CID itself) that the days of cosmetic surgery were over.

Early in 1976, Kelland was ready to move; and on the morning of 28 February twelve former or serving police officers were arrested at their homes on charges of corruption. The scene was set for the final act in a sordid drama stretching back as far as the early days of Simpson's regime.

The cases of the accused men were heard at three separate trials at the Central Criminal Court, two of them presided over by Mr Justice Mars-Jones who had conducted the 1964 inquiry.

At the first trial, which started on 8 November, six officers, including two detective inspectors, were separately charged with accepting bribes of £4,680 over a period of seven years. Five were convicted and sentenced to a total of thirty-six years' imprisonment. The sixth was acquitted.

The second 'pornography' trial began in March 1977, when ex-Commander Virgo, former DCS Moody and four others were accused on twenty-seven different counts of corruptly accepting bribes totalling £87,485. All were convicted and sentenced to a total of forty-eight years' in prison.

Finally in June 1977 (by which time Mark had been succeeded as Commissioner by David McNee) three former Flying Squad officers, Drury, Ingram and Legge, faced fourteen charges of corruption. Legge was acquitted. Drury and Ingram went to jail for eight and four years respectively.

There was an epilogue to follow. On 15 March 1978, ex-Commander Virgo's conviction was quashed by the Appeal Court and his sentence was set aside. The appeals of ten other defendants were rejected. On 8 June 1978 the sentences of Drury and Ingram were reduced, on appeal, to five years and three years respectively.

*

The pornography trials and the events leading up to them are not simply a moral tale. They are a timely reminder that while all power corrupts, absolute power—in this case personified by Robert Mark in his office of Commissioner—alone possesses the instruments which, resolutely used, can excise the cancer of corruption. It is readily understandable that men of the professional experience and personal integrity of Waldron and Brodie found it impossible to believe that they could be betrayed by men in whom they had reposed a proper trust. The fault of underlings lies not in their stars but in themselves, as Meiklejohn and his associates had long ago demonstrated; and between Harry Benson and James Humphreys there is a difference only of degree. It is therefore more than a coincidence that during the precise period when the Metropolitan Police was passing through one crisis, it was also giving proof, in uniform and detective branches alike, of its efficiency, its courage, and its devotion to public duty in another. The battle against terrorism in the Metropolis is a chapter in the history of the force which will be remembered long after Drury and Moody are forgotten.

*

In September 1964, a young Scotsman named James Stuart Christie was arrested in Madrid in possession of a rucksack containing a complete bomb-making kit which he had brought from Paris for a group of Spanish anarchists planning to assassinate Franco. He was sentenced to twenty years' imprisonment; and from this remote and seemingly routine exercise in political protest there was to emerge in the Metropolis an organized conspiracy to undermine by terrorism the whole fabric of a democratic society. Once more, across nearly a hundred years,[1] history was to repeat itself.

On 20 September 1967, after serving only three years of his sentence, Christie was released from prison in Madrid and returned to London. Within a fortnight he had given two interviews to *The People* in which he admitted that he was an active and dedicated anarchist, that he had deliberately and knowingly carried the bomb-making kit to Spain, and that he was an enemy of all organized forms of government. 'But,' he concluded, 'I'll never carry a bomb again.' Nor did he. There were plenty of others of his extremist persuasion ready to soil their hands in the cause of anarchy.

While Christie was still in prison in 1966, a militant group had been formed styling itself the '1st of May Group' and dedicated in the first instance, both in Britain and on the Continent, to the

[1] At the two subsequent 'Angry Brigade' trials, most of the defendants were charged under the Explosive Substances Act of 1883.

cause of Spanish and Italian revolutionaries. By 21 August 1971, when the international aims of that conspiracy had changed significantly to purely domestic objectives and most of the leading conspirators had been arrested, there had been twenty-one actual or attempted bombing incidents in the MPD; and the CID, at first with no special expertise or organization for counter-measures against this kind of terrorist activity, had demonstrated that patience, persistence and the weapons of forensic science are an irresistible combination. There was no gravy-train running through Barnet on the night of 12 January 1971; no hand-outs, no sweeteners; only a small group of ordinary policemen who realized that they had a critical problem on their hands. Fate is not only a matter of stuffed eelskins, for no one could then have known that within two years the Metropolis would be subjected to a far more ruthless assault, and that Commander Ernie Bond's modest Bomb Squad would become a highly sophisticated and, in the end, uniquely effective anti-terrorist organization. Fortunately for every citizen of London, there are many more men of the calibre of PC Stephen Tibble, murdered by an IRA gunman in the execution of his duty, than there are pigs at the Soho trough.

*

In a confidential police report written in March 1971, there is this classic definition of the nature of anarchism in our time:

> In addition to the overt revolutionary activity which pervades the far Left of the political spectrum, there is a sizeable 'underground' composed of persons intent upon grasping every opportunity to challenge, denigrate and, if possible, overthrow the form of society which finds acceptance by the majority of the population. These persons are, in the main, in their early twenties, follow no employment, have no settled address, but live fleetingly in various 'communes' . . . They will attach themselves to any cause, however hopeless or impractical, which they consider will aggravate or cause embarrassment to authority. They are, in the main, persons of considerable intelligence and cunning and have usually had the doubtful benefit of university or collegiate training.

Such were the members of the 1st of May Group and its later derivative, the 'Angry Brigade'.

The first incident in the Metropolis, shortly before Christie's release from prison, was a hit-and-run machine-gun attack on the American Embassy in August 1967. There was a lull of some seven months until 3 March 1968 when two bombs exploded outside the Spanish Embassy and the American Officers' Club in Lancaster Gate (three similar attacks occurred on the same day in The Hague). Between then and the middle of August 1970 there were six further bomb attacks in London, all (except for an incident at Paddington police station) directed against Spanish targets, including an attempt to sabotage an aircraft of Iberia Airlines at Heathrow with an incendiary device concealed in baggage.

Curiously, no attempt was made by the police to coordinate investigations,[1] not even when two men were caught running away after depositing a bomb at the Bank of Bilbao in King Street on the evening of 15 March 1969 and subsequently convicted; nor, even more inexplicably, when suddenly the target pattern changed. On 30 August 1970 a bomb exploded outside Sir John Waldron's house in Putney, followed nine days later by a similar incident at the flat of the Attorney-General, Sir Peter Rawlinson. The international anarchists had given way to the urban guerillas. In fact, although the police were not to know this until November, the 1st of May Group had been replaced by the Angry Brigade whose aims were no less extreme but concentrated on domestic political issues.

On 20 November the Angry Brigade announced its presence when, after the explosion of a device under a BBC van at the Miss World contest, it issued its 'Communiqué No. 1' claiming responsibility and franked with a rubber-stamp of unusual design with which the police were to become all too familiar. Three weeks later, after a Day of Protest against the Industrial Relations Bill, a bomb exploded in the basement area of the Department of Employment in St James's Square. It was followed by 'Communiqué No. 2'. There was still little sense of urgency at the Yard, and it was not until the evening of 12 January 1971 that matters reached a climax. At 10.04 p.m. the first of two bombs exploded

---

[1] A coordinated investigation would have shown that the bombs used in all the first fifteen incidents were of the acid-delay type and that all contained Nitramite or Nitratex, explosive substances only obtainable in France; also, that they were identical to the bomb-kit found on Christie in Madrid.

outside the Barnet home of Robert Carr, Minister of Employment. It was by far the most serious act of terrorism and its implications were of a clear conspiracy—how widespread no one yet knew—against the established social order.

On 12 January the senior detective officer of S Division (which included Barnet) was DCS (now Commander) Roy Habershon. He was not to know that by a geographical fluke he was to be involved closely not only with the Carr bombing but with the long pursuit and ultimate defeat of the Angry Brigade and subsequently with the IRA campaign in the Metropolis.

Habershon's CID team, reinforced by three Special Branch officers, carefully reviewed the whole catalogue of incidents which had followed Christie's return from Madrid and it was not long before they began to pick up a number of trails. The hottest scent, however, came from an unexpected quarter.

On 20 January police in Notting Hill arrested a paroled convict named Jack Prescott in possession of three stolen cheque-books and a quantity of cannabis. Remanded to Brixton, he obligingly confided to a fellow-prisoner his part in the Carr bombing and some revealing information about a 'commune' of anarchists engaged in revolutionary activities from a house in North London. Equally obligingly, the fellow-prisoner decided to make a detailed statement to Habershon on 3 February, the day on which Prescott was released on bail.

Prescott, it was established, had served a sentence in Albany Prison and had been paroled on 17 September 1970. While in prison he struck up a close friendship with another inmate, Ian Purdie, a professional militant, who was serving nine months for throwing a petrol bomb at the Ulster Office in Berkeley Street. Purdie had been released on 10 July 1970, and by the end of September had resumed his association with Prescott. As the inquiries, ranging as far as Manchester and Edinburgh, continued, Habershon's list of potential conspirators began to grow.

On 13 February Prescott (on bail) was arrested and charged with conspiracy to cause explosions. Purdie at once went into hiding but on 6 March he was picked up in Battersea, taken to Barnet for interrogation, and subsequently charged. Committal proceedings began on 22 April, but not before another bomb explosion, this time at the Ford Motor Company offices at Gant's Hill on 19 March and accompanied by another Angry Brigade communiqué.

Prescott and Purdie were duly sent for trial. The case was heard at the Old Bailey in November, by which time eight more alleged members of the Angry Brigade had been arrested.[1] Both men were accused of conspiring together to cause explosions. Prescott was found guilty and sentenced to prison for fifteen years. Purdie was acquitted.

The second and final phase of the Angry Brigade campaign started with the Gant's Hill explosion. There followed—between May and 15 August (an attack on the Territorial Army Centre in Holloway)—six widely scattered incidents,[2] which were at first investigated by local CID officers on the ground but supervised by Roy Habershon's small team in S Division. Plainly, however, the Angry Brigade had grown from a militant cell to a dangerous and well-organized body of anarchists. Accordingly, Waldron at last took steps to create a centralized team to plan and carry out counter-measures, and on 1 July the Bomb Squad came into existence, based on Scotland Yard and headed by Commander Bond and Roy Habershon. Its original strength was about 30 men (two-thirds from Special Branch and one-third from general duties CID officers). By 1975, when the IRA campaign was at its height, the squad had been increased to 108 and had become a highly sophisticated and expert organization, with a team of 42 surveillance officers, 8 explosives officers, forensic experts, and 8 Labrador dogs trained in explosive detection.[3] This brave and determined body[4] of men, women—and animals—were to meet and defeat the most ruthless demonstration of terrorism to which any city had yet been subjected. Their quality was matched by provincial forces (Birmingham, Guildford and the M.26, among many others, were to be the scenes of particularly savage incidents), but between August 1973 and the end of 1978 the Metropolitan tally was as follows: 184 bomb incidents, 15 shooting incidents,

---

[1] Throughout the summer of 1971 Habershon's team had arrested a number of other persons in connection with a related fraud conspiracy.

[2] The last six Angry Brigade bombings used a device of a different pattern, activated by a clockwork mechanism.

[3] Describing the back-up team of 13 anti-terrorist 'attack' Alsatians, Commander Huntley, who succeeded Bond as head of the Bomb Squad on 1 April 1972, has written: 'If there were such a place as a home for canine criminally insane these would qualify.'

[4] On 1 March 1976, the Bomb Squad was renamed the Anti-Terrorist Squad (C.13).

58 killed, 685 injured. Throughout the country, 148 terrorists had been arrested and a massive arsenal of weapons and explosives recovered. 'I doubt very much,' said Robert Mark, 'whether any country or capital city in the world can match that record in dealing with this conscienceless activity.'

Meanwhile Commander Bond's team had work to do. By the time of the Holloway explosion, they had built up a precise picture of the Angry Brigade and on 20 August, acting (in the police phrase) 'on information received', they raided a flat at 359 Amhurst Road, N.16 and arrested four persons, two men and two women. They also discovered a mass of documentary evidence and a complete bomb-making factory.[1] The following day detectives arrested Christie and a sixth suspect when, unaware of the earlier raid, they visited the Amhurst Road flat.

On 30 May 1972, eight persons (four men and four women) stood trial at the Central Criminal Court charged with conspiracy to cause explosions. The verdict was not arrived at until 6 December after a lengthy adjournment, largely owing to the inability of the jury to reach a unanimous decision. Eventually, by a majority of 10 to 2, two men and two women (the occupants of the Amhurst Road flat) were found guilty and sentenced to ten years' imprisonment each; the remaining four defendants, including Christie, were acquitted. It was the end of the Angry Brigade and a fitting testimony to the skill and determination of the Bomb Squad, to which Mr Justice James paid special tribute in court. But it was to prove only a prologue; the main drama was yet to come.

*

The curtain-raiser was short, sharp and unexpected. On 18 September 1972, while the Angry Brigade defendants were still on trial, a letter-bomb was received at the Israeli Embassy in London. It was opened by the Cultural Counsellor, Ami Shachori, and exploded, killing him. It was the first—and fortunately the only fatal—incident in a world-wide campaign orchestrated by the 'Black September' movement, an Arab terrorist group, and aimed at Jewish targets. In the four months to 25 January 1973, 181 such letter-bombs were posted to Israeli individuals or organizations

---

[1] The detailed components of this factory fill a foolscap page in a subsequent confidential Bomb Squad report.

(43 in England) from addresses as widely separated as Holland and
Malaysia. Almost all were intercepted at the point of delivery or
defused on receipt, and casualties were few and slight. These
incidents had no connection with the Angry Brigade, but they
underlined the ugly face of international terrorism. The Bomb
Squad, still only 30 strong, remained on the alert; and wisely so,
for in March the Provisional IRA came to England.

*

There had been a grim warning. In February 1972 a massive
car-bomb had exploded outside the Officers' Mess of the Parachute
Regiment in Aldershot. The 'Official' IRA had claimed responsibility as part of the 'Bloody Sunday' protest, but when it learned
that the victims of its 'military' coup consisted of five women
cleaners, a gardener, and a Roman Catholic priest, it retired behind
a barricade of moderation and made it known that its future
policy would be that of political persuasion. But it had not counted
on its militant wing; and in 1973 the 'Provos' took over.

7 March was the day of the Ulster referendum. It was an obvious
occasion for a major demonstration of IRA militancy, and at the
Yard contingency plans were made to counter any likely terrorist
activity in the Metropolis. Despite a steady flow of intelligence
reports reaching Special Branch,[1] there was no firm evidence of
the timing of any attack and no indication of probable targets or
methods; there were two clear assumptions, both of which proved
correct: that the targets would be buildings of major publicity
value in Central London and that the weapon would be the
'Provos' ' favourite car-bomb.

In mid-February, four cars were hijacked in Belfast and driven
across the border into the Republic where they were resprayed and
fitted with false number-plates. They were then each packed with
150 lb of explosive connected by an electrical circuit to an alarm-
clock. By 5 March, a task-force of ten 'Provos'—seven men and
three women—had assembled in Dublin.

The first 'wave' of two cars crossed by ferry to Liverpool on the
morning of 5 March, followed a day later by the second 'wave'.
Incredibly, all four cars succeeded in passing through port controls

---

[1] It will be remembered that Vincent had originally called it the 'Special
Irish Branch'. Once more history was repeating itself.

despite the fact that they bore false number-plates, displayed no tax discs, and reeked unmistakably of explosives. It was a not very distinguished security performance; and by 7 March the 'Belfast Ten' had assembled in London, reconnoitred the ground, and made their preparations.

There was a railway strike on 8 March. It was to have a significant effect on the events of that day, for while it resulted in the lifting of normal parking restrictions, it also meant that the only escape route for the terrorists was through Heathrow. By 7.30 a.m. all four cars had been parked at their targets—the first by the Post Office opposite New Scotland Yard in Broadway, the second outside the Old Bailey, the third near the Army Recruiting Office in Great Scotland Yard and the fourth at the British Forces Broadcasting offices in Dean Stanley Street, Westminster. All the bombs were primed and set to detonate at 3 p.m.; and by 9 o'clock the ten terrorists were at the West London Air Terminal on their way to catch the morning flight to Dublin.

About 8.30 a.m. two constables of the SPG patrolling outside Scotland Yard (so much for the 'riot squad' myth) noticed a Corsair with no tax disc and with number-plates which did not match the year of manufacture. Explosives officers were called from across the road, and found the rear compartment packed with a substance known as 'Co-op mix' and sticks of gelignite. Within half an hour, they had defused this massive and lethal bomb and Commander Huntley at once issued the order to 'close England', sealing off all ports of exit. At the Air Terminal, the 'Belfast Ten' were eating a hearty breakfast. By noon they had all been arrested (two were already aboard the 11.20 a.m. Trident for Dublin).

But a team of that size suggested at least two or three other car-bombs. The explosives officers at the Yard had correctly estimated that the timing device was set for 3 p.m. and thus there remained six short hours in which to seek out and neutralize. But where? The 'Belfast Ten' at Heathrow were not talking.

Shortly before 2 p.m., a telephone call was received at the *Times* news-desk giving details (slightly garbled) of the four car-bombs. The fact that the caller was obviously unaware of the discovery of the Corsair in Broadway suggests that he was speaking from Dublin. *The Times* alerted the Yard and sent out its own team of reporters, and by 2.30 p.m. the three remaining cars had been located. The Vauxhall Viva in Dean Stanley Street, close to the

Yard, was quickly de-fused by explosives officers. Elsewhere they were too late, although the police had in each case done their best to clear the areas. At 2.44 p.m. the Hunter in Great Scotland Yard detonated while explosives officers were carrying out preliminary tests on it. There were sixty-one casualties, most of them slight.[1] Seven minutes later the Cortina outside the Old Bailey exploded, causing widespread damage and 162 casualties, many of them serious. It had been a day to remember.

The trial of the 'Belfast Ten' opened at Winchester Crown Court on 10 September 1973 and lasted for forty-five days, during which most of the defendants behaved with histrionic arrogance, claimed the right to be treated as prisoners of war, and impudently accused the police of planting evidence. Eight were sentenced for life, one for fifteen years and one, a girl, acquitted on the grounds of diminished responsibility. But meanwhile the Provisional IRA had returned again to England; and this time they adopted very different tactics.

*

The 'Belfast Ten' could claim a macabre sort of victory, but they had shown a complacency and a lack of attention to detail which meant that such an operation was unlikely to be successful again. The Provisional IRA therefore changed their technique by organizing groups of 'sleepers', sympathizers with 'the Cause' who had lived and worked in England for several years and had become an unsuspected part of the community. With their romantic obsession with war games they named these groups Active Service Units (ASUs), each independent of and unknown to the others. They were to test the resources of the police and the fortitude of the public to the full.

The new campaign opened on 8 August 1973, with a series of incendiary attacks at Harrods and other department stores, chiefly in Oxford Street (always a prime target). The pattern plainly indicated an assault on public morale. It was urban terrorism in its most elementary and ruthless form.

The battle—which soon extended to the provinces—was to be fought out over more than two years until it culminated in the

[1] This incident occurred within a few feet of the Fenian bombing of Great Scotland Yard on 30 May 1884.

siege of Balcombe Street on 6 December 1975. It is neither possible nor necessary here to describe it by blow by blow. The methods ranged from time-bombs, throw-bombs, book-bombs and letter-bombs to shootings and hit-and-run attacks. The target pattern constantly changed. Public buildings, shops, clubs, pubs, public transport, pillar-boxes, restaurants, hotels; and, inevitably, private individuals—the murder of Ross McWhirter, the aimless killing of the cancer specialist, Hamilton Gordon-Fairley, two attempts on the life of Edward Heath. Not even the Fenians of the 1880s aimed so high or struck so low. Notable among targets were Madame Tussauds, the Hilton Hotel, the Armoury at the Tower of London, and the Naval and Military Club in Piccadilly. 'I almost preferred the Blitz,' said an old newspaper-seller. 'At least we were at war and we knew what to expect.'

'At least we were at war.' It is a nice point whether the Government should have treated the 'Provos' ' campaign as an act of open aggression against the safety of the realm. After all, service in Ulster qualifies the armed forces for a campaign medal. There were no campaign medals awarded in the Metropolis.

It was not long before Bob Huntley's Bomb Squad began to achieve notable victories—the 'Uxbridge Eight', the discovery of bomb factories in Southampton and Baron's Court, and a series of brilliant successes for the forensic scientists.[1] The climax was to come at the end of 1975.

On the evening of 6 December (his original plan had been disgracefully 'blown' by the *Evening News* two weeks earlier), Mark set a trap for the top terrorists. By 6 p.m. a task force of 700 policemen, including the Bomb Squad and the SPG, ringed the Mayfair area, confident of an IRA attack. They did not have long to wait. At 8 p.m. a car drove past Scott's Restaurant in Mount Street and the occupants opened fire with automatic weapons. Abandoning their car, the terrorists fled on foot and took refuge in Flat 22b in Balcombe Street, holding the occupants, Mr and Mrs John Matthews, as hostages. The siege was on.

It was to prove a classic of its kind, conducted under the full glare of television and radio publicity.[2] The operation was orches-

[1] The long list of incidents appended to Commander Huntley's confidential history of the Bomb Squad is a grim testimony to the mindless versatility of IRA terrorism.

[2] For a brisk account of the affair, see Mark, *op. cit.*

trated by Wilford Gibson, then DAC 'A' (Ops) and now AC 'A', and the Home Office delegated complete responsibility to the Commissioner, including the provision of a stand-by unit of the SAS in case the siege might develop into another Sidney Street. In the event it did not. A few weeks earlier, the police had learned some valuable lessons at the Spaghetti House siege at Knightsbridge. The basic premise in such situations was that, however difficult the decision, hostages were not 'negotiable'. Mark, when asked by a reporter what he would do if the terrorists held a politician, or even a cabinet minister, replied: 'Ask them if they would like a few more.' It was the kind of answer that endeared him to the press, and to a public which shared his sense of black humour.

After a little less than six days the terrorists had had enough. They surrendered, not as heroes, but as the cowards that they were; 'mindless brutes,' said Mark, 'devoid of reason, devoid of humanity, deserving only the contempt of their fellow-men.' They were the richest haul that the Bomb Squad had achieved, for when their flats were searched they were found to be not only the killers of Ross McWhirter, but involved in forty bombing and shooting incidents and guilty of seven counts of murder. They all received life sentences, with a recommendation of the judge, Mr Justice Cantley, that they should serve a minimum of thirty years in prison.

*

It is a measure of the political and social climate with which Robert Mark had to contend that IRA terrorism was by no means the only demonstration of public disquiet. One particularly sensitive area was that of race relations, a new phenomenon to which Simpson had first addressed himself in 1964. By the 1970s it had become a major issue, concerned not only with colour but with the whole field of community behaviour. Pious words were not enough. To Mark it was clear that people living in deprived areas— especially young people—had to be persuaded that the law was impartial, that it must be obeyed, and that the police were even-handed in carrying out their duties, irrespective of class or colour. It was a massive exercise in public relations, not greatly assisted by left-wing politicians and the inevitable civil libertarians who made mountains of black prejudice out of every hillock of honest endeavour.

Mark started by setting up a Community Relations Branch (A.7) at the Yard and by appointing community liaison officers in each division whose task was to carry the gospel into schools and youth institutions. He had two simple precepts: public tranquillity and the statistical fact that today's juvenile delinquent is tomorrow's potential convinced criminal. He was not helped by the events of August 1976.

The Notting Hill Carnival riots are a classic example of the vulnerability of the Metropolitan Police to the historic inability of the English to distinguish between liberty and licence. What began as a cheerfully exuberant Caribbean festival soon turned into a thieves' paradise and ultimately a brutal display of violence. The confrontation was planned and deliberate, and predictably the police became the whipping-boys, despite the fact that 400 officers were injured and damage was estimated at £250,000. As Mark has pointed out, the number of men on duty ('provocative!' cried the libertarians) was less than those at a Wembley Cup Final. And if there had been *no* police presence? What then would have been the libertarian answer? It is the statutory obligation of the Commissioner of Police of the Metropolis to maintain the Queen's Peace; and over the subsequent and disgraceful leniency of the magistracy, the best comment is no comment. 'You know,' said a young contable, 'you can't win in this game.' He was both right and wrong.

Likewise with political demonstrations, of which Mark had his fair share, as had Simpson and Waldron. The most serious confrontation was the battle of Red Lion Square on 15 June 1974 when the National Front clashed with a conglomerate of left-wing organizations calling itself 'Liberation'. The police presence, which included the SPG and mounted officers, was under the command of John Gerrard, now AC 'D'. They were violently attacked by the International Marxist Group, and in the ensuing mêlée a young man, Kevin Gately, received injuries from which he subsequently died. Mark at once played an ace. Instead of waiting for the inevitable libertarian reaction, he asked for an inquiry into the conduct of his men and the death of Gately. This was duly conducted by Mr Justice Scarman. His Report[1] is a fascinating commentary on the whole spectrum of political militancy and a virtually complete vindication of police conduct. Since, however,

---

[1] Cmnd. 5919.

the inquiry had been brought at the Commissioner's request, the cost fell on the Police Fund. Wryly, Robert Mark has noted that the legal bill to both taxpayer and ratepayer was £33,642. '*O, fortunatos nimium, sua si bona norint!*'

Mark's reforms had soon begun to pay dividends and by 1973 the rate of recruitment had significantly increased. There was a noticeable improvement in the relationship between uniform and plain-clothes branches, and the morale of the force was better than for many years. Mark now felt ready to deploy his formidable skills of communication in an area where no previous Commissioner had ventured to tread. He had prepared the ground by inviting the media to join in the war on crime. Henceforth the policy was to be not 'how little should we tell them?' but 'how much can we freely disclose?'. This policy of 'open government' was extended down to the level of individual police stations and it worked wonders in Fleet Street. It was one of the most successful of Mark's idiosyncratic contributions to the policing of the Metropolis, and presently he was to be given a public platform on which to mount his favourite hobby-horse. In November he was invited by the BBC to give the Dimbleby Lecture. It proved to be a highly controversial occasion.

Mark, as if he was clearing some unpleasant garbage from his front door, dealt first with the matter of crooked policemen, a subject which his audience, who had read their newspapers, digested without difficulty. He then turned to the matter of crooked lawyers and the shortcomings of criminal procedure. His audience sat up, with ears cocked.

Mark's argument—greeted over the next few days with widespread approval from the press and cries of dissent from much of the legal profession—was simple. There are corrupt policemen and it is the responsibility of chief officers to investigate and remove them. There are corrupt lawyers, but who will investigate and debar *them*? Under the adversary principle of the English legal process the function of defence counsel is to defend his client. But, said Mark, that obligation does not extend to presenting false evidence, fabricating alibis, or imputing dishonest motives to prosecution (usually police) witnesses; what, in fact, **Lord** Salmon in another context called 'highly paid forensic trickery'.

No Commissioner had spoken so bluntly before. It was a

virtuoso performance and a theme which Mark was to pursue with increasing obsession until his resignation. The scales of justice, he insisted, were heavily loaded in favour of the defence and particularly of unscrupulous lawyers, and he paraded disturbing statistics of the growing percentage of acquittals. Few police officers, who knew only too well the true extent of forensic trickery, would have disagreed with him; nor, over 200 years earlier, would Henry Fielding with his reference to 'the dirtiest money upon earth'.

Mark's forthright views were to be reinforced by his successor in his evidence to the Royal Commission on Criminal Procedure. For example, in his 1977 Report David McNee pointed out that 'of 230 people arrested for major crimes by the Robbery Squad between January 1976 and September 1977, 52 were already on bail.[1] If bail had been refused many serious crimes, including the use of firearms, would have been prevented.' The law has much to answer for.

McNee's reference to the use of firearms underlines both a problem and a dilemma. Ever since the appearance of highwaymen, dangerous criminals have resorted to the use of such weapons (Sir John Fielding and Sampson Wright did not hesitate to arm the Bow Street Horse and Foot Patrols in return); but with the formation of the Metropolitan Police and the public obsession with 'militarization', the constable's sole means of offence or defence were his truncheon or his bare fists, even during the Fenian troubles and the growth of anarchism.

What was then still the exception among violent criminals has increasingly become the rule—the Shepherd's Bush murders, the shooting of PC Miles, PC Tibble, and the innocent bystander Antiquis are sombre reminders—and the armed robber has become a symbol of our disorderly society.

This poses the dilemma. The police have no wish to be armed on a continental or American scale, but desperate criminals invite stern counter-measures and despite libertarian objections there is an unassailable case for issuing firearms to officers employed on such duties as the protection of Royalty or in situations where it is reasonable to expect extreme violence; and to provide guns and refuse permission to use them is demonstrably absurd.

Probably no more than 3,000 members of the Metropolitan

[1] The new and highly contentious Bail Act came into operation in April 1978.

Police are trained in the use of firearms, and since the Second World War fewer than half a dozen criminals or suspected criminals have been killed by police action in the MPD. It is not always possible to prevent serious crime by the simple exercise of sweet reason, but the idea of a London transformed into a Chicago is pure fantasy. The issue of weapons is controlled with exceptional strictness; and since the Commissioner is accountable to Parliament for the use or abuse of his powers, the system of checks and balances is entirely adequate.

In March 1974 Roy Jenkins returned to the Home Office in the new Wilson government. During his previous period in that office he had instituted several important reforms including the reduction of police forces in England and Wales to forty-three, and the introduction of majority verdicts in trials by jury. During the intervening years the Metropolitan Police had been much in the news with the revelation of serious malpractices among the CID and it was to one important aspect of this long-running serial that Jenkins now addressed himself. On 30 July he sent for Mark and read him the text of a statement which, later that day, he made in the Commons. The statement was, in effect, the genesis of the 1976 Police Act.

Jenkins's proposals dealt with the procedure for investigating complaints against the police. Under the 1964 Act, all deputy chief officers had been designated *de facto* disciplinary authorities in their respective forces; all, that is, except in the Metropolitan Police, the one force for which the Home Secretary had statutory responsibility. There, under a system hallowed by history, allegations of crime against officers were, as we have seen, investigated until 1972 by the CID. The provincial procedure, defined under section 49 of the Act, had worked well and all Jenkins need have done was to extend it to the Met. Instead, he decided to drag the police service into the political arena by setting up a Police Complaints Board consisting of lay members nominated by the Prime Minister, with power to appoint tribunals to consider all complaints other than those alleging crime, which would continue to be forwarded to the DPP. If he decided to take no action, or in the event of a subsequent acquittal, the papers would go to the Board for further consideration.

Mark galloped into battle. He was not without allies, for all forty-three chief police officers opposed the change—'the only time I have known them to be unanimous about anything controversial in my twenty years as a chief officer'. He made it abundantly clear that he would do all in his power to oppose the Bill both publicly and privately and that in the last analysis he would resign rather than administer it. Apart from its political overtones he took particular exception to the decision to remove from the chief officer the responsibility for deciding guilt and awarding punishment, contrary to the unanimous recommendation of the 1960–2 Royal Commission. Here at least he won a small victory, for on 15 July 1975 an amendment was made to the draft Bill restoring this vital right to deputy chief officers; but that was the limit of his success. In midsummer 1976 the new Police Act became law.[1] With it A.10 ceased to exist at the Yard and was duly replaced by a Complaints Investigation Bureau (CIB).

By 1976, terrorism had been largely contained,[2] there was a lull in violent political demonstrations, and the police were achieving considerable success in the fight against serious crime. To Mark it seemed a proper moment to step down, and on 27 October he submitted his formal resignation to the Home Secretary, to take effect on 12 March 1977 when he would have reached the minimum retiring age. There was no attempt by the Home Office to dissuade him.

In November he explained his reasons to the Metropolitan Branch of the Federation. These included his known opposition to the 1976 Act, the adverse effect on his net pension if he continued to serve beyond the age of sixty, and a feeling that he had largely completed the task he had set out to do. Each of these reasons was sufficient in itself, but in the autumn of 1976 he looked—and was— a tired man. He had driven himself hard and the going had been rough and with little respite. It was perhaps the best reason of all.

He had been a memorable, if often controversial, Commissioner, with a clear and uncomplicated view of the police function and an

[1] Mark was to have his moment of satisfaction. On 18 December 1978 a survey conducted by Dr Kenneth Russell of Leicester Polytechnic concluded, after the most detailed study, that the PCB 'is a very expensive, toothless, neutered watchdog, foisted on the public for political expediency'.

[2] The IRA provided several sharp reminders on either side of Christmas 1978; and on 30 March, the Conservative MP, Airey Neave, was murdered within the precinct's of the Palace of Westminster.

articulate ability to communicate his ideas shared by none of his predecessors. If his critics point to his obsession with publicity, that is no great fault. For far too long Commissioners had been remote, unidentifiable figures, even to their own men. That, at least, could never be said of Robert Mark. By the end he had become a household face and the Metropolitan Police had increasingly shared his public esteem. He is remembered with respect and even affection in the force, for he was an 'original'.

There was some brisk betting at the Yard over his successor. Would it be his Deputy, Colin Woods, or even one of the ACs? Or one of the Inspectorate? Or a provincial chief officer? In the event most of the punters would probably have lost their money when Merlyn Rees, a Welshman, chose David McNee, a Scot, to be head of the largest police force in England.

McNee was an interesting choice. He had joined the City of Glasgow Police in 1946. In 1968 he had been appointed Deputy Chief Constable of Dunbartonshire, returning to Glasgow as Chief Constable three years later. In 1975 he had become Chief Constable of the newly-created Strathclyde Police. Thus his entire service had been confined to one area, so that he could well be described as a 'parochial' rather than a provincial policeman. He was the first chief officer to be appointed from outside direct to the commissionership; and he was the first Scot. Rowan could trace his origins to Greenock, but McNee's police ancestry goes even further back to a fellow-citizen, Patrick Colquhoun. Along the way he had acquired the absurd newspaper tag of 'the Hammer'.

It was not long before McNee discovered that London is a long way from Glasgow. Recruiting had begun to fall again and the true position was concealed by an increase in the number of policewomen. Throughout the summer the Jubilee celebrations kept the force busy; and so, less happily, did a renewal of political violence on the streets. During most of the year pickets and police confronted each other outside the Grunwick film-processing plant at Willesden. During the summer and autumn there was a massive escalation accompanied by extreme violence and abuse. At times as many as 4,500 officers—a startling proportion of available uniform strength—were required to control the situation, and by the end of the year more than 300 policemen had been injured. In August the scene switched south of the river to Lewisham where in a pitched battle between members of the National Front and the Socialist Workers' Party, 270 police officers were injured in attempts to separate the rival factions. In both instances the courage and restraint shown by the police were exemplary, as a horrified public watched political extremists in action on their television screens; and by the end of the year the reputation of the force had never stood higher. The men might be forgiven for thinking that virtue had not received its just reward. They now decided to have their say.

*

During the summer, growing dissatisfaction in the service over the implementation of the Government's pay policy resulted in the appointment of a committee under Lord Edmund-Davies in August. It is indicative of the ill-advised tactics of Whitehall that this was originally called the Review Body on Police Negotiating Machinery and its terms of reference were restricted to 'reviewing the machinery for negotiating police pay and examining the constitutions of the police staff associations'. It looked—as indeed it was—like a sop to the TUC and a crude attempt to stall for time. The Federation would have none of it, and in the face of growing militancy (at a mass meeting Federation members gave the Home Secretary a rough passage) the Government beat a hasty retreat; in December the Review Body's terms of reference were extended to include a study of the proper basis of police pay[1] and it was re-named the Committee of Inquiry on the Police.

Edmund-Davies reported in July 1978.[2] The second half of his findings and recommendations relating to the extended terms of reference have been described by, among others, Robert Mark as the most important evaluation of the place of police in society since the 1829 Act. It is by no means an exaggerated claim, for even more important than the recommendations themselves is the unassailable logic of the arguments advanced in support of them. It is a document which, in its entirety, no student of social history can afford to ignore.

On the central issue of Metropolitan Police pay scales at the

---

[1] In his first Report (1977) David McNee commented sharply both on the existing sense of grievance and on the need to give the Metropolitan Police 'a substantial pay lead over their colleagues elsewhere'.

[2] Cmnd. 7283.

point of entry, the rates may be summarized thus (maximum basic rates after fifteen years' service in the rank of constable are shown in brackets):

	Before Edmund-Davies (*1 September 1977*)	After Edmund-Davies (*1 September 1978*)
	£2,208 (£3,990)	£3,600 (£5,700)
London allowance	£74 (£74)	£650 (£650)
London weighting	£245 (£245)	£319 (£319)
	£3,127 (£4,309)	£4,569 (£6,669)

The recommendations then went further:

1. The London weighting should count for pension, but not the London allowance.

2. All rates should be reviewed annually on 1 September and should be index-linked to average earnings (new series).

3. The same rule should apply to pensions.

4. In no circumstances should the right to strike be granted (see footnote to p. 203).

The Government, like many before it, had caught a tiger by the tail and had been severely mauled in the process. Ranged against it was the full weight of press and public opinion, but instead of smiling in the face of adversity, it demonstrated its injured dignity by accepting the recommendations on the basis of payment in two stages at intervals of twelve months (a decision which the Opposition immediately reversed on its return to office in May 1979). It was, in every sense, a typically Fabian device since with indexation the deferment of the second stage proved an illusory economy.

Thus, exactly 150 years after the creation of the 'New Police', the pay of a newly-joined constable had increased almost 100 times. It is too early to say whether Edmund-Davies has found the solution to the man-power problem which has bedevilled the police since the Second World War (in any event his proposals were based simply on natural justice). His Report predictably produced a marked increase in interest among young people seeking a career in the police service. But the police cannot afford to buy its way out of its difficulties. Edmund-Davies may have offered an incentive. He could not—and did not—attempt to influence imperative standards. One effect of his recommendations has been to reduce the wastage of experienced officers by premature retirement; but this may only be a temporary palliative until the implementation of the second stage provides pensions at the higher rate. The true problem still remains.

1978 was a year of comparative tranquillity. The terrorists still came and went but now they were chiefly Middle-Eastern extremists who chose London as a convenient setting in which to conduct their political and private vendettas. They posed a particular problem for Special Branch and for the Diplomatic Protection Group which Mark had set up in 1974, but counter-measures proved to be highly effective. Protests and demonstrations continued, but in a much lower key than during the previous year. Community relations still involved a high proportion of police time in divisions.

McNee could concentrate on his priorities.[1] His style differed completely from that of Robert Mark, less flamboyant but equally professional; and he must plainly have made an impact, for in September a Labour Party speaker accused him of having 'the morals of Canute'—an inadvertent compliment, for it equated him with one of the wisest and most reverent of English kings. The war on crime went well, especially in the fields of bank robberies and vehicle hijackings where the Flying Squad, the Central Robbery Squad, and No. 9 Regional Crime Squad operated as a single command unit.

McNee now turned to an old plan—'eight by eight'—which had been proposed by the team of management consultants in Simpson's time. In 1976 this had been revived by Mark's deputy, Colin Woods, under the name of RUFUS. Within days of taking over, McNee had set up a steering committee to examine the feasibility of what was, in effect, a radical re-shaping of the whole MPD and its component parts; and in Police Orders for 3 March

[1] The old malpractices had by no means been eradicated. At a Christmas gathering of retired policemen at the end of 1977, a veteran congratulated McNee on having inherited a 'clean' force. 'He looked extremely surprised when I told him that as of that moment there were over seventy officers under suspension.' And in January 1979 a provincial team was investigating allegations of serious corruption among Metropolitan and City of London officers.

1978 he announced his decision not to proceed with Woods's plan. Instead he appointed another steering committee under the Deputy Commissioner, served by a working party headed by DAC 'C' (Admin), Ray Anning, to study the operational responsibilities of the Area Inspectorate and the delegation to it of various existing functions from force headquarters. The proposals of this committee, which in the event followed a somewhat different pattern, were adopted on 1 January 1979 (see below).

'A force as large and complex as the Metropolitan Police,' remarked McNee, 'has to be constantly changing and adapting to new conditions. It cannot stand still.' One such change during the summer of 1978 was the transfer of the Finger Print Dept and the Criminal Record Office (C.3 and C.4) to B Dept as B.12 and B.13. It was a curious decision, justified on the grounds that all technical support services should come under one head (a new £9,000,000 communications system had been authorized shortly before) but privately an admission that B Dept was under-employed. Work continued meanwhile with the transfer of the entire finger-print collection on to video-file, and by the end of the year sixty-six subdivisions had been equipped with terminals linking them directly with the Police National Computer at Hendon. It had indeed been a period of consolidation and change.

*

As the Metropolitan Police entered its 150th year, it marked the occasion with the planned re-structuring of the force which, after David McNee's decision in March not to proceed with RUFUS, was duly christened 'Son of RUFUS'. The new organization—which brings the Metropolitan Police into line with provincial forces—is, in effect, a logical extension of the movement away from that 'too heavy a hand from above' and a practical delegation of responsibility to the lowest command level of policing. Mark had started this process with his CID reforms but had not stayed long enough to see it through. Now the men at the 'sharp end'—the new divisional chief superintendents—have been given the incentive and authority to be in a full sense lords of their 'manors', and it remains to be seen whether this overdue stimulant results in greater efficiency and flexibility.

The new structure may be summarized thus: the four *areas* remain unchanged; the twenty-four divisions become *districts*;

existing sub-divisions become eighty *divisions* (with a further division covering the Palace of Westminster); and existing sections become *sub-divisions*. In addition there are now five traffic divisions, but these are superimposed on the land districts and form part of B Dept. Thames Division,[1] while still retaining its old and honoured title, has become A.10, a branch left vacant since the creation of the Police Complaints Board and CIB. Thus horses, dogs, and boats have been, so to speak, 'brigaded' together under A Dept. This would have appealed to Charles Rowan's orderly and logical mind, for all, except the 'sniffers', are *preventive* arms of the law. The Policy Committee also considered the transfer of traffic divisions to A Dept on the premise that all uniform functions should logically be under a single command; but a conservative tradition runs strong in the Metropolitan Police and since B Dept had long been the home of 'Traffic', it was decided to leave well alone.

As an important extension to these structural changes, McNee went back to the short-lived experiment of 1967 by reviving or, more exactly, re-creating the post of Inspector of the Force. 'An organisation such as ours,' he wrote, 'if it is to be efficient, needs an effective system of monitoring itself.' Thus Area DACs—the old 'Inspectorate'—were directed to concentrate on their operational duties; and a new office—Inspector of the Force—working to the Deputy, and provided with that necessary muscle which Jim Starritt was never given, was formed.

At 1 January 1979, the actual strength of the Metropolitan Police was 22,196 (against an establishment of 26,628) and that of the civil staff 15,491. The gross budget for the financial year 1979–80 was £400,000,000.

Robert Peel could not have foreseen the sheer arithmetic of modern policing. Much of its vocabulary—computer, video-file, radio-car, bat-phone—would have been incomprehensible to him. But nothing in the intervening years would have changed his conviction that 'the principal object to be obtained is the Prevention of Crime'. Nor would he have altered a word of the speech in which he introduced his Police Bill to the Commons on 15 April 1829:

---

[1] 'The Thames,' commented McNee, 'is now virtually a dead river.' As a result, Thames Division has been halved in size to an establishment of 145 men and 36 boats (*Police Orders*, 10 November 1978).

'It is the duty of Parliament to afford to the inhabitants of the Metropolis and its vicinity the full and complete protection of the law and take prompt and decisive measures to check the increase of crime.'

Epilogue

WHEN AT 6 p.m. on 29 September 1829 the first Metropolitan policemen marched out of their station-houses—turning left and right on the *outside* of the pavement—they symbolized much more than one man's vision of a society in which the old Adam might be exorcized by patient example rather than by exemplary punishment. They represented, however few their numbers and however elementary their expertise, a physical presence, a public statement of the primacy of law and order in a Metropolis—indeed a whole country—where men and women (for deep and often deeply-felt reasons) no longer trusted in the historical truth which forty years later another visionary, out of the same mould as Peel, was to spell out: that democracy is government of the people, by the people, and for the people.

We know nothing of those men who set out on that September evening 150 years ago to keep the Queen's Peace except that they were 'of the people'; that, in Wellington's word, they looked very 'respectable'; that their average age was twenty-seven; that they were grossly underpaid; that they frequently got drunk; and that they were for many years subjected to every form of public attack and humiliation. What we do know is that they were sustained and encouraged in their lonely journey by two devoted public servants; and that the Metropolitan Police today owes its very existence to Charles Rowan and Richard Mayne.

Looking back over a century and a half, the reader may judge for himself the extraordinarily ambivalent attitude which the citizens of London, the politicians, the press, and even the judiciary have shown towards the Metropolitan Police. There have been moments —many of them—when a visitor from another planet might have imagined that the prevention and detection of crime were held to be an impertinent invasion of civil liberty. There have been occasions when the behaviour of police officers might have justified the belief that if liberty is sacrosanct, licence is more profitable. But if familiarity has sometimes bred contempt, it has also over the years created a much more fundamental identity of interest and a proper understanding of the place of the policeman in society, even though the constable on the beat may often have had good reason to wonder from whence cometh his help. When Cicero wrote that the safety of the people is the highest law, he was doing no more than anticipate Rowan's General Instruction Book; and when civil libertarians question police powers, they forget that those powers differ very little from those which in common law they also possess. The word 'duty' does not often feature in their vocabulary. It is only necessary to contemplate the tidal wave which would engulf the Metropolis in the event of a police strike to understand the true measure of Cicero's words, and the dangerous logic of the libertarian alternative.

For 150 years the Metropolitan Police has been lectured, lampooned,[1] humiliated, damned with faint praise, and occasionally—to its surprise—commended without reservation. That it has produced its Meiklejohns and Goddards, its Robsons and its Moodys is simply to demonstrate that a blue fig-leaf is no absolution for original sin. Always there has been a suspicion, if not an expectation, of impropriety; always there has been an irrational fear of 'militarization', fostered by opponents of the police idea and based on nothing more substantial than the natural relationship between uniforms and discipline. Indeed, the police constable is in many ways the antithesis of the private soldier. Desborough emphasized this when he wrote: 'The burden of *individual* discretion and responsibility placed upon a constable is much greater than that of any other public servant of subordinate rank', an observation repeated in almost identical terms by the Royal Commission of 1960–2; and if Peel had had the first word, it was left to Edmund-Davies to have the last:

> We live in a parliamentary democracy. The concepts of law and its impartial enforcement are fundamental to it. The instruments essential to the continued fulfilment of these concepts are an independent judiciary to interpret the law, the police to maintain and enforce it, and the armed forces to protect us from

---

[1] 'It is not,' remarked *Judy*, 'that their boots have become too big for policemen, but that policemen are becoming too big for their boots.'

external aggression. These three groups of people are unique in our society and essential to its continuation.[1]

This special status of the police has not until now been recognized by comparable rewards. Every major settlement—Desborough, Oaksey, Willink, Edmund-Davies—has been forced upon reluctant governments of every complexion by the pressure of events and the spur of public opinion. When in 1977 *The Times* spoke of 'the anger of the police', it drew particular attention to the long-standing feeling in the service that political advantage was being taken of a policeman's civil disabilities in law (a feeling shared for much the same reason by the armed forces). The wonder is not at the extent of militancy but at the degree of restraint, for in conversation, policemen of every rank, no longer an urban peasantry but a highly intelligent cross-section of the community, reflect the truth of Rowan's cardinal precept: 'There is no qualification more indispensable to a Police Officer than a perfect command of temper.'

It is against this background that the Metropolitan Police has to determine its own future. It is the most public institution in this country, its every action open to scrutiny, its every member personally accountable in law for the manner in which he executes his office of constable. For a century and a half it has listened to pious platitudes, learned to live with prejudice, and succeeded, through moderation, in maintaining the Queen's Peace in a society not always dedicated to the pursuit of public virtue. If, in the process, it has grown cynical, that is not surprising. 'I sometimes wish,' said a superintendent, 'that I was a civil servant. Then I would have the power but not the responsibility.'

Yet this most public of institutions is a very private world. The day a newly-attested constable makes his declaration, he becomes a man apart. He may not live where he pleases nor incur any debts. Neither he nor his wife may engage in any form of business enterprise without permission, nor may he indulge in any political activity. He is forbidden by law to withdraw his labour and his personal conduct is strictly governed by Police Regulations. All this he knows and accepts. What he does not so readily accept is his vulnerability to those fellow-citizens—and they are many and vocal—who seek to degrade his honourable office and visit him

[1] Cmnd. 7283 (1978).

with the sins of every wayward colleague. In no other profession would the formidable machinery of a Royal Commission have been invoked because a police constable became involved in an altercation with a popular comedian and a passer-by.

It is not simply a matter of money or of sophisticated equipment. The problem lies far deeper; and it lies with the people, who are themselves the police. It rests on two simple propositions which Robert Peel, in his greater wisdom, identified. Is society prepared to bring its irresistible power to bear against those who mock the rule of law and defy the democratic imperative of order? And does there still remain, among young men and women, the sense of duty which puts public service before private convenience? On the answers to those two questions depends the future of the Queen's Peace.

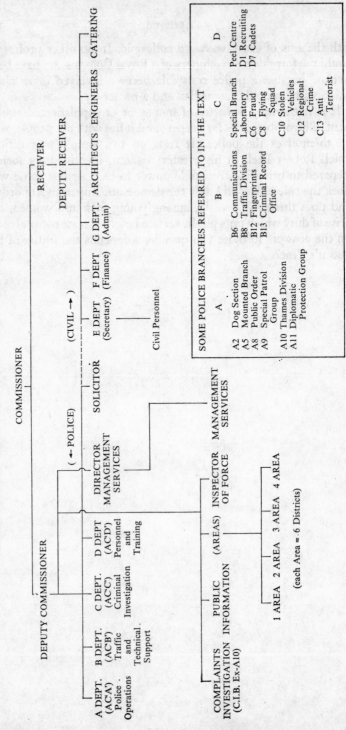

Appendix A

METROPOLITAN POLICE - OUTLINE ORGANISATION 1979

COMMISSIONER

DEPUTY COMMISSIONER

(← POLICE)   SOLICITOR   RECEIVER

(CIVIL →)   DEPUTY RECEIVER

A DEPT. (ACA') Police Operations

B DEPT. (ACB') Traffic and Technical Support

C DEPT. (ACC') Criminal Investigation

D DEPT. (ACD') Personnel and Training

DIRECTOR MANAGEMENT SERVICES

E DEPT (Secretary)

F DEPT (Finance)

G DEPT. (Admin)

ARCHITECTS   ENGINEERS   CATERING

Civil Personnel

COMPLAINTS INVESTIGATION (C.I.B. Ex-AI0)

PUBLIC INFORMATION

(AREAS)

INSPECTOR OF FORCE

MANAGEMENT SERVICES

1 AREA   2 AREA   3 AREA   4 AREA

(each Area = 6 Districts)

SOME POLICE BRANCHES REFERRED TO IN THE TEXT			
A	**B**	**C**	**D**
A2 Dog Section	B6 Communications	Special Branch	Peel Centre
A5 Mounted Branch	B8 Traffic Division	Laboratory	D1 Recruiting
A8 Public Order	B12 Fingerprints	C6 Fraud	D7 Cadets
A9 Special Patrol Group	B13 Criminal Record Office	C8 Flying Squad	
A10 Thames Division		C10 Stolen Vehicles	
A11 Diplomatic Protection Group		C12 Regional Crime	
		C13 Anti Terrorist	

APPENDIX B

THE FINANCING OF THE METROPOLITAN POLICE

1829 A police rate limited to 8d in the £.

1833 First Exchequer grant-in-aid not exceeding £60,000 out of the Consolidated Fund.

1839 A further Exchequer grant-in-aid of £20,000 p.a. to cover the transfer of the Bow Street Horse Patrol and the Thames Police. The Treasury directed to pay a yearly sum equivalent to a rate of 2d in the £ on additional rental value arising from the extension of the Metropolitan Police District.

1857 An Exchequer contribution not exceeding 2d in the £ for the whole MPD in lieu of the 1833 and 1839 sums.

1868 Police rate limited to 9d in the £, of which one quarter contributed by the Exchequer (i.e. 2¼d in the £).

1878 Treasury contribution fixed at 4d in the £, the balance of 5d being met by the police-rate.

1880 Exchequer grant of 1839 merged in general Treasury contribution.

1888 Local Government Act, by which Government contribution was made a charge on the Local Taxation Account in the same proportion as laid down in 1878. Source of rate income now the county councils and county borough councils lying wholly or in part within the MPD.

1890 First direct Exchequer grant for purposes of police superannuation. Under the Local Taxation (Customs and Excise) Act of this year, £300,000 p.a. was provided, half of which was paid in aid of the Metropolitan Police pension fund.

1909 The above sum proving inadequate, an additional police-rate was levied, but there was no corresponding increase in the Treasury grant.

1909 An Exchequer payment of £100,000 p.a. for services rendered by the Metropolitan Police for 'imperial and national' purposes. (In 1978 this payment stood at £2,400,000.)

1912 Police-rate limit raised to 11d in the £, but no increase in the Treasury proportion.

1918 Direct supplementary grant which increased the Exchequer contribution to one half of total net police expenditure, including pensions.

1929 Exchequer contributions previously received by the Police Fund from the Local Taxation Account replaced by equivalent additional payments by way of direct grant.

1979   The position remains, broadly, that about half of net expenditure comes from the rates and the remainder by way of Government grant, except that ratepayers are responsible in full for payments under the Riot (Damages) Act 1886, and for the full cost of school crossing patrols.

BIBLIOGRAPHY

The literature of law and order and of the preventive and detective functions of police institutions is legion. Most of it is very specialized; very little of it deals in any detail with the Metropolitan Police alone. Only two Commissioners (Sir Harold Scott and Sir Robert Mark) have written about their terms of office, although Macready described his brief period at Scotland Yard in his autobiography. A few senior officers have made their cosmetic contributions to the history of their times but none with particular distinction, with the notable exception of Howgrave-Graham who was Secretary from 1927 to 1946. The chief 'cottage industry' has been the reminiscences of assorted CID officers who, in the afterglow of long service, have largely confused fact with fiction. The three standard works remain Patrick Colquhoun's celebrated *Treatise* of 1796; Melville Lee's charmingly Victorian *History* which is a mine of information on the earliest period; and Tom Critchley's lapidary *History of Police in England and Wales* which, written from the vantage-point of the Home Office, is essential reading for a proper understanding of the complicated development of provincial police forces.

I have often thought that extensive bibliographies are part of an historian's defence mechanism designed to demonstrate his industry and scholarship. As I make no claim to be a professional historian, I feel free to cast away this shield and buckler. I have done my stint of reading and have my honourable scars to prove it. But it is in the source material, describing events as they happened, that I have found the greatest profit and pleasure; and in talking to policemen of all ranks and ages who have recreated the past, illuminated the present, and projected the future. For the reader who may wish to draw water from wells other than mine, I would commend this selected list of books:

WELCH, SAUNDERS: *Observations on the Office of Constable.* (1754)
COLQUHOUN, PATRICK: *A Treatise on the Police of the Metropolis.* (C. Dilly, 1796)
GASH, NORMAN: *Mr Secretary Peel.* (Longman, 1961)
RAMSAY, A. A. W.: *Sir Robert Peel.* (Constable, 1928)
LEE, W. MELVILLE: *A History of Police in England.* (Methuen, 1901)
WATSON, E. R.: *The Trial of Adolf Beck.* (William Hodge, 1924)
CLARKSON AND RICHARDSON: *Police!* (Field and Tuer, 1889)
MACREADY, SIR NEVIL: *Annals of an Active Life.* (Hutchinson, 1924)
DILNOT, GEORGE: *The Trial of the Detectives.* (Geoffrey Bles, 1928)
Scotland Yard. (Geoffrey Bles, 1929)

HOWGRAVE-GRAHAM, H. R.: *Light and Shade at Scotland Yard.* (Murray, 1947)
MOYLAN, SIR JOHN: *Scotland Yard.* (Putnam, *new ed.*, 1934)
BOYLE, ANDREW: *Trenchard—Man of Vision.* (Collins, 1962)
SCOTT, SIR HAROLD: *Scotland Yard.* (Deutsch, 1954)
REITH, CHARLES: *The Blind Eye of History.* (Faber and Faber, 1952)
A New Study of Police History. (Oliver and Boyd, 1956)
BROWNE, DOUGLAS G.: *The Rise of Scotland Yard.* (Harrap, 1956)
CRITCHLEY, T. A.: *A History of Police in England and Wales.* (Constable, *new ed.*, 1978)
COX, SHIRLEY AND SHORT: *The Fall of Scotland Yard.* (Penguin, 1977)
MARK, SIR ROBERT: *In the Office of Constable.* (Collins, 1978)

SOURCE MATERIAL

The most important sources have been conversations and correspondence with police officers and civil staff ranging from the present and past Commissioners to pensioners who joined in the time of Sir Edward Henry seventy years ago. I have kept to a simple principle. Both conversations and correspondence are private except where I have been given permission to quote names. This is proper. I am not an investigative journalist.

As for printed and manuscript sources, these are the most relevant:

MEPO papers, Public Record Office.
HO papers, Public Record Office.
Statute Book.
Parliamentary Debates.
Reports of Royal Commissions, Select Committees, Committees of Inquiry, etc.
The Annual Register, *passim*.
Commissioners' Annual Reports.
Reports of HM Inspectors of Constabulary.
New Scotland Yard, internal files.
Police Orders.
Police Regulations.
Police Studies, Vol. 1, No. 1.
Police Journal.
Police Review.
National newspaper files.

Index